Myth, Migration
and the Making of Memory

Myth, Migration and the Making of Memory

Scotia and Nova Scotia c.1700-1990

Edited by

Marjory Harper and Michael E. Vance

Published for the
Gorsebrook Research Institute for Atlantic Canada Studies
by Fernwood Publishing
and John Donald Publishers Limited

Editing: Douglas Beall
Design and production: Beverley Rach
Printed and bound in Canada by: Hignell Printing Limited

Published for The Gorsebrook Research Institute for Atlantic Canada Studies by
                Fernwood Publishing
                Box 9409, Station A
                Halifax, Nova Scotia
                B3K 5S3
                and
                John Donald Publishers Limited
                Unit 8 Canongate Venture
                5 New Street
                Edinburgh, Scotland
                EH8 8BH

Fernwood Publishing Company Limited gratefully acknowledges the financial support of the Ministry of Canadian Heritage and the Canada Council for the Arts for our publishing program.

Le Conseil des Arts | The Canada Council
du Canada | for the Arts

A catalogue record for this book is available from the British Library
ISBN 0-85976-521-0

Canadian Cataloguing in Publication Data

Main entry under title:

Myth, migration and the making of memory

Includes bibliographical references.
ISBN 1-55266-015-X

1. Scots -- Nova Scotia -- History. 2. Nova Scotia -- History. 3. Scotland -- Immigration and emigration -- History. 4. Nova Scotia -- Immigration and emigration -- History. I. Vance, Michael E. (Michael Easton), 1959- II. Harper, Marjory.

FC2350.S3M98 1999   971.6'0049163   C99-950123-2   F1040.S4M98 1999

303 - 482

Contents

Introduction

Myth

Migration

Memory

Illustrations

Contributors

Rusty Bitterman is Assistant Editor, *Acadiensis*, University of New Brunswick, Fredericton, New Brunswick.

Fiona A. Black is Reference Librarian, Information Services, Regina Public Library, Saskatchewan.

Keith Branigan is Professor Emeritus, Dept. of Archaeology, University of Sheffield.

J. M. Bumsted is Professor of History, St. John's College, University of Manitoba.

Barry Cahill is Senior Archivist, Government Archives, Nova Scotia Archives and Records Management.

E. J. Cowan is Professor of Scottish History, University of Glasgow.

Phillip Girard is Professor of Law, Dalhousie University, Nova Scotia.

Marjory Harper is a Senior Lecturer in History, Aberdeen University.

Colin D. Howell is Professor of History, Saint Mary's University, Nova Scotia.

Michael Kennedy is a graduate of the doctoral program in Scottish Studies, University of Edinburgh.

Cameron Pulsifer is Senior Historian, Canadian War Museum, Ottawa.

Eric Richards is Professor of History, Flinders University of South Australia.

James Symonds is Executive Director, Archaeological Research and Consultancy, University of Sheffield.

Michael E. Vance is Associate Professor of History, Saint Mary's University, Nova Scotia.

Uwe Zagratski is Professor of English, Osnabrück University, Germany.

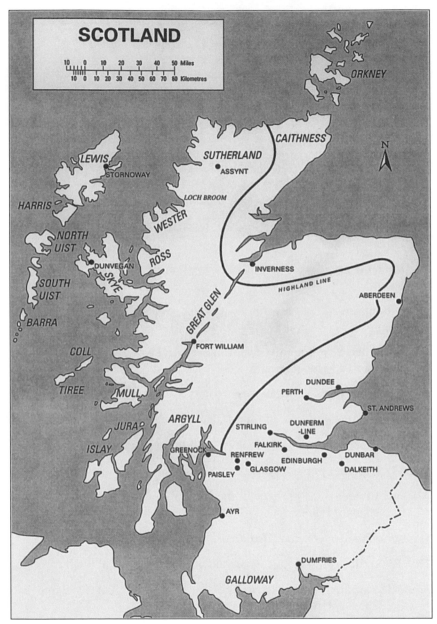

Map A   Scotland

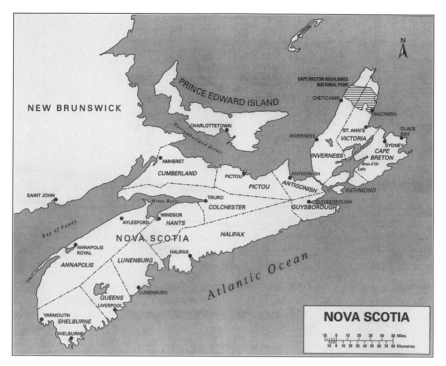

Map B   Nova Scotia

Preface

The collection of essays on offer here originally developed out of *Scotia - Nova Scotia*, an international conference held at Saint Mary's University, Halifax, Nova Scotia in September, 1996. The conference, which attracted twenty-seven speakers and sixty-two delegates, representing a variety of disciplines and interests, was designed to achieve three scholarly goals and the editors have borne these in mind while developing this volume. The first was to provide a critical evaluation of popular perceptions of the historical connection between Scotland and Nova Scotia; the second was to encourage an expansion of the range of scholarly inquiry on the topic; and the third was to promote discussion among scholars of different disciplines. This volume still retains much of that original intention, as the thematic structure and wide-ranging contributions attest, but it is hoped that the collection will also prove useful as an introduction to the inter-related histories of the two regions. That said, as our authors indicate, a great deal more research remains to be done before anything like a standard account of the Scottish-Nova Scotian connection can be written.

All scholarship is part of a collective endeavour, but this is particularly true of a multi-authored volume. As a consequence, the editors would first like to thank the contributors for agreeing to have their work published here. Two of the essays have already appeared in different versions elsewhere—Fiona Black's in *The Bibliotheck* and Marjory Harper's in *Acadiensis*—but the remainder are appearing for the first time after a very long wait. We commend our authors' patience, but there would not have been a volume at all if it were not for the support of a large number of public and private organizations. Although the idea for the conference originated with myself and was encouraged by Scott McLean of the Canadian Association of Scottish Studies, which co-sponsored the event, the Social Sciences and Humanities Research Council of Canada, through its occasional conferences grant, is largely responsible for making it possible. That support was supplemented by the non-profit *Scottish Studies Foundation* as part of its ongoing commitment to the promotion of research into the Scots in Canada, as well as *The Scots: The North British Society* of Halifax, the oldest Scottish organization in North America. In addition, a number of speakers were able to present their contributions in part due to the support of their home institutions and this was paralleled by the support given to the conference by the host institution, Saint Mary's University. The Senate Research Committee, particularly when it came time to publish this collection, and the offices of the Academic Vice President and the Dean of Arts, were particularly encouraging, while the Gorsebrook Research Institute for Atlantic Canada Studies was unstinting in its support. We are particularly indebted to Jackie Logan for her tireless organizational efforts, from the original conference grant application to the copy-editing stage of this volume.

Turning a collection of papers into a book is no easy task and a number of people have greatly aided the process. Douglas Beall's scrupulous copy-editing has been much appreciated, as have the efforts of the editors and staff at Fernwood Publishing. Finally, Chauna James' work on the original type-script made the publisher's task much easier and the aid and encouragement of Marjory Harper, my co-editor, were of invaluable assistance to myself. Ultimately, though, it is you, the reader, we thank for your interest in this book and we trust that it does not disappoint.

Michael E. Vance
Saint Mary's University,
Halifax, Nova Scotia

INTRODUCTION

1

Myth, Migration and the Making of Memory:
An Introduction

Marjory Harper and Michael E. Vance

Myth

A certain tale is told by tour guides as they conduct visitors through Point Pleasant Park in Halifax, Nova Scotia. According to this story, the heather that grows wild throughout the park originally found its way to Nova Scotia in the blankets of Highland troops sent to garrison the town: as they disembarked from their transports, the soldiers shook their bedding and the seeds that fell out found a new home across the Atlantic. Whether the story is an accurate account or perhaps simply an apocryphal tale explaining the activities of a zealous imperial botanist, its retelling reflects the importance of such myths in maintaining a sense of connection between Old and New Scotland. Nor is it solely the tourist industry that finds such tales useful. Recently a number of scholars have begun to take seriously the role of myth in shaping regional and national identity.[1] The heather story suggests that this kind of analysis of myth may also be instructive in a transatlantic context.

The first group of essays in this volume seeks to explore the importance of myth in shaping our understanding of the relationship between Scotland and Nova Scotia. Naturally enough the investigation must begin with emigration, which in the Scottish case is invariably associated with the Highlands. This is particularly true in literature, where the mythologizing of the emigrant experience has been most pronounced.

In the National Library of Scotland, for instance, one may find a late-eighteenth-century chapbook version of Henry Erskine's *The Emigrant,* described by the printer as a "very beautiful and pathetic Poem . . . written upon occasion of the frequent Emigrations from Scotland, more especially from the Highlands." The poem runs for fourteen stanzas and tells the tale of an elderly shepherd forced to leave his Highland home for exile on a "Foreign Shore." Erskine attributed the origin of this forced emigration to the introduction of ill-suited commercial agriculture and a new grasping landlord class that had little understanding of its paternalistic responsibilities.

> But ah, sad change! those blessed days are o'er,
> And Peace, Content, and Safety charm no more.
> Another lord now rules those wide domains,
> The avaricious tyrant of the plains,
> Far, far from hence he revels life away,
> In guilty pleasures, our poor means must pay.
> The mossy plains, the mountain's barren brow,
> Must now be tortur'd by the rearing plough,
> And, spite of nature, crops be taught to rise,
> Which to these northern climes wise Heav'n denies.
> In vain, with sweating brow and weary hands,
> We strive to earn the gold our lord demands,
> While cold and hunger, and the dungeon's gloom,
> Await our failure as its certain doom.
>
> To shun these ills that hoary my head,
> I seek in foreign lands precarious bread;
> Forc'd tho' my helpless age from guilt be pure,
> The pangs of banish'd felons to endure;
> And all because these hands have vainly try'd
> To force from art what nature has deny'd;
> Because my little all will not suffice
> To pay th' insatiable claims of Avarice.

The poem ends with a plea for readers to intervene in this state of affairs in order to reclaim the elite's paternal role and avoid a Highland depopulation that would leave Britannia defenceless "if in some future hour the foe should land."[2]

Erskine's condemnation of the landlords was, however, less strident and explicit than Robert Burns' scathing attack upon Lord Breadalbane, who in 1786 was trying to block the emigration of tenants from his estates.

> THEY! An' be d-mn'd! What right hae they
> To Meat, or Sleep, or light o' day,

Far less to riches, pow'r or freedom
But what your lordships PLEASE TO GIE THEM?[3]

Ethical objections to the implementation of commercial agriculture in the Highlands, which Peter Womack has argued were first raised by Scots poets like Burns and Erskine, were by the early nineteenth century tamed and transformed into the purely sentimental and somewhat vacuous recounting of emigrant departures. This change was already apparent in Erskine's poem but it found full expression in works like the *Emigrant's Lament* (1803):

Ye wilds and ye mountains, farewell!
Ye springs, and ye murmuring streams!
Though forc'd to forsake you by day,
We'll visit you oft in our dreams. . . .

Though dimm'd by our tears as they flow,
Their image becomes more obscure,
We wish that the ship might sail slow,
And the picture for ever endure.[4]

Sentiment, as a vehicle for understanding the process of emigration, was an integral part of the Romantic movement which Scottish authors such as Walter Scott, James Hogg and Robert Louis Stevenson did so much to develop. The fact that it was Scotland's literati who initially shaped our understanding of eighteenth- and nineteenth-century emigration may indeed support the claims of Katie Trumpener, who sees the Scottish Romantics as the most recent heirs of what she has termed "bardic nationalism." While earlier bards had provided the myths for the ancient kings of Ireland, Scotland and Wales, the nineteenth-century novelists were providing a unifying fiction of empire.[5] This was reflected on both sides of the Atlantic, as the Scottish Romantics' sentimental emigration poetry became part of popular culture[6] through works such as the "Canadian Boat Song"[7] and, later, "Farewell to Nova Scotia," with its chorus:

Farewell to Nova Scotia, the sea-bound coast,
Let your mountains dark and dreary be,
And when I am far away on the briny oceans tossed,
Will you ever heave a sigh and a wish for me?[8]

These words would not be out of place in the *Emigrant's Lament*.

The romantic mythic understanding of Scottish emigration as a reluctant or forced exodus, which became dominant in the nineteenth century, has continued to hold sway up to the present. In 1987 a Scottish vocal group, The

Proclaimers, had considerable success on both sides of the Atlantic with their song entitled "Letter from America."

> I've looked at the ocean,
> Tried hard to imagine,
> The way you felt the day you sailed,
> From Wester Ross to Nova Scotia,
> We should have held you,
> We should have told you,
> But you know our sense of timing,
> We always wait too long.

This poetic rendering of Highland emigration also pairs "Lochaber no more" with "Methil no more," "Bathgate no more," "Linwood no more" and "Irvine no more," thus linking the nineteenth-century depopulation of the Highlands with the late-twentieth-century collapse of heavy industry, coal mining and car production in the urban Lowlands.[9] Similarly, with the current renaissance of Cape Breton folk music, a sentimental version of Scottish emigration is also being maintained in post-industrial Nova Scotia.[10]

A recent article in *Scotland on Sunday* demonstrates the lengths this mythic version of events can reach. This article, headlined "Siege Mentality," reports on one Jack Ross, a descendant of a group of Scots who had emigrated to America after the Jacobite Rebellion. The accompanying photograph shows the kilted, targe-holding and claymore-wielding Ross standing in front of his Nova Scotia home, a 1:100 scale version of Dunvegan Castle on the Isle of Skye. Ross's house also reportedly contains a cardboard cut-out of the actor Mel Gibson dressed as William Wallace. Despite such homage to ahistorical Hollywood dreaming, Ross confidently asserts that his family's two hundred-year isolation from Scotland makes him "more Scottish than the Scots as far as ancient culture goes."[11] The fact that the article does not identify the location in Nova Scotia of Mr. Ross's Dunvegan is also revealing because this merely reinforces the image carefully cultivated by the Nova Scotia department of tourism that the entire province—despite the large percentages of English, Welsh, Irish, French, Blacks and Natives among its population—is essentially Scottish.

As in all myths, an element of historical reality lies behind the later fiction, and many scholars have done much to analyze the complex set of circumstances that link the introduction of commercial agriculture, the transformation of Highland society and Highland emigration to North America, including that to Nova Scotia.[12] Despite such correctives, however, recent work suggests that we have to look deeper into the Scottish past in order to understand the pervasive role of myth, not only for interpreting emigration, but for defining Scottishness itself. E.J. Cowan has argued that origin myths for royal lineage are entwined with early Scottish identity, and Bruce Webster has pointed out that such interpretations were modified by the introduction of feudal order through Norman families and continental Christianity, and that these images were in turn transformed by the experience of the late medieval Wars of Independence—each event taking on its own mythic aspect. Murray Pittock has continued the theme into the era when Scotland lost its constitutional independence, claiming that the fortunes of the Stewart monarchy and Scottish independence had become so intertwined that the creation of a "stateless nation" by the parliamentary union of 1707 was directly attributable—especially in popular Jacobitism—to the fall of James VII. The Romantics, notably Walter Scott, have been credited with taking the sting out of Jacobite identity by portraying the struggles of Scotland's past as heroic failures.[13] Romanticizing these conflicts was an integral step in Scotland's assimilation into the Victorian British Empire and worked equally well to neutralize both Jacobitism and the trauma of emigration.

Professor Cowan's chapter, "The Myth of Scotch Canada," in this volume also places much earlier in Scotland's past the origin of the *mythos* connecting Scotland and Canada. The early seventeenth-century colonization scheme to plant a Scottish colony in Nova Scotia has long been heralded as the beginning of the connection between Old and New Scotland. Recently, John Reid has pointed out that although William Alexander's settlement was abandoned and no effective British presence was maintained in the region until the eighteenth century, various ambitious New England Scots, as well as strategists in the Colonial Department, succeeded in keeping the name "Nova Scotia" alive throughout the seventeenth century when the region was in fact occupied by French Acadians and the native Mi'kmaq.[14] Cowan points out that the polemic surrounding the Alexander venture did much to create the image of escape and success that purportedly awaited emigrants in the New World and to suggest that Highlanders were best suited to the enterprise. However, Cowan notes that in its earliest incarnations the myth was Lowland in its orientation. The place names on Sir William Alexander's map are Lowland, not Highland. The post-'45 migrations to the Americas and the Victorian fascination with and creation of Highland ceremony and regalia have helped to transform Nova Scotia's Scottish identity into a Highland identity. As Cowan points out, this contemporaneous transatlantic development was perhaps best represented by the simultaneous creation of Highland games. Ironically, as Scottishness became more formalized through games, clubs and societies, the original culture, which survived only in Gaelic enclaves such as Cape Breton, the Highlands and the Western Isles, began its precipitous decline.[15]

By approaching the subject from an archaeological perspective, James Symonds' chapter, "Surveying the Remains of a Highland Myth," provides another method for qualifying much of the mythic account, while simultaneously demonstrating how the romanticized interpretation of transatlantic migration continues to inspire new research. This is particularly true in the case of Flora MacDonald. While in the Hebrides, her involvement in the events of the '45 scarcely rates a mention; beyond the Highands, her youth and gender, her clandestine involvement with "Bonnie Prince Charlie" and her subsequent "flight" to America all firmly established her as an enduring romantic heroine. As Hugh Douglas has pointed out, the desire to be associated with MacDonald has resulted in the establishment of colleges and memorials in the United States, and her visit to Nova Scotia, where her experience of a dreadful winter convinced her to leave for Skye, never to return to America, is also still commemorated.[16] Like Acadia's Evangeline,[17] another heroine (this time fictitious) created outside the community, Flora's migration to America came to symbolize the decline and dispersal of her society. Symonds suggests, however, that preliminary archaeological investigation of MacDonald's birthplace reveals a complex picture of land settlement that, while generally materially impoverished, was not without luxury items. The reorientation of field boundaries appears to conform to the historically known phases of clearance that had helped to make migration attractive, but the intricate nature of land use and re-use does not suggest one cataclysmic event. In addition, preliminary work at settlement sites in Nova Scotia has suggested both material improvement for emigrants and the persistence of housing designs suited to a Gaelic lifestyle. Thus, by focusing on the commonplace of her South Uist community, the Flora MacDonald Project has been able to assemble a more complete picture of Highland life than the myth can allow.

Symonds' chapter illustrates one method of transcending the romantic account in order to develop a fuller understanding of the experiences that anticipated and followed emigration, and in his chapter, entitled "Scottishness and Britishness in Canada, 1790–1914," Bumsted offers another. He tests the myth of Scotch Canada by studying the resilience of the immigrant community's Scottish identity in the face of an expanding sense of Britishness. Both Linda Colley in the British context and Phil Buckner in the Canadian one have argued that the sense of Britishness itself was partly forged in the process of the colonization and settlement of imperial possessions.[18] By examining a wide range of topics, including Scottish institutions, diet, sport and societies, Bumsted argues for both the persistence of Scottish ethnicity and an accommodation with Britishness. All the same, with the creation of Canada out of British North America in 1867, Scots were faced with a new focus for their allegiance and this event, combined with decreasing direct migration from Scotland, tended to weaken if not obliterate the obvious symbols of Scottish ethnicity. In fact, some aspects of Scottishness, such as the sports of golf and curling, became so incorporated into the dominant culture that they all but lost their Scottish associations by the end of the nineteenth century. Bumsted finds, however, that it is in Gaelic-speaking Prince Edward Island and Cape Breton that Scottishness has persisted most clearly into the twentieth century.

Cowan's, Symonds' and Bumsted's evaluations of the multifaceted relationship between romantic myth and actual experience in Scottish emigration to Nova Scotia lay the foundation for this volume's second set of essays, which seek to delve further beyond the myth and develop a more complete understanding of the shape and significance of Scottish settlement. Inevitably it is the Highlanders who have received the closest scrutiny.[19]

Migration

When writers have turned their attention to the mechanisms by which the Atlantic was bridged, the separation between poetic pathos and migration history has not always been obvious. In retelling the tale of the *Hector*'s much-celebrated voyage from Loch Broom to Pictou, Nova Scotia, in 1773, Donald MacKay could not resist including imaginative romantic speculation with his otherwise straightforward narrative:

> The *Hector* sailed on in bad weather and good. . . . It was one of those autumnal hurricanes which harry the east coast every year. Imagine, then, the black clouds building on the southern horizon. Seas breaking, sails reefed until there was barely steerage way, and a great wind swooping down at nightfall, with decks awash, the hatch was battened and only the light of swinging oil lamps in the pitching hold; the strong, the sick, the moribund, thrown into each others arms among slithering baggage of sacks and boxes. Amid the cries of the children they prayed, perhaps, sang hymns, composed themselves for death. . . Wasted by illness and hunger, shaken by the storm, the people of the *Hector*, for all their brave show of salt-stained plaids, broadswords and bagpipes, can only have stirred the pity of the settlers who hurried through the woods of Brown Point [Pictou] to greet them.[20]

MacKay's depiction of the emigrants as brave, suffering pioneers involved in an epic struggle is merely the latest in a long line of sentimental retellings that has done much to influence the "Highland" self-image of Pictou County and could, on occasion, find its way back to Scotland. Angus Robertson, President of the Highland Association of Scotland, while participating in the 1923 celebrations to commemorate the 150th anniversary of the *Hector*'s arrival, investigated the possibility of bringing 200,000 Highlanders to the province, in order that "this spiritual asset of the Empire may remain intact" and be prevented from "drifting to all parts of the world because their own country will do nothing for them."[21] In many ways, the *Hector* tale has served as a Nova Scotia "foundation myth" analogous to the role played by the *Mayflower* for New England. Recent scholarship has, however, penetrated the sentimental epic, placing the *Hector* emigrants in both their North American and Nova Scotian settlement contexts.[22] In the same vein, the essays in the second part of the volume explore some of the neglected dimensions of Highland migration, as well as the range of experiences of other Scots of differing regional and class backgrounds who came to Nova Scotia during the nineteenth and twentieth centuries.

Eric Richards' chapter, "Leaving the Highlands," reminds us that during the nineteenth century the Highland migration to Nova Scotia was part of a larger international movement which encompassed Australia and New Zealand as well as eastern Canada. Although the voyage of the *Hector* can be paralleled by many examples of desperate, heroic journeys to the Antipodes, Richards demonstrates that several other less dramatic migrations were of considerable numerical significance. Certainly, the fact that Highlanders played a prominent role in the destruction of Australian aborigines should caution us to avoid portraying them as simply hapless victims,[23] and the range and variety of emigrant types should encourage some consideration of the role of choice in determining the pattern of nineteenth-century Highland overseas migration. It was not only cleared tenants who found themselves in Nova Scotia, Australia and New Zealand, but members of the Highland elite, soldiers, gold-seekers and religious enthusiasts. Richards finds that, by the 1850s, Highlanders were constructing "remarkable inter-continental links" and "some of them, even among the poorest of their numbers, had become globe trotters, mobile spirits in the international labour market." Simplistic models highlighting landlord oppression or demographic and economic forces cannot account for the complexity of this international movement.

This is equally true in Nova Scotia, where the contours of Highland migration and settlement should alert us to the dangers of subscribing too closely to the *Hector* foundation myth. The Loch Broom emigrants were, in fact, anticipated by the Highland veterans of earlier American wars.[24] In addition, the activities of clergymen and emigration agents had begun to attract significant numbers of Highlanders to the eastern mainland of Nova Scotia and Cape Breton Island from the 1770s. Encouraged and organized by priests, Roman Catholics were predominant in the first wave of settlement, congregating mainly in Antigonish and Guysborough counties, and along the southern and western coasts of Cape Breton. First coming out on the *Hector*, Presbyterian Highlanders, after colonising Pictou County, extended settlement westward into Colchester and Cumberland counties, to the east coast of Cape Breton and to the area to the west and north of the Bras d'Or.[25] After the American Revolution, substantial numbers of Highlanders were also prominent among the Loyalists settled by the government further west and south, in the Minas Basin, Annapolis and Shelburne, but the most recognizable areas of settlement continued to be Cape Breton Island and the adjacent mainland, where new arrivals in the 1800s, attracted by the ready availability of land for community settlement among their countrymen, reinforced the pioneers' denominational distinctiveness. These migrations, however, were relatively small compared to later nineteenth-century transatlantic settlement.

That these movements were conflated into a single account of "emigration as tragedy" was a consequence of the experiences of the later and more numerous Highland migrants. Between 1815 and the late 1830s a downturn in the Scottish economy contributed to the largest phase of settlement in the province. Impoverished Highlanders from Caithness, Sutherland and the Hebrides, still drawn primarily to Cape Breton because of its proximity and delayed colonization, discovered a shrinking availability of cheap land in Nova Scotia and were forced to squat without title on infertile backlands, to such an extent that it was estimated in 1837 that more than half the island's population was squatting on Crown land.[26]

Keith Branigan's chapter, "Historical Archaeology and Migration," surveys recent archaeological work on Barra and confirms the greatly impoverished circumstances at sites which sent emigrants to Cape Breton in the early nineteenth century. Unlike the investigations on South Uist, the excavations of blackhouses on Barra have yielded remarkably few artefacts, often a few buttons or clay pipe fragments, with "seconds" pottery being the most prevalent type of find. Much of this cheap ceramic was the cast-off from Glasgow potteries, where it does not appear to have been used, and fragments of the same type have also been located in association with Hebridean settlement sites in Cape Breton.[27] The impression of meagre means reflected in the dispersal of these inferior artefacts is also confirmed by the physical context of the excavated Barra blackhouse settlements. Evidence of lazy-bedding for potato cultivation in settlements huddled into the landscape confirms the well attested circumstances of impoverishment in the Western Isles, but Branigan's archaeological evidence adds much greater precision to the study of blackhouse abandonment. The material evidence clearly illustrates why, despite a lack of official encouragement, stricter colonial land regulations and a deteriorating standard of living in the colony, some Highland Scots continued to migrate to Nova Scotia in the early nineteenth century. Branigan believes that as early as about 1820 abandonment was begun, perhaps establishing the preconditions for the large exodus to Nova Scotia during the late 1830s subsistence crises and the Highland potato famine of 1846–57. The number of Highland emigrants remaining in Nova Scotia began to wane thereafter, as more moved on to Upper Canada or the United States, many in the wake of Cape Breton's own famine of the 1840s.[28]

Elsewhere in Nova Scotia, other processes were at work in drawing Scots to the colony. Continued British military presence, particularly during the American War of Independence and the subsequent French Revolutionary and Napoleonic wars, brought many Scottish soldiers and seamen to Maritime ports, and several elected to stay after the conflicts had ceased. Cameron Pulsifer's chapter, "A Highland Regiment in Halifax," demonstrates that during the later nineteenth century, even in peacetime, the arrival of a Highland regiment at the Halifax Citadel could reinvigorate the Scottish community's sense of identity. Nevertheless, Pulsifer also argues that in that period Scots could not assume an ascendant position in Halifax society without creating tension. The conflicts over the Sir Walter Scott celebrations of 1871 reveal the extent to which Irish and English identities competed with the Scottish. Equally revealing is the fact that many members of the mercantile community, such as Falkirk native and local brewmaster Alexander Keith,[29] were Lowland Scots who demonstrated themselves to be the most influential supporters of the Tartan troops, thus reflecting the extent to which they too had adopted the mythic Highland national identity. Many merchants were in fact drawn to Nova Scotia by the trading opportunities that had been created during the same conflicts which had brought the Scottish soldiers. Some were from the former colonies to the south, while others came straight from Scotland.

Prominent in the Halifax business community at the end of the eighteenth century, for instance, was William Forsyth, a general merchant who built up a profitable sailing fleet, acquired a network of Scottish agents and went into partnership with two Scots-born timber merchants and shippers with interests in New Brunswick and Lower Canada, as well as Nova Scotia. Equally influential on the other side of the province in the same era was Edward Mortimer from Keith in Banffshire. He went from Halifax to Pictou as a representative of the Glasgow-based timber firm, William Liddell and Company, and soon established it as the region's leading timber merchant, exporting lumber from newly cleared land to the Clyde ports.[30]

The timber trade, which in the 1790s began to create new shipping routes and trading links between ports in Britain and North America, was an undoubted aid to immigration and settlement in the Maritimes during the first half of the nineteenth century. From small beginnings as a supplier of oak and pine masts to the Navy, the timber trade developed into the major hinge of Britain's commerce with the American colonies until the 1840s, and was dominated by Scots. Organised by local merchants such as Mortimer, who advanced capital to a multitude of farmer-lumberers and sawmillers for cutting and floating operations, it also offered a crucial incentive to migrants, not only by creating employment, but more importantly, by offering passages on the many timber ships which regularly plied the Atlantic.[31]

As Fiona Black's chapter, "Advent'rous Merchants and Atlantic Waves," illustrates, trade dominated by Lowland Scots was significant for reasons other than facilitating ocean voyages. Black explores the careers of a group of Halifax merchants whose influence on the colony cannot be measured solely by the cash value of the goods traded. Bookselling Scots such as Alexander Morrison, Archibald McColl and James Beith ensured Nova Scotians a supply of reading materials in English and Gaelic from a host of Scottish printers. These publications were often religious in content but also included practical works, leading fiction, poetry and works of philosophy and history. In fact,

Black demonstrates how these Lowland merchants ensured that Haligonians had reading material comparable to that available in Scottish "provincial towns" and, as a consequence, contributed to the circulation of ideas then current in the wider British literary world.

Barry Cahill's chapter, "Mediating a Scottish Enlightenment Ideal," demonstrates how this connection could at times allow Scots settled in Nova Scotia to contribute to wider transatlantic debates. Rev. James MacGregor's late-eighteenth-century antislavery tract is significant not only for its precociousness—Cahill claims it as the first example of its kind in Canada—but because his connections to Enlightenment circles in Glasgow provided Scottish polemicists with a practical lesson in the ills of Black slavery. The secessionist missionary's views were a product of both his education in Glasgow, where he had been exposed to, among other influences, the philosophy of John Millar, and his observation of slavery as it was practised by American colonists, primarily in former Acadian lands in eastern Nova Scotia. What is equally intriguing is that his tract was directed in the first instance against a fellow Scottish secessionist, the seventy-year-old Rev. Daniel Cock, who, despite his calling, had begun to engage in the slave trade himself. This allowed MacGregor, like David Hume, to highlight the truly corruptive nature of the institution. It should be noted, however, that Rev. Cock was not the only Scot exploiting Blacks, or for that matter the native Mi'kmaq, in Nova Scotia and the relationships between Scots and these groups still requires investigation.[32] The Enlightenment influences transported by Scots across the Atlantic to the more southern American colonies have received considerable attention, but MacGregor's contribution to the antislavery debate clearly demonstrates how they could extend to Nova Scotia as well.[33]

We also find, however, that Scots could bring with them more practical educational baggage that, along with their personal connections, allowed them a remarkable influence on the emerging colonial professional classes. Alan Karras has drawn attention to the importance of Scottish "sojourners" among the professional classes in Jamaica and the Chesapeake colonies during the eighteenth century. Scots not only administered the lucrative sugar and tobacco trade associated with each, but also provided these colonies with a class of lawyers, teachers and physicians. Although most were frustrated in their ambition to transfer an improved social status earned in the colonies back to Scotland, their shared patronage networks provided both a Scots domination of the professions and an awareness of the utility of being Scottish.[34] Colin Howell's chapter, "Scottish Influences in Nineteenth-century Nova Scotia Medicine," demonstrates that, for Scottish physicians, a similar patronage network was created in Nova Scotia. Howell highlights the importance of personal contacts between the colony's first "gentlemen" physicians and the mercantile community, also dominated by Scots. By the mid-nineteenth century, this was reinforced by the professional esteem that an Edinburgh qualification continued to confer on both Scottish and non-Scottish physicians alike. Ironically, by the end of the century the professionalization of medicine, which the Edinburgh medical school had been instrumental in promoting, meant that connections based on personal relations with other Scots, and a Scottish medical education itself, became far less important than a rational, scientific training that could be acquired just as easily in the United States or, after the founding of the McGill medical school at Montreal, in Canada itself. Nevertheless, Howell's chapter not only demonstrates the role of patronage in reinforcing the importance of Scottishness but also, like Cahill's chapter, alerts us to the fact that, for the Nova Scotian elite, Scottish institutions, ideas and processes could extend their reach across the Atlantic long after the first emigrants had arrived.

Professionalization, however, was a universal phenomenon in the western world. By the last decades of the nineteenth century, when physicians were concentrating on bolstering their authority on the basis of professional credentials rather than Scottish connections, emigration to Nova Scotia was itself becoming bureaucratised and professionalised. For much of the early nineteenth century, the activities of those encouraging Scots to emigrate to the Maritimes had been unofficial and sometimes incidental, based more upon private recommendations than any organised campaign. In 1869, however, each of the four provinces in the newly created Dominion of Canada appointed an immigration agent in Britain and, sixteen years later, William Annand, former Liberal prime minister of Nova Scotia, became the province's first agent-general. When he died two years later, he was succeeded in this unremunerated post by Sir Charles Tupper, who held the office in tandem with his position as Canadian high commissioner. Tupper served as high commissioner until 1896, and his successor, John Howard, was agent-general from then until his death in 1929, being awarded a salary of $2,000 a year in 1905, and being supported in his efforts by the creation of a provincial Department of Industries and Immigration in 1908, to ascertain employment needs and distribute immigrants accordingly. Howard's daughter succeeded briefly to the post of agent-general on her father's death, before the office was closed in 1931 as a consequence of the Depression, although Iris Howard continued to promote Nova Scotia unofficially for some years.[35]

The ability of Iris Howard to perform the function of agent-general is particularly intriguing, given the hosility directed against the earlier activities of Emma Stirling. Phil Girard's chapter, "Victorian Philanthropy and Child Rescue," demonstrates that during the late nineteenth century private philanthropy continued alongside government efforts, but that Stirling's refusal to accept conventional gender roles, along with her sometimes insensitive, patronising, Edinburgh upper-class attitudes, in large part accounted for the failure of her plan to "rescue" abandoned or neglected children from urban Scotland and bring them to the more healthful environment of Nova Scotia's

Annapolis Valley. As a consequence of the hostility she generated, Stirling's contribution to the development of the Edinburgh Society for the Prevention of Cruelty to Children was written out of offical accounts, and her attempt to establish a home for Scotland's "waifs and strays" at her Nova Scotian farm ended in a dramatic fire that was probably set by local inhabitants.

In addition to illustrating the dangers of flouting late-nineteenth-century gender, class and community norms, Emma Stirling's failed experiment also reflects the turn-of-the-century characterization of Nova Scotia, the Maritimes and much of Canada as a rural idyll ready to restore the physical and moral health of Scotland's urban degenerates. The orchards at Stirling's Aylesford farm were easily transformed into an Eden-like paradise in the philanthropist's self-promotions. Notions concerning the healthfulness of rural life versus the degrading effects of urban society had become a common theme by the turn of the century and, as Marjory Harper's chapter suggests, this imagery continued to exert its influence on Scottish emigration to the Maritimes well after the First World War.[36] In particular, the Glasgow-born philanthropist George Cossar, when advocating the benefits of his Lower Gagetown "training" farm in New Brunswick, also highlighted the healthful effects of agricultural labour for boys from Scotland's cities.

Conceived as part of an imperial solution to Scotland's urban unemployment and poverty, Cossar's New Brunswick establishment was tied to his Craigielinn farm, in Scotland, which provided the recruits and was part of a system that supplied young "agriculturalists" for the Maritimes, the rest of Canada, and Australia. Despite Cossar's claims, not all the young men appreciated the regenerative power of hard farm labour, and some returned to the life of misdemeanour and petty crime which had prompted reformers to advocate their emigration from urban Scotland in the first place. Many boys and parents claimed that the trainees had suffered ill-treatment, poor wages and inadequate living conditions on Canadian farms, and the boys' apparent recidivism may have been the product of this exploitation. Cossar was able to weather such criticisms but not the onset of the worldwide depression. Although Cossar's scheme collapsed in 1932, his activities demonstrate that private philanthropy continued to exert its influence on Scottish emigration well into the twentieth century, if not always with positive results.[37]

As these juvenile emigration schemes suggest, by the early twentieth century, emigrant Scots were no longer desired in the Maritimes as a pioneering population but were officially and privately encouraged as an aid to the existing agricultural economy, which was itself experiencing outmigration. As early as 1910, agent-general John Howard was able to recommend Nova Scotia to conservative, less adventurous immigrants, for whom "the pioneer life on the prairie or in the woods does not appeal," with the following appraisal:

Nova Scotia is a province which has not yet come into its own. Its pioneers have made a competence and retired, and the sons of the farmers, attracted by town life or the glamour of Western prairies, have left the homestead for others to cultivate. Thus, fine farms, which only require the ordinary skill of a Scotch farmer to produce large and profitable crops, are in the market at very low prices. . . . No part of Canada offers greater attractions to the middle-aged farmer with a good Scotch training than some parts of Nova Scotia and New Brunswick. . . . One who wishes to ensure himself a comfortable old age and good openings for his children will find the Maritime Provinces a very homelike country, nearer to Great Britain than any other of our over-seas Dominions. He will find perfect security for money and labour invested in the improvement of his land, a rising market for farm produce, and, in the mines, factories, and engineering works of the seaboard provinces, a start in life for all his children, no matter what their talent or inclinations.[38]

It is likely that many of the juvenile immigrants "assisted" to New Brunswick in the 1920s would have sent less glowing accounts, but by that same decade such evaluations of prospects in the factories and mines of Nova Scotia would have been seen as pure fantasy. As in much of Britain, the economic depression was well under way by the 1920s with the postwar decline in demand for goods such as coal and steel, which had been mainstays of the regional economy. Several Nova Scotian industries had disappeared altogether, while others became the focus of severe labour unrest. The strikes against the British Empire Steel and the Dominion Coal companies in Cape Breton were as intense, bitter and violent as any in Britain, including the 1926 General Strike.[39] David Frank has pointed out that, in this context, Cape Breton's Scottish heritage was incorporated into the trade union movement in order to promote greater worker solidarity. Although some members of Cape Breton's industrial workforce had emigrated directly from Scotland, most of the labourers had been drawn from areas of previous Scottish settlement in the region. In the new mining towns, the older Gaelic culture, reflected in music and dance, was married with more recently imported Lowland influences, such as the music hall caricatures of Harry Lauder or the nascent socialism of Robert Burns' "A Man's A Man for A' That." This new "emergent" culture became radicalized during the industrial conflicts of the 1920s and as a consequence became firmly associated with working class identity in Cape Breton. No longer the sentimental romantic cultural lament of the dejected, downtrodden exile, Scottish culture in this context became the combative "Gaelic war cry" which, it was claimed, the miner's progenitors used to "shout on the field of battle."[40]

New research is thus transforming our understanding of the variety and character of the Scottish connection with Nova Scotia. As the chapters in Part

2 of this book indicate, Scottish emigrants included, among others, Highland crofters, Lowland merchants and Edinburgh philanthropists, and their arrival influenced the development of the province's class identities. Nevertheless, when any serious attempts have been made to quantify the migration, scholars have been confronted with the problem of serious gaps in provincial immigration records, giving rise to much vague and ill-informed speculation about the actual significance of Scottish settlers in the province. However, as early as 1942, J.S. Martell provided a systematic survey of the immigration statistics available in the Public Archives of Nova Scotia. His findings confirm that, for some time in the nineteenth century, Scots were indeed the most numerous immigrants, accounting for 21,833 of the 39,243 known arrivals at Nova Scotian ports between 1815 and 1838.[41] In only six years did Irish arrivals exceed those from Scotland, and particularly large numbers of Scots arrived from 1817 to 1819 and in 1828, 1829, 1830 and 1832. Vessels disembarked their human cargoes at an increasing number of ports, among which Halifax, Pictou and Sydney were the most prominent. But deficient statistics for these major ports (particularly the latter two), and non-existent records for the outports along the Cape Breton coast and Northumberland Strait where many migrants were landed, suggest that the figure of 21,833 Scots may be a considerable underestimation.[42]

During the later nineteenth century, the initial Scottish settlement was supplemented by more recent arrivals, who had often been encouraged by previously successful settlers, whose glowing correspondence was quoted in the agent-general's annual reports. Nevertheless, Scottish immigrants were outnumbered by the English throughout the professional agency period—a point not always noted in migration studies, which tend to highlight the remarkable Scottish influx of the early to mid-nineteenth century. By the 1921 census, the 148,000 Nova Scotians of Scottish origin represented just over 28 percent of the province's total population of 523,837, whereas those of English origin represented about 39 percent of the total.[43] Some potential immigrants may have been deterred by occasional rumours of fraudulent agencies (although these rarely surfaced in published propaganda), while others were positively discriminated against.[44] E.B. Elderkin, the provincial government's travelling representative in Britain, admitted in 1914 that crofters from the mainland around Inverness would do well in Cape Breton and southwest Nova Scotia, but claimed that this was not true for their countrymen from the Western Isles whose forbears had pioneered settlement on Cape Breton a century earlier.

> From my observations I would say that the Hebrides are the most hopeless places that I have ever seen in which to secure suitable emigrants for Nova Scotia. . . . I did not meet a single individual whom I would have felt justified in recommending, even had they

been willing to go. . . . The wants of these people are few, and easily supplied, and I cannot help but say that in my judgement it would be next to a crime to put forward an organised effort to transplant them into a different climate and conditions.[45]

Such blatant discrimination was repeated by investigators across Canada[46] and it was not entirely restricted to the Hebrideans. Until about 1925, Scottish immigrants were either portrayed as uncivilised, quarrelsome and litigious or, by the late nineteenth century, were increasingly ignored as irrelevant, pre-industrial bystanders in celebrations of Nova Scotia's material progression to cosmopolitan status. A commentary on the Pictou Scots in 1859 disparaged them as "a canting, covenanting, oat-eating, money-griping tribe of second-hand Scotch Presbyterians: a transplanted, degenerate, barren patch of high cheek-bones and red hair, with nothing cleaving to them of the original stock, except covetousness and that peculiar cutaneous eruption for which the mother country is celebrated."[47] Yet, paradoxically, by the 1930s, Nova Scotia Premier Angus L. Macdonald had begun promoting his province's "tartan" heritage—a process that continues to this day. Certainly, we must look beyond numbers, areas of settlement and the range of Scottish immigrant types if we are to understand the apparent contradiction between declining numbers and the increasing celebration of Scottishness in late-twentieth-century Nova Scotia.

The Making of Memory

One way of reaching an understanding of the late-twentieth-century preoccupation with "tartanism" is to examine how the link with Scotland has been remembered. In other words, how has the memory of Scotland been reflected in Nova Scotian culture? Studies elsewhere have demonstrated that the memory of individual and collective experience is often moulded in order to accommodate prevailing orthodoxies.[48] As discussed above, the standard account that emerged during the nineteenth century was that of the Scottish Romantics. On both sides of the Atlantic, this first entailed cultivation of powerful victim imagery which highlighted the plight of exiled Highlanders and obscured the contributions of Scottish labourers, artisans, farmers and even business elites; later this was reduced to a sentimentalized "Kailyard" celebration of the virtues of the rural life from which many Scottish emigrants had apparently been drawn and had recreated in Nova Scotia. The chapters in Part 3 of this volume address the extent to which the Scottish population of Nova Scotia accommodated their collective memories to this orthodox version of events.

Rusty Bitterman's chapter, "On Remembering and Forgetting," examines how Highland memory was invoked to help immigrants adjust to the realities of settlement in Nova Scotia. He stresses the importance of understanding the chronological and class factors that could induce some members of the community to "remember" and others to "forget." The initial response in Gaelic songs, such as those of Donald Chisholm, was to blame the landlords for unwanted emigration. The "plague on the landlords" called for by such poets echoed the disillusionment of late-eighteenth-century Gaelic bards in Scotland itself. These men, often from the "middle and upper strata" of Highland society, articulated a criticism that highlighted landlord betrayal, abandonment of custom and the placing of profits above people. As a consequence, these poems became a central part of the Highland victim imagery. Bitterman argues, however, that although these poets, by virtue of their prominent social position, had some claim to speak for their communities, the varied experience of the settlers in large part accounts for whether or not they maintained such interpretations. For instance, on Prince Edward Island, where the commercialization of agriculture became a hotly contested issue in the 1830s, the "memory" of landlord oppression continued to be invoked, while in Nova Scotia, where many Highland Scots had successfully integrated into the colonial elite, symbolized by the creation of Highland societies on the London model, the criticisms of the commercialization of Highland agriculture were conveniently ignored. Instead, greater emphasis was placed on the Highlanders' martial traditions and history of loyalty, especially in North America.

Bitterman acknowledges the great difficulty of measuring the extent to which those responsible for selecting and constructing these versions of events shaped or simply reflected wider emigrant opinion. Michael Kennedy, in his chapter, "Lochaber no more," rises to this challenge by exploring how alternative Gaelic understandings of migration failed to be incorporated into the dominant narrative. After closely examining the oral Gaelic folklore of Nova Scotia, it becomes apparent that, along with the lamenting of the emigration as a forced exile, there was an equally strong tradition of celebrating the migration to the new land. Kennedy accounts for this dichotomy by highlighting the personal experiences of those who composed the songs, particularly John the Hunter and his critic, Alan the Ridge, and he also points out that Gaelic song was a public form of expression which encouraged diversity of opinion. This not only makes the oral tradition more dynamic than is commonly understood but also renders it a valuable source of broader opinion in the settler community. Although Kennedy cautions that the oral tradition does not allow a single Gaelic version of events to be isolated, he concludes that, contrary to expectations created by the dominant mythic tradition, on balance the majority of Maritime Gaelic songs celebrate the emigration from Scotland rather than lament it. On rare occasions, as the oral tradition of Strathalbyn, Prince Edward Island, indicates, this could even result in criticism of those who would abandon their settlements in the New World to return to Scotland. Kennedy accounts for the failure of the more favourable Gaelic memory of emigration and settlement to have an impact on the dominant narrative by pointing to the highly selective reading of the folklore by authors external to the community. Essentially, only those songs which confirmed the romantic interpretation of the Highland emigrants as victims were selected, translated and incorporated into the dominant English language tradition.

Kennedy's exhaustive treatment of the Gaelic oral sources highlights two problems which must be faced when attempting to recover the collective memory of Highland emigration. The first is common to all preliterate cultures and concerns the need for sensitivity to the ways in which memory can survive in nonwritten form. This is not only true for Gaelic Scotland and Nova Scotia, but also for colonial West Africa or native North America. Secondly, we need to be conscious of how the memory of marginalized peoples can be distorted or ignored by the dominant culture.[49] The implication of Bitterman and Kennedy's chapters is clear: the power to construct collective memory often rests with the most successful and the most powerful. All the same, resistance to the pervasive victim narrative has been attempted, particularly in twentieth-century literature.

In the final chapter of this volume, "Above and Below Ground," Uwe Zagratzki argues for a detectable "decolonizing strategy" in the regional fiction produced in both Scotland and Nova Scotia. In this century a number of Scottish authors, particularly Lewis Grassic Gibbon, have situated their literature in the northeast. Zagratzki believes that this is significant, not only because it is a region largely ignored by English or English-influenced Edinburgh authors, who tend to focus on the Highlands, but because the agricultural rhythms of the community reflected in these tales recall a "genuine" democratic tradition, which in the work of Gibbon traces its ancestry from the Picts to the 1930s. The control that Gibbon's Lowland peasants are determined to exercise over their work combats both the Calvinist ideology of the Reformation and the socially destructive effects of agricultural capitalism. In Cape Breton the Gaelic past and Highland mythology are invoked as forms of resistance. Zagratzki points out that in the work of Alistair MacLeod the miners' fate is linked to that of their ancestors. Just as landlord-directed clearances were held to be responsible for the exodus from Scotland, so economic pressures brought to bear by industrial capitalism are portrayed as forcing the miners underground.[50] Yet, ironically, it is in the mining communities where Highland culture is maintained and preserved, perhaps most dramatically in the pickling jars of Sheldon Currie's *The Glace Bay Miners' Museum*. In addition to restricting industrial capitalism by being involved in her community's ceilidhs, storytelling and Gaelic language, Margaret McNeil makes a dramatic gesture of defiance by preserving some of her dead husband, brother and grandfather's body parts in a private museum, refusing to allow the memory of their death in the mines to be forgotten.[51]

Zagratzki's chapter demonstrates how the dominant narrative can be subverted and made to accommodate these more democratic concerns, although even those providing criticism expressed their views in romantic, naturalistic and rural terms. It is, after all, the act of "digging" which symbolically links

Gibbon's Lowland peasants with MacLeod's Cape Breton miners—a socialism of the earth. This mythic, agrarian Scottishness developed on both sides of the Atlantic and continues, as Zagratzki's examples demonstrate, to hold a dominant position in contemporary image making. In Scotland, focus was initially placed on an invented Highland landscape that owed more to the images created by Landseer and Sir Walter Scott than to the demographic reality of a country in which four-fifths of the population lived in the urban-industrial central Lowlands.[52] It subsequently became more closely associated with the "Kailyard" genre of literature, which sentimentalised the rural life of the "but and ben"[53] for a mass audience in the late nineteenth- and early twentieth-century popular publications.[54] Perhaps it was precisely because it offered an escape from the demographic and industrial realities of urban Scotland was the Kailyard genre so appealing. In Nova Scotia, argues Ian McKay in his seminal article on "tartanism", the primitive rusticity celebrated in such fiction did not become an admired quality in the province until after World War One, when, in an era of industrial decline and then worldwide economic depression, faith in material progress was lost. Instead Nova Scotians began to construct an alternative notion of heritage, in which Scottishness was equated with manliness, probity and success. Simplicity was now commended rather than condemned, and the emphasis of a previous generation of Nova Scotian writers on the virtues of economic development was replaced by a celebration of pre-industrial traditions which were claimed, inaccurately, to represent the essence of Scottishness.[55]

McKay also argues that, in the 1930s, desire to portray Nova Scotia as a pre-industrial Arcadia where the common folk continued the ancient ways brought with them from Scotland was particularly encouraged by the Scotophile premier Angus L. Macdonald, who apparently saw this as a way of bolstering Depression-era tourism to the province.[56] Macdonald also appears to have been at least partially motivated by political concerns. The calming influence of a sanitized past was particularly attractive to a premier who had to face demands on the left for a halt to unfettered industrial capitalism as a solution to 1930s crises.[57] Nevertheless, McKay points out that Macdonald was personally attached to a romantic understanding of the Scottish past and applied this understanding of his own heritage to the entire province.

In promoting the Scottish rural folk ideal, Nova Scotians like Macdonald were participating in wider inter-war intellectual developments. Pyrs Gruffudd has pointed out that in Britain, particularly Wales, the romanticization of landscape and simple life came to be closely associated with nationalism. Although initiated by the nineteenth-century Romantics' celebration of the wilds of Wales, Scotland, and rugged areas of England such as the Lake District, by the 1930s the preservation movement sought to link the maintenance of the countryside with protection of the community. Preservation of identity, whether local, regional or national, came to be identified with the conservation of rural landscape. Even though this could, as in Wales, be associated with radical "Celtic nationalism," the countryside movement tended to act, like heritage development in Nova Scotia, as a socially conservative force.[58]

The power to construct collective memory, however, no longer appears to reside in the community's oral tradition, the creations of literary artists, the concerns of political leadership or even the campaigns of preservation movements, but rather in the commercial dictates of "heritage." Economic vulnerability and the quest for an acceptable corporate identity have given a particular potency to the heritage hunters' search for an imagined past in which the myth is so much more attractive than the truth. This is exemplified in Nova Scotia by the simultaneous creation of the Cape Breton Highlands National Park and the Cabot Trail during the 1930s.[59] Since the late nineteenth century, travellers had come to Cape Breton in search of the "preserved" Gaelic culture of the region. As early as 1886, Charles H. Farnham, an American writing for *Harper's Weekly*, described his grand tour of the region in a style borrowed from Johnson and Boswell, and celebrated the simple life of the region.[60] By 1932 the construction of a highway into the more remote, mountainous parts of the island was seen by the government as having several economic benefits. In particular, it would provide work for the region's unemployed and it would draw tourists, largely from the United States, to the region. The creation of the national "Highlands" park was similarly motivated, and spurious parallels with the Scottish Highlands were deliberately constructed. Tourists, like those who had journeyed to the Scottish Highlands from the second half of the nineteenth century, were expected to be enthralled by the rugged beauty of Cape Breton's mountains, but they were also encouraged to reflect on the heroism of the Gaelic emigrants who had settled the region.[61] The extent to which this could reach is best exemplified by the "Lone Shieling," an alleged replica of a Scottish Highland original habitation built in stone and thatch along the northernmost stretch of the Cabot Trail. Constructed in 1947 with the aid of a bequest from Donald S. MacIntosh, a Dalhousie University geology professor and settler grandson, the Shieling bears no relation to actual dwellings constructed by the Highland emigrants who, as James Symonds' chapter points out, naturally made use of the abundant supply of wood to construct their buildings. The thought of assembling the necessary stones in order to construct a remembrance of home could only have occurred to later generations with sufficient resources and leisure to indulge such sentimental inclinations.[62]

The coupling of tourism and romantic Scottishness continues to be reflected in contemporary heritage promotion. Every summer at the Halifax Citadel, which was only surrendered to the Canadian army in 1906 and was not converted into a heritage site until 1951, visitors are treated to the spectacle of a company of mid-Victorian, kilted, 78th Highlanders going through their drills.[63] Despite having housed numerous units of the British army, the cura-

Figure 1.1   The "Lone Shieling" Cape Breton Highlands National Park
(D. Kaufman photo)

tors of the Citadel chose to recreate a period when a Highland regiment was ensconced in the fortress. By doing so, the site meets tourist expectations better than, say, a company of Welsh Fusiliers could. This coupling of the mythic, sentimental understanding of Nova Scotia's Scottishness with the concerns of the tourist industry is seen even more clearly in Pictou, Nova Scotia, where a replica of the *Hector* is currently under construction.

Employing the *Hector* as a tool for promoting the province has had a long history. The 150th anniversary celebrations of its landing demonstrated that as early as 1923 the ship was emerging as an important element in Nova Scotia's tourism.[64] The current scheme continues to view the vessel as a key element in the regeneration of the local economy. The harbour site of the new *Hector* boasts a museum and gift shop, and the planners hope that the entire area will aid in the renewal of the town's waterfront. Ironically, however, the former wealth of Pictou was generated not by Highland pioneer agriculturalists but by merchants and later industrialists. A pulp mill on the opposite side of the harbour still dominates the town's environs, and Pictou's association with the industrial past has led one local historian to claim the epitaph "Canada's Cradle of Industry" for the community.[65] Nevertheless, the cover of her popular history illustrates a distinctly pre-industrial group of Highland emigrants struggling ashore from the *Hector*. Only when one delves beyond the surface does the mercantile and industrial character of the community become apparent, while the harbourside reconstruction itself involves a similar masking of the community's actual historical experience.[66]

Figure 1.2   Illustrated cover of *The Birth Place of New Scotland: An illustrated History of Pictou County, Canada's Cradle of Industry*, by Judith Hoegg Ryan, Halifax, 1995 (courtesy of Formac Publishing Ltd.)

The adoption of romantic Scottishness for commercial advantage has also been patently apparent in Scotland itself, as David McCrone and his colleagues have recently demonstrated in *Scotland—The Brand*.[67] Their study concludes that Scotland suffers from "too much heritage," the manufacture of which has given rise to a spurious, ersatz image of the country's past that, in the absence of a distinct national state, provides Scots with a ready-made and saleable group of trivialized national symbols—Bannockburn tea towels, Bonnie Prince Charlie shortbread tins, Mary, Queen of Scots, playing cards—while tours of the empty Highland landscape, particularly by North Americans, have had the added bonuses of supplying customers for remotely located gift shops and reinforcing the notion of a land fossilized since the Battle of Culloden and the Clearances. Hence, until recently it was places such as Inverness, Skye and Pitlochry that, in addition to the ancient capital of Edinburgh, were promoted as heritage destinations. Only now, in its reinvented form as "city of culture" or "city of architecture", has Glasgow been subjected to the same packaging. An example of how this idealized Scotland has become so far removed from its actual landscape is that of Arthur Freed, the producer of "Brigadoon," who had toured the country in 1953 in search of a suitable Highland village for his film, only to return to Hollywood to claim that his visit had yielded "nothing that looked like Scotland."[68]

Again, it is a Romantic, Sir Walter Scott, who has been credited as the founder of Scotland's modern tourist industry. His novels and poems have not only popularised Scotland's past, they have also sent an ever-rising tide of domestic and foreign tourists in search of a vicarious historical experience to the sites celebrated in his writings. By the late nineteenth century, the government too was beginning to recognise heritage as a national commodity, and in 1882 Parliament passed the Ancient Monuments Act, taking sixty-eight structures under its protection. By 1982, this number had mushroomed to over 12,000, along with 330,000 listed buildings and more than 5,000 conservation sites, often spurred on by the lobbying of embattled aristocratic proprietors anxious to find a means of supplementing declining fortunes while maintaining their ancestral residences, at least during their own lifetimes. Most of the growth in heritage sites has occurred since 1970, an era in which the changing demands of tourists also gave rise to concepts of participatory heritage experiences instead of passive observation of static historic sites.[69] One such example is Edinburgh's Royal Mile, where tourists can now sample, in addition to the numerous tartan shops along the route from the Castle to Holyrood Palace, the diorama of the route's newest addition, the Scotch Whisky Heritage Museum. As with many other such Disney-fied sites in the United Kingdom and elsewhere, visitors are treated to full-scale mock-ups, worthy of Madame Tussaud, illustrating the history of whisky making, and to an obligatory shop where one can purchase the industry's more recent efforts.

Such developments are part of what Stephen Haseler has termed, in a different context, the creation of the "Theme Park" nation,[70] implying the reduction of complex and contentious national sites into sanitized, trivialized, recreational heritage destinations packaged for the ever-expanding tourist trade. Although these creations may appear innocuous and even desirable, given the economic benefits, David Lowenthal, in *Possessed by the Past*, has recently highlighted the danger of allowing heritage to continue to expand in its present uncritical form. He notes that "because heritage concerns are passionately partisan, they are also seamed with paradox." In summing up both the proponents and detractors of current preoccupations, Lowenthal provides a pithy encapsulation of the most prevalent concerns:

> Heritage brings manifold benefits: it links us with ancestors and off-
> spring, bonds neighbors and patriots, certifies identity, roots us in
> time honoured ways. But heritage is also oppressive, defeatist and
> decadent. Miring us in the obsolete, the cult of heritage . . . immures
> life within museums and monuments. Breeding xenophobic hate, it
> becomes a byword for bellicose discord. Debasing the "true" past for
> greedy or chauvinist ends, heritage . . . [can undermine] . . . historical
> truth with twisted myth. Exalting rooted faith over critical reason, it
> stymies social action and sanctions passive acceptance of preordained
> fate.[71]

Heritage can empower, but it can also exclude and victimise. Combatants in the Balkans cite their heritage as justification for brutality, just as extremists in Northern Ireland have used it as an excuse for their violence. Even in Nova Scotia, although seldom leading to direct conflict, the romanticized Scottish heritage can feed racial tension. Zagratzki's chapter notes that despite the decolonizing purpose of Cape Breton's Scottish-influenced literature, its crea-tion has, ironically, retarded the development of a regional literature of indig-enous peoples. The colonized become the colonizers. This is seen even more dramatically in *Speak It!*, a National Film Board of Canada documentary on Blacks in Nova Scotia, in which a youth is interviewed in the Halifax Public Gardens with a piper playing in the background, which prompts him to declare that "you don't have to be Scottish to have a heritage."[72] In addition, the distilled Scottish heritage with its emphasis on tartan, clans and Highland soldiers is extremely masculine in character. As can be seen from the contribu-tions in this volume, women are seldom viewed in anything other than sup-portive roles. Emma Stirling's career suggests that this exclusion has had a very long history, and certainly a great deal more research is required before we can address this imbalance.[73]

Conclusion

Who controls the memories of Scotia and Nova Scotia? Whose interests are served by the presentations of that past? The "commodification of culture" that the contemporary heritage industry represents has had the effect of perpetuat-ing distortions and trivialising the impact of Scottish settlement, ultimately producing a tartan travesty in which Scottish identity has become little more than a series of unconnected marketable goods. As Lowenthal points out, we cannot do without heritage, nor is it desirable to do so; nevertheless, since ancestral loyalties often "rest on fiction as well as truth," we must learn "to face its fictions." A fuller understanding of the past is not only as exciting, entertaining and authentic as the prevailing romantic-mythic interpretations, but also vital because it challenges us to face the difficult issues that have affected both the historical connections between Scotland and Nova Scotia and our own contemporary society. The project that professional academics, heritage agencies and the wider public must undertake is to broaden our collective memory, even beyond the detailed recounting of individual migrations, in order to incorporate the experiences of Scots men, women and children who have been left out of the narrative. Furthermore, we must also strive to reach a better understanding of how Scots related to the peoples they encountered in Nova Scotia. It is hoped that this book represents a modest contribution to that wider purpose.

Notes

1. In particular, Benedict Anderson's notion that nations are in fact "imagined communities" supported by shared mythological understandings of origin and character has had considerable influence on scholarship; see Anderson, *Imagined Communities: Reflections on the Origin and Spread of Nationalism* (London, 1983). For the role of myth in historiography, see R. Samuel and P. Thompson, *The Myths We Live By* (London, 1990). The importance of myth in shaping the identity of Scotland is surveyed in D. Broun, R.J. Finlay and M. Lynch, eds., *Image and Identity: The Making and Re-making of Scotland Through the Ages* (Edinburgh, 1998), and the essays in I. Donnachie and C. Whatley, eds., *The Manufacture of Scottish History* (Edinburgh, 1992), set out to revise some of the more persistent myths of Scottish history. For a related history of the creation of English identity, see Stephen Hasler, *The English Tribe; Identity, Nation and Europe* (London, 1996). An extremely helpful analysis of myth and identity in a comparative British colonial context is Richard White, *Inventing Australia: Images and Identity, 1688–1980* (Sydney, 1981); and, for a broader Australian historiographical analysis, see James Walter, "Defining Australia," in G. Whitlock and D. Carter (eds.), *Images of Australia: An Introductory Reader in Australian Studies* (St. Lucia, Queensland, 1992). A useful study which explores one of the more persistent mythic identities elsewhere in Canada is Norman Knowles, *Inventing the Loyalists: The Ontario Loyalist Tradition and the Creation of Useable Pasts* (Toronto, 1997).
2. Hon. Henry Erskine, "The Emigrant: A Poem," 2nd ed., 1796, *Scottish Chap Books*, LC 2894(19), National Library of Scotland. The poem was first published in the *Weekly Magazine*, vol. 31 (1776). Erskine was an Edinburgh lawyer with Whig inclinations.
3. Robert Burns, "Address of Beelzebub," in *The Poems and Songs of Robert Burns*, 3 vols., J. Kinsley, ed., no. 108 (Oxford, 1968). The poem was not published until 1818. In the meantime, Burns had, under the earl's patronage, composed a much more flattering poem, still preserved in the author's own hand on the wall of Kenmore Inn, on the natural beauty of the Breadalbane Estate.
4. Quoted in Peter Womack, *Improvement and Romance: Constructing the Myth of the Highlands* (London, 1989), p. 123.
5. Katie Trumpener, *Bardic Nationalism: The Romantic Novel and the British Empire* (Princeton, 1997).

6. This was also true of Nova Scotian literary culture. Thomas McCulloch, a native of Paisley, founder of Pictou Academy and the first president of Dalhousie College, was particularly influenced by the literary models of *Blackwood's Edinburgh Magazine* and Sir Walter Scott. See the summary of his career by Susan Buggey and Gwendolyn Davies in *Dictionary of Canadian Biography* (hereafter *DCB*), vol. VII, pp. 529–41. The colony's most renowned early author, Thomas Chandler Haliburton, whose parents were from England, used the first line of Scott's *Lay of the Minstrel*, "This is my own, my native land," as the epitaph for his *Statistical Account of Nova Scotia*. See *DCB*, Vol. IX, pp. 348–57.

7. See the Cowan and Kennedy chapters in this volume.

8. The verses to the song also parallel sentimental Scottish poetry:

> The sun was setting in the west,
> The birds were singing on ev'ry tree,
> All nature seemed inclined to rest,
> But still there was no rest for me.
>
> I grieve to leave my native land,
> I grieve to leave my comrades all,
> And my aged parents whom I always held so dear,
> And the bonnie, bonnie lass that I adore.
>
> The drums they do beat and the wars do alarm,
> The captain calls, we must obey,
> So farewell, farewell to Nova Scotia's charms,
> For it's early in the morning I am far, far away.
>
> I have three brothers and they are at rest,
> Their arms are folded on their breast,
> But a poor simple sailor just like me,
> Must be tossed and driven on the dark blue sea.

Intriguingly, this "traditional" song was first published in 1932 as "The Nova Scotia Song" by the folklorist Helen Creighton, whom Ian McKay identifies as one of the leading contributors to what he has termed the early twentieth-century anti-modernist "Quest of the folk." According to McKay, such sentimental folk songs and tales provided an illusory escape from the rigours of modern capitalism and allowed Nova Scotians to reinvent themselves as custodians of a unique pre-industrial "simple life." See Helen Creighton, *Traditional Songs from Nova Scotia* (Toronto, 1950), pp. 264–65; and Ian McKay, *The Quest of the Folk: Anti-Modernism and Cultural Selection in Twentieth-Century Nova Scotia* (Montreal, 1994).

9. The chorus and remaining verses are as follows:

> When you go, will you send back
> A letter from America?
> Take a look down the railtrack
> From Miami to Canada.

Broke off from my work the other day
I spent the evening thinking about
All the blood that flowed away
Across the ocean to the second chance.
I wonder how it got on when it
reached the promised land?. . .

. . . Lochaber no more
Sutherland no more
Lewis no more
Skye no more . . .

I wonder my blood,
Will you ever return
To help us kick life back
To a dying mutual friend
Do we not love her?
Do we not say we love her?
Do we have to roam the world
To prove how much it hurts?

Bathgate no more
Linwood no more
Methil no more
Irvine no more.
The Proclaimers, "Letter from America," *This is the Story* (Chrysalis
Records, 1987) .

10. For a review, see Kenneth Donovan, "Reflections on Cape Breton Culture: An
    Introduction," in *The Island: New Perspectives on Cape Breton's History, 1713–
    1990* (Fredericton, 1990), pp. 1–29. A philosopher's critique of the phenomenon
    is John E. MacKinnon's "Sentiment and Community," *Scottish Tradition* 22 (1997),
    pp. 44–55.
11 *Scotland on Sunday*, 14 December 1997, p. 20.
12. See, for example, J.M. Bumsted, *The People's Clearance: Highland Emigration
    to British North America* (Edinburgh, 1982); Eric Richards, *A History of the
    Highland Clearances. Vol.2, Emigration, Protest, Reasons* (London, 1985); Allan
    I. Macinnes, "Scottish Gaeldom: The First Phase of Clearance," in T.M. Devine
    and R. Mitchison (eds.), *People and Society in Scotland. Vol.1, 1760–1830* (Edin-
    burgh, 1988); Marianne McLean, *The People of Glengarry: Highlanders in Tran-
    sition, 1745–1820* (Montreal, 1991); J.I. Little, *Crofters and Habitants: settler
    society and economy in a Quebec township* (Montreal, 1991); and T.M. Devine,
    *From Clanship to the Crofters' War: The social transformation of the Scottish
    Highlands* (Manchester, 1994). Rosemary Ommer's "Primitive Accumulation and
    the Scottish Clan in the Old World and the New," *Journal of Historical Geogra-
    phy* 12, no. 2 (1986), pp. 121–41, examines the persistance of clan allegiances as
    reflected in Nova Scotian landholding practices, while Allan MacNeil, "Scottish
    Settlement in Colonial Nova Scotia: A Case Study of St. Andrew's Township,"

Scottish Tradition 19 (1994), pp. 60–79, stresses instead the importance of economic factors over kinship in Antigonish County.

13. See E.J. Cowan, "Myth and identity in early medieval Scotland," *Scottish Historical Review* 63 (1984), pp. 111–35; Bruce Webster, *Medieval Scotland: the making of an identity* (New York, 1997); Murray G.H. Pittock, *The Invention of Scotland: The Stuart Myth and the Scottish Identity* (London, 1981), pp.1–5, 73–98. Pittock also suggests that echoes of this mythological coupling of the Stewarts and Scottish nationhood have been seen more recently in the folksinging revival and in the renewed popular and academic interest in Jacobitism (pp. 160–65). For the development of the Jacobite folk tradition, see also William Donaldson, *The Jacobite Song: Political Myth and National Identity* (Aberdeen, 1988). The sanitizing impact of Scott's romanticism is debated in M. Ash, *The Strange Death of Scottish History* (Edinburgh, 1980). For a detailed analysis of the role of myth in the creation of Scottish identity in all eras, see Broun et al., *Image and Identity*, and, most recently, William Ferguson, *The Identity of the Scottish Nation: an historical quest* (Edinburgh, 1998).

14. John G. Reid, "The Conquest of Nova Scotia: Cartographic Imperialism and the Echoes of a Scottish Past," in Ned C. Landsman (ed.), *Nation and Province in the First British Empire* (East Linton, forthcoming). For a summary of recent archaeological investigations of Alexander's settlement, see Brigitta Wallace Ferguson, *The Scots Fort: A Reassessment of its Location* (Halifax, 1994). The most recent celebration of the venture is Mark Finnan's *The First Nova Scotian* (Halifax, 1997).

15. V.E. Durkacz, *Decline of Celtic Languages* (Edinburgh, 1983).

16. Hugh Douglas, *Flora MacDonald: the most loyal rebel* (London, 1993).

17. As an American, Henry Wordsworth Longfellow also used his poem *Evangeline*, which began the legend, to criticise of the brutality of the British Empire; a link that latter-day Scottish nationalists have also made with respect to the Highland Clearances. For the character and influence of the legend, see Naomi Griffiths, "Longfellow's *Evangeline*: The Birth and Acceptance of a Legend," *Acadiensis* XI, no. 2 (Spring 1982), pp. 28–41. See also Barbara LeBlanc, *The Dynamic Relationship between Historic Site and Identity Construction: Grand-Pré and the Acadians* (unpublished Ph.D. thesis, Université de Laval, 1994).

18. Linda Colley, *Britons: the Forging of a Nation, 1707–1837* (London, 1992); Philip Buckner, "Whatever happened to the British Empire?," *Journal of the Canadian Historical Association* (1993), pp. 3–32.

19. Sec, for example, Charles W. Dunn, *Highland Settler: A Portrait of the Scottish Gael in Cape Breton* (Toronto, 1953); D. Campbell and R.A. MacLean, *Beyond the Atlantic Roar: A Study of the Nova Scotia Scots* (Toronto, 1974); Neil MacNeil, *Highland Heart in Nova Scotia* (New York, 1948); and, most recently, David Craig, *On the Crofters' Trail: In Search of the Clearance Highlanders* (London, 1990), which follows the migrations to the rest of Canada as well as Nova Scotia.

20. Donald MacKay, *Scotland Farewell: The People of the Hector* (Toronto, 1980), pp. 102 and 135; MacKay also recounts numerous unattributed stories of the Highlanders' naivety, including one of incredulous emigrants mistaking a porcupine for a bear and trying to eat the bark of trees in a search for sugar (p. 145)—a clearly stereotypical and most likely fabricated account.

21. Although Robertson's ambitious scheme, which he did not cost or formulate in

detail, was never implemented, even in part, it does represent the longevity of the influence of the *Hector* saga. John Howard's "Report" in *Journals and Proceedings* (1924), p. 44 (Public Archives of Nova Scotia [hereafter PANS], microfilm 9192).

22. Bernard Bailyn, *Voyagers to the West: A Passage in the Peopling of America on the Eve of the Revolution* (New York, 1986), pp. 390–96.

23. Don Watson, *Caledonia Australis: Scottish Highlanders on the Frontier of Australia* (Sydney, 1984); see also Henry Reynolds, *The Other Side of the Frontier: Aboriginal Resistance to the European Invasion of Australia* (Ringwood, Victoria, 1982).

24. Don Smith, "From Swords to Ploughshares: The Scottish Soldier and Settlement in Central Nova Scotia, 1749–1775" (unpublished Master's thesis, Saint Mary's University, in progress).

25. Campbell and MacLean, *Beyond the Atlantic Roar*, pp. 35–75.

26. Stephen J. Hornsby, *Nineteenth Century Cape Breton: A Historical Geography* (Montreal, 1992), p. 54.

27. See Symonds' chapter below. The Glasgow manufacturers were so embarrassed by the product that they often sent it unstamped. Some of the production sites, such as Bell's Ltd., have been the subject of archaeological investigation by GAURD, University of Glasgow (editors' communication with James Symonds).

28. By 1871, 87 percent of the island's population of 75,000 had been born in Nova Scotia, and the depression of that decade provoked a further wave of outmigration to Halifax, the industrial towns of Pictou County, other parts of the Maritimes, and Boston; Hornsby, *Nineteenth Century Cape Breton*, pp. 121, 186–87, 191–95. For the impact of the famine on Scottish Highland emigration, see T.M. Devine, *The Great Highland Famine: Hunger, Emigration and the Scottish Highlands in the Nineteenth Century* (Edinburgh, 1988).

29. *DCB*, vol. X, pp. 395–96.

30. In 1813 he went into business on his own account, providing credit and goods— usually Scottish imports—to the settlers and storekeepers involved in the timber trade, against their future deliveries of timber. By this means, as well as through his extensive landholdings, fishing, and mining rights, he became extremely powerful, and when he died in 1819 he was owed £10,554 by 151 Nova Scotian debtors, most of them probably fellow Scots; *DCB*, vol. V, pp. 611–12.

31. Lucille H. Campey has recently argued that "the timber trade was the sole reason why ships left in such numbers from Scottish ports for Pictou or the Miramichi, and without those ships the takeover of this part of the eastern Maritimes by Scots could not and would not have happened"; L.H. Campey, "Scottish Settlement Patterns in Canada" (unpublished Ph.D. thesis, University of Aberdeen, 1998). For the central importance of the trade for neighbouring New Brunswick, see Graeme Wynn, *Timber Colony: a historical geography of early nineteenth century New Brunswick* (Toronto, 1981). The timber merchants were effectively emigration agents, in an era when Nova Scotia's attitude towards settlement changed from one of welcome before 1815 to one of indifference or hostility in the 1820s and 1830s, at least to those without means. Scottish novelist and Canada Company director John Galt proposed to establish a land and emigration company in the province in 1834, but his plan was rejected by the Colonial Department on the grounds that it had been "conclusively proved to the Emigration

Commission that Nova Scotia is unfit for the reception of a large number of Emigrants. It contains little good [unsettled] land in all, and that little is scattered in patches separated from each other by Rock and impenetrable Forest. People in this Province frequently become dependent on charity, and the arrival of a ship full of Passengers is looked for [by] the Inhabitants with dread"; J.S. Martell, *Immigration to and Emigration from Nova Scotia, 1815–1838* (Halifax, 1942), PANS publication no. 6, pp. 25–26, from CO 217/157, 14 January 1834.

32. The starting point for examining the history of Blacks in Nova Scotia is Robin Winks, *The Blacks in Canada: a history* (Montreal, 1997, new. ed.), and James W.St.G. Walker, *The Black Loyalists: the search for the promised land in Nova Scotia and Sierra Leone, 1783–1870* (New York, 1976). John Reid and Naomi Griffiths have noted that the Alexander colony enjoyed positive relations with the Mi'kmaq, but by the eighteenth century a good deal of animosity had developed between the Native population and the British. See N.E.S. Griffiths and John G. Reid, "New Evidence on New Scotland, 1629," *William and Mary Quarterly* 69 (July 1992), pp. 491–508; Bill Wicken, "Encounters with Tale Sails and Tall Talks: Mi'kmaq Society, 1500–1760" (unpublished Ph.D. thesis, McGill University, 1994); and *Scots and Aboriginal Culture*, a soon to be published collection of papers given at a conference of the same title at the University of Guelph, 1996.

33. See R.B. Sher and J.R. Smitten, eds., *Scotland and America in the Age of the Enlightenment* (Princeton, 1990).

34. This was compounded by the hostility which many experienced while in the colonies, particularly in the Chesapeake. Alan L. Karras, *Sojourners in the Sun: Scottish Migrants in Jamaica and the Chesapeake, 1740–1800* (Ithaca, 1992); Michael E. Vance, "Scottish Emigration to North America: A Review Essay," *Scottish Tradition* 20 (1995), pp. 65–75.

35 John Howard's appointment in 1896 coincided with the Laurier government's increased commitment to promoting British immigration through federal and provincial agencies, manifested mainly in an injection of $4 million into the federal immigration budget. Recruitment was targeted successfully not only on the traditional categories—farm workers and domestic servants—but also on more affluent immigrants, who were encouraged to invest, particularly in fruit farming. Through lectures, pamphlets, maps, exhibitions of produce, lantern slides, films, and even advertisements on London buses, Howard and his staff tried to convince Britons that Nova Scotia was "not located in the Arctic Circle nor permanently snowbound" and to win recruits who would bolster the provincial economy at a time when people were leaving the Maritime Provinces rather than entering them. The later Atlantic House experiment of 1958, under which one agent-general was meant to represent all the Maritime Provinces, proved to be unworkable, and after Newfoundland and Prince Edward Island had withdrawn from the agreement, Nova Scotia and New Brunswick eventually reverted to separate agents-general in 1968; Shirley B. Elliott, *Nova Scotia in London: A History of its Agents General, 1762–1988* (London, 1988).

36. Raymond Williams, *The Country and the City* (London, 1973). For the impact of these notions on Maritime sporting history, see C. Howell, *Northern Sandlots: a social history of Maritime Baseball* (Toronto, 1995), pp. 27–28. Andrew Sackett's, "Inhaling the Salubrious Air: Health and Development in St. Andrews, New Brunswick, 1880–1910," *Acadiensis* 24, no. 1 (Autumn 1995), pp. 54–81, illus-

trates how these ideas affected the development of one Maritime tourist destination.

37. Recently, the sometimes painful legacy of this type of emigration has been recognised by the opening of the British records dealing with the "Home Children." It is now apparent that in the name of charity many philanthropic agencies had continued to send children to Canada and Australia against their wishes, breaking apart families and leaving deep psychological scars. For an overview of child migration to Canada, see Joy Parr, *Labouring Children: British Immigrant Apprentices to Canada, 1864–1924* (Montreal, 1980).

38. Howard was not beyond employing stereotypes in order to encourage emigration: "The inhabitants are largely of Scotch extraction, with the result that educational facilities in Nova Scotia are very good, and the familiar Scotch institutions, religious, teaching and recreation, are much the same"; undated issue of *Aberdeen Free Press*, quoted in *Annual Report of the Agent General for Nova Scotia, 1910*, pp. 29–30, PANS, microfilm 3610.

39. See John Reid, "The 1920s: Decade of Struggle," in his *Six Crucial Decades: times of change in the history of the Maritimes* (Halifax, 1987), and David Frank, "The 1920s: Class and Region, Resistance and Accommodation," in D. Muise and E. Forbes (eds.), *Atlantic Provinces in Confederation* (Toronto, 1993).

40. According to David Frank, the satirical songs of Dawn Fraser amounted to a cultural wing of J.B. MacLachlan's radical working class political campaigns. Both men were Nova Scotia–born but of Scots ancestry; David Frank, "Tradition and Culture in the Cape Breton Mining Community in the Early Twentieth Century," in K. Donovan (ed.), *Cape Breton at 200: Historical Essays in Honour of the Island's Bicentennial, 1785–1985* (Sydney, 1985), pp. 203–18.

41. Scottish immigration was clearly not easing in 1828, as had been alleged by some commentators. Of the other individuals entering the colony during the same period, 12,949 were Irish immigrants, 2,120 were English and 228 were Welsh, with another 2,113 designated as "passengers." J.S. Martell, *Immigration*, p. 95.

42. Martell, *Immigration*, pp. 10, 92–93.

43. Ian McKay, "Tartanism Triumphant: The Construction of Scottishness in Nova Scotia, 1933–1954," *Acadiensis* 21, no. 2 (Spring 1992), p. 8.

44. In 1909, for instance, Joseph Christie, of Aberdeen, Scotland, abandoned nine female fishworkers in Halifax after recruiting them on the promise of a free return passage and a year's employment at good wages, while a year later the false promises made to a Scottish farmer by a "quondam real estate agent" brought about the discontented immigrant's return to Scotland and a complaint to the agent-general; see Marjory Harper, *Emigration from North East Scotland, Vol. II, Beyond the Broad Atlantic* (Aberdeen, 1988), pp. 241–42, and "Report of the Secretary of Industries and Immigration," *Journals of the House, 1910*, pp. 8–9, PANS, microfilm 3610.

45. Elderkin's Report (1914), in *Report of the Secretary of Industries and Immigration, Journals of the House, 1915*, pp. 32–33, PANS, microfilm 3614.

46. See Michael E. Vance, "British Columbia's Twentieth-Century Crofter Emigration Schemes: A note on new sources," *Scottish Tradition* 18 (1993), pp. 1–27, and Wayne Norton, *Help Us to a Better Land: Crofter Colonies in the Prairie West* (Regina, 1994).

47. Frederick S. Cozzens, *Acadia: or a month with the Blue Noses* (New York, 1859),

pp. 150 and 199.

48. Some of the most intriguing studies in this regard have been of twentieth-century soldiers. See Paul Fussell's classic study, *The Great War and Modern Memory* (Oxford, 1975), and his more recent *Wartime: Understanding and Behavior in the Second World War* (Oxford, 1989), both of which draw on literary evidence. Jonathan Vance's *Death so noble: memory, meaning, and the First World War* (Vancouver, 1997), and Alistair Thomson's *Anzac Memories: Living with the Legend* (Oxford, 1994), are based on oral interviews. The contributions in Kate Darian-Smith and Paula Hamilton, eds., *Memory and History in Twentieth Century Australia* (Oxford, 1994), examine how the popular memories of women and aborigines, as well as soldiers, are accommodated and manipulated by prevailing orthodoxies. John Bodnar's *Remaking America: Public Memory, Commemoration and Patriotism in the Twentieth Century* (Princeton, 1992), and Michael Kammen's *The Mystic Chords of Memory: The Transformation of Tradition in American Culture* (New York, 1991), are two influential studies that examine the intimate relationship between popular memory and national identity in the United States.

49. See John Tosh's extremely useful chapter "History by word of mouth," in *The Pursuit of History: Aims, Methods and New Directions in the Study of History* (London, 2nd ed., 1991). The extent to which the Native perception can be written out of history is ably demonstrated in Robert F. Berknafer, *The White Man's Indian: Images of the American Indian from Columbus to the Present* (New York, 1978). Unfortunately such mistreatment has spawned a plethora of "advocacy" polemics, such as Daniel N. Paul, *We Were Not the Savages: A Micmac Perspective on the Collision of European and Aboriginal Civilizations* (Halifax, 1993), that are just as cavalier with written and oral testimony. The promise of a more balanced approach toward the oral history of a doubly marginalized group is discussed in Nancy Shoemaker, *Negotiators of Change: historical perceptions on Native American Women* (New York, 1995).

50. See also Mary F. Finnigan, "To Live Somewhere Else": Migration and Cultural Identity in Alistair MacLeod's Fiction" (unpublished Master's thesis, Saint Mary's University, 1996). She argues that MacLeod was also influenced by peculiarly Canadian concerns, such as the 1960s preoccupation with finding an authentic identity in the lead-up to the centennial celebrations.

51. Sheldon Currie, *The Glace Bay Miners' Museum: The Novel* (Wreck Cove, N.S., 1995). For an historian's criticism of the recent film version of the novel, see David Frank, "One Hundred Years After: Film and History in Atlantic Canada," *Acadiensis* 26, no. 2 (Spring 1997), pp. 112–36. Frank notes that the focus on the folkish nature of the Glace Bay community ignores the strong influence of the trade union and co-operative movements in modifying the worst effects of industrial capitalism, and that the conflicts portrayed in the film are more in keeping with the turn of the century rather than the apparent 1940s setting.

52. Charles Withers, "The Historical Creation of the Highlands," in Ian Donnachie and Christopher Whatley (eds.), *The Manufacture of Scottish History* (Edinburgh, 1992), pp. 143–56.

53. The *but* referred to the kitchen or outer room, and the *ben* to the inner or best room in a two-room dwelling; Mairi Robinson, *The Concise Scots Dictionary* (Aberdeen, 1987).

54. G. Shepard, "The Kailyard" in D. Gifford (ed.), *A History of Scottish Literature, Vol. 3, Nineteenth Century* (Aberdeen, 1988). For the role of the Kailyard in the popular press, see W. Donaldson, *Popular Literature in Victorian Scotland: language, fiction and the press* (Aberdeen, 1986).

55. This is elaborated upon in McKay's broader intellectual history of the province, *Quest of the Folk*, in which tartanism is seen as part of a more general rustification of Nova Scotia. Industrial realities were excluded in the idealized writings of Gordon Brinley and Neil MacNeil, while Dorothy Duncan perceived them as an encroaching pollutant of the last stronghold of the Gael in North America. Scottish history in relation to the province, as in Scotland itself, was reduced to a selection of isolated, largely rural, romantic incidents. See G. Brinley, *Away to Cape Breton* (New York, 1936); MacNeil, *Highland Heart*; and D. Duncan, *Bluenose: A Portrait of Nova Scotia* (New York, 1942).

56. McKay, "Tartanism Triumphant," pp. 17–20.

57. See E. Forbes, "The 1930s: Depression and Retrenchment," in Muise and Forbes, *Atlantic Provinces in Confederation*.

58. Pyrs Gruffudd, "Heritage as National Identity: Histories and Prospects of National Pasts," in David T. Herbert (ed.), *Heritage, Tourism and Society* (London, 1995), pp. 49–67, and "Remaking Wales: nation-building and the geographical imagination, 1925–50," *Political Geography* 14, no.3 (1995), pp. 219–39. See also Michael Bunce, *The Countryside Ideal: Anglo-American Images of Landscape* (New York, 1994), and Simon Schama, *Landscape and Memory* (New York, 1995).

59. Named after the famous explorer Giovanni Caboto (John Cabot), who explored the Cape Breton coast for the English crown in 1497. The trail begins in Baddeck, which boasts the family home of Alexander Graham Bell, winds by the Gaelic College at St. Ann, and passes "Keltic" Lodge, the government-owned resort at Ingonish, before proceeding through the Highland Park. Only when the traveller comes out of the park and enters Chéticamp, a French Acadian settlement, is it apparent that people other than Highland Scots have a claim to the region.

60. Reprinted with an introduction by Stephen F. Spencer in *Acadiensis* 8, no. 2 (Spring 1979), pp. 90–106.

61. The foundation of the park and construction of the trail are outlined in a park pamphlet entitled "The Cabot Trail, 1932–1992" (University College of Cape Breton, n.d.). The researchers rely on Alan A. MacEachern's unpublished paper "In Search of Eastern Beauty: Establishing the Prince Edward Island and Cape Breton Highlands National Parks, 1935–1939," delivered at the Canadian Historical Association annual meeting, 1992.

62. MacIntosh's grandfather had arrived in the area from Skye via Aberdeen and had been part of a larger Hebridean community that had settled the Pleasant Bay region. Professor MacIntosh, who was also a past president of the Halifax North British Society, donated one hundred acres of the ancestral lands as a park and location for the shieling in the hope that it would be "a visible link between the old Scottish home of our forefathers in the Isle of Skye and [the] new home in the highlands of Cape Breton." His bequest appears to have been inspired by the "Canadian Boat Song," also sometimes known as "The Lone Shieling"; Clara Dennis, *Cape Breton Over* (Toronto, 1942), and McKay, "Tartanism Triumphant," pp. 33–34. A similar sentimental memorial is the cairn commemorating the battle

of Culloden at Knoydart on the Pictou-Antigonish county line; it was constructed in 1938 and has subsequently been the site of an annual service commemorating the victims of the battle.

63. H. Piers, *The Evolution of the Halifax Fortress, 1749–1928* (Halifax, 1947); C.W. Pulsifer, "Highland Officers in Halifax: A Social, Cultural, and Military Study of the Officer Corps of the 78th Highland Regiment of Foot in Halifax, Nova Scotia, 1869–71" (unpublished Ph.D. thesis, Queen's University, 1992); B. Dunn, *The Halifax Citadel, 1906–51: The Canadian Period* (Parks Canada, 1977).

64. Michael Boudreau, "A 'Rare and Unusual Treat of Historical Significance': The 1923 Hector Celebration and the Political Economy of the Past," *Journal of Canadian Studies* 28, no.4 (Winter 1993–94), pp. 28–48.

65. Judith Hoegg Ryan, *The Birthplace of New Scotland: An Illustrated History of Pictou County, Canada's Cradle of Industry* (Halifax, 1995).

66. For an historian's critique of the development, see Michael Boudreau, "Ship of Dreams," *New Maritimes* September/October 1992, pp. 7–15.

67. David McCrone, Angela Morris and Richard Kiely, *Scotland—The Brand: The Making of Scottish Heritage* (Edinburgh, 1995).

68. Forsyth Hardy, *Scotland in Film* (Edinburgh, 1990), p. 1.

69. There are currently three main guardians of Scottish heritage and although they operate side by side, each works to a different agenda. Since the priorities of the Scottish Tourist Board (STB) are to generate income and promote employment, the promotion of heritage is only part of its remit. Its approach is moulded by its marketing priorities, which, interestingly, dictate a romantic, heritage-based promotional campaign for the North American market, and a modified, practical emphasis for British consumers. Whereas the STB defines heritage as a commercial product, Historic Scotland is concerned more with education and the conservation of artefacts than with entertainment and seeks to promote the three hundred properties in its care through publications and information plaques. It has a much lower public profile than the third main promoter of heritage, the National Trust for Scotland, the only agency not funded directly by the state. Founded in 1931 as a largely aristocratic body, and concerned that the (English) National Trust was neglecting Scottish interests, it emphasizes, with considerable success, the collective role of its 230,000 members as stewards of the natural and built environment; McCrone et al., *Scotland—The Brand*, pp. 2–4, 114–34. Also see John R. Gold and Margaret M. Gold, *Imagining Scotland: Tradition, Representation and Promotion in Scottish Tourism since 1750* (Aldershot, 1995).

70. Haseler, *The English Tribe*, p. ix; McCrone et al., *Scotland—The Brand*, p. 5. For a critical discussion of the vogue for Heritage sites, see John Richard and Peter Spearitt, eds., *Packaging the Past? Public Histories* (Melbourne, 1991, a special issue of *Australian Historical Studies*); William J. Murtagh, *Keeping Time: The History and Theory of Preservation in America* (New York, 1990); and David Lowenthal, *The Past is a Foreign Country* (Cambridge, 1985).

71. David Lowenthal, *Possessed by the Past: The Heritage Crusade and the Spoils of History* (New York, 1996), pp. ix–xiii.

72. *Speak It! From the Heart of Black Nova Scotia* (NFB, 1993), directed by Sylvia Hamilton.

73. For the masculine character of Scottish heritage, see McCrone et al., *Scotland—The Brand*. A recent volume that seeks to redress the gender imbalance for Nova

Scotian history in general is Janet Guildford and Suzanne Morton, eds., *Separate Spheres: women's worlds in the 19th-century Maritimes* (Fredericton, 1994). For the role of "standard" political history in minimising the significance of women in Canadian history, see Veronica Strong-Boag, "Contested Space: The Politics of Canadian Memory," in *Journal of the Canadian Historical Association* 5 (1994), pp. 3–17. For similar concerns regarding Scottish history, see Joy Hendry, "Snug in the Asylum of Taciturnity: Women's History in Scotland," in Donnachie and Whatley, *Manufacture of Scottish History*.

MYTH

2

The Myth of Scotch Canada

Edward J. Cowan

It is a strange thing that a nation can hold within itself an ancient race, standing for the lost, beautiful, mysterious, ancient world, can see it fading through its dim twilight without heed to preserve that which might yet be preserved, without interest even in that which once gone cannot come again. The old Gaelic race is in its twilight indeed, but now alas!, it is the hastening twilight after the feast of Samhainn when winter is come at last, out of the hills, down the glens, on the four winds of the world.
—Fiona Macleod, *The Winged Destiny* (1904)

The lament for times, places and peoples past has long been a theme of Celtic, and thus Scottish, literature. William Sharp was an Englishman who, through his pen name, Fiona Macleod, invoked the feminine side of his personality to explore a Celtic twilight which existed largely in his imagination and nowhere else. He thus represents a mindset which was shared by many Scottish immigrants to Canada who realised that what is "once gone cannot come again" but who nonetheless attempted to preserve that which had been lost in myth and memory of their own imagining. Such manifestation of "the kingdom of the mind" might take the form of nostalgic poetry sometimes composed, as will be shown below, by people who had never seen their ancestral home and could barely remember the languages of its people. "Scottishness," which is a notoriously difficult term to define, might be reaffirmed, experienced or invented though such community activities as meetings of Scottish societies or Caledonian games. Music, literature or costume might all play their part, as have revivals of interest in genealogy or clan organizations in the present century.

What is included in such activities is an ongoing process of self-mythologization by people who, for one reason or other, feel themselves to be Scots, or "Scotch," to use the preferred term of the nineteenth century. Here I will argue that such mythologization was already detectable when the Scots first made contact with Canada and that it would remain an important component of the emigrant experience. In the seventeenth century, Sir William Alexander and Sir Robert Gordon of Lochinvar, neither of whom visited what is now Canada, attempted to redefine it in the image of Scotland as successive immigrants continued to do.

If Sir Robert Gordon of Lochinvar had had his way, Cape Breton would now be known as New Galloway. Shortly after Sir William Alexander, Earl of Stirling and Viscount of Canada, received his charter for Nova Scotia, in 1621, he allotted Cape Breton to Gordon, who promptly renamed the island New Galloway after the area of southwest Scotland where his estates were situated. In 1622 he was the promoter of the first expedition from Scotland to Nova Scotia, though the episode was largely a fiasco.

Sir Robert Gordon was a glorious enigma, described by his peers and admirers as a man of robust physical and mental strength who would have been conspicuous in any era, a skilled courtier, an accomplished swordsman and one of Galloway's finest sons. Locally, however, he was known as a hell-raiser who was involved in several feuds. In 1620 he was in debt to the tune of £100,000. In the course of his life, which ended, along with his transatlantic dreams, in 1627, he was accused of seizure of property, of several slaughters and murders, of organising illegal convocations, of oppressively seizing ships and, for good measure, of arson, abduction and adultery. He killed his own servant, a Gordon kinsman, on the grounds that his victim had had an affair with his wife, of whom Sir Robert wished to rid himself and thus sought to discredit. On one occasion his own mother sought protection against his violence. He was, in short, the perfect man to embark upon a colonial project.[1]

Alexander sent a ship for Gordon's use to Kirkcudbright in Galloway in May 1622 so, as he said, "the businesse might beginne from that kingdome which it did concerne." In what was truly the first Scottish colonial scheme, the participants displayed little of the flair and enterprise for which successive generations of Scots later became so famous. Gordon himself was nowhere to be seen; the Galwegians were reluctant to embark; locally the price of victuals had tripled. The ships did not arrive off the coast of Nova Scotia until mid-September and were forced to winter in St. John's, Newfoundland. After further setbacks, they eventually, in the summer of 1623, discovered the joys of Cape Breton:

> delicate medowes, having roses white and red, growing thereon with
> a kind of wilde lilly, which had a daintie smel . . . very good fat earth,

> having severall sorts of beries growing thereon, as goose-berries, straw-berries, hind-berries, rasberries, and a kind of red wine berie, as also some sorts of graine, as pease, some eares of wheate, barly and rie growing there wilde,

as well as plentiful supplies of timber, fish, fowl and game.[2]

This visit, however, represented the highpoint and the expedition was effectively over.

As well organised a pamphlet as the expedition was chaotic, Alexander's *Encouragement to Colonies* surveyed the history of colonization from the time of Columbus, noting by implication where others had gone wrong. He had a shrewd grasp of the appeal, importance and potential benefits of the enterprise upon which he had embarked. He speculated on the idea that the native peoples had entered the American continent by way of the polar land and ice bridge. He was full of admiration for the achievements of his predecessors and, remarkably for the period, he did not allow religious conviction to cloud his judgement. Moderation in all things inspired Alexander's vision for Canada, in which country his views deserve to be much better known. No less remarkable, in view of Gordon's well-attested ruffian-like behaviour, was *Encouragements For such as shall have intention to bee Under-takers in the new plantation of Cape Briton, now New Galloway in America, by Mee Lochinvar* (1625), which is, quite simply, a masterpiece of the literature of colonization. Conventionally, the author noted conversion of the heathen as one of the main motives for plantation, but he then went on to anticipate the key justifications for emigration which would be reiterated ad nauseam by future generations, namely, enlargement of the dominions—in this case, specifically Scottish—national and personal enrichment, the bridling of sedition at home and settling "security against enemies abroad." Other motives included glory, adventure, the removal of "that unbeliefe, which is so grounded in the mindes of men, to the discredite most noble and profitable endevoures with distrust," and the benefit of his fellow human beings.

> Wee are not borne to our selves: but to help others, and our abilities and meanes are not so much unlike at the first houre of our birth, and the last minute of our death: and it is our deedes good or bad that all of us have to carrie to Heaven or Hell after this life.[3]

Gordon's short pamphlet followed Alexander's in theme and moderate tone. For example, he recommended that conversion would be most effectively accomplished "by daily conversation where we may see the life, and learn the languages of others," and he took care to give the aboriginal words for certain plants and roots. He considered the highest calling of any person to be the acquisition of territory for the mother country, condemning the feebleness of those who were content to pursue unadventurous and impecunious existences, which were a disgrace to the memories of their heroic and patriotic ancestors. Gordon highlighted the classless nature of emigration by pointing out that, in recently planted Ireland, gentlemen had become peers, and artisans gentlemen, but he was particularly interested in encouraging people of his own class, together with their younger sons, to become involved, in order that they might escape prodigality, lack of preferment and the universal distress occasioned by debt, and become more like Italians, who were not afraid to dirty their hands on trade. Anyone who failed to hearken to his words of wisdom was unceremoniously dismissed as

> either the bastard of generosity, or the nursling of simplicity, or the abject of frugality: and shall either become for ever, the prostitute of infamy, or consecrated to perpetual oblivion: and when he is dead, his actions, his means, his name and all, shall die with himself; and if he shall ever happen to be remembered, that remembrance shall only be in ignominy, as the wretch of his country, the curse of his kindred; and an unthrift for himself.[4]

Lochinvar's appeal came to nothing; in his case the old Scotland defeated the new.

Alexander, like Gordon, was confident that his fellow Scots were as well suited as any in the world for emigration, "having daring minds that upon any probable appearances do despise danger, and bodies able to endure as much as the height of their minds can undertake, naturally loving to make use of their own ground, and not trusting to traffique (trade)." Swarms of Scots had traditionally departed their homeland for different parts of Europe. There was thus a considerable element of mythos embedded in these two tracts, produced right at the beginning of the Scottish experience in Canada, that is still with us today. Gordon can be seen as one of Caledonia's "hardy sons," prone to adventure, violence and forthright condemnatory speech, a type of rugged individualist in contrast to the cannier and more moderate Alexander. There are echoes of the Promised Land in the descriptions of Cape Breton. There is evidence of a sympathetic interest in native language and culture, perhaps anticipating a certain capacity for assimilation. The notion is intruded that emigration is a patriotic act, reminiscent of the later couplet, "True patriots all, for be it understood/We left our country for our country's good." And there is the idea that Scots, numerous as they were and surplus to the requirements of a small country, somehow had a natural aptitude for emigration.

In view of the profile presently projected by Nova Scotia, it is of interest that Alexander conceived of his New Scotland in Lowland, rather than Highland, terms. The St. Croix River was briefly renamed the Tweed "because it

Figure. 2.1   Map detail from William Alexander *An Encouragement to
Colonies*, London, 1624 (courtesy of the John Carter Brown
Library, Rhode Island)

doth divide New England and New Scotland." The location of the Solway,
disgorging into the St. Lawrence, is unclear (at least to me), though the Clyde
would appear to be the Saint John River. The nomenclature dearest to his own
heart would have been that of the Forth which he could view from his castle at
Menstrie and which united the two wealthy halves of eastern Scotland, as the
Miramichi linked, though it appeared to divide, the eastern part of Nova Scotia,
as it then was, from the south shore of the St. Lawrence to the Atlantic.[5] The
Scoticization, and hence mythologization, of the landscape would become a
popular ploy wherever in the world the Scots settled, but it is noteworthy that
the rivers he chose were all emphatically Lowland. The Gaels, however, were
not forgotten. Charles I in 1629 reported to the Scottish privy council that
Alexander had agreed on, with the heads of some of the chief clans of the
kingdom, measures for transporting themselves and their followers to Nova
Scotia, "so debordening our kingdom," he approvingly noted, "of that race of
people, which, in former times, had bred soe many troubles."[6] The Highlanders were thus almost present from the beginning, as was the idea that the new
colony would make a fitting destination for a troublesome, unwanted and—in
the eyes of some—alien population.

53

To the elements of *mythos* which were already present in the early seventeenth century successive generations would apply layer upon layer of their own manufacture, right down to the present day. Indeed, the tradition could be taken back much further, for *Eirik's Saga*, which describes the Norse expeditions to Vinland in the late tenth century, tells of a Scots couple, "a man called Haki and a woman called Hekja," who could run faster than deer, who were put ashore on the eastern seaboard of North America to jog southwards for three days and returned bearing grapes and wild wheat, recalling the land of plenty of the Book of Numbers.[7] The St. Lawrence pilot with Samuel de Champlain was one Abraham Martin *dit l'Ecossais*,[8] possibly the same individual who gave his name to the Plains of Abraham where Scottish regiments under General Wolfe were to win a famous victory over Montcalm in 1759— or so we used to believe until Parks Canada reinvented the episode on the plaques and markers which now interpret the field of battle.

Captain John Mason graduated from hunting Hebrideans to the position of governor of Newfoundland and vice-admiral of New England; to his wife and other female emigrants, the poet Robert Hayman composed the lines:

> Sweet Creatures, did you truely understand
> The pleasant life you'd live in Newfoundland,
> You would with teares desire to be brought thither.
> When you are there, I know you'll ne'er come thence.[9]

Mrs. Mason should have consulted Susanna Moodie;[10] it would be some time before the "thousand dollar cure" would be available to either lady.

The word "Scotch" is now reserved for whisky, to which North Americans added rocks in order to create in the glass a mystical microcosm of the universe—fire, ice and water—although the novelist Neil Gunn posited a counterview when he observed that the Celtic race "brewed its own death potion and with disintegrating irony called it the water of life."[11] Until the late nineteenth century, "Scotch" was the label the Scots applied to themselves, but by 1920 one commentator could lament:

> The term Scotch has silently and without any obvious reason been replaced by Scottish. It has now been restricted by common and tacit consent to things that are bought and sold such as Scotch tomatoes, Scotch whisky, Scotch herring and Scotch M.P.s.[12]

The *Oxford English Dictionary*, which was edited by an erudite Scot, Sir James Murray, who thus should have known what he was talking about, relates that it was permissible to speak of such items as Scottish literature, Scottish history and the Scottish character, but that "it would sound affected to say a Scottish girl or a Scottish gardener and there is no alternative for expressions like Scotch tweeds or Scotch whisky."[13] Therein lies the clue to changing usage: "Scotch" would be reserved for subordinates, be they girls or gardeners, and for "things." At the height of Empire, Scots appeared to run not only the world, but worse, England, and the English retaliated, in the insidious class fashion still favoured in some quarters, by turning all Scots into subordinates. W.J. Rattray, in his four volume study, *The Scot in British North America*, uneasily noted that there existed "an amount of prejudice against the Scot which seems perfectly inexplicable." He complained that ever since the seventeenth century nothing had become so common as virulent criticism of the Scottish character; religion, caution, thrift and clannishness had been made "the unmerited butts of ridicule and sarcasm."[14] His explanation was that the hostility was driven by sheer jealousy of Scottish success and he was probably correct.

T.W.H. Crosland produced an hilariously humourless book, *The Unspeakable Scot* (1902), which was devoted to a kind of literary genocide of his subject, detailing what he considered to be irrefutable historical points which would destroy the Scots and their reputation, once and for all. His penultimate thesis was that "the Scotch are in point of fact quite the dullest race of white men in the world and that they 'knock along' simply by virtue of Scottish superstition, coupled with plod, thrift, a gravid manner and the ordinary endowments of mediocrity." Finally he posited the notions that "it was a Scotchman who introduced thistles into Canada and that very likely it was a Scotchman who introduced rabbits into Australia"! On the latter point he may have been correct, for an emigrant handbook much favoured by Scots actually recommended the importation of those pestiferous creatures in their luggage.[15] At time of writing the Scots seem to have survived Crosland's assault, though the term "Scotch" is still sometimes used in England to offend[16] and, since it sometimes takes the New World a while to catch up with the Old, "Scotch" seems to have entered the canon of North American English.[17]

Language was, for many, an important register of assumed identity. The Rev. A.J. Lockhart, a native of Nova Scotia and an individual who, so far as is known, never set foot in Scotland, penned the following effusion:

> O think ye o' the auld hame,
> Brither dear?
> O think ye of the auld hame,
> When nicht is near?
> The sun frae the lift is sinkin',
> Let fa' a tear
> For the auld time, an' the auld hame,
> Brither dear![18]

The poem is perhaps not quite in the same league as the better known

"Auld Scotch Sangs" by the Rev. G.W. Bethune, a native of Brooklyn, whose composition was a smash hit on both sides of the Atlantic in the later nineteenth century, but both belong to a remarkable genre of central concern to the present investigation, since in each case the writer was articulating an experience which was no part of his own memory, while bathing it in nostalgia, using a language which was not his own, and for good measure imagining a country which was ancestral but which he personally had never seen. They and hundreds of others like them, by no means all touched by the muse, were greatly to elaborate the myth of Scotch Canada. Scottish societies and clubs throughout the country, often aided and abetted by the folks back in Scotland through literature, music, Highland games and the rest, would further perpetrate the myth.

Myth will be used here in two contradictory senses: in the nineteenth-century sense of something which is untrue, but also, and more importantly, as a codification of historical experience, real or imagined, past, present or yet to come, an essential construct which people feel compelled to devise for themselves for the sake of self-preservation.

Historians, particularly in Scotland perhaps, have been all too ready to debunk the myths, whereas it should be their obligation to attempt to understand them. Since the Scots, arguably, have perhaps the greatest capacity for self-mythologization of any nation on the planet, outside the United States, the search for Scotch Canada also involves the parallel quest for Scotch Scotland. The subject is a vast one, and here only a few suggestions can be made, since many questions will remain.

The Scottish contribution to Canadian history was undoubtedly immense, but it cannot be properly investigated until parallel studies are in place which scrutinise the role of all the other ethnicities which make up the mosaic. Why do we hear so much about the Scots and the Irish in Canada, and so little about the English? How is it that the Scots, who were up to their necks in the skullduggery of Empire, have managed to leave the English with the burdensome responsibility of imperialism? What follows is to be construed as a clear-eyed view of Scottish-Canadian history by one who is both a Scot and a Canadian, and does not recognise the tartan saints that some historians and biographers have written about.

If the Scots produced some of the most admirable figures in Canadian history, they also contributed some of the most despicable. Just as Scots were responsible for some of the greatest literature in the world, they also manufactured some of the worst. The cries of "Here's tae us, wha's like us?" derive from an inferiority complex. The frequently quoted dictum that the world is divided into two categories—those who are Scots and those who would like to be—is erroneous for there is a third category: those who are and do not want to admit it. When? When the wrong team loses a football match. When one peruses the latest issue of the *Sunday Post*. When one has suffered yet another rendition of "Stop Your Tickling Jock" or "These Are My Mountains." It is Scots, and not Canadians, who are responsible for such deplorable productions, though representatives of both nations have conspired to produce much of the filopietistic nonsense, which blatantly and unforgivably has been passed off as serious investigation of the Scots-Canadian experience.

Consider the following:

> Our pioneers were not the outcasts of European, Asiatic, or any other nations that would gladly give to the far-off forests of the Western world their scrofulous, their vicious and their vile. They were the progeny of noble ancestors. Not infrequently were they the very cream of their respective clans. Many of them were amazingly agile and athletic. Look and movement told of energy, strength, and will-power. They were mentally vigorous, eager and alert. Their big bodies were captained by big brains. They were men and women of marvellous faith, magnificent courage, of tremendous zeal and undaunted valour. Worthy were they of the best traditions of their native lands, distant, far, but ne'er forgotten.[19]

This repugnant material is drawn from a local history of Aldborough Township, which contained places with such names as West Lorne, Killfinlay, Crinan and Port Glasgow. Aldborough's assessment role in 1820 lists eighty-seven names, all Scots and overwhelmingly Highland. In this absorbingly offensive little work we are told that the cabin of the Scots settler often became "a veritable sanctuary for the seeking soul of the storm-strayed straggler, who, like the way-worn minstrel, in the days of Sir Walter Scott, wandered from door to door." On the long winter nights the "patriarchal sire, with locks silently growing silvered," would entertain his attentive brood by relating "the amazing deeds done by their ancestors in the din and gore of bravest battles, or in the distant days of deserving peace."[20] This is just one example of hundreds, or thousands, of such productions throughout Canada and, like them, it manages to evoke elements of a bogus Scott-land redolent of racism, romance, rant and rhetorical invention. It was first published about 1933 by well-intentioned folk and so it was of its time, but what is alarming is that it was reprinted as recently as 1984.

A most useful collection of essays, and probably the most common starting point for people who wish to investigate the subject is *The Scottish Tradition in Canada* (1976), edited by the late Professor Stanford Reid of the University of Guelph. In his introduction "the editor hopes that the following chapters do not sound too much as though the Scots are boasting," yet in over three hundred largely uncritical and upbeat pages the reader is treated to a parade of distinguished achievers who pioneered Canada, exploring it from sea to shining sea, who were leaders in the fur trade and giants in the church, the military, business, politics, education and literature. There is hardly one word of qualification throughout. It is thus of some interest to note a review published the same year that Stanford's book appeared. The volume in question was Marjorie Wilkins Campbell's *Northwest to the Sea: A Biography of William McGillivray*. The reviewer, Heather Robinson, confessed that she cringed every time she read a phrase such as "the tough, intrepid . . ." and in this respect Ms. Campbell did not disappoint:

> What follows is another astonishing exercise in Canadian double-think, another failed attempt to manufacture a Canadian hero out of a greedy, selfish, small-minded, unimaginative, disagreeable Scots clerk. . . . Tough, intrepid, phooey. The fur traders who rose to become robber barons were distinguished primarily by their ability to rob the Indians, cheat their competitors, and shaft their friends. A more reprehensible lot would be hard to find in any nation's iconography. [McGillivray] . . . owed his success to nepotism, the North West Company owed its success primarily to rum.[21]

Three years earlier, Wayland Drew, in his novel *The Wabeno Feast,* had his hero Mackay remark, "We have skewered this country like a fat ham from Quebec to Athabaska."[22] There is undoubtedly some substance in both points of view, and they should be taken seriously, but their main importance lies in the evidence they provide of Scotophobia in the minds of two modern commentators who were not, themselves, totally unsympathetic to the Scots.

While Robinson and Drew provide suitable correctives well-rooted in historical reality, the career of Alexander Mackenzie, also of the North West Company, presents a rather different perspective. When he made his epic journey to the Pacific in 1793, Mackenzie made it clear that he could not have done it without the aid of the native peoples in whose customs, culture, artifacts, and language he manifested a consuming interest. Already he could lament that the old way of life was under serious attack, and perhaps he detected parallels with his native Island of Lewis. Much of the land west of the Great Lakes was hunted out. Smallpox, spread by the whites, had taken a severe toll. Mackenzie believed that Christian missionaries had done untold harm and the loutish and criminal behaviour of certain fur traders had poisoned relations with the native population. Worst of all, many aboriginals had a great fondness for alcohol which the whites were only too ready to indulge. In addition, many of these people, whose sacred customs had become contaminated through association with the incomers, had become hopelessly dependent on handouts from the British government.[23] John Rae, from Orkney, was able to survive four trips to the Arctic by closely observing the conventions, and especially the diets, of the Indians and the Inuit, though his fondness for the natives earned him suspicion from his fellow whites.[24] Robert Dickson from Dumfries, who married To-to-win, sister of Red Thunder, a Sioux chief, and who associated with James McGill in the fur trade and with Lord Selkirk at the Red River settlement, wished to establish an aboriginal republic extending all the way from Lake Superior to the Pacific.[25] None of these men was a plaster saint; all of them had their flaws and faults like anyone else, but, more importantly, they shared an empathy for the peoples among whom they lived, and they had no illusions about the negative qualities of many of their countrymen.

Robert Louis Stevenson observed in "The Foreigner at Home" that "in spite of the difference of blood and language, the Lowlander feels himself the sentimental countryman of the Highlander. When they meet abroad they fall upon each other's necks in spirit."[26] Although Stevenson lived for a time in upper New York State, he knew little of Canada; in point of fact, the often considerable antipathy between Lowlander and Highlander which existed in the Old Country was frequently exported to the New World. The first permanent white settler in London Township, Ontario, was a man named Mackenzie. When the Rev. William Proudfoot arrived in 1832, he was advised of the desirability of Gaelic-speaking ministers, though he considered the language barbaric and thought even less of the people who spoke it, who were, in his view, stubborn, lazy and obsessed with simply recreating a redundant society. To him the Gaels were a "stiff-necked race," not understanding "anything that requires thought." At a wedding service he conducted between two Gaels, he lamented the presence of "whisky and bagpipes and the gibberish of Gaelic." Those who (understandably) deserted his congregation were dismissed as "a set of ignorant bigots whose ignorance is in many instances beyond the reach of teaching."[27] Those Scots who founded towns in southern Ontario such as John Galt (Guelph), Robert Hamilton (Hamilton), William Dickson (Dumfries) and William Gilkison (Elora) positively discouraged Gaels. Following the potato famine of the 1840s, Scots settlers initially proffered their charity to destitute Highlanders at Fergus, but by the early 1850s they had become an embarrassment and were persuaded to move on, usually towards the townships around Lake Erie.[28] Through time, of course, the barriers came down and even in Ontario many communities such as Puslinch, Bruce County and Embro had earlier welcomed Highlanders. Embro was largely settled by people cleared from Sutherland. From nearby Woodstock, Donald Macleod published the third, enlarged and improved edition of his classic of the Clearances, *Gloomy Memories* (1857).[29] Thriving Gaelic-speaking communities were established elsewhere in Canada, as is well known, such as in Nova Scotia, the Selkirk-inspired settlements of Prince Edward Island and Red River, and the Eastern Townships of Quebec, but, as in Scotland, the phenomenon of tartanization was to be long delayed.

After the failure of the Forty-five rebellion, kilts were outlawed except for use in regiments such as the Black Watch and the Fraser Highlanders. The

Gaels had taken to trews or breeches by the time the ban was lifted in 1789, in which year a member of the ruling royal family had his portrait painted while wearing a kilt. Sir Walter Scott devised the ploy of having everyone—at least the great and the good—decked out in tartan for George IV's visit to Edinburgh in 1822. At that historic moment, tartan mania was born: books on clan tartans appeared, tweed manufacturers in the Lowlands made fortunes, and kilt-wearing received a further boost when Victoria and Albert built their holiday home at Balmoral on Deeside. The kilt, however, was emphatically an upper-class article of clothing until comparatively recently, since it was, and remains, a somewhat expensive garment.[30] It used to be said that if one encountered a kiltie on Edinburgh's Princes Street he was either a visiting American or a prospective Tory MP. Since many Canadian settlers were former soldiers, kilts would not have been unknown, but the garment only gained in popularity, slowly, as Highland games developed. Otherwise it was the preserve of the elite at St. Andrew's balls and of pipers, who were generally ex-military men. The fanciful notion of starving Highlanders in ragged kilts struggling ashore at Pictou off the *Hector* in 1773[31] is thus entirely false.

Pipes are another matter. It is well attested that they were featured at weddings, barn raisings and impromptu ceilidhs throughout the country. The Scots were an audible minority from the beginning. A Vancouver paper allegedly carried a notice that a pipe band would depart from Hastings Street the following day: "We make this announcement in order that ordinary citizens who are not Scotch may take to the woods."[32]

The Scots were to contribute to the cultural life of Canada in other ways. Dougall McKinnon from Tiree figured out how to harness a pair of moose to provide traction for his cart.[33] Whisky frequently accompanied the pipes, but Peter Stewart from Puslinch found a more practical application:

> At one logging bee when whiskie was plentiful and good . . . I was driving a neighbour's oxen and they were very heavy and lazie and I got tired driving them and in the afternoon I gave each ox a bottle of whiskie . . . and in the afternoon I had the liveliest team in the field.[34]

In Peter's Township the last communion service in Gaelic took place in 1908.[35] As late as the 1920s certain office-bearers in the Zorra Caledonian Society had to be Gaelic speakers.[36] Much Gaelic literature was composed in Nova Scotia and elsewhere.[37] The contribution of English-speaking Canadian and Scots-Canadian writers to the maintenance of the Scottish profile and the fabrication of Caledonian fantasy is a subject which would richly repay study, as Elizabeth Waterston has demonstrated.[38] Scots controlled much of Canadian publishing—newspapers and journals, as well as books—and, true to character, they favoured their own.

One of the most familiar, loved and influential poems associated with the creation of Scotch Canada was written by an unknown person who was not Canadian and had never been to Canada, yet his or her "Canadian Boat Song" has exerted a powerful fascination upon the Scottish and Canadian imaginations since it was first published in *Blackwood's Magazine* in September 1829:

> From the lone shieling of the misty island
> Mountains divide us, and the waste of seas,
> Yet still the blood is strong, the heart is Highland,
> And we in dreams behold the Hebrides.[39]

(If this anonymous Scot conferred a Scottish identity on Canada, it was to be left to another, almost three-quarters of a century later, to confer a Canadian identity upon Canada when a bank clerk in Whitehorse launched upon the world a modest book of verse entitled *Songs of a Sourdough*.)[40]

The further creation of mythos, and the prominent profile of the Scots in Canada, were alike enhanced by the creation of Scottish societies, too many of which were already in existence, according to one authority, at the beginning of this century.[41] In the United States the earliest such society, the Old Scots Charitable Society of Boston, dates to 1657, followed by the St. Andrew's societies of Charleston (1729), Philadelphia (1749) and New York (1756). The oldest in Canada is the North British Society of Halifax, founded in 1768. The fur traders celebrated St. Andrew's Day (30 November) and Hogmanay (31 December) before the end of the eighteenth century.[42] St. Andrew's societies rapidly spread throughout Canada during the nineteenth century and they would reward thorough investigation, although complete runs of records seldom exist and all too often they are in the hands of former members who treat them as private property. They functioned as benevolent societies which gave financial assistance to recent immigrants and to needy causes. Guelph, for example, donated £20 in 1863 to the Lord Provost of Glasgow "for the relief of the unemployed and indigent cotton spinners." They also existed to promote Scottish history and culture, most notably on St. Andrew's Day. Because their memberships usually embraced the elites of towns and cities, their activities attracted a disproportionate amount of coverage in the local press. At Guelph the festivities included a concert, followed by a dance. At 12:30 a.m., supper was served and dancing resumed until five in the morning.[43] Many societies also organised Burns nights or picnics. All had an official piper. Back home, the St. Andrew's night celebrations would have been well beyond the social and financial reach of most of the emigrants; in Canada, apart from somewhat exclusive gatherings in cities such as Montreal and Toronto, they could participate and indeed may have almost felt an obligation to do so. Another benevolent society which rapidly gained hold in the later Victorian era was the "Sons of Scotland," though already by 1911 it was under fire for failing to inculcate "race-patriotism," while degenerating into an "ordinary, cheap, insurance benefit association."[44] Whether attending balls or Burns suppers, there was an element of the carnivalesque involved; one or two annual wallowings in Scottish culture, bathos and nostalgia enabled people to act like normal human beings (such as Canadians) throughout the rest of the year.

Another area of activity in which Scots were notably conspicuous was sports, there being broadly three categories to which they contributed: (1) sports introduced by the Scottish regiments, namely, curling, golf, shinty and dancing; (2) more complex (because recently invented) games such as Canadian football, allegedly developed by Scots at McGill University; and (3) folk sports and games played at Caledonian games throughout the country. Space will permit a brief look at only two of these categories.

Historians of the subject in Scotland recognise the first Highland games as those organised by the St. Fillans Highland Society in 1819. In that same year, Bishop Alexander Macdonell, William McGillivray of the North West Company, and John MacDonald of Garth established a Highland Society in Glengarry County, Ontario, for the purpose of organising games. Highland games therefore were as much a Canadian initiative and development as they were Scottish. Activities had to be cheap and accessible like folk sports worldwide. Events at Highland games were often martial in origin, but they were not exclusively, or particularly, Scottish. Caber tossing, for example, was popular in Sweden, though it is now considered to be characteristically Highland. Games were held in Charlottetown, P.E.I., by 1838, in Halifax in 1845 and in Toronto in 1847. The Montreal Athletic Games borrowed some sports from their Caledonian cousins and, lest it should be thought that the Games were too closely identified with Scots, their title was changed to the Montreal Olympics in 1844. As it happens, Scottish games such as the annual gathering at Braemar, patronised by the royals, and thus by persons of influence from Europe and elsewhere, contributed directly to the revival of the Olympics in 1896, because it was believed, erroneously, that traditional Scottish sports preserved ancient forms extending back to Greece itself.

Piping was conspicuous at Highland or Caledonian Games, as was dancing, although women were excluded until after the First War. About the same time, kilts became mandatory for competitors in the heavy events such as the shot-put, hammer throwing and the caber toss; previously they had worn tights or long shorts. During the nineteenth century, competitors would participate in virtually all of the events, racing and heavyweight, and still have energy for dancing. At early Canadian games fully accoutred Highlanders would take on one another with broadswords. The loser was the combatant who was tapped on the head five times, mild stuff according to an Irish observer: "In my land we have a better method when men fight with shillelaghs until one of them can no longer defend himself—and sometimes even longer!"[45] The prize for innovative lunacy, however, must be awarded to the organizers of the Northern Meeting at Inverness, Scotland, in the 1820s, who invented a contest to lift a

252-pound boulder over a bar five feet off the ground. Inspired by heroic tales of the Celtic past, they also arranged a cow-dismembering competition, using live animals and bare hands. Someone had clearly been tapped on the head once too often.[46] Prizes in Canada, as in Scotland, were items such as a book of Ossian's poems, a sporran or a snuff box. Some canny Scot must have organised the Toronto Games in 1859, for "although no prizes were given each athlete strove to the utmost to win his spurs." The Games were not exclusively patronised by Scots, but they represented Scottish identity at its most colourful and most conspicuous and provided fertile fields for the invention of tradition.

One other massively popular sport was curling, perhaps the supreme example of a Scottish game which the Canadians made their own. It has been claimed that the Montreal Curling Club, founded by Scots in 1807, was "the first organised sports club in British North America."[47] At a match between Montreal and Québec held at Trois Rivières in 1835, the participants were disappointed that there was neither haggis nor "good or even tolerable whiskey to be had"—they had to settle instead for turkey and champagne.[48] Curling had been a working class sport in Scotland and, despite aristocratic or elevated patronage, in Canada it continued to blur social and class barriers. Alexander McLachlan (1818–96), a native of Johnstone, Renfrewshire, migrated to Ontario where he earned a reputation as the "Robert Burns of Canada"; he celebrated the sport in his "Curling Song":

> For on the rink distinctions sink,
> And caste aside is laid,
> Whate'er ye be, the stane and tee,
> Will test what stuff ye're made.
> And this the school to teach the fool,
> That only nerve and mind,
> Acquired skill and stubborn will,
> Are leaders o' mankind.[49]

Curling is central to the theme of this investigation because one remarkable aspect of the curling dinners which always followed matches was that someone invariably stood up and recited his or her (since women played too) composition in the form of a poem or song. These were usually dismal sentimental effusions which were quite often published in the local press. The same feature was also associated with St. Andrew's nights, Burns suppers, church socials and private or semi-private gatherings. Indeed, it appears that almost anywhere the Scots congregated, somebody recited a poem or sang a song about the auld country. There were as many local poets in Canada as there were in Scotland.[50] Some were first-generation immigrants composing in Gaelic or Scots, but a remarkable group consisted of second- or even third-generation Scots who had never seen Scotland but who nonetheless felt compelled to drone on, in Lallans, about an imagined homeland, a never never landscape of hills and grannies and hame. One such was John Simpson of Elora, who actually wrote something called "Nobody's Child," though the following is drawn from "The Scottish Emigrant's Lament":

> My own native land! thou art dear to my heart,
> The thought of thee fills me with deepest emotion;
> Stern Fortune condemned me from thee to depart,
> To cross the rude waves of the deep-rolling ocean.
>
> Though fair is the landscape that greeteth my eye,
> I pine for the sight of thy dark, rugged mountains;
> No beauteous heather, no gowans are nigh,
> No more can I bask by the clearest of fountains.[51]

The theme of the poem is that the emigrant spends his entire life in a state of lament, pining for the scenery of the homeland, even though heather and gowans are rarely juxtaposed in nature and the clearest of fountains are non-existent.

Rather different in tone is a satirical effusion entitled "Scotch Dainties" by John Imrie, a Glaswegian who settled in Toronto:

> Gie a Scotchman a guid cog o' brose,
> Wi' milk just new-drawn frae the coo',
> Feth, ye'll no see him turn up his nose,
> But tak' them, an' then smack his moo'!
>
> Chorus: Brose, parritch, kail, haggis, an' bannocks,
> Are dainties abune a' compare!
> Nae English, French, Yankees, or Canucks,
> Could mak' such a gran' bill o' fare![52]

If such a poem, or song, continued to circulate in a society which was forgetting the language, the humour was also likely to be lost over time, resulting in a situation encountered at Burns suppers today, on both sides of the Atlantic, when Burns' "Address to the Haggis" is often declaimed as if it were a mournful psalm, so ignoring the playful intentions of the poet.

The manufacture of Scottish identifiers throughout the nineteenth century masks the decline in Scottish identity. One notable feature of emigrant letters is how quickly people called themselves Canadians. Such people, weaned on Henry Mackenzie, James Hogg and Walter Scott, were almost programmed for nostalgia. John Scott was fairly typical: "After the lapse of six years my heart still warms when I think on many localities in my native land which I used to frequent, and the friends and acquaintances I have left behind." Five years later he observed, "We are now of course all Canadians. I shall fondly yet wish again to see my old fatherland and friends there, although I could not make my home there." In 1873, James Hunter returned to his native Annandale. He stood at the Devil's Beef Tub near Moffat enjoying the vista and reflecting on his good fortune to have been born in such beautiful countryside. "But," he confided to his diary, "I am a Canadian now."[53] In personal discussions with descendants of the settlers who went to Dumfries Township from Hawick in the Scottish Borders, it emerged that in the 1920s or '30s they had no special awareness of their Scottish heritage and assumed that everyone celebrated Robert Burns and St. Andrew, yet by the seventies or early eighties they were flying the Atlantic in search of their roots. The final stage in the process of mythologising Scotch Canada belongs to the twentieth century.

The province of Nova Scotia began parading its Scottishness in the 1930s under the premiership of Angus MacDonald as a calculated and self-conscious promotion for the tourist industry.[54] Fergus Chamber of Commerce was established in 1946, the same year in which it sponsored the first Highland games day. The chief instigator was a Mr. Alex Robertson, who felt compelled to remind patrons that the day was "an athletic event, not a political event."[55] Fergus was a Scottish creation and it still displays an architecture (complete with dormer windows) which is faintly reminiscent of the main streets of Callandar or Pitlochry in the Old Country, yet by 1875 the predominant population was Irish and the Scots were already in decline. The games apparently lost money until about 1972, yet now they are among the largest in Canada. Each year the Fergus publicity machine concocts new and ever more elaborate "traditions" about the games, now forever buried under many layers of bogus accretion. So appealing was the first gathering in 1946 that the Service Club of neighbouring Elora, not to be outdone, and despite the town's Scottish origins, proposed to organise a rodeo![56] That the games picked up in 1972 is diagnostic, for the majority of clan societies in Canada and the U.S. have come into being since 1970, a direct response, it seems, to the phenomenal success of Arthur Haley's *Roots* and the mass impact of the television series. It has been argued that some such societies, hopefully few—and be it noted that they have nothing whatsoever to do with "clans" as understood in an historical context— are covert racist organizations with their headquarters in the southern United States. Furthermore less than one-third of people participating in recognizable Scottish recreations such as Highland dancing or piping have Scottish surnames.[57] Scots and their culture have travelled far since that ship, with its would-be colonists, left Kirkcudbright in 1622.

More than an element of mythologization was present at the very beginning of the Scottish journey. While some sought a new life and more prosperous circumstances, others clearly went in search of a world they had lost.[58] During the nineteenth century they developed a self-myth of the trustworthy, hardworking, common-sensual, thrifty and reliable Scot. Many were also religious and law-abiding. They were educated to be literate, but perhaps more important, they were numerate. Many biographies of prominent Scots-Canadians seem to share the same stereotypical introductory chapter in which the hero is born in poor circumstances, has the essential Scottish values dinned into him, acquires a modicum of education and a hefty dose of religion, usually of the presbyterian variety, emigrates (preferably in strained and uncomfortable circumstances), obtains a humble position on the shop floor, usually through the patronage of a fellow Scot, works his way up to the presidency of the company and then launches into a career as one of Canada's luminaries in politics or whatever else. Such Scottish figures had become the models for aspiring immigrants, irrespective of ethnic origin, around the time of Confederation.[59] The Scots preserved their identity through business and entrepreneurial activities, settlement schemes, the church, societies, annual events such as St. Andrew's balls and Burns suppers and, of course, Highland games. Bucketloads of execrable sentimental verse and song sustained the myth of paradise lost. In that myth the Scots created a flattering portrait of themselves, but there is abundant (and frequently non-Scottish) evidence to indicate another, more critical and less self-serving picture. Although Scottish prestige and influence were in decline throughout the period, the twentieth century was to embellish the canvas with details that were quite alien to Scotland itself.

The Scottish community in Canada now looks back wistfully to a time, not all that distant, when the country actually welcomed recruitment from the "Land o' Cakes," for emigration has now become a trickle. Gone are the halcyon days when the curling facilities could be advertised as an attraction to would-be immigrants.[60] The authors of *The Scotsman in Canada* (1911) self-consciously constructed their volumes as monuments to the achievements of their fellow countrymen, but both manifested their disappointment that Scottish precedence was slipping. Wilfred Campbell advocated a federation of Scottish societies and the dedication of a Scottish building in Ottawa, to overcome what he distinguished as the great weakness of the Scottish people: "They seem ever afraid to act as a community and uphold their most sacred ideals, for fear of offending some other national influence; a lamentable weakness in an otherwise great people."[61] He thus inadvertently highlighted the Scottish desire to assimilate, a subject which has received far too little attention. His colleague, George Bryce, believed that his book had demonstrated "how congenial to Canadians is a Scottish life atmosphere" including literature, customs and ideals which in turn would "make Canada a most acceptable home for the Scottish immigrant." Although Nova Scotia and Ontario beckoned, as a resident of Winnipeg, he commended

> the broad and hospitable West, with its Scottish-like climate, its hearty
> warmth for the industrious stranger, its liberal expenditure for educa-

tional advantages, its predominant religious atmosphere suited to his taste [to which] the Scottish immigrant will be especially attracted, and where he will find a favourable, remunerative, and socially suitable sphere of action for himself and his children.[62]

In his view, for Scots, Canada would prove a home away from home, or, in John Buchan's phrase, an extension of Scotland. That it was neither the immigrants would discover for themselves.

Future research must place the myth of Scotch Canada in the context of Polish, Portuguese and Chinese Canada, to name only a few components of the modern mosaic, but a further point to be considered is the question of symbiosis and mutual cultural reinforcement. Scotland is to England what Canada is to the United States, northern countries co-existing with wealthier and more powerful southern neighbours. It may be worth asking whether the North American experience of Scottishness, manufactured or otherwise, had any impact on the Old Country? Emigrants are notoriously conservative. For example, the French often have difficulty recognising the French values preserved in modern Quebec. Calabrian emigrants retain a view of the homeland which few there would share.

The Scottish experience on both sides of the Atlantic is anomalous, because the myth of Scotch Canada is not all that different from the myth of Scotch Scotland. Burns and Scott, together with the near cults which they engendered—through no fault of their own, it must be said—were almost as popular in Canada as they were at home. The Kailyard—perhaps the Canadian equivalent would be the pumpkin patch—school of literature was created with the emigrant market very much in mind—saccharine tales of couthy Scots living the rural idyll. Such productions had a tremendous appeal for the emigré mindset, but it could be argued that they were actually designed to cater to the assumptions and expectations of the overseas market, in the Canadian part of which a subgenre was developed. That such literature appealed to exiles in the dark satanic mills of Lowland Scotland as well was perhaps as fortuitous as it was significant. One Scots-Canadian was incensed that when a Scot allowed "literary emotion" to engulf him: "He began to spout cheap sentiment to his neighbours (and) became an object of ridicule to the serious-minded . . . became a very commonplace buffoon in the hands of Ian Maclaren and his ilk, who made a burlesque of what the Scotsman might have been at his worst."[63] Such sentiment was reinforced by music hall performers such as Sir Harry Lauder, who led what would become a lengthy procession of exponents of ersatz culture to the wilds of Canada, and they continue to come as the twentieth century reaches its end, though thankfully they are now being repelled by increasing numbers of talented Canadian musicians, particularly from Nova Scotia. Meanwhile, Scots apparently exist in a post-"Braveheart" mythopoetic fantasy, carefully nurtured by the Scottish Tourist Board. Yet, when all is said and done, many of the symbols that we use, whether we are Scots or Canadians, are simply aids to the confrontation of our own reality. Perhaps it is only academics who get hot under their kilts about such matters.

This chapter began in Cape Breton and there it can fittingly end. Possibly one of the most powerful writers about that part of the world, and certainly one of the most attractive, is Alistair MacLeod, one who has recently been exonerated from the charge of creating a bogus past.[64] In his beautifully realized short story, "The Road to Rankin's Point," MacLeod's hero, Calum, almost replicates the experience of Sir Robert Gordon's men 350 years earlier, as his car noses its way through the rich vegetation of the roadside:

> The wild flowers burst and hang in all their short-lived, giddy, aromatic profusion. . . . The sweet red-and-white clover swarms with bees. The yellow butter-cups flutter and the white and gold-green daisies dip and sway. The prickly Scottish thistles are in their lavender bloom and the wild buckwheat and rioting raspberry bushes form netted tapestries of the darkest green.[65]

When the storyteller absorbs his grandmother's death, the present confronts the past and the lights go out forever: "For the first time in the centuries since the Scottish emigrations there is no life at the end of this dark road." This is moving, non-intrusive and believable as we share his grief, not only for his grandmother and himself, but for the generations between her and the emigrant ships which set sail from the Minch so long ago. What, however, are we to make of the following?

> High on the rafters of the barn that stands outside, my grandfather had written in the blackest of ink the following statement: "We are the children of our own despair, of Skye and Rum and Barra and Tiree." No one knows why he wrote it or when, and even the "how" gives cause for puzzlement. In that time before ballpoint pens or even fountain pens, did he climb such heights holding an ink bottle in one hand and a straight nibbed pen in the other? And what is the significance of ancestral lands long left and never seen? Blown over now by Atlantic winds and touched by scudding foam.[66]

Does this seem likely? Is this the subjective voice of an author who has read too many books and is engaged upon the manufacture of a new mythos? Is MacLeod, who clearly sees the Clearances as a metaphor for the economic decline of his own Maritime province, using his poetic licence to state an historical truth which is otherwise inexpressible? He furnishes a clue elsewhere in his brilliant story, one which addresses the central conundrum with which this chapter has been concerned: "Sometimes when seeing the end of our present our past looms ever larger because it is all we have or think we know."[67]

Sometimes, in dreams, we behold more than the Hebrides.

Notes

1. David Laing, ed., *Royal Letters, Charters, and Tracts Relating to the Coloniza-tion of New Scotland and the Institution of the Order of Knight Baronets of Nova Scotia, 1621–1638* (Edinburgh, 1869), pp. 107–9; *The Scots Peerage* J.B. Paul, ed., 9 vols. (Edinburgh, 1904–14), Vol. V, pp. 113–16.
2. Sir William Alexander, *The Mapp and Description of New-England; Together with A Discourse of Plantation, and Collonies etc.*, in Laing, *Colonization of New Scotland*, pp. 32–35.
3. Sir Robert Gordon, *Encouragements*, in Laing, *Colonization of New Scotland*, B-B2v.
4. Gordon, *"Encouragements*," Article 3 and Conclusion.
5. For a parallel discussion of these matters, see John Reid, "The Conquest of 'Nova Scotia': Cartographic Imperialism and the Echoes of a Scottish Past," in Ned Landsman (ed.), *Nation and Province* (forthcoming). I am grateful to Dr. Reid for a copy of his paper.
6. Laing,*Colonization of New Scotland*, p. 48; on the Highlands and Islands at this period, see Edward J. Cowan, "Fishers in Drumlie Waters: Clanship and Campbell Expansion in the time of Gill-easbuig Gruamach," *Transactions of the Gaelic Society of Inverness* 54, 1984–86 (Inverness, 1987), pp. 269–312.
7. *The Vinland Sagas: The Norse Discovery of America*, translated by Magnus Magnusson and Hermann Palsson (Harmondsworth, 1965), p. 95; Northrop Frye, *The Great Code: The Bible and Literature* (New York and London, 1982), pp. 42–43.
8. J.M. LeMoine, *The Scot in New France: An Ethnological Study* (Montreal, 1981), pp. 7–8. On Quebec, see also Lynda Price, *Introduction to the Social History of the Scots in Quebec, 1780–1840*. National Museum of Man Mercury Series, History Division paper no. 31 (Ottawa, 1981).
9. Laing, *Colonization of New Scotland*, p. 6.
10. Susanna Moodie, *Roughing It in the Bush*, edited by Carl F. Klinck (Toronto, 1962; London, 1852); Carl Ballstadt, Elizabeth Hopkins and Michael Peterman, eds., *Letters of a Lifetime* (Toronto, 1985). Both Susanna and her sister Catharine married officers from Orkney. Susanna's "gentle" upbringing notoriously ill-prepared her for life on the frontier, the barbarism of which she eloquently discussed in her book which is now regarded as a Canadian classic.
11. Neil Gunn, *Whisky and Scotland: A Practical and Spiritual Survey* (London, 1935), p. 98.
12. David Rollo, ed., *The Wisdom of Oliver Brown* (Stirling, 1992), p. 17.
13. Sir James A.H. Murray, *A New English Dictionary* (Oxford, 1888–1928).
14. W.J. Rattray, *The Scot in British North America*, 4 vols. (Toronto, 1880–84), vol. 1, pp. v–vi. Rattray "never had the opportunity of visiting North Britain" (p. vii). Such publications helped foster the myth of Scotch Canada. See John Murray Gibbon, *Scots in Canada: A History of the Settlement of the Dominion from the Earliest Days to the Present Time* (London, 1911), which is liberally illustrated

with pictures of Scots engaged in heroic endeavours, including one of a kilted rustic ploughing a field in Manitoba. See, too, Wilfred Campbell, *The Scotsman in Canada: Eastern Canada, including Nova Scotia, Prince Edward Island, New Brunswick, Quebec and Ontario* (London, c. 1911), and George Bryce, *The Scotsman in Canada:Western Canada, including Manitoba, Saskatchewan, Alberta, British Columbia, and Portions of Old Rupert's Land and the Indian Territories* (Toronto, 1911). Although not entirely uncritical, both books are written in celebratory mode. A supreme example of the genre is Duncan A. Bruce, *The Mark of the Scots: Their Astonishing Contributions to History, Science, Democracy, Literature and the Arts* (Secaucus, 1996).

15. T.W.H. Crosland, *The Unspeakable Scot* (London, 1902), pp. 27–28; William Cattermole, *Emigration: The Advantages of Emigration to Canada* (London, 1831), pp. 91–92.
16. For example, A.J.P. Taylor, *English History*, 1914–1945 (Oxford, 1965), p. v.
17. Most memorably in the small classic by John Kenneth Galbraith, *The Scotch* (Toronto, 1964).
18. Daniel Clark, ed., *Selections from Scottish Canadian Poets: Being A Collection of the Best Poetry Written by Scotsmen and Their Descendants in the Dominion of Canada* (Toronto, 1909), p. 248.
19. N.a.,*The History of Pioneer Days in Aldborough* (reprinted Aylmer, 1984), p. 120.
20. N.a., *History of Pioneer Days*, pp. 13, 92–94.
21. Heather Robinson in *Toronto Star*, January 31, 1976. I owe this reference to Hugh P. MacMillan of Guelph.
22. Wayland Drew, *The Wabeno Feast* (Toronto, 1973), p. 160.
23. Alexander Mackenzie, *Voyages from Montreal on the River St. Laurence through the Continent of North America to the Frozen and Pacific Oceans in the Years 1789 and 1793 with a Preliminary Account of the Rise, Progress and Present State of the Fur Trade of That Country* (London, 1801; reprinted Edmonton, 1971).
24. Robert I. Richards, *Dr John Rae* (Whitby, 1985); Ian Bunyan et. al., *No Ordinary Journey: John Rae Arctic Explorer, 1813–1893* (Edinburgh, Montreal and Kingston, 1993).
25. Louis Arthur Tohill, "Robert Dickson, British Fur Trader on the Upper Mississippi," *North Dakota Historical Quarterly* 3, no. 1 (1928); 3, no. 2 (1929); 3, no. 3 (1929); 3, no. 3, pp. 191–97.
26. Robert Louis Stevenson, *Memories and Portraits* (London, 1887), pp. 1–23.
27. Stewart D. Gill, "A Scottish Divine on the Frontier of Upper Canada: The Reverend William Proudfoot and the United Secession Mission," unpublished Ph.D. thesis, University of Guelph, 1984, pp. 44–45.
28. Information kindly communicated by Mr. James Dow, Fergus.
29. Donald Macleod, *Gloomy Memories in the Highlands of Scotland: versus Mrs Harriet Beecher Stowe's Sunny Memories in (England) a Foreign Land or a Faithful Picture of the Extirpation of the Celtic Race from the Highlands of Scotland* (Toronto, 1857). Macleod dedicated his edition to Donald Matheson, MPP for North Oxford, Canada West, and William Manson, Captain of the Highland Guards, New York. He also prefaced his work with a history of the Gaels down to the Clearances which he addressed to his fellow countrymen in both Scotland and Canada. Sadly, the best efforts of Hugh P. MacMillan (Guelph),

Brian Mearns (now repatriated to Sutherland where he teaches Gaelic) and myself have failed to find any trace of Macleod's grave, or of his papers, in the Woodstock area.

30. The best account of tartan and its history is to be found in Hugh Cheape, *Tartan, The Highland Habit* (Edinburgh, 1991).

31. Donald MacKay, *Scotland Farewell: The People of the Hector* (Toronto, 1980).

32. Bryce, *Scotsman in Canada*, p. 415.

33. Margaret Mackay, "Poets and Pioneers," in Billy Kay (ed.), *Odyssey: Voices from Scotland's Past* (Edinburgh, 1980), p. 67.

34. Quoted by Mark Spenser, "Scottish Immigration to Crieff, Ontario," unpublished paper, University of Guelph, 1988, p. 22. In 1897 a resident of Puslinch, Matthew McPhatter, invited surviving immigrants to write down their experiences. This quotation is taken from these McPhatter "Letters." In the same paper, Spenser memorably quotes an informant, Donald A. Stewart, as saying that when Puslinch was settled, "The Scots headed for the hills, the English got the good land and the Irish got the rest." (p. 23).

35. Margaret McCormick, *The History of Knox Presbyterian Church* (Crieff, 1975), p. 11.

36. Information supplied by Mr. Woody Lambe from his research on the minute book of the Zorra Caledonian Society.

37. George S. Emmerson, "The Gaelic Tradition in Canadian Culture," in W. Stanford Reid, ed., *The Scottish Tradition in Canada* (Toronto, 1976), pp. 233–47; Margaret MacDonell, *The Emigrant Experience: Songs of Highland Emigrants in North America* (Toronto, 1982).

38. Elizabeth Waterson, "The Lowland Tradition in Canadian Literature," in Reid, ed., *Scottish Tradition*, pp. 203–31.

39. For discussion of the circumstances surrounding the publication of the poem and for ideas about its possible author, see "The 'Canadian Boat-Song': A Mosaic," compiled by D.M.R. Bentley, *Canadian Poetry* no. 6 (1980), pp. 69–79.

40. Edward J. Cowan, "The War Rhymes of Robert Service, Folk Poet," *Studies in Scottish Literature* 28 (1993), pp. 12–27.

41. Bryce, *Scotsman in Canada*, p. 422.

42. Bryce, *Scotsman in Canada*, p. 411.

43. Information derived from the minute books of the St. Andrew's Society of Guelph.

44. Campbell, *Scotsman in Canada*, pp. 419–21.

45. Henry Roxborough, *One Hundred—Not Out: The Story of the Nineteenth Century Canadian Sport* (Toronto, 1966), pp. 109–10. On some of what follows, see Edward J. Cowan, "Ethnic Sports in Canada: The Scottish Contribution," in *Sports and Ethnicity, Polyphony: The Bulletin of the Multicultural History Society of Toronto* 7, no. 1 (1985), pp. 17–20.

46. David Webster, *Scottish Highland Games* (Edinburgh, 1973), p. 126.

47. Gerald Redmond, *The Sporting Scots of Nineteenth Century Canada* (East Brunswick, 1982), p. 20.

48. Nancy Howell and Maxwell L. Howell, *Sports and Games in Canada, 1700 to the Present* (Toronto, 1969), p. 36.

49. Alexander McLachlan, *Poetical Works of Alexander McLachlan* (Toronto, 1900).

50. For some indications, see Waterston, "Lowland Tradition," pp. 223–24.

51. Clark, *Scottish Canadian Poets*, p. 19.

52. Clark, *Scottish Canadian Poets*, p. 45.
53. Edward J. Cowan, "From the Southern Uplands to Southern Ontario: Nineteenth-Century Emigration from the Scottish Borders," in T.M. Devine (ed.), *Scottish Emigration and Scottish Society* (Edinburgh, 1992), p. 74. I was privileged to be given access to the James Hunter diary before it was due to be deposited in the Provincial Archives of Ontario. At the time of writing it did not appear to have been accessioned.
54. Ian McKay, "Tartanism Triumphant: The Construction of Scottishness in Nova Scotia, 1933–1954," *Acadiensis* 21, no. 2 (1992), pp. 5–48. See also Ian McKay, *The Quest of the Folk: Antimodernism and Cultural Selection in Twentieth Century Nova Scotia* (Montreal and Kingston, 1994). That McKay's powerful theses have not yet been entirely heeded is indicated by the recent appearance of Carol Corbin and Judith A. Rolls, eds., *The Centre of the World at the Edge of a Continent: Cultural Studies of Cape Breton Island* (Sydney, 1996).
55. Vikki Walsh, "A History of the First Fergus Games," in *36th Annual Fergus Highland Games Official Programme* (Fergus, 1982), p. 7.
56. Minutes of the Fergus Chamber of Commerce, Wellington County Archives.
57. On these and other matters, see the illuminating discussion in Rowland Berthoff, "Under the Kilt; Variations on the Scottish-American Ground," *Journal of American Ethnic History* 1, no. 2 (1982), passim.
58. Cowan, "Southern Uplands to Southern Ontario," p. 78.
59. I owe this point to Dennis Blake, onetime graduate student at the University of Guelph, based upon his study of nineteenth-century Canadian newspaper caricatures.
60. John Kerr, *History of Curling* (Edinburgh, 1890), p. 323.
61. Campbell, *Scotsman in Canada*, pp. 421–23.
62. Bryce, *Scotsman in Canada*, p. 430.
63. Campbell, *Scotsman in Canada*, pp. 24–25. Ian Maclaren was the pen-name of John Watson (1850–1907). His *Beside the Bonnie Brier Bush* (1894) and *The Days of Auld Lang Syne* (1895) are the best known fiction of the Kailyard genre. Between 1896 and 1907 he made three lecture tours of North America where his books were immensely popular.
64. Mackay, *Quest of the Folk*, pp. 310–11.
65. Alistair MacLeod, *The Lost Salt Gift of Blood* (Toronto, 1976), p. 158.
66. MacLeod, *Lost Salt Gift of Blood*, pp. 169–70.
67. MacLeod, *Lost Salt Gift of Blood*, p. 184.

3

Surveying the Remains of a Highland Myth:
Investigations at the Birthplace of Flora MacDonald, Airigh-mhuilinn, South Uist

James Symonds

> We know that the Highlands of Scotland are romantic. Bens and glens, the lone shieling in the misty island, purple heather, kilted clansmen, battles long ago, an ancient and beautiful language, claymores and bagpipes and Bonny Prince Charlie—we know all that, and we also know that it's not real.[1]

The "Highland Myth" has been constructed, often by outsiders, over the course of the last 250 years. In the middle of the eighteenth century, the Gaels were demonised as lawless and volatile barbarians, a threat to the English state. But by the middle of the nineteenth century, a remarkable transformation had taken place, most notably with the formation of Highland regiments, which provided the backbone of British imperial armies. In addition, the Highland landscape, made newly accessible by improved roads and steamships, had been tamed, romanticized and appropriated by the Victorian upper classes, who viewed their recently acquired estates as places of leisure, recreation and deer hunting. The region's inhabitants were regarded by these elites as anthropological curiosities, as an anachronistic race of noble savages collected in photographs by ethnographic voyeurs.[2] They were, in the words of Dr. John MacInnes of the School of Scottish Studies (himself a Gael from Raasay), the "aboriginals of the British Isles." This loaded expression encapsulates the feeling of disinheritance and injustice felt by many inhabitants of the Western Isles.

In many ways, the legend of Flora MacDonald, which focused on her heroic ferrying of Bonnie Prince Charlie over the sea to the Isle of Skye after his defeat at the Battle of Culloden, highlighted that sense of disinheritance. Her brave act came to be viewed, in song and folklore, as part of the last stand of the doomed, ancient Highland order. Her subsequent *exile* to America came to symbolise the clearance and migration of the loyal Gaels and the subsequent destruction of the clan "system."[3]

In more recent years, the mythic understanding of Highland clanship has been modified as crofting has come to dominate the landscape of the Outer Hebrides. Although this method of tenure replaced the earlier clan-based land systems, crofters have come to be perceived as the heirs of a timeless tradition and as stoical and egalitarian (usually perceived of as masculine in gender), eking out a self-sufficient existence in a marginal environment, their life guided by the needs of smallhold agriculture and strict religious observance.[4] However, crofting and the crofting landscapes encountered by visitors today have emerged from a little understood train of events, and in many localities this system of land tenure is less than two hundred years old.[5]

The Flora MacDonald Project is a multi-disciplinary research project that sets out to explore the physical and cultural landscape of eighteenth- and nineteenth-century South Uist. Our study area is centred upon Airigh-mhuilinn, the township where Flora MacDonald was born in 1722. Flora MacDonald was chosen to provide a thread linking the various elements of our research. For her part in the '45 rising, Dr. Johnson wrote, her name shall be "mentioned in history." Two and a half centuries later this is indeed the case, and Flora MacDonald is known and celebrated around the world as the most famous of Scottish heroines.

Flora's life spanned a turbulent period of history in which the Highlands were irrevocably transformed. The widespread adoption of agrarian capitalism ushered in new patterns of rental and radically different attitudes towards landholding. As the daughter, and later wife, of a tacksman, Flora experienced the social upheaval of "improvement" and emigration at first-hand. When she and her husband, Allan, left Campbeltown on the *Balliol* for Wilmington in North Carolina in 1774, they could not have anticipated that within two years they would be caught up in the American War of Independence. Having lost her home and possessions to revolutionary forces following the battle of Moore's Creek, Flora fled to Nova Scotia, before taking the unusual step of returning back across the Atlantic to Skye.[6]

The notoriety accorded to Flora for her brief involvement in the '45 has ensured that the colourful episodes and occasional trivia of her life have been closely documented by historians. The same cannot be said for the ordinary people of the Highlands and Islands whose lives are overshadowed by the upper echelons of clan genealogies. By using historical archaeology, our aim

Figure 3.1   Cairn erected on the purported birthplace of Flora
MacDonald, Airigh-mhuilinn, South Uist (J. Symonds photo)

is to redress this imbalance and to throw light upon the lives of the hidden people of South Uist, people who, though living in the eighteenth and nineteenth centuries, are poorly represented in historical records.[7] In giving voice to these "silent men and women of the modern past,"[8] we strive to recover the commonplace, rather than the exceptional, and to enter their minds and context through an examination of the routines of their daily lives.

I

The Outer Hebridean chain of islands, situated off the northwest coast of Scotland, stretches two hundred kilometers north-south from the Butt of Lewis to Barra Head. The principal islands of Lewis, Harris, North and South Uist, Benbecula and Barra have a wide range of topographies. The Uists, however, are low-lying and their treeless landscapes are peppered with vast numbers of inland lochs. This landscape is both diverse and beautiful, ranging from the western fertile machair (shell-sand soils), which support a varied flora unique to the islands, to the eastern moorlands. The eastern side of South Uist is hilly, with the peaks of Beinn Mhor and Hecla rising to six hundred meters.

The current understanding of the last thousand years of human settlement on South Uist is heavily based upon historical sources, but recent fieldwork has exposed numerous potential weaknesses in an exclusively document-based approach. Evidence of extensive Viking and Norse settlement on the machair, for example, has only been recovered by archaeological excavations in the last four years. It is possible that settlement continued to be concentrated on the machair until the seventeenth century, when a series of violent and destabilizing sand-blows ravaged the west coast of the island. Perhaps in response to these rapidly deteriorating climatic conditions, or else because of changing tenurial agreements, new settlement sites were established further inland on the *Gearraidh*, the black peatlands traditionally reserved for seasonal grazing.

The settlement at Airigh-mhuilinn has several phases of development, each of which has left a mark on the landscape. Through much of the eighteenth century and into the early nineteenth century, the land was held as a "tack," and the homes of subtenants clustered around the dwelling of the headman, or "tacksman," to form a township. After a period of proto-crofting in the 1820s, the land was parcelled up to form a sheep farm in 1827. From this date until 1917, when land at Airigh-mhuilinn was divided once again, this time to create two crofts, the sheep farm at Milton dominated the landscape. In the wake of these wholesale reorganisations of the landscape, the tenants and cottars of Airigh-mhuilinn were moved on a number of occasions.

Archaeological evidence suggests that the majority of the population of Airigh-mhuilinn were cleared off the land by 1850. The few individuals who remained would have worked as farm labourers at Milton farm. The dispossessed were scattered to several locations. Some were cleared to the east coast of Uist, to the "back of the hill," or to the small and hitherto virtually uninhabited island of Eriskay, in the Sound of Barra. Others left, either voluntarily or involuntarily, for the New World on ships chartered by the owner of the estate, John Gordon of Cluny. Over the course of a single decade, the population of South Uist fell from 7,500 to 5,000.[9]

While the phasing of land use is detectable from documentary sources, the records are largely silent on the lives of the community's inhabitants. In order to move beyond the historical framework and recover the lived experience of the majority of inhabitants, a landscape survey is being conducted. This approach seeks to map the physical landscape in which the community lived and worked and which they modified for their needs. The energy these people expended in carving out and tending to fields and livestock left permanent traces in the landscape. The fields of rural settlements are in many ways as important to our understanding of rural lifeways as the domestic structures, not least because the fields provided much of the diet of the population and were also where they spent most of their days.

Initially our survey focused on the agricultural traces which cover the area around the settlement. These mostly take the form of hand-dug lazy-beds for potatoes, and small clearance cairns. It soon became obvious, however, that such information made little sense without also considering the paths of movement, patterns of drainage, areas of quarrying and other features which showed how people in the past had moved through and used the landscape. We found that there was no identifiable logic to the size of lazy-bed patches, their width, orientation and location, although certain constraints imposed by the local environment could be identified. Almost every available patch of land in this area bore traces of agricultural activity.

One of the problems we faced was trying to establish if this extensive coverage was the result of prolonged occupation, or whether it resulted from a shorter episode of lazy-bed cutting, abandonment and relocation. In a few cases we were able to detect a chronological relationship between different patches of lazy-beds, but positive identification of re-use was more difficult to determine. Absolute proof of prolonged re-use of lazy-beds will probably only be forthcoming from a detailed program of soil micromorphology, something well beyond our meagre research budget.

Although the survey results highlighted the seemingly precarious nature of existence in this environment, we could not establish any obvious territorial units related to particular buildings, beyond the ubiquitous kailyards, perhaps indicating that the community saw many subsistence-related activities as a shared endeavour. While the agricultural traces hinted at a very fluid interaction with the landscape, we found that some of the paths and trackways were well defined, a testament to their prolonged use. This was very noticeable in the transition zone between the blacklands and the machair to the west, suggesting long-established routines of movement between these areas. Similarly, understanding the complex pattern of drainage ditches was an important part of tracing the patterns of mobility as well as the development of land use during the last two centuries. Present-day loch levels are the result of extensive drainage undertaken to prepare the land for sheep. Earlier loch levels would have meant less land for cultivation but increased possibilities for movement, since access by water played an important role in the past.

One of the most intriguing discoveries of our survey, apart from the sheer density of features, was the way in which boundaries had been systematically dismantled. This is in sharp contrast to our experience in the English countryside, where boundaries, particularly parish boundaries, tend to become "fossilised." The simplest explanation for the widespread stone-robbing would be that inhabitants of the Hebrides were keen to re-use stone. But in areas where stone is plentiful, an alternative explanation may be called for. Many of the surviving boundaries relate to the laying out of the sheep run for Milton Farm. Older boundaries appear to have been removed as part of deliberate policy. Removal of old boundaries may have had a dual appeal to landlords: it opened up the landscape for use by sheep and at the same time erased the form, and therefore the social memory, of earlier land use.

This shifting land-use pattern is reflected in the number of construction techniques which were employed to divide the land within the township through time: turf walling, orthostatic walling and drystone walling. Most of the earlier boundaries were probably erected in piecemeal fashion, perhaps during seasonal lulls in the agricultural cycle, by small groups of family and close kin. The later, massively constructed walls of the sheep run have a uniform design and suggest the mobilization of gang labour for construction. This raises the possibility of investigating landlord-tenant mechanisms of cooperation and coercion, and suggests that a detailed study of agricultural landscapes could recover the physical manifestation of landlord policy at the local level.

Taking the survey approach further, one of our principal long-term goals is to study the entire township of Airigh-mhuilinn. The Uist townships consist of broad divisions of land which cross the island from coast to coast, enabling each community to exploit the island's full ecological range. In order to make best use of this range, township communities were seasonally mobile. So any full survey should extend to traces of farming activity beyond the settlement itself, including the seasonal use of upland shielings, and the gathering of seaweed for kelp production. Similarly, another aspect of our investigation is a focus upon the material life of people, the built environment and portable material culture, in order to develop a more complete understanding of daily life within the settlement.

The Flora MacDonald Project has completed a detailed archaeological field survey of Airigh-mhuilinn and has located the remains of more than twenty structures. Over the last three summers a program of excavation has run concurrently with this field survey. These excavations have generated important findings that not only highlight the multi-use occupation but present considerable technical difficulties for the excavators. The apparent simplicity of many structures at surface level is misleading. Many stone-built structures, despite being relatively short-lived, have complex histories of use. Dwellings (often in use for as little as one generation) pass into use as byres and may later be re-occupied briefly by the dispossessed. Turf-built structures (a traditional technique in the Uists) leave little trace but can be recognized with experience.

The most impressive structures within the core of the settlement are a series of blackhouses. The term "blackhouse" is frequently misapplied to describe almost any house in the Hebrides which is more than a hundred years old and in a ruinous state.[10] A blackhouse will be defined here as a house with double-thick drystone walls and a thatched roof. Houses of this type were rectangular in plan, with rounded corners to deflect the wind. Inside, the houses were divided into a series of activity areas. Some, but by no means all, blackhouses incorporated a cow byre beneath the same roof. The houses did not usually have windows, although sometimes small panes of glass were inserted into the thatch to allow light to enter. Warmth and heat for cooking were provided by a peat fire which burned on a hearth in the centre of the floor. There was no chimney, and smoke filled the house, rising to escape through a smoke-hole in the roof. The first blackhouse to be investigated, Structure E, was completely excavated in July 1996. The excavation revealed that it had been erected in the last quarter of the eighteenth century and occupied until c.

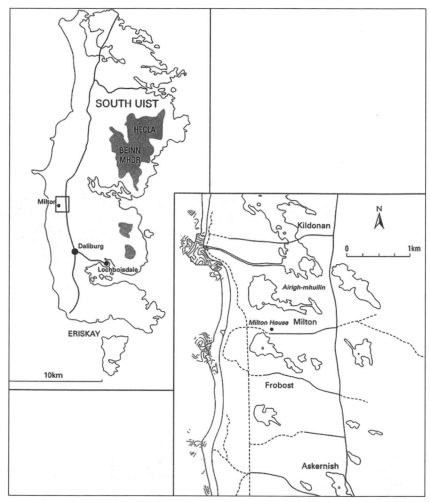

Figure 3.2   Area of archaeological investigation, South Uist

1830. It is tempting to associate its abandonment with the establishment of the sheep farm at Milton, a short distance away.

We know from travellers' descriptions that the homes of high-ranking Highlanders at this time were a blend of the sophisticated and the primitive. Dr. Samuel Johnson, who visited the Hebrides in the 1770s, tells how he stayed at one house where the bed sheets were made of the finest Indian cotton but little attention had been given to the floor of the bedchamber, which comprised waterlogged earth.[11] It appears from the excavation of Structure E that while little modification was made to the traditional long house structure, investment was made in portable wealth, apparently confirming eighteenth-

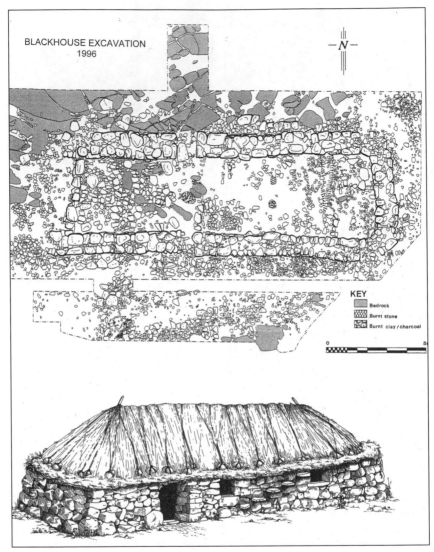

Figure 3.3   Plan and artist's reconstruction of House E, Airigh-mhuilinn,
            South Uist

century reports.

Finds recovered within the blackhouse included wine bottles and bronze
implements, indicating a degree of sophistication and challenging the myth of
the savage Gael. During its long history of use, the house was remodelled
several times, finally serving as a sheep barn. Such multiple use was reflected
in one of the most surprising findings of our excavation, that the blackhouse

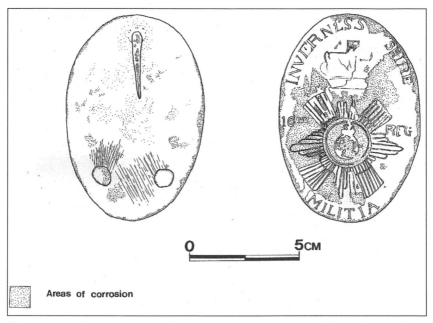

Figure 3.4 Drawing of a military belt plate excavated from House E

was built on top of a dump of iron slag which filled a natural depression in the bedrock. The material derived from a bloomery for roasting iron-ore with wood charcoal, and had been intentionally placed at the end of the spur, in a windy location.[12] The most spectacular artifactual find was made just outside the doorway of Structure E: a bronze belt-buckle inscribed with the insignia of the Inverness-shire Militia, a regiment established in the Napoleonic era. We will never know the identity of its owner or the circumstances of its loss, but the find serves to remind us of the important part that military service played in the life of Highlanders in both Scotland and North America.[13]

The eighteenth and nineteenth centuries brought the culture of mass consumption to the Highlands. The material changes brought by access to mainland markets were profound. Mass-produced glass and ceramic vessels from the factories of Edinburgh, Glasgow and Stoke-on-Trent entered South Uist in quantity for the first time and percolated down the social hierarchy. Contact with the wider world of the British colonies is also attested by the adoption of tea drinking, tobacco smoking, and the use of sugar and molasses to sweeten food.

The influx of new objects and foodstuffs allowed new forms of social expression to be developed in South Uist. This is an important point, as the commercial transaction necessary to acquire a dinner service also enabled the purchaser to buy into a wholly new mind-set of polite, mannered behaviour. Of course the mere possession of a dinner service need not imply that it was used frequently, or indeed that it was used in a way that was considered to be "correct" by outsiders. It does, however, suggest that the dinner service, along with the types of behaviour to which it gave expression, were thought to be desirable and worthy of emulation.

A couple of points are worth raising here. First, the ceramic material excavated from blackhouses at Airigh-mhuilinn demonstrates an unusual degree of curation. Some vessels show evidence of clumsy repairs; for example, some china plates and bowls are held together by lead staples. Does this mean they were highly prized because of their expense? And was it considered acceptable to dine off broken or repaired vessels? Second, the overall assemblage recovered from excavations shows a disproportionately high percentage of hemispherical bowls to flat dinner plates and side plates, and cutlery is almost completely absent. The implication is that food, in the form of potatoes, oats and various broths, was prepared in a pot over the fire and eaten, using the hands, from a bowl.

The hemispherical bowls unearthed at Airigh-mhuilinn are relatively low-status factory-made slipwares, and sponge-decorated wares. Spongeware was mass-produced in the potteries of Glasgow and Edinburgh from the early nineteenth century and found its way to the Outer Hebrides on the steamships that operated out of the Clyde. The bowls were decorated with colourful flowers, and some bore thistles and other distinctive Scottish emblems. It is a moot point whether or not the emblems employed reflect the whims of individual urban artisans or were deliberately chosen by the factory owners to appeal to Scottish consumers. Preliminary research by the author has revealed that similar spongeware bowls were found in areas settled by Scots on mainland Nova Scotia and Cape Breton Island. It seems likely that the distribution of bowls, which are also found in abundance along the coasts of Labrador and the Cape of Good Hope, reflects the high-liquid-content diet of poorer communities in marginal locations; it may also be the case that these areas relied upon trade and exchange with passing fishing boats and therefore had to make do with such low-status, utilitarian ceramics.[14]

The example of hemispherical bowls demonstrates that, in order to understand the ways in which material culture was used and transferred, we need to develop an archaeology which goes beyond localized landscape survey and artifact analysis. As Flora's own brief flight illustrates, we need an archaeology of emigration in order to fully understand Airigh-mhuilinn. We must broaden our canvas to encompass research on both sides of the Atlantic and realise the international potential for analysis that is possible by means of historical archaeology.[15]

II

A great deal has been written by historians about the Scottish emigrant experience. The process is nonetheless still imperfectly understood, as relatively few scholars have attempted to trace the movement across the Atlantic. In the words of Edward J. Cowan, "Scottish historians seem to lose interest when the emigrants embark, while their North American counterparts deem them fit for study only when they arrive in the New World."[16] British archaeologists have also been largely silent on the subject, perhaps reflecting a widely held but erroneous belief that archaeology has little to add to eighteenth- and nineteenth-century history.

In the popular imagination, emigration from the Hebrides is sometimes conflated into a single catastrophic episode: the forced eviction and transportation of the peasantry during the Highland Clearances of the 1850s. The reality was rather more complex. Emigration from the Highlands was part of a continuum, the migrations of the mid–nineteenth century being conditioned by a long-lived "culture of mobility" in Highland society.[17] It is interesting that many Maritime Canadians of Scots descent seem determined to believe that their ancestors were "impoverished sheep thieves" hounded by unforgiving landlords.[18] This reductionist stance denies the fact that differences in wealth and motivation existed among emigrants. The willing Roman Catholic emigrants who left South Uist in 1772, led by John MacDonald of Glenaladale, were keen to escape the religious intolerance of their Protestant laird, Colin MacDonald of Boisdale. They would have taken with them a different sense of place and social order and a very different set of memories than the destitute crofters exiled from South Uist in 1851. The latter, dragged onto ships at Loch Boisdale, had clung on to the bitter end to a sense of clan and kinship which their lairds had long since abandoned.[19]

The life which these people sailed to in the New World was very different to that which they had left behind. We must expect that, because of different experiences of life and emigration, different "New Scotlands" were created. One example concerns the ways in which oral tradition has been preserved in South Uist and Cape Breton. In South Uist, tales of nineteenth-century emigration are rare. The storytellers emigrated long ago and those who remained have erased the sorrow from their collective memory. Unlike in Cape Breton, there is no imagined "Golden Age" of rural harmony.[20] The past is remembered, if it is recalled at all, as a time of great pain and poverty.

The main point is that social changes in South Uist and Nova Scotia were interrelated. We cannot fully understand the rich texture of one without the other. This might seem a simple point, but it is equally clear that such an understanding has not informed previous archaeological approaches to Hebridean settlements on either side of the Atlantic. By reharnessing the Old World to the New, we can gain an invigorating new perspective for collaborative research. The vast potential for integrated archaeological investigation has already been identified by economic historians and historical geographers.[21]

But the role of religion and government in shaping the material life of community and the thick weave of kith and kin has yet to be explored by archaeologists. For example, the dominance of staple export economies in Nova Scotia before 1900 meant that much of the personal wealth generated by timber and mining flowed back to British locations.[22] So one must look, for example, to some of the substantial town and country houses of England and Scotland to understand this layer of the region's heritage.

Family and community ties were also transported across the Atlantic and lie buried to await the archaeologist's trowel. The influence of extended kin in determining patterns of settlement is well documented. Rosemary Ommer's study showed that 71 percent of the pioneer population of Broad Cove–Margaree District in Cape Breton were related to each other before they left the Highlands, suggesting that whole "neighbourhoods" were transported intact, as a kind of mental map of social relations and obligations redrawn in the New World. This leads us to ask whether some emigrants might have accepted poorer quality land in order to be closer to kith and kin.[23] Some Highland emigrants, to be sure, practised close cousin and brother-sister exchange marriages as a direct reaction to their radically changed circumstances, and had "no inclination to mix with strangers."[24]

Social relations may be embedded in the landscape in other ways, as Stephen Hornsby has shown. The economic divisions between "frontland" and "backland" in Cape Breton had their origins in the character and timing of emigrations from Scotland. The few relatively prosperous tacksmen who arrived in Cape Breton between 1800 and 1820 acquired good quality "frontland." After 1820, only the thin-soiled "backlands" were available.[25] Archaeological field surveys and excavations combined with census data and oral history could assemble a fine-grained picture in these different areas of farming practice, along with mechanisms of trade and exchange, and the construction of community and individual identities. This kind of archaeological work has the potential to supplement the historical research by Rusty Bitterman, for example, on the improvisatory economic strategies of the "backlanders" of Cape Breton.[26] Looking beyond Cape Breton, one of the most exciting prospects is the possibility of making detailed comparative studies between the conditions of everday life before and after emigration that will allow us to answer questions such as, how did exiles from South Uist adapt to the New World and its new social and economic conditions?

But before we can approach a study of this complexity, we must break from the continual retelling of the migration myths, such as the Flora MacDonald saga, and examine instead the remains of the houses and fields occupied by Hebridean emigrants in Nova Scotia. The Highland Settler Project is the first purpose-led attempt to recover traces of eighteenth- and nineteenth-century Scottish rural settlement in Nova Scotia. Preliminary reconnaissance of MacKinnon's Brook at Mabou, Inverness County, and Rossfield in Pictou

Figure 3.5   A Cape Breton House of the 1820s. The MacDonald House at the Highland Village Museum, Cape Breton (J. Symonds photo)

County has demonstrated that a remarkably rich store of buildings and field systems is available for study, although often obscured from view by a canopy of regenerated pasture spruce.

One in particular was the cellar of the Neil MacPhee house. Born near Ormiclate in South Uist in 1785, MacPhee emigrated to Mabou with his wife Margaret via Prince Edward Island in the first decade of the nineteenth century.[27] The frame houses of the type which covered this cellar were in widespread use in Nova Scotia by 1820 and their use by Uist emigrants reflected an adaption to new circumstances.[28] But the frame structures would have also changed the immigrant Highlander's experience of domestic space. Hebridean blackhouses were essentially single-storey longhouses made of drystone, with turf roofs. They had no chimneys and were choked with smoke. The wooden houses of Cape Breton were altogether lighter and brighter. Gone was the tradition of stalling cattle within the house, but the hearth (though enclosed in a stone chimney-stack) still stood at the centre of the house, a kind of fulcrum around which Gaelic daily life revolved. The long-standing symbolism of the central hearth was retained in the new wooden houses, no doubt affording some spiritual comfort. At the same time, practical improvements were made: a chimney channelled smoke away, and partitioned rooms introduced new possibilities for private space and segregated activities. Aside from the use of new construction materials, the greatest change came in the conversion from a horizontal plan to a vertical house form. The house now had two storeys and an attic; the ground floor contained a kitchen and utility room, and a parlour for occasional use. Above this were the rooms where the family slept. The half-room created in the attic frequently held a loom for weaving.

III

As this brief discussion has suggested, historical archaeology can make a valuable contribution to an understanding of the life of eighteenth- and nine-teenth-century communities. Although the Flora MacDonald myth has been useful in drawing attention to the South Uist–Nova Scotia connection, our investigations have endeavoured to reconstruct the entire community by exploring the landscape setting and materiality of day-to-day life. We have taken a contextual approach based upon detailed microregional case studies which have demonstrated a considerable complexity and adaption not usually reflected in romantic versions of Highland emigration such as the MacDonald legend. The exciting possibility which we are now exploring is that of extending these surveys to the New World, to allow comparisons of Old and New World mentalities and practices.

Notes

1. Peter Womack, *Improvement and Romance: Constructing the Myth of the Highlands* (London, 1989), p. 1.
2. Womack, *Improvement and Romance*. For a more general treatment, see Linda Colley, *Britons: Forging the Nation 1707–1837* (London, 1992), pp. 113–32; T.M. Devine, *From Clanship to Crofters' War* (Manchester, 1994), pp. 19–31; and Charles Withers, "The Historical Creation of the Highlands," in Ian Donnachie and Christopher Whately (eds.), *The Manufacture of Scottish History* (Edinburgh, 1992), pp. 143–56.
3. See Ruairidh H. MacLeod, *Flora MacDonald: The Jacobite Heroine in Scotland and North America* (London, 1995), and Hugh Douglas, *Flora MacDonald: The Most Loyal Rebel* (London, 1993), pp. 216–33.
4. Francis Thompson, *The Crofting Years* (Luath Press, 1984), pp. 131–35.
5. See James Hunter, *The Making of the Crofting Community* (Edinburgh, 1976), p. 3; Devine, *From Clanship to Crofters' War* (Manchester, 1994); and Allan Macinnes, *Clanship, Commerce and the House of Stuart, 1603–1788* (East Linton, 1996).
6. See MacLeod, *Flora MacDonald: The Jacobite Heroine*.
7. Brian M. Fagan and Charles E. Orser Jr., *Historical Archaeology: a brief introduction* (New York, 1995), pp. 202–04.
8. Charles E. Orser Jr., *A Historical Archaeology of the Modern World* (New York, 1996), p. 160.
9. T.M. Devine, *The Great Highland Famine: Hunger, Emigration and the Scottish Highlands in the Nineteenth Century* (Edinburgh, 1988), pp. 79, 177, 181–85, 199–200, 207–8.
10. The Hebridean "blackhouse" has become synonymous with island culture. See Alexander Fenton, *The Island Blackhouse* (HMSO, 1978). Within the islands,

Gaelic speakers prefer to refer to this older type of structure as "thatched houses," perhaps illustrating an old confusion among English speakers between the Gaelic word for "black" and "thatch" (i.e., *dubh* and *tubha*).

11. Samuel Johnson, *A Journey Through the Western Isles of Scotland* (Harmondsworth, 1984; first published in 1775), p. 106.

12. Cf. H. Fairhurst, "The Deserted Settlement at Lix, West Perthshire," *Proceedings of the Society of Antiquaries of Scotland*, 1968–69, pp. 160–99.

13. See James Hunter, *A Dance Called America: The Scottish Highlands, the United States and Canada* (Edinburgh, 1994), and D.M. Henderson, *The Highland Soldier: A Social Study of the Highland Regiments 1820–1920* (Edinburgh, 1989).

14. Charles Burke, Fortress Louisbourg, personal communication;. J. Webster, "On Dressers," unpublished paper presented to the CNEHA Conference, Fortress Louisbourg, October 1995.

15. James Deetz, *Flowerdew Hundred: The Archaeology of a Virginia Plantation* (New York, 1993), p. 163.

16. E.J. Cowan, "From the Southern Uplands to Southern Ontario: Nineteenth Century Emigration from the Scottish Borders," in T.M. Devine (ed.), *Scottish Emigration and Scottish Society* (Edinburgh 1992), p. 61.

17. T.M. Devine, "The Paradox of Scottish Emigration," in Devine, *Scottish Emigration and Scottish Society*, p. 5. See also J.M. Bumsted, *The People's Clearance* (Edinburgh, 1982); John Prebble, *The Highland Clearances* (Harmondsworth, 1963); and W.C.A. Ross, "Highland Emigration," *Scottish Geographical Magazine* (May 1934), pp. 155–66.

18. P.M.Toner, "Lifting the Mist: Recent Studies on the Scots and Irish," *Acadiensis* 18, no. 1 (Autumn 1988), pp. 215–26.

19. See, for example, A.D. Cameron, *Go Listen to the Crofters: The Napier Commission and Crofting a Century Ago* (Stornoway, 1986), for a discussion of the injustice felt, as recorded in oral testimony from crofters to a royal commission on crofting, published in 1884.

20. Robert McKinnon and Graeme Wynn, "Nova Scotian Agriculture in the Golden Age: A New Look," in D. Day (ed.), *Geographical Perspectives on the Maritime Provinces* (Halifax, 1988), pp. 47–59.

21. See, for example, the lead suggested by the work of Rusty Bitterman: "Farm Households and Wage Labour in the North East Maritimes in the Early Nineteenth Century," *Labour/Travail* 31 (Spring 1993), pp. 13–45, and "The Hierarchy of the Soil: Land and Labour in a Nineteenth Century Cape Breton Community," *Acadiensis* 18, no. 1 (Autumn 1988), pp. 33–55. Also see Rosemary Ommer, "Highland Scot migration to south western Newfoundland: a study of kinship," in John Mannion (ed.), *The Peopling of Newfoundland* (St. John's, 1977).

22. MacKinnon and Wynn, "Nova Scotia Agriculture," p. 58.

23. Ommer, "Highland Scot migration"; Graeme Wynn, *Timber Colony: a historical geography of early nineteenth century New Brunswick* (Toronto, 1981).

24. M. Molloy, "'No inclination to mix with strangers': Marriage patterns among Highland Scots migrants to Cape Breton and New Zealand, 1800–1916," *Journal of Family History* 11, no. 3 (1986), pp. 221–43.

25. S. Hornsby, *Nineteenth-Century Cape Breton: A Historical Geography* (Montreal, 1992), and "Migration and Settlement: The Scots of Cape Breton," in Day, *Geographical Perspectives*.

26. Bitterman, "Farm Households and Wage Labour" and "The Hierarchy of the Soil."
27. Research into the genealogy of this family and the Scottish settlement of Cape Breton was generously provided to the author by James Sinclair of Mabou, Cape Breton.
28. This type of frame house was in widespread use in New England in the mid–eighteenth century and appears to have spread into Nova Scotia with the influx of New England Planters into the province in the 1760s (David Christianson, Nova Scotia Museum, Halifax, personal communication).

4

Scottishness and Britishness in Canada, 1790–1914

J.M. Bumsted

It was in 1976 that I first went to Edinburgh to begin research on the Scots in Canada. Over the years, the Scots—while not my only topic of research—have been the underlying glue that holds much of that research together. I began my Scottish research with Lord Selkirk, expanded to early Highland emigration to Canada, moved on to the settlement of Prince Edward Island and more recently have been trying to wrestle with an overview of the Scottish presence in Canada. It is hard to believe that my book on Highland emigration, published as recently as 1982, now serves mainly as target practice for younger scholars.[1] In any event, I have been struggling with Scots and Scottishness, mainly in the Canadian context, for a long, long time. I would like to begin by offering some general observations on the subject which represent my cumulative wisdom.

In the first place, it seems to me almost axiomatic that any understanding of the role of the Scot in Canada has to begin with the history of Scotland itself. Interpreting that history has always been extremely controversial. Fashions in scholarship are subject to surprisingly rapid change, and one generation's wisdom quickly becomes the next generation's straw man. Scots in the nineteenth century knew that they had been a distinct national group, members of "a country that will ever be embalmed in the hearts of all true Scotchmen," most distinguished for its acknowledgement of God and the Bible and its institution of a system of parish schools.[2] The study of ethnic or national groups has altered substantially over the course of the twentieth century. Studies on the Scots in Canada at the close of the nineteenth century assumed that the topic could be covered by telling the story of the settlement of people from

Scotland and then shifting to recounting the Canadian achievements of everybody of Scottish birth or ancestry.[3] More recently, the study of ethnic groups in Canada has become considerably more theoretically sophisticated, and there has been increasing recognition of the need for more appreciation of the historical background of the country of origin, as well as more precise notions of what particular contributions have been made to the country receiving the immigrants. Nevertheless, the bulk of research in the new ethnic studies revolves around immigrant groups whose record in Canada does not go back into the eighteenth century and for whom appreciation of the vagaries of a long historical sweep in the context of multiple regions on both sides of the Atlantic is not so urgent. Indeed, the very duration of the Scottish experience in Canada has militated against its study.[4]

As we all know, until 1603, Scotland was an independent kingdom of the British Isles. In that year, dynastic developments found Scotland and England sharing the same monarch, James I in England and James VI in Scotland. James's successor was executed by the Puritan Commonwealth, and with the Restoration the choice of monarchs fell largely to the initiative of the English. In 1707 came the union of Scotland and England.[5] That union, produced at least partly by the economic need for Scotland to gain access to trade within the expanding British Empire, was what the fathers of Canadian Confederation called a "legislative union," as opposed to a "federal union," which was what Canada received a century and a half later. Canadians at the time of Confederation, it must be added, saw legislative unions as a good deal more centralizing than federal ones.[6] In any case, the previously separate legislatures of Scotland and England were merged into one, and a separate Scottish national parliament disappeared, leaving behind only local municipal government. The legislative merger had its own anomalies. The English had opposed admitting all members of the Scottish nobility to the new House of Lords, for example, and the compromise worked out saw the Scottish nobility represented in the Lords by eighteen of their number, democratically elected by their colleagues. There was something ironic about this democratically elected group in a British Parliament which was profoundly undemocratic.[7] Moreover, Scotland was allowed to keep its own law, its own courts, its own national church, its own system of weights and measures, as well as its own banking system and currency, so that the legislative merger did not produce total integration. In some ways, legislatively unified Scotland had more institutional autonomy than did federally unified Canada.

The status of these distinctively Scottish institutions within the farflung British Empire, however, was not at all clear. There is considerable evidence that England assumed that its law, church, courts, and weights and measures would be the ones extended throughout the Empire, and in any case this is essentially what happened in what became Canada and elsewhere. I discovered to my surprise a few years ago that the initial royal commission of 1769 to the lieutenant-governor of the island of St. John insisted only that those laws conform to the "laws and statutes of our Kingdom of Great Britain," although the more usual understanding of the formula for colonial law was that it conform to the "laws of England," especially the common law.[8] What a contemporary would have taken to be the "laws of Great Britain" is not at all clear. In any event, while Scottish law had some influence in the expanding empire after 1707, chiefly because some lawyers and jurists had been trained or educated in Scotland, the dominant law of the colonies became the English common law. Scots were readily admitted to the ranks of those who administered and governed the Empire, but what they administered tended to be substantially more English than British. It must be emphasized that the situation of Scotland within Great Britain after 1707 was hardly unique, even within the British Isles. The distinguished Welsh historian Gwyn A. Williams produced a wonderful book with the title *When Was Wales?* His answer is:

> Wales has always been now. The Welsh as a people have lived by making themselves in generation after generation, usually against the odds, usually within a British context. Wales is an artefact which the Welsh produce. If they want to. It requires an act of choice.[9]

In any case, after 1707 Scotland ceased to be a nation-state, although it is considerably more open to debate whether it ceased to be a "nation." Academics often get too wrapped up in terminology and subtleties of conceptualization. What matters about places like Scotland or Wales is not whether they are nations or regions, but whether they have a sense of their own identity. What matters about that identity is not whether it is real or mythological, whether it is based on historical record or the imagination of its inhabitants, but whether it exists and whether a large number of inhabitants subscribe to it.

As scholars have demonstrated over the past few years, the impact of the Union upon Scotland and Scottish national consciousness was quite variable, depending upon where and when one looked. Two resistances from the Highlands of Scotland, in 1715 and 1745, had to be brutally suppressed by the British authorities. In this suppression they had the assistance, or at least support, of large numbers of the people of Scotland, but it is not at all clear whether the resistances could be characterized as inspired by Scottish "nationalism," since most of the resistors probably operated within a prenationalistic framework and saw themselves as the personal lieges of Jacobite monarchs rather than defenders of a Scottish nation-state. What the "'15" and the "'45" did was to focus attention upon the Scottish Highlands and upon the Celtic/Gaelic culture which existed there.[10] That culture, at least, was sufficiently insulated from the English to be regarded as distinctive, and there was a tendency in the eighteenth century, as now, to insist on distinctiveness as the main criterion for national identity.

The loss of an independent parliament and of nation-state status had considerable impact upon Scottish national identity, especially on the writing, and meaning, of Scottish history, however. In a century in which history was largely politics—the eighteenth century—historical writing about Scotland floundered. As one recent scholar has put it, "the vital heart of the nation's history has been lost—the link between liberty and nationhood." The loss of this link, moreover, "inhibited the growth of a nineteenth-century nationalist intelligentsia."[11] The lack of political continuity, for a variety of reasons, threw many Scots back upon the Gaelic fringes for symbols of the meaning of Scotland.

There was thus a new emergence of Highland Scottishness in some circles. Considerable fuss occurred a few years ago when the historian Hugh Trevor-Roper insisted in a much-discussed article that most of the visible symbols of modern Scottish identity—especially plaid tartans and kilts—had been invented during the eighteenth century, possibly even by Englishmen![12] There was even more controversy over the very title of the book, *The Invention of Tradition*, in which Trevor-Roper's article appeared, with large numbers of people shocked at the concept that "traditional" could be invented rather than mysteriously seeping out of the mists of the folk past. But there was no doubting that the eighteenth-century attempts of James Macpherson and the Rev. John Macpherson to create for Celtic Scotland an indigenous literature that seeped out of the mists involved blatant forgery of texts. More successful were the literary efforts of Robert Burns and Sir Walter Scott. These authors were content with ersatz distinctiveness rather than the truly authentic package. Burns created a vocabulary and a series of metaphors that Scots of all social origins could identity with and carry with them around the world, while Scott resurrected older myths of Scotland and gave them new fictional life. Much of the Scottish identity that at least Lowland Scots took with them into Canada during the nineteenth century had been forged by Burns and Scott.

A recent study by Linda Colley has attempted to argue, with substantial documentation, that the period between 1707 and the 1830s saw the development—even *invention*—of a new British nation and nationality.[13] Accepting the conceptualization of Benedict Anderson, she sees a nation as "an imagined political community" and argues that we can plausibly regard Great Britain as an invented nation "inevitably superimposed on much older alignments and loyalties."[14] That new British nation was anchored by the opportunities of the British Empire and, formed in the crucible of international warfare against the French and Spanish, carried forward a fine old sense of anti-Catholicism that helped unify Scots, English, Welsh and some Irish. Great Britain defined itself in terms of the enemy, in Colley's words, in terms of "the other." There is no doubt that there was a new sense of Britishness developing after 1707, although it is interesting that a number of reviewers were not entirely convinced by Colley's arguments. There was an overwhelming sense of "Yes, but so

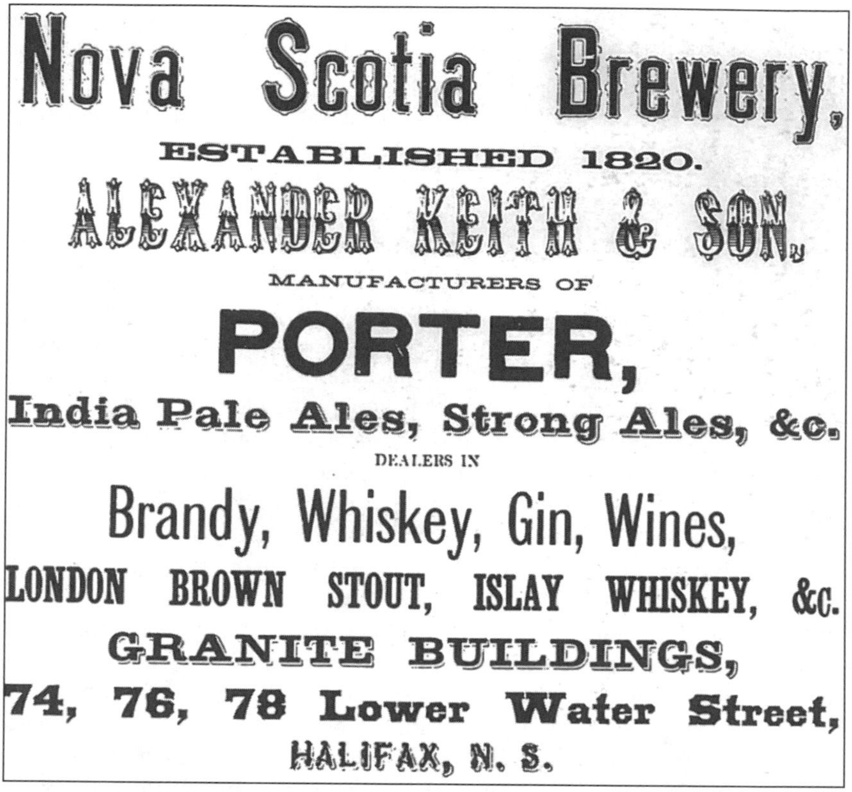

Nova Scotia Brewery,

ESTABLISHED 1820.

ALEXANDER KEITH & SON,

MANUFACTURERS OF

PORTER,

India Pale Ales, Strong Ales, &c.

DEALERS IN

Brandy, Whiskey, Gin, Wines,

LONDON BROWN STOUT, ISLAY WHISKEY, &c.

GRANITE BUILDINGS,

74, 76, 78 Lower Water Street,

HALIFAX, N. S.

Figure 4.1   Keith Brewery advertisement, 1871 (courtesy of Nova Scotia Heritage Trust)

what?"[15] While on one level we have a unifying Protestant hostility to Catholicism, on another level we have a constant series of extremely divisive schisms within the Protestant churches of Great Britain. The new nationalism was undoubtedly important for the ruling classes and intelligentsia of the British Isles, but how far it reached into the ranks of ordinary people is quite another matter. Ruling-class Scots moved easily in and out of a colonial administration that was largely English in emphasis, but, then, ruling-class Scots had always been most assimilable. Even the Highland lairds had been turned into English landholders by a process of allowing them to "own" the traditional lands of their subordinates. Several of Colley's reviewers resorted to the distinction made by George Orwell between "nationalism" and "patriotism," the latter being far more important and far more rooted in association with place and landscape than with nation-states.[16] Colley's effort to see Britishness as a superimposed set of attitudes suggests the extent to which the "superimposition" is really not an assimilation out of the older values, which still remain

93

crucial, especially at the subliminal level. Moreover, once we allow nations to be imagined or invented communities, the questions become: whose imagination or invention and of what community?

Whatever else one wishes to say about it, the nationalism of the nation-state has very political overtones. Nevertheless, there are profound distinctivenesses and local preferences that lurk beneath the political level. To give but one example, there is the matter of diet and demography. Scotland in our own times has the highest incidence of heart disease, diet-related cancers, congenital diseases (such as spina bifida) and strokes of any place in the Western world. Scots eat too much sugar, junk food and fat, and not enough green vegetables and fruit. They smoke and drink too much. We do not know enough about the history of these preferences, although they are deeply rooted in the historical past, and especially in the relative poverty of the average Scot. Neither the dietary preferences or their statistical consequences have very much directly to do with politics or government.

But it seems clear to me that many of Canada's drinking habits and institutions, if not its food choices, are descended far more from Scotland than from England, and the concept of an overarching "British" diet or cuisine, while plausible, does not take us very far. I have always felt the kinship between the Canadian beer parlour and the traditional Scottish pub, for example, for in both drinking was done somewhat guiltily and with the deliberate intention of getting drunk as quickly as possible. In both, drinking was serious business, the primary purpose of a visit. The notions of enjoying oneself or visiting with one's neighbours were quite alien. Because Scots drank more seriously, deliberate non-drinking was a popular reaction. Teetotalism flourished in Presbyterian communities.

While it is true that Scots allowed themselves to be drawn into Great Britain on some levels, it is equally true that they remained separate on other, more profound ones. Drinking customs and institutions are only one example. If we look at soccer football, the first of the "mass" spectator sports of the nineteenth century, we find the establishment of an English league and a Scottish league. Efforts to amalgamate the two foundered over differences in philosophy between the English and the Scots, exacerbated by English attitudes of superiority that the Scots found understandably offensive.

Colley is most different from other scholars and commentators, not in her documentation of the development of notions of Britishness, but in her assumptions that this ever intended to be (or became) genuinely all-encompassing rather than mere camouflage. An equally plausible view among scholars of Great Britain is the claim that what we had essentially was an English state, which made certain concessions to the outer fringes.[17] As Canadian scholar Philip Buckner has pointed out, "The English did become the dominant group in Britain; English became the dominant language, the English monarch the British monarch, the English aristocracy the dominant social group and the capital of England the capital of Britain. Clearly the English themselves saw the creation of Britain—and indeed the British Empire—as the expansion of England and they confused our understanding by continuing to use the words British and English indistinguishably."[18] Not only was the history of Canada until our own century studied as an integral part of the history of Great Britain and the British Empire, but Canada's development was often seen as an extension of the history of England, which was the important part of Great Britain and the Empire. A few years ago an old friend gave me a copy of a little book published in Toronto in 1891 by Copp, Clark Company, Limited. This work was entitled *High School History of England by Arabella B. Buckley (Mrs. Fisher) and W.J. Robertson, B.A., LL.B., and History of Canada by W.J. Robertson, B.A., LL.B.*[19] It noted on its title page that it was "Authorized by the Education Department of Ontario" and so was presumably employed in the Ontario high school system in the age of imperial federationism. Buckley and Robertson did not entirely ignore the Scots, Irish and Welsh on either side of the Atlantic; they simply assumed that the important imperial history was that of England, concluding with the Imperial Exhibition of 1886. They then observed,

> for the inhabitants of India and the colonies are all subjects of the same Empress-queen, and in the Australasian and Canadian colonies at least, nearly all are English in speech, in race, and in heart. Surely there is every encouragement to lead the English-speaking race to look forward hopefully to the future; and if a watchword is needed to bind together England's sons in all parts of the world, it is found in Nelson's noble words—"ENGLAND EXPECTS EVERY MAN TO DO HIS DUTY."[20]

Nelson's words remind us that not everyone who fought the French thought they were British, and the entire passage reverberates with controversial assumptions.

No doubt Lorne Murchison, the protagonist of Sara Jeannette Duncan's 1904 novel *The Imperialist*, had studied Buckley/Robertson in school.[21] It would at least explain his declamatory monologue to Dora Milburne before his departure for London as secretary to the head of a deputation of the United Chambers of Commerce of Canada to press the British government for improved communications within the Empire. Lorne understood perfectly well about that empire:

> We'll get off easy if the street boys don't shout: 'What price Canucks at us! But I'll see England, Dora; I'll feel England, eat and drink and sleep and live in England, for a little while. Isn't the very name great? I'll be a better man for going, till I die. We're all right out here, but

we're young and thin and weedy. They didn't grow so fast in England, to begin with, and now they're rich with character and strong with conduct and hoary with ideals. I've been reading up the history of our political relations with England. It's astonishing what we've stuck to her through, but you can't help seeing why—it's for the moral advantage.[22]

Not surprisingly, this view of Great Britain and the British Empire distressed many in Scotland, Ireland and Wales, particularly since it influenced the way the history of the British Isles was written throughout much of the nineteenth and early twentieth century.

We end up not merely with academic controversy, of course, but academic controversy that has contemporary politics lurking behind it. One of the results of a community, nation or region acquiring a sense of exploitation and marginalization is often a resurgence of assertions of separate identity. Such reassertions do not follow a predictable pattern, nor are they necessarily the inevitable result of the natural increase in any identifiable positive public manifestations of distinctiveness except anger and outrage. It may well be that the quest for national identity and self-determination is exacerbated as the real socio-cultural differences disappear. In Scotland, for example, the post-1945 growth of Scottish nationalism has come in the face of a seemingly unstoppable erosion of Gaelic language and customs, which were once thought to be the ideal manifestations of Scottish distinctiveness.[23] In Canada, Quebec has become far more assertive on the nationalist front since it has joined the remainder of industrialized and urbanized Canada on the socio-economic level. Socially, the Quebecois are more like the people of the remainder of Canada than they care to admit. Moreover, Canada itself becomes far more concerned about its overt cultural identity the more it assimilates into a continent dominated by the United States.

The resurgence of separatism, alienation or nationalism produces a counter-reaction, which in turn not only polarizes opinion but significantly affects our interpretation and understanding of what is happening out there in the world. In adjusting our explanations, we usually end up not only overreacting in the present, but in altering our understanding of the past. The re-emergence of Quebec separatism and Scottish nationalism over the past few decades has greatly influenced the historical interpretation not merely of Quebec and Scotland but of the larger states of which they have been a part. This is only to emphasize what most historians now accept: our understanding of the present greatly conditions our interpretation of the past. I do not wish to pursue this theme further at this point, since it really deserves a separate treatment of its own. But matters like nationalism, multiculturalism and ethnicity are concepts of high political importance, and our present debates and discontents resonate through our consideration of the past, and vice versa, whether intentionally or unintentionally. Even the most innocently academic of exercises can be enlisted on behalf of a contemporary argument.

If the history of Scotland and Scottishness, especially in the context of Great Britain, is a highly contentious, complex and controversial subject, so too is the history of the Scottish experience in Canada. The complexity of the subject, when once we dig beneath the surface, is mindboggling. The variables that have to be taken into account over a lengthy timespan are numerous. We have to deal with three nationalities changing over time: Scotland's, Great Britain's and Canada's. We must keep in mind the several regional differences within Scotland itself, and the regional shifts in the flow of Scottish immigration, which, while relatively constant in numbers over time, greatly altered in composition. We have to take into account the differing capacities of the territories of settlement to absorb new settlers. Uninhabited or underpopulated wilderness has a far different assimilative effect than densely populated territory; cities are different from farming areas. New wilderness was continually being opened up in Canada, at least until 1914 and even beyond, but the cumulative effect of the settlement process was to reduce the comparative extent and influence of the ever-decreasing wilderness areas. Scots immigrants between 1815 and 1850 entered a quite different Canada than those a century later. Generalizing about the Scottish experience in Canada is a bit like generalizing about the Canadian identity. Everything is plausible and very little that is said can be documented.

One other simple reality has to be remembered. While in Scotland everyone associates with other Scots most of the time and is exposed to Scottish institutions as a matter of course—whatever these things mean, the "default" is "Scots"—the Scot in Canada, at least to some extent, is a Scot by choice. He or she has to push a button or strike a key in order to become Scottish. There are several ways to identify Scottishness overseas. One is through individual self-ascription; anyone can be Scottish if they feel Scottish, a piece of wisdom you will hear often enough at social gatherings like Burns Night suppers in Winnipeg, often intended by more "chuks" than "macs." Another is by concentrating on the symbols and public expressions of Scottishness: the kilts, the pipes, the tartans, the Gaelic language and the creation of a membership in various Scottish organizations. The symbols are, of course, meaningless "tartanry," and the public expressions, including instruction in Gaelic, Gaelic newspapers, and Scottish societies, usually signal the decline of a culture rather than its vitality, since they are often made to prevent perceived cultural loss. The more important question is the extent to which Scots abroad *choose* to associate with other Scots. We know very little about these choices, because they are exceedingly hard to document. Careful analysis of diaries might demonstrate, as Alan Karras showed a few years ago about Scots in the eighteenth-century Caribbean, that Scots went out of their way to have both social and business connections with other Scots.[24] We have not yet done such an analysis for

Canada. Institutions such as churches, schools and even colleges that do not so much trumpet their ethnicity as quietly assume it are probably more important than the manifestations of the self-consciously Scottish. St. Francis Xavier University was a Highland Catholic educational institution that throughout its nineteenth-century existence found substantially more than half of its student body in those of Highland Catholic descent; it introduced classes in Gaelic only at the end of the century, when the Highland Catholic identity was clearly in trouble. But in 1897, when St. F.X. graduated its first four females, those graduates' surnames were MacDonald, Bissett, MacDonald and MacDougall.[25]

One of the few generalizations that can be made about the Scottish experience in Canada over the course of the nineteenth century is that it becomes less visibly distinct and identifiable as the century goes on. The rate of the decline of distinctiveness is another matter entirely, depending on where you look in a very large country. I would distinguish four periods, each of which has its own characteristics that affect the distinctiveness question. For me the four periods are: (1) up to 1815; (2) from 1815 to 1840; (3) from 1840 to 1870 and (4) from 1870 to 1914. I will discuss each of these periods briefly, in turn.

1. Up to 1815: The period up to 1815 is characterized by a relatively small flow of emigration from anywhere, even the British Isles, to some very scattered, largely underdeveloped and isolated provinces in British North America.[26] That flow of emigration is dominated by Highland Scots heading in privately financed but organized parties chiefly to Prince Edward Island, Nova Scotia, Cape Breton, Red River and Upper Canada. The emigrants are for the most part poor but proud and self-sufficient. They are often led by the natural leaders of their local society: tacksmen and clergymen. Group settlement is the norm and, indeed, religious and linguistic preferences are as important as national ones. Gaelic-speaking Highland Catholics settle apart from Gaelic-speaking Highland Protestants, and these groups settle apart from English-speaking Highland Protestants. The British government intervenes in emigration only to attempt to regulate the passenger traffic, largely on behalf of Highland lairds who fear the depopulation of their estates. The importance of the timber trade for supplying vessels to carry immigrants is established in these years. Much of the timber trade is controlled by Scottish-born merchants operating out of Halifax, Montreal and a number of smaller seaports. Difficulties of inland transportation make it difficult for the new communities to interact with one another. Some, as in western regions, which are dominated by Scots-born fur traders, are almost totally isolated. For all these reasons, Scots are both distinctive and highly prominent among new settlers in this period.

2. 1815 to 1840: In this period we see increased activity by the British government in assisting emigration, as well as a greatly increased flow to

British North America from all parts of the British Isles.[27] Scotland ceases to become the overwhelmingly predominant source for British immigration, as Scots are joined by the Welsh, the Irish (from both the North and South) and the English as well. Gaelic-speaking Highland Scots become a much smaller percentage of the Scottish total. Gaelic continues to decline in the Highlands, partly because of the large numbers of Gaelic speakers who emigrate. While some of the emigrants settle in groups in ethnic communities, most come alone or in family parties, and they often settle in cities or on the land cheek by jowl with other emigrants regardless of origin. Many newly settling regions, especially in the Canadas, or growing cities anywhere, become veritable melting pots of immigrant groups who share, on one level, a common origin in the nation-state of Great Britain rather than some other national culture. The Scots manage to hang on to some aspects of dominance in this period. They continue to control the management of the western fur trade and, as Scottish fur traders retire to Red River, they come to dominate that settlement's society as well. Scottish-born or Scottish-descended merchants continue to be important in the major seaports, although they no longer monopolize any trade. Nevertheless, the Scots of Montreal are the largest single component of the Montreal trading community. Significantly, the local political tensions between French-Canadians and British-Canadians convert the Montreal Scots into "Anglos." The conflict becomes not between Scots and Quebeckers but between those supported by the Anglophile colonial establishment and those opposing it. In this period, Scots firmly establish the Church of Scotland as an ethnic church in the colonies and experience schisms that merely echo those at home. Scottish Catholics take the lead in seeking a non-francophone (and non-Quebecois) administrative structure for the Church outside Quebec, and lead that structure until mid-century. Scottish educators are important, but are not the only, influences in creating the educational system of British North America. Scottish attitudes toward alcoholic beverages, abolitionism, the relationship of church and state, and political reform are exported to British North America and form a base for early political parties. Scottish sports, especially curling, golf, the Highland games and hockey, are exported as well. Scottish charitable and friendly organizations expand and flourish in this era, led by the St. Andrew's and Robert Burns societies. The poetry of Burns serves as a major model for early poetic efforts in British North America, and not just among Scots. For much of the period it covers, Helen Cowan's book on British immigration to Canada misleads because it does not distinguish the national groups among the immigrants.[28] This creates a statistical nationality with the wave of a pen, but one which does not reflect the actual situation. Scots, Irish and Welsh, if not English, are each still all conscious of their national origins.

3. 1840 to 1870: This is probably the critical period for Scottishness. After 1840, British North America ceases to be the only colonial destination for

emigration from the British Isles, as Australia, New Zealand and, to some extent, South Africa assume increasing importance. Among Scottish emigrants to British North America, the Highland component becomes even less important. The Scottish proportion of new immigration from Britain decreases. Group settlement becomes far less common. We do not really know whether Scottish immigrants from this period had less strongly Scottish identifications, although since this was an era of great industrial and agricultural transformation, it is entirely possible (and consistent with theory) that a sense of distinct Scottishness was on the wane in Scotland itself. The confederation of Canada offers another competing national identity for its people, and the successful expansion of the British Empire, especially in Asia, only enhances the willingness of those whose origins are in the British Isles to see themselves as part of that Empire. A resurgence of formal institutions fostering Gaelic probably reflects the growing realization among the Gaelic-speaking community that the younger generation is rapidly losing the language, rather than any genuine revival. The process only partly involves the loss of distinctiveness by the Scots. It also involves the appropriation of elements of formerly Scottish distinctiveness by non-Scottish groups. Formerly Scottish sports are now adopted by the larger community, for example, and their play by itself ceases to be an ethnic determinant. Highland paraphernalia, such as kilts and bagpipes, become part of the general Canadian military heritage. Increased intermarriage by representatives of the second and third generations of earlier Scots immigrants helps to reduce the sense of Scottishness. Nevertheless, we need to be careful about assuming that the loss of distinctiveness and Scottish identity is either sudden or total. A long-standing hostility between Irish and Scots plays itself out in frequent Canadian confrontations. Joseph James Hargrave, (himself educated in Scotland, reported in 1869 that the original Scotch settlers of Red River "were a persevering pig-headed party of Presbyterians, who practised what little they knew, and bequeathed it all as a heritage to their successors."[29] Beneath the sarcasm, one catches more than the hint of a persistent ethnicity. The Red River Scots had finally obtained a Presbyterian clergyman and established a Presbyterian church more than thirty-five years after their emigration to the west, large numbers of them in the process abandoning the Church of England, which had served them as an interim religious home. Presbyterianism continued to flourish elsewhere in communities with large numbers of Scots. The celebration of St. Andrew's Day continued to be an important occasion. Virtually every newspaper in British North America reported extensive St. Andrew's Day celebrations on 30 November. Many of the orations that were, along with a procession, a feature of the day suggest a Scottish-British ambivalence among the orators. The Reverend W. Taylor in 1857, for example, distinguished a false from a genuine Scottish patriotism: "It is quite possible to be devotedly attached to our own country, without assuming a defiant attitude towards any other; and to uphold her honour, without undervaluing or disparaging the

Figure 4.2 "The Curlers" by Harvey (courtesy of the National Galleries of Scotland)

excellence of other people and races." He went on to insist on fraternalism with "those allied countries, England and Ireland, which, together, with Scotland, form the triple confederacy of Great Britain."[30]

4. 1870 to 1914: Scottish distinctiveness further declines in the period after 1870. There were several factors behind this decline. With a few exceptions, such as the largely unsuccessful crofter colonies in Manitoba and Saskatchewan, group settlement involving Scots was a thing of the past in Canada. The number of Highlanders amongst the Scots immigrants is now very small as well. The new frontier in the Canadian West was initially opened by Canadians, Americans and British immigrants who formed a substantial Anglo-Saxon community united as much by the ever-expanding British Empire as by Great Britain itself. Most assisted settlement to Canada was done by British imperial organizations that mixed their clients indiscriminately. This was the era of imperial federation, and while it was true that one could be an imperialist and a Canadian simultaneously, it was equally true that one could be an imperialist, a Canadian and a Scot as well. Nevertheless, the processes of intermarriage and of the erosion of symbols of Scottish distinctiveness via their appropriation by the larger Canadian community continued unabated. By the time the Great War broke out, for example, the Highland military tradition had been fully merged into the Canadian one; indeed, in their mess halls Canadian officers today still drink toasts "Across the Water." Most Canadians of Scottish origin by 1914 had been born in North America, and the number of Scottish-born remained fairly constant through this period at under 200,000 people.

Scottish identifications never entirely disappear, however. Over the years I have read a number of immigrant letters and diaries from the settlement period in the Canadian West. Historians talk of these immigrants as "British."

But in these documents I have always been struck by the paucity of the use of the term "British" to refer to customs, culture or the nationality of one's friends and neighbours.[31] The letter-writers and diarists are far more likely to use national or even local labels—"a Scot from Glasgow," "a Cockney from London"—than a more all-inclusive term. "British" is used far more often in formulistic ways: "British pluck," for example. Almost all of the early literary figures in early Manitoba—Alexander Ross, Alexander Begg, Joseph James Hargrave, George Bryce—were of self-consciously Scottish backgrounds and often educated in Scotland. None of them thought of themselves as "British" Canadians; rather, they were "Scottish" Canadians.

Some places remained considerably more Scottish than others. A good deal depended, of course, on the concentration of Scots-born and of Scottish descent in the local population. The greater the proportion of Scots, the more likely that Scottishness remained alive and important. Large numbers of Scots survived only in out-of-the-way places. By 1900, Prince Edward Island and Cape Breton Island were the true centres of Scottishness in Canada, the latter being the only place keeping alive the Gaelic language and the old customs and traditions. For the most part, however, the Scottish identity in Canada had suffered from several quite different tendencies. One was for the British identity to take precedence over the Scottish, often as part of a self-conscious strategy to improve oneself economically, while Highland Scots in eastern Nova Scotia gave up their distinctiveness fostered by generations of poverty on farms and fishing boats, for example, in favour of assimilation into the larger British Canadian society. Another tendency was for the traditional symbols of Scottishness to be increasingly appropriated by both the larger British and even the general Canadian society. By World War I, Scottish sports (except perhaps for the Highland games) had only distant ethnic identifications. Developments in Scotland occasionally reassert an awareness for past Scottishness. The rise in importance and public recognition of the St. Andrew's Golf Club as the "birthplace of gold" means that its Scottish origins have been re-established.

In the twentieth century, Scottish ethnicity has been kept alive mainly by the latest generation of Scottish-born immigrants to Canada. I recently spoke to the Burns club in Vancouver, for example. Few of those present were under sixty years of age, and almost all had immigrated to Canada after World War II. They freely admitted that they did not know what would happen to their club after their demise, since their children had very different interests. With the recent decline of substantial Scottish (and British) immigration to Canada, we can probably foresee the virtual disappearance of overt ethnicity, at least until the children start searching for their roots.

Notes

1. *The People's Clearance: Highland Emigration to British North America, 1770–1815* (Edinburgh and Winnipeg, 1982).

2. "Thoughts of Home; A Sermon Preached on St. Andrew's Day, 1856, before the St. Andrew's Society, of Montreal, by the Rev. W. Taylor, D.D., One of the Chaplains of the Society, in the United Presbyterian Church" (Montreal, 1857).

3. See, for example, W.J. Rattray, *The Scot in British North America*, 4 vols. (Toronto, 1800–1884).

4. See Jean R. Burnet with Howard Palmer, *Coming Canadians: An Introduction to a History of Canada's Peoples* (Toronto, 1988).

5. Bruce Galloway, *The Union of England and Scotland, 1603–1608* (Edinburgh, 1986); P.W.J. Riley, *The Union of England and Scotland: A Study in Anglo-Scottish Politics in the 18th Century* (Manchester, 1978).

6. For the distinction between legislative and federal unions made in the 1860s, see P.B. Waite, *The Life and Times of Confederation, 1864–1867: Politics, Newspapers, and the Union of British North America* (Toronto, 1962).

7. William Robertson, *Proceedings Relating to the Peerage of Scotland, from January 16, 1707 to April 19, 1788* (Edinburgh, 1790); Michael W. McCahill, "The Scottish Peerage and the House of Lords in the late Eighteenth Century," *The Scottish Historical Review*, 51 (1972), pp. 172–96.

8. Frank MacKinnon, *The Government of Prince Edward Island* (Toronto, 1951), appendix A ("Commission to Governor Walter Patterson, August 4, 1769"), p. 322.

9. Gwyn A. Williams, *When Was Wales?* (Harmondsworth, 1985), p. 304.

10. Charles Withers, *Gaelic Scotland: The Transformation of a Culture Region* (London and New York, 1988).

11. Colin Kidd, *Subverting Scotland's Past: Scottish Whig Historians and the Creation of an Anglo-British Identity, 1689–c. 1830* (Cambridge, 1993), p. 268.

12. Hugh Trevor-Roper, "The Invention of Tradition: The Highland Tradition of Scotland," in Eric Hobsbawm and Terence Ranger, eds., *The Invention of Tradition* (Cambridge, 1983), pp. 14–42.

13. Linda Colley, *Britons: Forging the Nation 1707–1837* (New Haven and London, 1992).

14. Colley, *Britons*, p. 373. See Anderson's *Imagined Communities: Reflections on the Origin and Spread of Nationalism* (London, 1991).

15. See Walter R. Johnson, "A Historiographical Sketch of English Nationalism, 1789–1837," *Canadian Review of Studies in Nationalism*, 19 (1992), pp. 1–7; John Brewer, "The binding of the free: Creating Great Britain and its Other," *Times Literary Supplement*, 16 October 1992, pp. 5–6; review of Colley by Bernard Crick, *The Political Quarterly*, 1993, pp. 160–63; review of Colley by Frederick Dreyer, *Canadian Journal of History*, 28 (December 1993), pp. 588–91.

16. George Orwell, "The Lion and the Unicorn: Socialism and the English Genius," in Sonia Orwell and Ian Angus, eds., *The Collected Essays, Journalism and Letters of George Orwell, Volume 11, My Country Right or Left, 1940–1943* (Harmondsworth, 1968), pp. 74–134.

17. Michael Hechter, *International Colonialism: The Celtic Fringe in British National Development, 1536–1966* (Berkeley and Los Angeles, 1975); Keith Robbins,

Nineteenth-Century Britain: Integration and Diversity (Oxford, 1988).

18. Phillip Buckner, "Whatever Happened to the British Empire?" *Journal of the Canadian Historical Association*, new series, 4 (1993), p. 9.
19. In many ways this little book is an admirable textbook.
20. *High School History of England*, p. 322.
21. Sara Jeanette Duncan, *The Imperialist* (Toronto, 1961).
22. Duncan, *The Imperialist*, pp. 98–99.
23. Withers, *Gaelic Scotland*.
24. Alan Karras, *Sojourners in the Sun: Scottish Migrants in Jamaica & the Chesapeake, 1740–1800* (Ithaca, N.Y., 1992).
25. James D. Cameron, *For the People: A History of St. Francis Xavier University* (Montreal and Kingston, 1996), especially p. 98.
26. See my "The Cultural Landscape of Early Canada," in Bernard Bailyn and Philip D. Morgan, eds., *Strangers within the Realm: Cultural Margins of the First British Empire* (Chapel Hill, 1991), pp. 363–92, and "The Scot in Canada, 1763–1815," in Ned Landsman, ed., *Nation and Province in the First British Empire* (East Linton, forthcoming).
27. Gerald Redmond, *The Sporting Scots of Nineteenth-Century Canada* (Toronto, 1982).
28. Helen I. Cowan, *British Emigration to British North America: The First Hundred Years*, revised edition (Toronto, 1961).
29. *Montreal Herald*, 11 October 1869.
30. *Thoughts of Home*, p. 10.
31. See, for example, the letters of Willie Wallace in Kenneth S. Coates and William R. Morrison, eds., *"My Dear Maggie . . ." Letters from a Western Manitoba Pioneer William Wallace* (Regina, 1991).

MIGRATION

5

Leaving the Highlands:
Colonial Destinations in Canada and Australia

Eric Richards

In his influential work on the Atlantic world of the eighteenth century, Bernard Bailyn uses a remarkable array of metaphors to dramatise migration. He conjures up great centrifugal forces at work, motioning people across the Atlantic in mysterious but momentous ways. He evokes their mobility as ant-like, so incessant that the phenomenon possesses no stable form. In another insect image, he finds the individual data of British emigration (during the flurry of departures of 1773–74 out of various places, notably the West Highlands) rising like a cloud of gnats from his computer print-outs. The point of Bailyn's resort to metaphor and the computer is, of course, to bring pattern and structure to these mesmerising movements. Eventually he produces a dual model of British emigration: first the "metropolitan" model, especially characterised by individualistic, young male migration out of the large towns and notably London. By contrast the "provincial model" was dominated by family migration with a high sense of social cohesion and communal purpose, usually originating in rural districts, for example, parts of Yorkshire. Many contingents from the Scottish Highlands figured in this second model, demonstrating also the precocious involvement of the Highlanders in the history of British emigration.[1] The provincial model, well known in emigration research, is much reinforced by Marianne McLean's work on early Highland emigration to eastern Canada in her *People of Glengarry*.[2]

In the nineteenth century, the story, if anything, becomes even less manageable as conditions in the donor and receiving countries became much more complicated. The scale changed greatly too, especially from the late 1820s, and the number of destinations increased dramatically. In effect, therefore,

105

there were far more "gnats," far more dispersion, and a much more complicated metaphor is required. When Bailyn's own work enters the nineteenth century, his quest for metaphor and pattern will face substantially larger challenges.

The Highland component of the story is writ smaller but is no less mesmerising. There is a danger of reducing it to a single and powerful image. Highland emigration was, most of all, the dramatic face of the Highland tragedy in the nineteenth century. The history of Highland migration contains some of the strongest images of communal clan-like movements in the history of European exoduses. The sense of family solidarity in the shadow of eviction and adversity is most commonly associated with Highland migrations. Clansmen trekking to West Highland ports, sailing in perilous conditions and reestablishing themselves in new Scotias is the common model.

The Highlanders are often invested with this tragic aspect which inevitably brings to mind parallels with the Irish story and the images of desperation and alienation so movingly evoked in Oscar Handlin's marvellous but outdated account of nineteenth-century emigration from Europe to North America in *The Uprooted*. It is not difficult to identify excellent examples of Highland desperation in both the North American and antipodean theatres of nineteenth-century emigration. Emigration to Canada and Australia certainly contains indelible accounts of dejected emigrants from the Highlands, many arriving in pitiful circumstances which can be related to eviction and associated poverty.

At other times the movement of people out of the Highlands was barely perceptible—small shifts, minor seepages, year after year. These leakages were persistent and widespread, unspectacular and unpublicised. Often they passed unrecognised by the commentators of the time. They were part and parcel of the general shifting of society: small and large movements, temporary and permanent moves, which blurred into each other. They were registered much more in the statistical aggregates of the censuses than in the contemporary literary record.

On many occasions the widely separated colonial claims on the Highlands, as a source of emigrants, intersected. Thus, for instance, both eastern Canada and Australasia reached deep into the straths and mountains of the north of Scotland for migrants. By the middle decades of the nineteenth century, these Highland fastnesses were releasing migrants to many destinations, none of them perfectly synchronised, often following different timetables, flowing in many directions and conforming to no single formation. Within the broad story there were several exotic variants which happened to connect three Scotias, namely the Highlands, Nova Scotia and the Antipodes. The last was, of course, regarded as the far rim of the emigrant world.

These intercontinental connections offer the full width of the spectrum of emigration as the Highlands responded to adversity and opportunity in the nineteenth century. It is the diversity of the departures that demands the sort of taxonomy after which Bailyn continues his quest. But beyond such organising principles is the greater fact that the Highlands contributed powerfully to the repeopling of two continents in that century. Distance and cost made the Australian option much smaller, requiring special mechanisms to bring it within the reach of Highlanders. In both arenas, however, they were usually the poor foot soldiers of the empire of emigration; yet Highlanders were also the entrepreneurs and the cutting edge of imperial advance; and they were as heavily implicated in the quasi-genocidal aspects of American and Australian empire as any other group from the British Isles.

Highlanders in the early American colonies have been depicted as the "shock troops" of empire, moving deep into the backwoods, doing the rough work of pioneering, confronting and dispersing the indigenous peoples.[3] In Australia and New Zealand, in the Victorian Age, Highlanders were again involved on the savage frontiers of settlement, thrusting into aboriginal space and taking an appalling toll of human life. Highlanders on the antipodean frontier, as on the more formal battlefields of empire, were undoubtedly red in tooth and claw.[4] In the Scottish Highlands, land hunger or resource hunger worsened in the nineteenth century; a growing population on a limited and ungenerous land was now forced to compete for the same land with the demands of industrialisation. It was an unequal contest from the start. The awful irony was that the Highlanders, leaving their own homelands, soon faced land hunger again in eastern Canada, and then became agents for the further intensification of land use in the rest of North America and Australasia, bearing down on the indigenous peoples of those places.

Mostly, however, the Highlanders tended to merge with the widening rivers of emigration that issued from the British Isles after 1830, spreading across new continents in the general manner of their fellow emigrants from England and Ireland. Pockets of Scottish and Highland concentration undoubtedly persisted, even in Australia. There were self-conscious efforts to recreate new Edinburghs, and even New Scotlands, in the outback. Religion and language were the most effective social cement in the colonies. But in the Australian colonies, ranged against communal cohesion, were the pressures of rural dispersion over huge distances, and Highlanders were considered most adaptable for the pastoral life. As an alternative, there were the cities of Australia where, by the end of the Victorian age, most Australians were concentrated. In cities the sheer human numbers weighed against the preservation of immigrant identity for anything longer than a generation or so.

It is tempting to tell the entire Highland expatriation story as a mechanical reaction to Malthusian crises and landlord oppression. Such matters unquestionably loom large in the account, but taken alone they diminish the variety and dynamism of the Highland participation in the imperial outreach. The long-distance Highland migrants, on the far fringes of the Victorian Empire, represented the widest spectrum of Highland society, which had been buffeted by severe economic transformation in the nineteenth century. Highlanders issued out of every stratum and district of their country. Most went to North America but many thousands reached the great southern continent. Their emigrations mirrored the diversity and turmoil of Highland society. Almost all of them were emigrating under the pressure of changing land use in the Highlands.

The Highlands contained some of the worst poverty in the British Isles; it also experienced one of the most rigorous and dislocating series of economic changes of any part of the nineteenth-century British Isles. There was undoubtedly a Malthusian element in many of the departures: of people fleeing population growth, poverty, and deprivation and the fear of worse, of indeed famine. But none of these processes operated automatically. Poverty itself often bred a growing reluctance to leave the squalor of the glens; it often gave rise to conservatism and a diminution of horizons.[5] None of this was unique to the Highlanders.[6] Migrants from other rural regions in Britain and the rest of Europe went through similar agonising before emigration, especially to Australia.

The paradox of the fate of the Highlanders was that their region contributed more strongly than ever to the advance of the national economy during the years when it was able to sustain a diminishing proportion of its own people. As Brinley Thomas points out, the so-called Celtic periphery fed the English industrial core before it turned to other sources of supply, eventually of course to Canada and Australia, the destination of many of the "surplus people" of the Highlands.[7]

Some economic historians have seen this process—which was almost a forced tribute of the "Celtic zones" to the industrialisation of the core—as a necessary adjustment, observed in all parts of the system. Thus Sara Horrell, Jane Humphreys and Martin Weale argued that the growth of agricultural productivity meant that industrialisation needed to take up the surplus labour released by the growth in the rural sector.[8] This is a schematic way of expressing the Highland change. The painful restructuring of the Highland economy (which sometimes takes the name of the Clearances) was premised on the reality of massive productivity gains in primary products such as wool, cattle and fish supplied to the rest of Britain in the nineteenth century. Up until the 1840s the expanding economy was associated with a rising population; but even then the increment of population increase was mainly lost by outmigration. After that, population fell absolutely as well as relatively. But this was not unique to the Highlands; it was the common experience of rural Britain, penalised for its own labour efficiency, which contributed so much to industrialisation.

The Highlands were therefore part of a rural world which everywhere lost population during industrialisation. This was the great shift that lay behind the Clearances, part of the structural change which altered the bases of life in this region in common with other parts of the British Isles.[9] But it was more explosive in the Highlands, where the change was most radical and little mitigated by governmental concern. Moreover the slow rate of internal migration out of the western Highlands in the nineteenth century diminished the impact of emigration and prevented a substantial fall of population.[10]

Economists and emigration historians look for the smooth transit of surplus labour to more favourable destinations. This process, in its fully rational mode, was marked by what is known as "convergence" in incomes and capital availability, in a world in which, in the long run, all was for the best of all possible worlds.[11]

The problem, in the real world, was the existence of frictions and resistances. For instance, the agricultural labourer in depressed southern England simply would not migrate in sufficient numbers to improve wage levels in that sector. This was frustrating to economists, planners and colonial recruiters. We might recollect Thistlethwaite's proposition that "the centripetal tendencies which kept people at home were at least as strong as the centrifugal tendencies which sent them abroad."[12] Similarly, in the Highlands there were impediments to structural adjustment. The peasantry did not smoothly evacuate the region. They moved in fits and starts, subject to resistance, friction, bloody-mindedness, and the perception of choice and opportunities. The evacuation of the Highlands was a stuttering, uneven and unpredictable process conditioned by collective urges and individual and familial eccentricities. They chose different exits too, notably to eastern Canada, but also to Australia, which emerged strongly by the 1840s.[13]

The earliest intersection of Canada and Australia as alternative destinations for Highland emigration occurred in 1815–17. There was a discontinuity in the evolution of emigration out of the British Isles, and the British government intervened, for the first time, to promote emigration, reversing its previous opposition. Its attention turned especially to the Highlands, where landlords were also beginning to switch from resistance to encouragement of emigration, though there was still a great deal of ambivalence on all sides.[14] Government policy began to turn toward a less negative and then a positively encouraging attitude toward emigration in response to the uneasy economic and political conditions which prevailed over much of the country in the years immediately following Waterloo. Severe depression, poor harvests and demobilisation produced great alarm in government circles. Assisted emigration was one among several nostrums suggested as a means of immediate relief to workers and rulers alike. Not everyone agreed: Francis Horner noticed that the government was desperate to find any "practicable palliatives" and that "the only thing the Government had thought of, for its relief, was to afford liberally every possible encouragement to emigration." Horner satirised the idea as "a forced emigration of our peasantry and artisans [which] . . . forms a sagacious and enlightened system of policy; the last result of all the political reasonings, and liberal ideas of the eighteenth and nineteenth centuries." It was a disgrace to a civilised community and a grotesque reversal of Enlightenment thinking.[15]

It was at this moment that the Colonial Office began to think of New Holland as a possible destination of voluntary emigration from the Highlands. Given the contemporary condition of North America, it was not a surprising suggestion. Thus Lord Bathurst at the Colonial Office, increasingly conscious of the dangerous signs of discontent and popular protest in the northern Highlands as new phases of clearance came to public notice, suggested to landowners that the antipodes might offer alternative locations for removed tenantry. This was one of the first occasions when the British government showed a positive interest in emigration, and the first time that Australia was given a serious hearing as a possible destination. In the end the schemes to promote emigration were small in scale and restricted to eastern Canada and the Cape of Good Hope. Nevertheless, the intellectual and political climate of British emigration had shifted significantly; and in the Highlands the clearing landlords and their agents began to think of the possibilities.[16]

It is almost always difficult to connect specific Highland clearances with actual emigration. Emigration from the region predated the Clearances, and the pressures outward were normally wider and more pervasive than particular episodes of clearance. But occasionally the nexus was obvious. From December 1817 there is evidence from the horse's mouth: James Loch, supervising the massive removals on the Sutherland Estate, told Lord Bathurst at the Colonial Office that "The gradual introduction of the Northumberland stock farmers has produced of late years the same removal of the people from the hills to the Coast and has produced in many the same desire to emigrate to the Colonies as existed some years ago." Loch denied that this was the intention of the Sutherland policy, but he acknowledged that it was the actual effect. The estate had made every effort to dissuade the emigrants and had arranged their resettlement within the Sutherland estate. But the people removed from the straths were headstrong, and the "young and active" preferred to go to Canada. Loch remarked that the prevailing Act of Parliament made emigration unnecessarily expensive because it forced "the shipowner to provide more animal food for each individual than a highlander ever consumes probably in a twelve month."[17]

New South Wales, at least until 1819, was still regarded, within and without government, as the exclusive preserve of convicts. At that time Bathurst made it known that voluntary emigration of persons of enterprise and integrity would now be welcomed in the colony. There was a minor flow from Scotland in the following decade, including a few from the Highlands.[18] The essential problem was that emigration to New Holland was too expensive for ordinary emigrants, and certainly for clearance victims.

The shift in attitudes to emigration, already telegraphed in 1815, was also manifest in the words of Patrick Sellar, the most infamous figure in the story of the Highland Clearances. Sellar was a sheep farmer from Elgin in Moray who became involved in the Sutherland estate and executed a series of massive evictions in 1813–15. He was charged with culpable homicide in 1816 and tried and exculpated in Inverness. He lived on to become one of the most successful sheep farmers of the new pastoral sector of the Highland economy. He expressed the extreme version of landlord policy during the acute subsistence crisis in the Highlands in 1816–17. Sellar, in correspondence with his landlord, advocated the subsidisation of emigration to facilitate the introduction of sheep farming. He asked, "Would not Lord Stafford throw about some bait to induce them to emigrate to America and carry a swarm of their dependents with them?" Sellar took the view that it was madness to maintain the Highlanders in beggary on the estate; it was better to pay them to go to Canada or New Holland. He suggested that Stafford purchase some land in Nova Scotia, to be called New Sutherland, and induce some of the people to emigrate from the interior. Whether they went slowly or quickly, he contended, there would still be discontent and heartbreak. It made no difference. The Highlanders, he argued, were perfect emigrants for Canada, specifically because "they are less advanced in society."[19] Sellar's was the voice of extreme realism but, between 1820 and 1850, such a prognosis of the Highland dilemma eventually became the conventional wisdom of many landed proprietors.

At the time of the Sutherland clearances, Sellar's advocacy of emigration was awkward because it cut against the idea that the estate would accommodate all the people dislodged by the removals. James Loch, Sellar's superior, remained significantly ambiguous. Loch put the matter of emigration in the context of rapid population growth on the Sutherland estate. It was, he said, "every day a more anxious and important subject." He thought that the time had come to bring the question before the government. The recurrent distress in the north warranted serious consideration of "affording some of the mountaineers a comfortable settlement at the Cape or New South Wales or in Van Diemens Land." He went on to say that "I almost hope this summer [1816] may incline come of the people to emigrate." In political terms it was premature to think that landlords could openly promote emigration even if their policies precipitated the partial evacuations of their small tenantries.[20] But Loch's employer, the Countess of Sutherland, privately talked of getting "rid of these inefficient people" who occupied the estate without "any profit to themselves" or to the owner. Emigration, under the impact of these assumptions, soon ceased to be an ambiguous matter.[21]

In the history of social protest during the Highland Clearances, the common people, even as late as 1820, continued to believe that it was possible to curtail landlord removal plans by threatening to emigrate. It was another sign of the changing structure of Highland life that this rapidly turned into an empty tactic as landlords became convinced of the advantage of emigration to their own finances.

The precise impact of some of the clearances on emigration from Sutherland is well documented. The infamous Sellar events of 1814–16 were followed in 1819 and 1820 by the great removals in Kildonan and elsewhere on the same estate (though without the direct involvement of Sellar). Of a total of 3,331 people removed, about 70 percent remained on the estate, most of the rest going to adjoining estates and counties. According to estate statistics, only about 2–5 percent emigrated. These data provide a good measure of the immediate dislocation caused by the Clearances. There was evidently an immediate and substantial offloading of the small tenantry at the very moment of clearance. Even where the estate was making a substantial effort to retain and succour the people (as the Sutherland estate claimed to be doing), the people cleared to make way for the sheep were on the move, set in motion by the cataclysm.[22]

The Sutherland statistics of 1819–20 unquestionably understated the dislocation caused by the Clearances. Clearance, in reality, operated as the first precipitant of mobility, which set off a sequence of change which was not played out for many years. In the longer run, many stayed on the estate for a matter of generations, but others moved on, probably in step-like formations, from the pre-clearance site to coastal village, then south and then perhaps abroad, possibly in the next generation. [23]

At the time of the great Sutherland clearances some of the cleared people went to Canada, but none to Australia. But there were already contemporaneous movements to the two destinations from other parts of the Highlands. Australia and New Zealand emerged in the 1830s as relatively late extensions of empire, a new theatre of imperial opportunity. Australasia required special mechanisms and incentives to attract migrants. These mostly took the form of large profits in the pastoral industry, high wages, the gold rushes and subsidised passages. Only in a few years in the late 1830s and the 1850s did Australia recruit and assist some of the "huddled masses" from the Highlands. Mostly Australia's immigrants derived from the middle rungs of the proletarian ladder.

Australia could not rely on a tradition of popular migration, unlike Canada, where "they knew they could find many of their own relations and friends; they know that they would find whole districts of the country peopled by Highlanders, speaking their own language, maintaining their own manners and customs, and, above all, they know that they would find their own church established by law."[24]

However, by the late 1830s, the provision of free passages, and favourable reports from the earliest recruits to the Australian colonies, created a minor diversion to Australia. From 1837 to 1840, one agent alone had seen 600 depart from the west Highlands to Australia while another 1,259 went to the Maritime Provinces of Canada. On the Sutherland estate in 1837 there were reports of "a temporary dread of Canada" and a switch to the Australian opportunities that were beginning to emerge. This was a consequence of the disturbed condition of Canada and the provision of assisted passages to South Australia and New South Wales, and soon also to New Zealand. Another factor in the matter was Australia's attempt to sway choice by improving the supervision of the emigrant trade to Australia so that its safety record and general efficiency became a byword for good organization.[25]

The numbers of Highland emigrants to Canada were always much greater though there were antipodean analogues in every class of immigrant. Thus, for instance, there was a parallelism among the soldier emigrants. Land grants to the military were the common impetus for settlement in both early New South Wales and eastern Canada. Half-pay and retired officers from the Highlands took advantage of these opportunities, which gave them an excellent escape mechanism out of the extremely competitive conditions which had overtaken the Highland economy in the years before and after Waterloo. Lachlan Macquarie, the governor of New South Wales in the 1810s, had taken the classic route out of the west Highlands. He had left the island of Ulva by way of the army in India to a commission in New South Wales, and then eventually to his illustrious governorship in the 1810s. He then become a conduit for other Highlanders to the antipodes. The military Highlanders were vital to the British Empire in both hemispheres, and the Empire was no less vital to them.

Highlanders emigrating in groups drawn from common clan, geographical and religious backgrounds have been the most photogenic in the historical imagination.[26] Most of the best-known examples of communal expatriation from the Highlands, which Levitt and Smout described as "coagulated emigration," were Canadian, but they were replicated in the southern continent also. For instance, Major Donald Macleod of Talisker in Skye took the classic route through the army into pastoralism and wide acres in Van Diemen's Land. He had inherited a failing estate in Skye which had been in the family possession for two hundred years; he served as a lieutenant in the East Indies and retired as a half-pay officer. Soon after Bathurst had announced that the Australian colonies were suitable destinations for civilian emigrants, Macleod negotiated a loan from his father-in-law, Alexander Maclean of Coll, and obtained a land grant in the convict island. Macleod sold off his property in 1819 and conveyed his family entourage aboard the *Skelton* to Hobart in 1820 where he established a new dynasty.[27] Here was the antipodean answer to Highland decline: an uprooting and a reestablishment of the fallen family. Some of Macleod's party were from Coll, and thirteen years later more of the Coll kinsfolk, another tacksman family, followed the Macleods to Van Diemen's Land in their own ship, the *John Dunscombe*.[28]

The greatest Highland story of collective emigration to Canada was that of the Macdonnell tenantry from western Inverness to Glengarry in Canada at the turn of the century. They were levered out of their ancestral lands by the Glengarry and their story has been told in fine detail by Marianne McLean.[29]

Curiously, McLean does not recount an exquisitely ironic final twist to the Glengarry story which was acted out in eastern Australia four decades later. This entailed the pathetic attempt at emigration by Aeneas Macdonnell, the last chief of Glengarry, to New South Wales in 1840. He was attended by his family and dependents in a classic communal migration. They were equipped with timber houses and agricultural implements "for residence in that distant region" and all planned, ready to start afresh in the antipodes. Macdonnell had inherited a bankrupt estate, mortgaged and encumbered by the extravagance of his famous father (a model for Walter Scott's Fergus MacIver). This was the common fate of west Highland estates which had not modernised. Thus in 1840 the estate was abandoned by sale, the proceeds used to finance the great revitalising emigration of the Macdonnells to Australia.

There were public displays of sentiment at the departure of the Macdonnell from Scotland and again on his arrival in Australia.[30] But the emigrant laird failed badly in the new country. He was both incompetent and unlucky. He swiftly lost his investment and returned to Scotland a broken man, to die an early death. The sins of the clan fathers were visited on the son in the most devastating manner. By exact contrast, the descendants of the earlier migrants to Glengarry fared much better than their chief who later fled to the opposite side of the globe. It was the perfect symbolic termination, and it is instructive to connect the Canadian and Australian chapters of the narrative. The story possesses the stereotyped figure of the romantic Highlander, the last of the clan, unfitted for the capitalist world, the personified collision of cultures in which the paternalist model of the old Highlands was subverted by the fast world of modern commerce.[31]

There are too many Highland success stories in both Australia and Canada to allow us to linger long with this recurrent caricature. Nor were these group/kinship migrations unique to the Highlanders. Even in the Australian context there were equivalent English and Irish families who emigrated in response to low agricultural prices and sharpened competition in the British Isles. The recourse to empire was a common strategy to stave off social and economic decline, and to recover caste in a new context. In the Highlands these pressures were proportionately more intense than in most other parts, with the notable exception of Ireland.

The parallelism between the Canadian and Australian variants of the story extended through the middle ranks of Highland society. Dynamic and youthful elements in the Highlands responded to the availability of land and profits across the entire English-speaking world. In Australia there were extraordinarily successful pastoralists among the Highlanders who may be set beside the melodramatic failure of Glengarry. Niel Black, in the western district of Victoria, was the most renowned of this class of entrepreneurial Highlander, a man who continued to recruit his labour from the Highlands long after his own migration.[32]

Networks out of the Highlands stretched in all directions, some of them by means of the army and trade through India to the Far East, then to Australia and the Pacific.[33] Sometimes this involved a flow of capital, often highly capitalistic and experienced in the ways of the world, with intercolonial communications. For instance, Donald Maclaine wrote back to his brother in Lochbuie from Batavia in October 1839: "I am as happy as the day is long, in town all day making money, and in the country all evening making love." This was not the usual image of the dour, tragic, expatriated clansman. Maclaine was a link further to west Highland investment and pastoralism in the new colony of South Australia.

Nor should any taxonomy of Highland emigration neglect the return flow of capitalistic Highlanders from their successful colonial adventures. They returned, nabob fashion, with colonial fortunes to fructify the old economy. The story of Matheson's millions from the trade of the Orient, by its colossal scale, tends to overshadow many other examples of Highland fortunes made in Australia and Canada whose earners often ended their days in retirement in Highland villages, lowland spas or even London suburbs.[34]

Generally, however, it was the pressure of adversity, or narrowing opportunities at home, which propelled Highland emigration from all strata of this "society in travail" (in Malcolm Gray's phrase). At the top, as Glengarry's case showed, even landlords were emigrating, often enough in distress. In 1841, during a parliamentary debate on the question of Highland emigration, Henry Baillie spoke of the current plight of a landowner who had been forced, by the collapse of the kelp trade, "to hand over his whole estate to his younger brothers, and he himself only last year had been sent out at their joint expense as a sheep farmer to Australia."[35]

But mostly it was small tenantry rather than landlords who took the ships to the colonies. By 1836, with the recurrence of famine in the west Highlands, the tone of opinion among estate factors perceptibly hardened. Now there was a growing desperation in their minds. James Loch, a relatively moderate voice in the region, described Assynt as "this vastly overpeopled district" and urged the importance of getting the people to emigrate to Nova Scotia. He said, "Privately I wish the one half of the whole population of [the Highlands] would go; it would add greatly to the interest and welfare of the remainder, and greatly to the interest of the landlord, and more especially if one could get quit of the worthless, retaining the more respectable."[36] The Duke of Sutherland thought of buying land in South Australia to enable "the surplus population of this estate to scttle as Colonists in that country." Sutherland eventually withdrew from the project, but Malcolm of Poltalloch in Argyll bought a large estate in the new colony with the idea of settling his unwanted Highland tenantry in the arid outback. Sensibly, they refused to go and Malcolm was left with a vast sheep station instead.

In 1837, when free passages were offered to New South Wales, several parts of the Highlands responded strongly. The mentality of some the Inverness-shire emigrants was caught by a Gaelic bard, marking the departure of a substantial group from Kingussie. They had trekked to Fort William and Oban to embark on the *St. George* for Sydney, leaving their parish on the day of the St. Columba Fair. The song, part of the oral record of the Highlands which is rarely so conveniently available, was composed for the occasion but was hardly a dirge. It celebrated the land of promise, a warmer climate, the special opportunities for the young women to "find men to marry them who'll put gold in their two ears." In Australia, sang the bard, they would live far better, with bread and butter, sugar and tea,—"we shall lack nothing." They would leave behind a land in which rising rents were putting shame on their faces, a land in which little would grow and where the potatoes rotted in the damp soil. In the land of promise they would be able to take a gun on the hill without the keeper forcing them to run; the women would be clothed in silk, satin and wool, and they would rise late in the day. It was evidently a song of jolly bantering, perhaps designed to make the wrench of departure more bearable.[37]

Half a decade later, in the potato famine of 1846–51, the urgency redoubled. By that time landlords and tenants were equally desperate to accelerate emigration to Canada, Australia or indeed anywhere. One landlord in this position was Lord Lorne, owner of the island of Tiree. In 1846 he assisted 160 tenants to Canada. He had the usual dual motivation: humanitarianism and profit. He wanted to sell the island, but the price would be hopelessly low unless the population was radically reduced. The sale was affected by the remains of Lorne's paternalism; he wanted the purchaser to be "a monied man who is likely to behave well to the people." Yet few outgoing landowners had the luxury of selling to a handpicked successor of proven benevolence. The succession was more usually a random matter, and the new generation of proprietors in the Highlands was a mixed bag.[38]

Clearances undoubtedly accelerated migration and most went to eastern Canada, the cheapest route beyond Scotland. Only a few went directly to Australia, partly because the selection procedures of assisted passages usually excluded large families with dependents. The Australian colonies would not normally subsidise families with dependents, the old or the sick. The usual migrations were, therefore, generally atomistic rather than family-based. The Australian account does, however, provide a few well-documented cases where evictions were associated with the provision of passages on emigrant ships. This was certainly an option which landlords employed on occasion, adding to the duress of poverty, to persuade people to evacuate their estates. In the early 1850s, Highland landlords co-operated with the Highland and Island Emigration Society to persuade their small tenants to accept free passages to Australia, subsidised jointly by landlords, charity and the colonial governments. There were certainly clearance victims among these five thousand emigrants to Australia and some of them carried memories and hatreds to the colonies which resurfaced in later years.

Among the Highland and Island Emigration Society emigrants—straight out of the worst subsistence crisis of the century and assisted in family groups to eastern Australia—were unambiguous examples of wretchedness. This scheme, for virtually the only time in the history of assisted immigration, catered to large family groups. The Australian colonies were desperate for labour during the era of the gold rushes and were prepared to compromise their usual restrictions regarding dependency levels among the migrants. The Highlanders, of course, confronted the desperate consequences of famine and associated evictions. This unusual conjunction of gold and famine produced a flow of refugees from the Highlands to southeastern Australia.

The story of emigration to colonial Australia generally yielded relatively few accounts of *extremis*, and cannot rival the worst examples of immigrant squalor associated with the Atlantic passage. But some of the people who left the Highlands for Australia at the end of the Great Famine under the auspices of the Highland and Island Emigration Society came closest to refugee status. Among them was the Campbell family of Uig leaving for Melbourne from Liverpool in September 1852. The head of the family had been employed on road construction in the west Highlands as a form of destitution relief. According to the official record, Campbell "left his home at one hour's notice to emigrate."[39] Others among the society's emigrants needed emergency feeding and strengthening before they could be readied for the ocean voyage. These people were part of a panic departure (given institutional impetus) and fit perfectly the catastrophe version of the Highland emigration story. Australia received Highland emigrants with the marks of famine and poverty upon them, comparable with the distress of earlier settlers in Nova Scotia.

Even when the exodus was fully co-ordinated, as in the case of the Highland and Island Emigration Society, the emigrations remained subject to great unpredictability. The society was seriously embarrassed in 1854–55 when the emigrant supply to Australia dried up with the onset of better harvests. The society was left bereft of emigrants and holding a surplus of unspent funds.

The parallels between Highland emigration to Canada and Australia are manifold. Direct connections between these widely separated destinations are more sparse but serve to demonstrate the remarkable articulation of the migrant world by mid-century.[40] There were enough Highland-Canadian stories which terminated in Australia to identify the broader processes. For instance, there were connections between Nova Scotia and the first Australian colonies from the start, the army providing a continuing network which Scots in particular were likely to utilise. Thus men who were involved in the foundation of New South Wales in 1788 had already served in Halifax.

The most renowned story of Australo-Canadian migration was, of course, that of Norman McLeod's double migration. His Noah-like saga began in the West Highland migration to Cape Breton in 1817 and finished in Waipu, New

Zealand, thirty-five years later, taking in Adelaide and Melbourne en route. It is one of the most remarkable instances of "coagulated migration" in the history of international migration. McLeod sustained communal solidarity and cohesion for more than forty years across three countries and two oceans.

In the wider context, two facets of this extraordinary story have particular significance. First, the Normanite people were clearly inspired and driven by a commitment to community-making which survived for thirty years in Cape Breton, resisting dislocation and economic hardship, as well as intercommunal friction and theological antagonism. More especially, both the great migrations coincided with famine and land hunger in the donor regions, first in Wester Ross in 1817 and then in Cape Breton in 1847–49. The language of hunger and despair in the Cape Breton petitions and the correspondence of the time were a perfect echo of the public debates in the Highlands in 1817 and 1847.[41] The petitions spoke of "the very jaws of death" tightening on the community, and the "alarming destitution" which was "threatening starvation." They drew images of a "famished population," their potatoes blighted, compelled to consume the seed before the following season, "the ghastly features of death staring in their very faces," supplicating for meal and oats. In effect, it was the story of land hunger and destitution of the Highlands transposed to Cape Breton.

Second, the Normanite exodus, in its practical requirements, was by any standard a sophisticated project. It was prefaced by communications with McLeod's own prodigal son who had previously departed the Cape Breton community without satisfactory permission. Later his father described it as "my dear son's random emigration to that distant, vastly extended and unoccupied country." The younger McLeod became a newspaper editor in Adelaide and his letters provided the spur to the great remigration out of Cape Breton.[42] In fact, the younger McLeod's advice proved faulty and the Normanites rejected settlement in Australia, ostensibly on moral grounds, and because of the inaccessibility of acceptable land. They were, in McLeod's own description, "a cluster of friendly emigrants [seeking] the advantage of settling together near good sea ports and fishing grounds, with the advantage of agriculture and salt water's refreshing breezes." The group decided to press on to New Zealand where they finally created the Waipu community. The Normanite migration, in fact, had combined the features of both atomistic and communal migration.[43]

This was an extraordinary international migration. The logistics and the solidarity of the double migration were unusual and impressive. So too were the organization and financing of the episode. The community in Cape Breton had evidently accumulated enough capital and collective trust to invest in a vast and expensive intercontinental migration.[44] Nevertheless, the singularity of the Normanite expedition to New Zealand, though it was remarkable enough, need not be overstated. Communal migrations, secular or driven by ideologies or millenarian passion, have been common enough in world history, and especially in Australian and Canadian immigration. There are mid-century parallels with other migrations to Australia such as the English Hentys to Victoria and the German Lutherans to South Australia. And, later in the century, there were exotic migrations from Australia to Paraguay that were matched in the opposite direction by Welsh migrants who left Argentina to live in Victoria and New South Wales. There are further parallels among religious communities such as those mobilised by the formidable presbyterian J.D. Lang in New South Wales, as well as by Samuel Marsden among the Anglicans. Lang and Marsden were both scourges of morals in the early colony, employing a mastery over their respective flocks which brings to mind the authority of Norman McLeod. It is useful to see even the most exotic Highland emigrants within the wider flow of humanity that shifted across the globe in the nineteenth century.

Most connections between Canadian and Australian Highlanders were sporadic.[45] The gold rushes caused considerable intercontinental migration, including trans-Pacific migration. The Highland component was small and not easily identified. Interest was certainly aroused in Nova Scotia. The voyage to Australia of the *Sebim*, a vessel built and sailed by men of Barrington, Nova Scotia, was a specific response to the magnetic attraction of the Victorian gold diggings.[46] John Ross of Halifax was registered as a shipbuilder in Hobart in 1854. Sir Simon Fraser (1832–1919) was born in Pictou, Nova Scotia, younger son of William Fraser of Inverness, and had worked in a family flour mill and farm. He arrived in Australia in 1853, also attracted by the gold diggings, and eventually accumulated enough capital to set up in commerce in Melbourne and Sydney. He became wealthy and politically influential, involved in large-scale railway investment. He maintained his Canadian connections and introduced a Canadian engineer in drilling for artesian water.

Frank Thistlethwaite, in his seminal paper on the history of international migration, urged historians to seek "the secret sources of movement." He also recommended that their research should work "to a finer tolerance," to differentiate within the national, regional and peasant mass.[47] Taken literally, his advice requires analysis at the levels of the village and the household.

In practice, Thistlethwaite's advice is often difficult or impossible to follow. Most emigrants who paid their own passages are practically invisible to posterity. It is in the survival of a relatively few batches of emigrant letters that we see the complexities of their lives and the stratagems of their intercontinental mobilities. These letters contain remarkable evidence of the continuity of connection with the old country, and also of individual family diasporas; for instance, the Highland family which kept contact with four brothers in Victoria, and others in western Canada, Buenos Aires and the United States. The sheer scale of movement and dispersion revealed in such accounts challenges simple classification.

The great variability in the quantity and direction of Highland emigration was exposed in the Poor Law Inquiry (for Scotland) in 1843. In parts of the central Highlands at that time, there were reports of people leaving for the United States, British North America, South Africa, New South Wales, Van Diemen's Land, the West Indies and Jamaica, and Demerara. Many of these were clearly single men and many were single female servants.[48] By mid-century, Highland emigration appears to have become increasingly atomistic. External assistance schemes reinforced this tendency through their particular selection requirements. Collective emigration continued, but the odds were generally against it unless landlords and tacksmen intervened to provide special assistance.

The estate of Francis Clerk of Ulva in Mull in 1851 offered local evidence of fine "tolerance." The island proprietor, Clerk, had embarked reluctantly on a course of clearance and had thereby reduced the population from 500 to 150. His account said that "Five of the families removed for crofts on other properties. Two of the crofters are in Tobermory—all the others went to America, Australia, or to the south of Scotland." Clerk argued that agriculture was no longer feasible in the Highlands. He was regarded as one of the most considerate of west Highland landlords, but his policies clearly propelled a wide dispersal of his small tenants.[49]

Only a microscopic knowledge of very small communities—single villages, single streets and single families—can fully reveal such a degree of atomistic scattering. Fortunately, this type of Thistlethwaitian focus is possible for the Sutherland parish of Dornoch in the 1850s. Enough local evidence survives to expose decidedly diasporic movements from within this east Highland village. It is clear that family members were leaving Dornoch for different continents and then conducting intercontinental correspondences in the increasingly sophisticated world of the nineteenth-century mass migrant. The data on the destinations of the Dornoch emigrants shows that 23 went to New Zealand, 122 to Australia and 46 to North America. These figures tell us nothing about other Dornoch people who went to other parishes, to other counties or to England. We know that two left for Glasgow, two for Edinburgh and one each for Aberdeen and Forres. Some of the Dornoch families departed in groups; thus one family of ten went to New Zealand, another of eight sailed to America, and families as big as fifteen went to Australia. The east Sutherland story suggests that decisions about emigration and destinations were made at a local level and also within each household—even in a family a dispersion was not rare. In Australia there were many examples of families, Highlanders included, with representatives from a single generation on three different continents. It is possible that families and individuals chose destinations based on costs, but this was not necessarily critical because distant destinations (especially in Australia) attempted to equalise the competition by systems of assistance. [50]

There also survives evidence of emigration for a single year, 1854, from a larger district in Sutherland, the Dunrobin agency. It indicates that twenty-seven groups of emigrants were granted aid, sixty-five people in all. They dispersed to eastern and western Canada, Sydney, Melbourne, Adelaide, Victoria, Geelong and New Zealand. In the Highlands there are many examples of people from the same parish, the same street and even the same family taking quite different paths during simultaneous emigrations. There is in this story no sense of coherence or solidarity of purpose. Instead there were departures to distant points of the globe without pattern among the married and unmarried, widowed, young and old, and different occupational groups. The emigrants from Dunrobin did not sail in the same vessels as they headed for identical destinations, and those going to Australia often chose different locations. Thus, among the twelve groups assisted to Australia in 1854, seven went to Melbourne (in five different ships), one to New Zealand, one to Moreton Bay, one to Adelaide and one to Portland. If they were intent on creating "new Scotlands," they were proceeding in a extraordinarily atomistic fashion.[51]

These village dispersions, of which there are many examples, are mystifying to emigration historians and historians of New Scotlands. Again, Highland families sometimes had representatives from a single generation on three different continents. And even when emigrants departed in groups, there was no guarantee or even likelihood of continued communal solidarity. Thus one-third of the population of St. Kilda travelled together to Australia in 1852–53 but then mainly dispersed across colonial Victoria. Religion certainly provided some colonial cohesion, the Waipu community being a spectacular example. But these well-publicised cases were almost certainly exceptional. Moreover, such a fracturing among the Highlanders in Australia was not unlike that of other emigrants from the west of Scotland and the British Isles generally.

Thus, in Australia the identification of persistent Highland communities is much more difficult than in eastern Canada, where concentrations were far greater and repeatedly revitalised by new blood from the Highlands. In Australia the Highlanders were far-flung, and the subsequent transfusions were slight. These realities weighed against a continuity of settlement and culture. Furthermore, the hurried departure of people in radically different directions to different continents may suggest a desperation among a panicking population. However, a more positive view of the matter is also possible: the mid-century Highland emigrants, often departing under duress, were nevertheless calculating how to fulfil their own needs among the available opportunities and expressing an adventurousness which remains impressive.

The evacuation from the Highlands was not a smooth exodus. There were many exits out of the Highlands, many models and many destinations. Over the long run, it manifested in all sectors of the society. The lowliest cottar and squatter responded to the differentials between the Highlands and the outside world. And so did landowners of every size and status, giving up the candle in the face of poor returns and overbearing responsibilities; they were replaced by new owners, some of whom took on the mantle of the paternalist laird, and some of whom transparently did not. In between was every stratum of Highland society, making adjustments with either reluctance or enthusiasm.

At the end of the day, Highland society underwent its transformation with or without bitterness. No part of Highland society was immune to the change and no destination was neglected. The greatest beneficiaries were clearly the colonies that received migrants who were often ideal for their socio-economic characteristics.

Every level of Highland society yielded emigrants. Even sheep farmers were not exempt, as the case of Patrick Sellar demonstrated. Sellar, of course, was one of the most notorious "immigrants" to the Highlands in the first decade of the century. He crossed the Moray Firth to Sutherland from lowland Elgin in 1809, carrying with him the full baggage of "Improvement" ideology. He raised a large and distinguished family but, at the end of a single generation, it became clear that the Highlands had little future even for the fittest. Sellar established himself up as a nouveau-riche laird in his own right at Ardtornish in the 1840s and died a wealthy man with property in three counties. But his own family—nine of them—were dispersed as much as any other family in the Highlands. Only one remained in the north, and he died young, oppressed by falling wool prices. The rest found their futures outside the region, in mercantile, political and academic pursuits in Glasgow, Liverpool, Melbourne, New Orleans, London and beyond. At least two of them emigrated, and one of them confronted other Highland emigrants in the Australian colonies, still retelling atrocity stories about the old Sellar.[52]

The Sellars became part of the general evacuation, though with rather more comfortable circumstances than most of the people involved in the Highland outflow. The new managerial and capitalist cadre in the Highlands had to adjust to the transformation which they themselves had wrought. Even their own families had no security in the new, depopulating Highlands.

The evacuation of the Highlands to all of its many destinations was never the orderly convergence posited by economic theory. It was too slow for that. It was also disjointed, discontinuous, unpredictable and subject to reversals. The range and diversity of these departures and responses were remarkable. Highlanders often responded with volition, calculating their own utilities and their own futures. Some departures were communal, some atomistic and the account cannot be simply homogenised. It was neither smooth nor unidirectional. By the mid-nineteenth century the Highlanders' mobility exhibited different velocities and was highly variegated, not unlike that of other contemporary emigrants.

There were many destinations and some of the detailed local evidence, from Sutherland at least, suggests that neither family nor chain migration was decisive. Bailyn's "provincial" model could no longer contain the people evacuating the Highlands. The Highlanders were constructing remarkable intercontinental links by mid-century. Even amongst the poorest of their numbers, some had become globetrotters, mobile spirits in the international labour market. Categorising these migrants requires discrimination. They were not merely the victims of negative circumstances. In scarcely visible fashion, these emigrants connected imperial outposts in ways that orthodox histories of empire always discount. The Highlanders were an imperial people.

Notes

1. Bernard Bailyn, *The Peopling of British North America, An Introduction* (New York, 1986), particularly Chapter 1; *Voyagers to the West* (New York, 1987).
2. Marianne McLean, *The People of Glengarry* (Montreal, 1991).
3. See W.R. Brock, *Scotus Americanus* (Edinburgh, 1982), pp. 1–2.
4. See, for instance, Don Watson, *Caledonia Australis* (Sydney, 1984).
5. On intermittent Highland reluctance to emigrate, see Malcolm Gray in T.M. Devine, ed., *Scottish Emigration and Scottish Society* (1992), pp. 22–24.
6. On the tardiness of surplus labour to leave much of rural England in the mid to late nineteenth century, see G.E. Mingay, *Rural Life in Victorian England* (1976), p.99. See also W.A. Armstrong in G.E. Mingay, ed., *Agrarian History of England and Wales, Volume VI, 1750–1850* (1989), pp. 835, 958, 967.
7. See Brinley Thomas, "Food Supply in the Industrial Revolution," *Agricultural History*, 56, (1980), pp. 328–42.
8. Sara Horrell, Jane Humphreys and Martin Weale, "An input-output table for 1841," *Economic History Review*, XLVII (1994), pp. 545–66.
9. Cf. Sanderson and Morse quoted in Devine, ed., *Scottish Emigration and Scottish Society*, p.7.
10. See Gray, p.12.
11. See Timothy J. Hatton and Jeffrey G. Williamson, *Migration and the International Labor Market, 1850–1939* (1994).
12. Thistlethwaite, "Migration from Europe Overseas in the Nineteenth and Twentieth Centuries," in *11th Congres International des Sciences Historiques, Rapports* (Upsalla, 1960), p. 50.
13. On the great variability of emigration rates in different parts of the Highlands and at different times, see: Marianne McLean "Achd An Rhigh: A Highland Response to the Assisted Emigration of 1815," in D.H. Akenson, *Canadian Papers in Rural History*, V (Gananoque, Ontario, 1986), pp. 181–97; and Ian Levitt and T.C. Smout, *The State of the Scottish Working Class in 1843* (Edinburgh, 1979), Table 10A, p. 251.
14. At various times before 1815 the drain of people from the western seaboard of the Highlands had been so heavy that landlords were sent into panic, beseeching the government to step in and staunch the outflows which threatened their rent rolls. Indeed, at the turn of the century, they succeeded in persuading the government to raise the basic requirements of food and space on board the migrant ships to such standards that the cost inflation radically reduced the possibilities of Atlantic migration.
15. Horner to Henry Hallam, 14 July 1816, in Kenneth Borne and William Banks

Taylor, eds., *The Horner Papers* (Edinburgh, 1995), pp. 91–92. On the 1815 scheme see McLean, *The People of Glengarry*, pp. 181–97, which argues that "the picture of the Highlander as the naive and victimised emigrant does not fit the evidence of the 1815 emigration" (194).

16. On the continuing hostility of several Highland landowners, see Michael E. Vance, "The Politics of Emigration: Scotland and Assisted Emigration to Upper Canada, 1815–1826," in Devine, ed., *Scottish Emigration and Scottish Society*, p.39.

17. Stafford County Record Office, Sutherland Collection [hereafter D593], D593/3/ K/1/3/5/ Loch to Bathurst, 3 December 1817.

18. See, for instance, *Inverness Courier*, 12 February 1819.

19. D593/ Sellar to Loch, 27 October 1816.

20. The official attitude of the Sutherland regime remained opposed to emigration. See [James Loch] *An Account of the Improvements on the Estate of Sutherland* (1815), pp. 11–12.

21. D593/K, Loch to Lady Stafford, 28 November 1816 and 23 December 1816; Lady Stafford to Loch 11 July 1817; Loch to Rev. Edwards, 29 September 1825; and S.R.O. Loch Muniments, GD 268/361 Lady Stafford to James Loch, 24 March 1824. Earlier, in 1816, cattle prices had collapsed and the harvest was very poor. Loch organised removals and relief measures, declaring that the people should be required to work for food. He also remarked at the time: "I wish they were safely in that beautiful country in new Holland, they are now so busy in exploring. When the present exceeding irritation of men's minds is somewhat composed I really think that some plan must be calmly thought of and considered much with the King's Government." SRO Dep 313/1587, Loch to Lady Stafford, 3 December 1816. I thank Dr. Malcolm Bangor-Jones for this reference.

22. D593/K, Suther to Loch, 3 February 1820.

23. The movement of people cleared from Sutherland into neighbouring Caithness created serious overcrowding in that county which was later expressed in a higher rate of emigration too. See Ian Levitt and T.C. Smout, *The State of the Scottish Working Class in 1843* (Edinburgh, 1979), p. 238. *Parliamentary Report*, 1841, pp. 528–29.

24. GB PD (Hansard), 3rd series, vol. 56, pp. 514–15 speech by H. Baillie. The unpredictable character of prospective migrants was captured in a parliamentary enquiry of 1841. For instance, John Bowie had arranged for a large party of bounty emigrants to leave from Skye in 1837. But when the time came for sailing, two-thirds of them had changed their minds. After further explanation to the people, the ship was "fully filled" and many others left behind, But the process was highly selective—generally the "middling sort," according to one witness, the able-bodied, a few with assets, some with many, like one who had £120. But the bounty system worked against dependents, even where the dependent had supporters galore, like the patriarch of seventy who had eighteen followers all able to meet the criteria but would not go "without the old man, who would not be allowed to go."

25. See R.G. Jameson, *Australia and her Gold Regions* (New York, 1852), p. 101.

26. See, for example, Maureen Molloy, "Kinship, Authority and Transitions to Adulthood: the Highland Scots at Waipu, New Zealand, 1854–1914," *Journal of Social History*, 22 (1989), p.488.

27. *Scotsman* 22 January 1840.

28. See James Dixon, *Narrative of a Voyage to New South Wales and Van Diemens Land* (Edinburgh, 1822), pp. 138–42. The family background is provided in James Fergusson, ed., *Letters of George Dempster to Sir Adam Fergusson, 1756–1813* (1934), pp. 175–88. Land grant was the great incentive. See also *Notes and Queries of the Society of West Highland Historical Research*, IV (1977).
29. McLean, *The People of Glengarry*.
30. For a description of the recently arrived Glengarry in Sydney, see John Hood, *Australia and the Far East* (London, 1843), p. 109, which also describes the much happier experience of Lachlan Mackay and "his former starving family in Coll," now prospering in the colony (133).
31. *Scotsman*, 22 January 1840.
32. See Margaret Kiddle, *Men of Yesterday* (Melbourne, 1961).
33. See the case of tenantry turned out of Uig parish in Lewis in 1838, several of whom went to Canada, assisted by a kinsman who had made some money in Calcutta. SRO Mackenzie Papers, GD 403/63/31, Murdo Mcleod to Mrs. Tolme, 26 June 1838.
34. See Eric Richards, "The Highland Passage to Colonial Australia," *Scotlands* (1995).
35. GB PD (Hansard), 3rd series, vol. 56, pp. 514–15 speech by H Baillie.
36. Quoted in Eric Richards, *Leviathan of Wealth* (London, 1973), p. 245.
37. Extracts from Thomas Sinton, *The Poetry of Badenoch* (Inverness,1906), with translation by D.R. Morrison (1974) in Mitchell Library, Sydney, ML 2265.
38. See Gray, p. 30.
39. Scottish Record Office, Highland Destitution Records, HD 4/5.
40. See Jim Bennett and Ian Fry, *Canadians in Australia* (Fyshwick, 1995). For another account of what I term "migrations of rising expectations," involving Scotland, New Brunswick and Australia, see John Lack, ed., *James Cuming: An Autobiography* (City of Footscray Historical Society, 1987).
41. As retailed in J.S. Martell, *Immigration to and Emigration from Nova Scotia, 1815–1838* (Halifax, 1942). See also Flora McPherson, *Watchman against the World* (1962), especially pp. 124–41, and Molloy, "Kinship, Authority and Transition to Adulthood", passim. For evidence of near famine in Cape Breton in 1848, see J.L. MacDougall, *History of Inverness County, Nova Scotia* (1922), p. 29.
42. "Letters of Rev. Norman McLeod, 1835–51," edited by D.C. Harvey, *Bulletin of the Public Archives of Nova Scotia*, II, no. 1 (1939).
43. For evidence of near famine in Cape Breton in 1848, see J.L. MacDougall, *History of Inverness County, Nova Scotia* (1922), p. 29.
44. See Thomas Dunbabin, "Australia and Canada," *Australian Quarterly* (March 1951), pp. 54–66.
45. The most remarkable case of Scottish-American-Australian migration is probably that of Ewan Gilles, originally from St. Kilda, whose roving career is a migration statistician's nightmare since his movements amount to at least *ten* migrations. See Richards, "The Highland Passage to Colonial Australia," pp. 28–44, and further detail in "The decline of St. Kilda: Demography, Economy and Emigration," *Scottish Economic and Social History*, 14 (1992), pp. 55–75, and "St. Kilda and Australia: Emigrants in Peril, 1852–3," *Scottish Historical Review*, LXXI (1993), pp. 129–55.
46. On the movements from North America to Australia in the first year of the rushes,

see Jameson, *Australia and her Gold Regions*, p. 101.

47. Thistlethwaite, "Migration from Europe Overseas in the Nineteenth and Twentieth Centuries," p. 43.
48. British Parliamentary Papers (1844) XX, *Report from the Commissioners appointed for inquiring into the Administration and Practical Operation of the Poor Laws in Scotland.*
49. British Parliamentary Papers (1851) XXVI, *Report to the Board of supervision by Sir John McNeil on the Western Highlands and Islands.*
50. N.L.S. Dep 313/2366.
51. N.L.S. Dep 313/2366, "Total Cost and Average paid per Head to Emigrants in the years 1847 to 1853." I am grateful to Dr. Malcolm Bangor-Jones for this reference.
52. See Richards, "The Highland Passage to Colonial Australia," passim.

6

Historical Archaeology and Migration:
Barra Blackhouse Abandonment and Mid-nineteenth Century Migration to Nova Scotia

Keith Branigan

Here I shall present some of the results of an interdisciplinary program of fieldwork and excavation begun in 1988 on the southern isles of the Outer Hebrides. This program has traced the human occupation of the islands from the last ice age up until the end of the Highland Clearances and has sought to identify and assess the interaction of humans with the natural environment over this time. Our work has focused on seven of the islands, but I shall restrict my discussion here to the Isle of Barra. Emigration from Barra to Nova Scotia and other parts of Canada is historically attested in the early to mid-nineteenth century. I seek to do two things in this chapter: (1) to provide an overview of the architecture, furnishings and material culture of the Barra blackhouses from which the migrants came and (2) to examine briefly the abandonment history of four blackhouse settlements and to discuss what extent they may be related to episodes of emigration.

Barra is a small island (Figure 6.1)—the main part of which is only some eight kilometres (five miles) across—with a northern peninsula. This peninsula is made up of machair grassland, which is also found, but only in small areas, further south, on the west coast of the island at Greian, Borve and Tangusdale. The west coast distribution of the machair is typical throughout the Outer Hebrides,[1] but Barra does not have quite as hostile and precipitous an east coast as the islands to the north. The extent and location of the machair and the nature of the coastline at the time of the Clearances are factors which have to be borne in mind.

Figure. 6.1 Blackhouse sites, Barra

Barra Blackhouses: An Overview

In our field survey, which has covered about 60 percent of Barra, we have recorded just over one hundred abandoned blackhouses. From the data base which these provide, we can identify certain characteristic features of the Barra blackhouses. Their construction is basically similar to that of other Hebridean blackhouses: thick, low walls with a core of earth and/or peat and rough-built, uncoursed stone inner and outer faces, often incorporating, particularly at foundation level, very large blocks of stone or boulders. The external corners of the houses are rounded, and the external wall faces are slightly battered. There is usually a single door, roughly central in one long wall and set well back into its depth; together with the frequent thickening of the front wall as it approaches the doorway, this provides much-needed shelter from the strong winds which are an everyday feature of life on Barra. The roof timbers sit on the broad top of the wall and are covered with turves, often of peaty material.

These features are typical of the blackhouses found throughout the Hebrides, but in one respect at least the Barra blackhouses seem to differ from those found on the islands to the north. There the houses are sufficiently long in relation to their width—as exemplified by the well-known houses at Arnol in Lewis and Sollas in North Uist—to have been compared to prehistoric and even Norse longhouses. Barra blackhouses do not share this characteristic. We find that over 80 percent of Barra blackhouses have length to width ratios below two and that a similar percentage have lengths below 11.5 metres. This seems to be a significant, but not exclusive or universal, feature of Barra blackhouses.

Inside the blackhouse, internal partition walls appear to be in a minority. Less than 20 percent of our recorded blackhouses show traces of a stone partition wall; these walls usually shut off between 20 and 30 percent of the interior space. As to the rest of the interior, we rely on evidence provided by our excavations of two blackhouses.

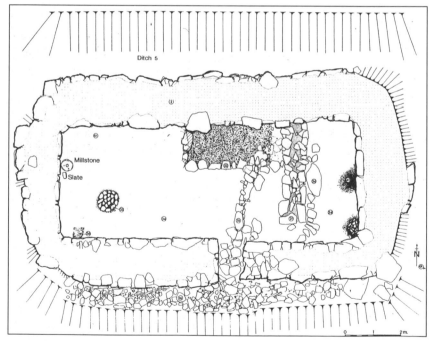

Figure 6.2   Plan of the blackhouse excavated at Allt Chrisal, Barra

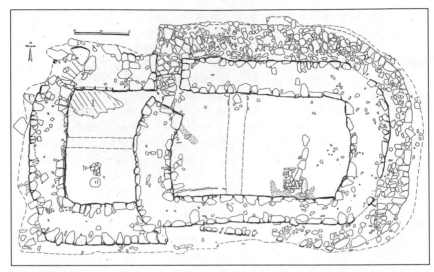

Figure 6.3   Plan of the blackhouse excavated at Balnabodach, Barra

The blackhouse at Allt Chrisal (Figure 6.2) is one of the largest on Barra and measures fourteen by seven metres overall.[2] The floor was compacted earth with no trace of surfacing. There was a circular hearth at the west end, close to which stood a small stack of peat. Although there is no structural evidence and no visible trace in either the wear pattern or the deposits on the floor, it seems likely that bed-boxes would have been placed against the walls at this end of the room near the fire and away from the doorway. Against the rear wall, and opposite the door, was a slightly raised platform with a cobbled surface, edged with a stone curb. This may have been a stand for a dresser, on which the occupants could have displayed their best crockery. A minimum of thirty-nine vessels of such crockery was found in and around the blackhouse. These include cups, saucers, plates, bowls, a teapot, a jug and storage jars. They appear to have been products not only of Glasgow but also of Stoke-on-Trent and Sunderland, and may have been acquired either from seasonal pedlars or returning fishermen. The other material culture is remarkably impoverished: only a single bronze button and a few fragments of clay pipes.

The picture is broadly repeated at Balnabodach (Figure 6.3). This blackhouse has a more complicated history, being originally a single-room house 9.5 by 6.8 metres, subsequently enlarged to 14 by 6.8 metres, at which point the interior was partitioned. Later the rear wall of the house was rebuilt. The floor was of trampled earth with no trace of surfacing. There was a small hearth and adjacent hard-standing in the area partitioned off at the west end of the building, and a brick hearth was built in the main room in its second phase. Almost opposite the second-phase door, a kerb of small slabs marked out an area against the rear wall too small to take a bed-box but large enough for a small dresser. The pottery found represents a minimum of fifty-one vessels, amongst which forty-six forms could be identified. Almost 40 percent of these were medium-sized multipurpose bowls, and just over 20 percent were plates. Cups and tea-bowls were few in number, and there were four jugs, three large bowls and two large storage jars. To what extent these sherds reflect the original vessel assemblage is open to debate, but one can suggest that whilst tea drinking was a rare occupation, broths or soups and gruel or porridge were probably common parts of the diet. As at Allt Chrisal, there was a scarcity of other material culture in the occupation deposit: a few pieces of clay pipe, three glass beads, three buttons, a thimble, a ring, a hinge from a small casket, and a coin or token (all of copper alloy), an iron wedge and blade, and a whetstone.

The impression gained from these two assemblages is that the material culture associated with blackhouse occupation was on the whole impoverished. The houses themselves were built entirely of locally available materials, although roof timbers would have come from either driftwood or timbers from old boats. Furnishings were also simple, and even the supposed dressers may have been homemade. A small quantity of generally cheap contemporary crockery was acquired either by returning seamen or from travelling pedlars who specialised in selling "seconds" to the islands. This came mostly from the Scottish potteries, but some was obtained from Stoke and small quantities perhaps came from Merseyside and northeast England. Other belongings were few and simple, and the only imported pleasures were a little tobacco and tea. The blackhouses were very dark inside and had earth floors, so that anything dropped or broken might be lost or only partially recovered. Equally, extensive excavations in the vicinity of the blackhouse at Allt Chrisal revealed no evidence of domestic rubbish dumps where unwanted material culture had been disposed of.

The poverty of material culture thus seems to be a reality rather than an illusion created by the biases of archaeological evidence. Certainly it is supported by contemporary descriptions of visitors to the islands[3] and by reports describing the arrival of impoverished Barra emigrants in Canada.[4] Barra blackhouses have three further features which may be interrelated and deserve comment. A first feature is the relative scarcity of houses with interior partitions. Such partitions are normally interpreted (without excavation) as evidence of a byre at one end of a blackhouse. In Barra, fewer than 20 percent of blackhouses yield evidence of partitions. Further, in the case of the two examples we excavated, such walls appear to be related to a subdivision of the living area rather than the creation of a byre, and in each case the partition is a secondary feature and not part of the original design.

The scarcity of internal byres may be related to a second feature, which is the frequency with which separate, external byres are associated with Barra blackhouses. Byres or probable byres have been recorded at close to thirty-two blackhouses. The frequency of external byres may help to explain not only the relatively low frequency of partition walls but also the tendency of Barra blackhouses to be relatively short compared to those on the islands to the north, where internal byres are commonplace.

Furthermore, the use of internal partitions to divide human living space, and the fact that in the two excavated examples these were clearly secondary alterations to the original plan, might be related to a third feature of Barra blackhouses. This is their appearance in pairs or trios. Forty blackhouses, almost half of the recorded sites, are found in pairs, and six in two trios. Could this phenomenon and/or the partition of human living space reflect the voluntary subdivision of tenancies or crofts for which Barra was notorious?[5] Another possible explanation of blackhouse pairs is the action of MacNeil of Barra (c. 1833), when he divided all his crofts in two.[6] In either case, the pairing of blackhouses on Barra may be interpreted as a socio-economic phenomenon related to factors either specific to or particularly dominant on the island. These same factors played a significant part in the stimulation of emigration from the island in the first half of the nineteenth century.

Blackhouse Abandonment: Four Case Studies

The excavation of two blackhouses and the survey and documentary study of two blackhouse settlements allow us to consider the timing and causes of their abandonments. Each site is briefly described and the date of abandonment proposed, before the problem of causal factors is discussed.

Gortein

The settlement at Gortein has a central focus on a long occupied site (Figure 6.4), four somewhat scattered houses to the east, and three small houses situated close together in a side valley to the north. Altogether, there are eleven blackhouses here, plus a drying shed. In addition, there are many clearance cairns and lazy-beds, several sheep pens, field and enclosure walls, and a kelp oven. The settlement was clearly active over a considerable time and took maximum advantage of the slender natural resources in the vicinity: reasonably well-drained if somewhat shallow soil on the main settlement area, some moderately sheltered and drained pasture in the valley to the north, a good supply of fresh water, and a beach from which to exploit the marine food resources in the Sound of Vatersay.

Parish records list six surnames amongst the occupants of Gortein in the first quarter of the nineteenth century and we believe that the main settlement focus and the eastern cluster were probably in occupation at that time—in all, perhaps seven or eight households. Births registered at Gortein were declining, however, and the last took place in 1834. It is difficult to envision Gortein occupied beyond c. 1840, and its abandonment appears to have been a process rather than an event.[7]

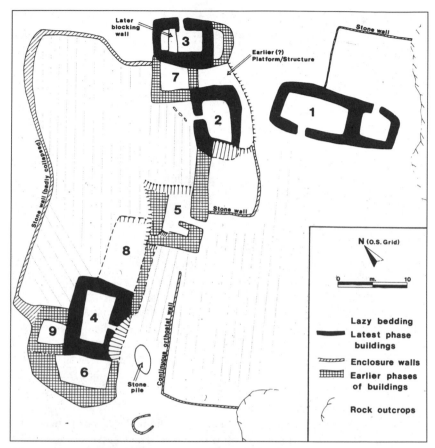

Figure 6.4 Plan of the main blackhouse settlement at Gortein, Barra

Allt Chrisal

The isolated blackhouse at Allt Chrisal has both a separate byre and drying shed. Clearance cairns immediately by the house indicate a vegetable plot, probably for potatoes, whilst across the stream there was a hard-standing, perhaps for small hayricks or to lay out seaweed to dry. Beyond that was an enclosed area of cultivated land on which barley and beare were probably grown. There were also two kelp ovens between the house and the shore, and a boat noost is a reminder that the fish and crab in the Sound of Vatersay were a valuable food resource.[8] By Barra standards the house was a good size (fourteen metres long), and pieces of small glass panes from a window in the front wall and of a bulls-eye window pane from the door perhaps reflect modest ambitions on the part of its occupants. There was a drain immediately to the right of, and running through, the door. Its position, and the absence of a contemporary partition, suggest that it served a domestic function rather than as a drain for an internal byre space. A partition wall was inserted only in a secondary phase of use.

The pottery associated with the occupation has already been described above and its diverse origins noted. All of the vessels found can be accommodated within the period c. 1775–1825 and there are no traces of typical mid-nineteenth-century wares. The available documentary evidence adds to this evidence and allows us to identify the occupant of the blackhouse. This was James Cambell, whose father had probably built the house in the late eighteenth century. He was recorded as living in Glen, immediately behind Castlebay, by 1835,[9] and there is no record of further inhabitants, so the Allt Chrisal blackhouse was abandoned c. 1825–35.

Crubisdale

The settlement at Crubisdale (Figure 6.5) is known only from survey.[10] It consists of seven buildings tucked against a steep southeast-facing slope, fronted by a stream and nestled in a hollow so it is invisible from all directions. There is one extensive area of lazy-bedding about seventy-five by forty-five metres, and several smaller ones, including three tiny patches on the steep slope behind the settlement which can only have been for potatoes. One enclosed cultivation patch also contains the remains of peat-cutting for fuel.

A persistent oral tradition holds that the settlement was used for boatbuilding, and although the settlement is a kilometre distant from the sea, there is a convenient natural "slipway" down which boats could have been taken to the water's edge at Nask.

There is little purpose in describing the individual buildings in detail, but we may note that house H (a very large house by Barra standards) has a drying shed alongside it, and that house D is the only one with traces of an internal partition. House E has a large annex added to its east end, beyond which is an enclosed natural platform. If boatbuilding took place at Crubisdale, this seems its most likely location, with the annex and enclosed area serving as a workshop area. Building C was far more heavily robbed of stone and its foundations more deeply embedded than the other houses, and it possibly predates some of them and was robbed for the construction of an adjacent house. In this case, we might see the settlement as occupied by three to five families, depending how one interprets the relationships between buildings A and B and D and E.

There is no trace of occupants at Crubisdale in the 1841 census and we therefore believe it was abandoned before 1840, at roughly the same time as Allt Chrisal and Gortein, although I would emphasize that we are not claiming that all the abandonments are contemporary, let alone monocausal.

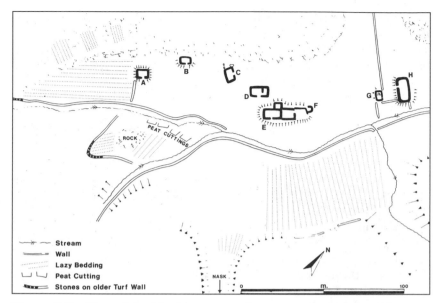

Figure 6.5   Plan of the blackhouse settlement at Crubisadale, Barra

Balnabodach

The settlement at Balnabodach is a fascinating one. It stands on the edge of a sea-loch approached by a narrow sea-filled dyke 400 metres long, so the settlement and its harbourage are well protected from storms. There are houses on either side of the stream which runs into the loch. Those on the west side of the stream were upstanding buildings built between c. 1850 and 1880 and abandoned between c. 1900 and 1930. To the east of the stream are remains of other houses, all reduced to grass-covered ruins. One of these, house A, was selected for excavation in 1996. As suspected, it proved to be multiperiod, but at the time of its abandonment it was a two-roomed house fourteen metres long. As noted earlier, we believe the extension was added for domestic use.

The date of production of the pottery recovered from house A ranges from c. 1750 to 1860. However, it is unlikely, given their relative remoteness, that the Western Isles would have received either the earliest or latest products of the kilns. If we plot the median production dates of the vessels, we find there was a clear peak in 1830 and 1840, and nothing after 1850. The pattern strongly suggests an abandonment c. 1850, since although we have to allow for a time lag from acquisition to breakage, there is not a single vessel that need have been acquired after c. 1845.

The census returns appear to provide us with confirmation of abandonment c. 1850, and before 1851. The 1841 census lists eight households and records a population of twenty-six at Balnabodach. The next census, ten years later, lists eleven households and records a population of forty-three. The significant difference between these dates is not the size of the population, but that the 1851 population is quite clearly a different one. Even making very generous allowances for the distortion of recorded ages that occurs in census data at this time, only three of the forty-three recorded inhabitants of 1851 can conceivably be identified with individuals found in the 1841 census. Since these three persons are named Donald McNeil (two individuals) and Mary McNeil—two of the commonest names found in nineteenth-century Barra— and their recorded ages are in each case at variance with the figures from the 1841 censes, even these three may well be new inhabitants. In any event, there is a total or almost total change of population at Balnabodach between 1841 and 1851, and we associate the abandonment of the settlement east of the stream with this change. The ceramic evidence suggests the date is probably nearer 1850 than 1840.

In summary, our four case studies all suggest blackhouse abandonments in the period c. 1820–50. It would be possible to collapse these dates down to a less than ten-year period, beginning with Allt Chrisal as late as 1834–35 and ending with Balnabodach as early as c. 1842, but this would be pushing the evidence to its limits and might encourage the search for a monocausal explantation.

Explaining Blackhouse Abandonment

We must obviously tread carefully in seeking an explanation for the abandonment of both isolated blackhouses and whole settlements in a relatively short time frame. First, we should bear in mind that in the case of isolated or individual buildings a whole range of personal and highly specific circumstances may be dominant factors but may also be invisible in the archaeological and documentary record. Second, there is a danger that we might too readily collapse a process into an event in order to relate the abandonment to a known historical date. In the four cases we are examining here, it seems best to look at each abandonment separately.

Allt Chrisal

The abandonment of Allt Chrisal appears to be a good example of personal or site-specific factors, for we can trace James Cambell from Allt Chrisal to Glen (in 1835), and thence to Nairn in 1851, and to Kentangaval by 1861. He clearly did not emigrate, and three decades after leaving his house at Allt Chrisal he was living less than two kilometres away. Local oral tradition has it that Allt Chrisal was abandoned abruptly due to rat infestation following a ship going down in the Sound of Vatersay. Excavation certainly confirmed extensive rat runs and nests in the house, but whether these were sufficient to cause its abandonment is doubtful.

Gortein

Documentary evidence indicates that Gortein was finally abandoned before 1841 but after 1835. However, it also suggests that abandonment was a process rather than an event, with a gradual reduction in the number of births recorded there, and we might place the process as taking place within the period c. 1820–35.

The frail subsistence economy of the Western Isles in this period has been carefully documented by Devine in exploring the socio-economic context of the potato famines of the period beginning in 1846.[11] In summary, the introduction of the potato and the development of the fisheries in the late eighteenth century had both diversified and strengthened the subsistence base of the islanders. With the outbreak of the Napoleonic Wars, kelp production had provided a further economic boost to the islands, whilst the increased opportunities for military service had opened up new possibilities for supplementing the income of island families. But these same factors contributed to the development of a crofting system in which not only was a croft no longer required to provide the entire subsistence needs of its tenants; it was actually considered desirable (by the landlords) that it did not. Equally, the buoyant economy of the islands at this time encouraged the growth of population and the subdivision of tenancies.

The frail underpinning of the economy began to collapse by 1820 as the end of the war years brought an increasingly sharper decline in the price of kelp and an abrupt end to widespread opportunities for military service. The white fisheries, particularly important to Barra, were also unpredictable,[12] so that pressure on cultivated land became ever greater at the same time as rent arrears began to grow and the number of cottars increased. Barra, still in the hands of McNeil, was largely unaffected by the growing demand for "improvements" and sheep farms, but in a misguided attempt to swim against the economic tide, McNeil built a kelp producing factory.[13] The only way he could finance it was to double his rent income, and in 1833 he achieved this by the simple measure of dividing all the crofts in half, but maintaining the rent per croft at the previous level. One immediate response to this was that five hundred of his tenants chose to emigrate to North America. It is certainly possible that some of the inhabitants of Gortein were amongst those who left of their own choice in the wake of MacNeil's rent rise around 1833. We must tread carefully, however, for research amongst the parish records by the Barra Historical Society reveals that some former inhabitants of Gortein migrated only a few kilometres, as far as Nask, Borve and Kentangaval. Furthermore MacNeil's rent rise may have taken place after outmovement from Gortein was already well under way, if not almost completed. Extensive emigration from Barra is recorded in the late 1820s,[14] almost certainly in response to the repeal in 1827 of the expensive restrictions placed on emigrant ships by the Passenger Act of 1803. With the cost of a passage cut by 300 percent, the opportunity for crofting families to escape from the downward spiral of the Hebridean economy was greatly increased. If crofters from Gortein were amongst those who emigrated to Canada in the period between 1820 and 1835, then they were more probably on ships which sailed around 1827–28 than those of the mid-1830s.

Crubisdale

The difficulty in discussing the abandonment of Crubisdale is that we only have a *terminus ante quem* of 1841. Abandonment before 1841 precludes both Gordon's clearances and the potato famine from consideration as causal factors, and MacNeil's only recorded clearances were at Kilbarr and Roll.[15] Local oral tradition has nothing to say on the abandonment of Crubisdale, and we can only speculate that economic conditions in the twenty years following the end of the Napoleonic Wars may have played a part in the settlement's demise, as we have suggested was the case at Gortein. In that event some families may well have been amongst the emigrants of either the late 1820s or the early 1830s, but more documentary research would be needed to establish this.

Balnabodach

With Balnabodach we are probably dealing with a different decade and different situation. If, as we believe, the old (eastern) settlement at Balnabodach was abandoned after 1841 but before 1851, and a total or near-total change of population is recorded by 1851, then we have a good prima facie case for identifying a migration. The events of the 1840s on Barra are well known, beginning with the purchase of the island in 1840 by Colonel Gordon of Cluny. In 1846 came the great potato famine, which continued with varying intensity for almost a decade. The deprivation and even starvation that this caused drove Gordon to decide on the enforced clearance and emigration of a large part of his tenantry, and this was carried out between 1848 and 1851. Nearly three thousand people from Benbecula, South Uist and Barra were shipped to North America in these years.[16] In 1850 alone, 660 were forcibly removed from Barra. At the same time, crofts were given over to sheep farms under a single tenant.

When we look at the census returns for Balnabodach in 1851, we see there is not only a total change of population but also a dramatic change of occupation. In 1841, of the nine households, five were occupied by crofters, two by cottars and two by paupers. In 1851 the occupations of the eleven households include not a single crofter, but there are now four fishermen, three boatbuilders, one cottar, one labourer and one pauper. In addition, there is a "farmer of 6 acres" who is the only individual not born in Barra, an outsider from Kintail in Ross. Even given all the caveats about the use of census figures, it is difficult to avoid the conclusion that the crofters of Balnabodach were amongst those forcibly shipped to Canada by Gordon in 1848–51, and that they were replaced by other Barra families who were given no crofting rights but were obliged to earn their living from the sea. Local oral tradition maintains that crofters from the rich machair pasture of Borve were settled at Balnabodach by Gordon, and this is something we are currently exploring in the census data.

Summary

Our research to date suggests that Barra blackhouses and blackhouse settlements may have some distinctive features which might have been reproduced, albeit in modified form and materials, by first-generation emigrants to Canada. These include "short, fat" blackhouses, often built in pairs, with separate byres and sometimes drying sheds. The occupants of these houses had a somewhat impoverished material culture but acquired and displayed both the colourful wares of the Scottish potteries and the blue transfer-printed wares of the Staffordshire kilns.

The four settlements to which we have paid particular attention were all abandoned c. 1820–50, and possibly within a shorter period than this, but they cannot all be related to a single historical event or episode. One (Allt Chrisal) was abandoned abruptly, probably as the result of very specific personal or local circumstances. A second (Gortein) appears to have suffered a process of abandonment, perhaps lasting a decade, most probably related to increasing economic fragility. This could apply to Crubisdale too, but the dating evidence is presently too imprecise in this case. Finally, a fourth settlement (Balnabodach) was almost certainly the victim of Gordon's clearances.

It is almost certain that some, if not all, of those evicted from Balnabodach were dispatched to Canada and that some of the voluntary migrants from Gortein were amongst the Barra immigrants arriving in Canada in the period 1827–33. But for confirmation of this, and of their destinations within Canada, we turn for help to Canadian archives and Canadian historians.

Notes

1. N. Owen, M. Kent and P. Dale, "The machair vegetation of the Outer Hebrides: a review," in D. Gilbertson, M. Kent and J. Grattan, eds., *The Outer Hebrides: The Last 14,000 Years* (Sheffield, 1996).
2. K. Branigan and P. Foster, *Barra: Archaeological Research on Ben Tangaval* (Sheffield, 1995), pp. 69–72.
3. J.N. MacLeod, *Memorials of the Reverend Norman MacLeod* (Edinburgh, 1898), pp. 221–22.
4. T. M. Devine, *The Great Highland Famine* (Edinburgh, 1988), p. 207.
5. Devine, *The Great Highland Famine*, pp. 8, 26.
6. J. Hunter, *The Making of the Crofting Community* (Edinburgh, 1976), p. 36.
7. K. Branigan and C. Merrony, "The abandoned settlements of Crubisdale and Gortein," in Branigan and Foster, *Barra*, p. 198.
8. P. Foster, "Excavations at Allt Chrisal, 1988–94," in Branigan and Foster, *Barra*,

pp. 62–64, 93–96.
9. M. MacNeil, personal communication, June 1995.
10. Branigan and Merrony, "The abandoned settlements of Crubisdale and Gortein," pp. 193–95.
11. Devine, *The Great Highland Famine*, pp. 1–32.
12. Devine, *The Great Highland Famine*, p. 154.
13. Hunter, *The Making of the Crofting Community*, p. 35.
14. J. Anderson, "Essay on the present state of the Highlands," in *Trans Highland and Agricultural Soc of Scotland* (1831), p. 30.
15. Devine, *The Great Highland Famine*, p. 184.
16. Devine, *The Great Highland Famine*, p. 325.

7

A Highland Regiment in Halifax:
The 78th Highland Regiment of Foot and the Scottish National/Cultural Factor in Nova Scotia's Capital, 1869–71

Cameron Pulsifer

Regiments and other units of the British army spent periods of service of varying lengths in Halifax virtually from the city's founding in 1749 until their final withdrawal in 1905.[1] Each of these units influenced the city in distinct ways, depending upon its particular social, national and personal make-up and also upon its own regimental or unit "ethos." This tends to have been lost sight of in accounts of the British military in Halifax published to date and under-lines the fact that the "definitive" account of the impact of the British military on Halifax has yet to be written.

This chapter is in the main a discussion of a single event in the life of mid-Victorian Halifax. It involves a Scottish regiment, the 78th Highland Regiment of Foot, which was in garrison from May 1869 until November 1871, and the Halifax Scottish community of the time, at least as it was represented in its major national/cultural organizations. Although the specific event is of no great consequence in the overall history of the city, it is interesting nonetheless as a case study of the cultural impact of a British military unit on Halifax, and as an exploration of the state of "Scottishness" that prevailed in Nova Scotia's capital city at the time. It is in fact a classic instance of Old Scotia encounter-ing Nova Scotia.

The 78th Highland Regiment of Foot is the same unit represented in the re-enactment program at today's Halifax Citadel. It was founded in 1793 by Francis Humberston Mackenzie, a descendant of the Earls of Seaforth, and should not be confused with the earlier 78th regiment that fought under Wolfe at Louisbourg and Quebec. The earlier 78th was raised mostly amongst members of the clan Fraser and was disbanded soon after the victory at Quebec. The later 78th was raised initially amongst the clan Mackenzie in the county of Ross and Cromarty and on the island of Lewis, and its regimental associations were all with that clan. A decade after leaving Halifax, it was to be linked with another one-time Mackenzie regiment, the 72nd Foot, to form the Seaforth Highlanders.[2]

The 78th was emblematic of a phenomenon that had been growing in strength in Scotland since the beginning of the nineteenth century, and along with the immense worldwide success of the novels of Sir Walter Scott. As is well known, the popularity of these novels, and the products of a horde of imitators, had fostered an image of Scotland that the international community and indeed Scotsmen themselves had come to equate with true Scottishness. This has been described by the historian H.J. Hanham in his book *Scottish Nationalism* as the Scotland "of the modern tourist industry."[3] The Highland warrior, who had only recently been thought savage and uncouth, was cleaned up and made into a dashing and romantic figure, acceptable in the most polite of drawing rooms. By the mid-nineteenth century, kilts, tartans, bagpipes and clans had become established as the prevailing icons of a pan-Scottish national mythology in the Highlands as well as the Lowlands.[4] Scott was the "original promoter", writes Hugh Trevor-Roper in his customary forthright style, "of the Highland take-over of Scotland: of the great retrospective violation of history whereby the whole country has been clanned and tartaned, kilted, plaided and piped for foreign tourists."[5] Such iconography is, of course, not unknown in the way that contemporary Nova Scotia presents itself to the world, as Ian McKay discussed in his insightful article, "Tartanism Triumphant: The Construction of Scottishness in Nova Scotia, 1933–1954."[6]

McKay's point is that the identification of Nova Scotia with a mythic Scottish past, and the promotion of the province as a little piece of Scotland transposed to this side of the Atlantic, is purely a twentieth-century phenomenon. He views this development as being a product, in the broadest sense, of a widespread anti-modernist trend and, in the narrowest sense, the active promotion of Premier Angus L. Macdonald and the Nova Scotia Department of Tourism. Here, writes McKay, "we have an illustration of the cultural impact of tourism as it was powerfully focused by the 20th century state." Previous to this, writes McKay, "we search in vain through thousands of Victorian and Edwardian words on the nature of Nova Scotia to find a solid argument for its Scottish essence."[7]

This mythologizing of the Scottish past has certainly had its detractors. Hugh Trevor-Roper, for example, in his well-known article "The Invention of the Highland Tradition," has drawn attention to the fact that there was a great deal of misrepresentation and even outright fraud on the part of some of

Scott's fellow antiquarians in promoting this particular view of the Scottish past.[8] He takes great delight, for example, in pointing out that the *feileadh beag*, the famous philibeg, or kilt, as it is known today, was invented by an Englishman, one Thomas Rawlinson of Lancashire, sometime around 1730. This Rawlinson did to facilitate the work of Highlanders he employed in his iron-ore smelting enterprise at Invergarry near Inverness. The traditional Highland garment, the *feileadh mhor*, or belted plaid or "big kilt," he considered too "cumbrous or unwieldy."[9]

Probably the tradition's most virulent critic, however, is the Scottish Marxist writer Tom Nairn, with his references to "vulgar Scottishism, or tartanry" and the "great tartan monster."[10] Nairn sees this phenomenon as the reflection of a "popular sub-romanticism" that looked backward to an irretrievably lost past, rather than as the expression of a "vital national culture" that looked forward to an achievable future. Nairn speaks of being in the crowd at one of the phenomenon's more popular twentieth-century manifestations, the Edinburgh military tattoo, in the following scholarly, dispassionate terms: "How intolerably vulgar! What unbearable, crass, mindless philistinism! One knows that *kitsch* is a large constituent of mass popular culture in every land: but this is ridiculous!"[11]

Whatever one may think of such historical deconstructions and political fulminations, one cannot deny the strong appeal that this Highland-centred view of Scottish heritage had and continues to have, or the fact that it had largely triumphed by the mid-Victorian period. It had indeed received the royal imprimatur, with Queen Victoria, from the 1850s on, "cherishing a romantic affection for Jacobites and Highland clans" at her seat at Balmoral in Aberdeenshire and indeed nurturing what some viewed as an unnaturally close association with her Highland ghillie, John Brown.[12] Nowhere was this national/cultural emphasis taken more seriously than in Her Majesty's Highland regiments, which managed the feat, none too strenuous in the Scottish context, of maintaining an unswerving loyalty to the contemporary monarch while regularly drinking toasts to the "king over the water."

The Highland regiments, most particularly the 42nd Foot, or Black Watch, had kept alive the Highland traditions of dress and music during the period when they were proscribed after the rebellion of 1745. The result was that, after 1782, when the proscription was lifted and something of a rage for Highland attire set in, civilian forms of the dress were heavily influenced by prevailing military fashion.[13] Repeated prominence in many military campaigns thereafter, and the growing strength of the so-called Highland revival as inaugurated by Scott and others, enhanced their reputation to the extent that by the mid-Victorian period the Highland regiments had become virtual figureheads for the new national mythology. Certainly by this period most Scotsmen seem to have viewed them as *the* national regiments, as is testified to by the fact that their membership was 85–95 percent Scottish. In contrast, the national make-up of Lowland regiments, whose dress and regimental culture bore few specifically Scottish features at this time, was indistinguishable from that of English units.[14]

One of five kilted regiments in the army at this time, the 78th came to Halifax equipped with the full panoply of contemporary Highland military costume. Though based upon apparel worn by clan warriors of the early eighteenth century, these uniforms had in fact evolved considerably over the years as dictated by military needs and evolving trends in military fashion. Thus the philibeg was worn, which had developed from and was the smaller version of the original Highland *feileadh mhor* (or belted plaid); the sett, or tartan, was that of the Mackenzies, which in reality was simply the government, or Black Watch, pattern with white and red stripes added.[15] Hanging in front just below the waist was the sporran, which, from the original simple leather pouch, had now sprouted horse hairs and tassels that hung down almost to the knees. The military doublet, with skirts or flaps extending beneath the waistbelt (the tunic worn by other regiments being too long for the kilt and sporran) stood in for the traditional Highland jacket. And crowning it all was an imposing ostrich feather headdress that had evolved from the eighteenth century practice of adding black feathers to the traditional "cow pat"–shaped Highland bonnet.[16]

Probably the core of the regiment's links with its Celtic warrior origins was the six-member pipe corps. The playing of the piper had traditionally stirred the military ardour of the clansmen before battle and kept it alive while the fray was in progress. Pipers were officially authorized for the army's Highland regiments as early as 1854, although they had been maintained unofficially since the beginning. Dressed in their "piper-green" doublets and glengarries, the members of this group were kept busy playing duty calls and parades during the day and performing at the officers' mess in the evening. Their leader, the pipe major, was in some ways the "keeper of the flame" of the regiment's links with its Celtic past and, indeed, many accounts of life in Highland regiments, particularly literary ones, impute an almost shamanistic quality to this individual. The 78th's pipe major in Halifax was the Ross-shire native Ronald Mackenzie. Besides being a champion player in his own right, he was taught by his uncle, John Ban Mackenzie, one of the most celebrated figures in the world of piping.[17]

The presence of this regiment for two and a half years in Halifax, replete as it was with costume and associations that in some circles had come to be held as the very embodiment of Scottish tradition and culture, naturally raises the question of its impact on the local community, and particularly its Scottish element. The last kilted regiment to serve in Halifax previously had been the 42nd Foot, or Black Watch, which was present in the city for eleven months in 1851–52; the last Scottish regiment of any sort, the trews-wearing 72nd Duke of Albany's Highlanders, had been in garrison for three years, between 1851 and 1854. In the meantime, Highland regiments had achieved additional public prominence and added further to their military reputation through their leading role in the Crimean War (where they constituted the "thin red line" at Balaklava) and in the quelling of the Indian Mutiny of 1857–58. The members of the 78th, for example, had for a time become great popular heroes as their regiment had led the way into Lucknow during the first relief of that besieged garrison in September 1857. Undoubtedly, interest in the 78th in Halifax would have been enhanced also by suspicions that this might be the last such unit that would be seen in the city, since rumours were then afoot (false as it turned out) that the British garrison was about to be withdrawn from Halifax, as it certainly was to be soon from the rest of Canada.[18]

There is no doubt that considerably more attention than usual greeted the 78th regiment's disembarkation, which after all was a fairly frequent event in the life of this garrison city. This would seem to have been almost entirely due to its Highland attributes. Thus, in an article entitled "The Kilties," the *Morning Chronicle* newspaper reported that the 78th "presented a fine appearance. It is a long time since Halifax had a regiment wearing the kilt, and the appearance of the men created quite a sensation."[19] Even the religious papers, usually indifferent to the comings and goings of the military, were moved to comment at length. The Presbyterian *Witness* enthused: "The men are as fine a specimen of 'the race' as have ever visited Halifax. The dress is highly picturesque, and does justice to their manly proportions."[20] The Baptist *Christian Messenger* doubtless reflected the susceptibilities of some, in an age when both male and female styles of clothing exposed as little of the human body as possible, when it commented: "Some of the more sensitive are shocked by their bare knees, and in cold weather suppose that they must suffer from the exposure."[21] The wearing of the kilt was certainly not unknown in Victorian Halifax, so, from the perspective of the twentieth century, when kilts are commonplace and even in some quarters viewed as Nova Scotia's provincial costume, one is struck by the relative strangeness this Highland attire seems to have had for these writers.

There were, of course, two distinct groups in the regiment: the officers and the rank and file. This chapter will be concerned almost exclusively with the officers. It is difficult to determine what the rank and file of Highland regiments, most of whom were from the Glasgow and Edinburgh regions, thought of their units' distinctive national/cultural emphases. It must have meant something to them, given that the great majority of the army's Scottish rank and file were concentrated in these regiments, but more work needs to be done in this area. It is easier to deal with the officers, given that their records tend to more personalized. Of the forty-six officers on the strength of the 78th during its years in Halifax (not all served in the city at once), nineteen were from Scotland, and four of its eighteen English-born officers and two of its eight Irish-born had strong Scottish connections. Ten of the Scottish officers were from the Highlands. The author has argued previously that the national/

145

cultural identity of Highland regiments, and the notion that they best represented the military traditions of Scotland, were of critical importance in motivating the Scottish officers, whether from the Highlands or the Lowlands, to choose to serve in them.[22] Such national/cultural preoccupations certainly were of significance in the ways the officers of the 78th interacted with the Scottish community of Halifax.

Nova Scotia was at this time one of the most heavily Scottish of Britain's overseas possessions, largely thanks to the waves of immigration that had come to Cape Breton and the province's eastern counties at the end of the eighteenth and first part of the nineteenth centuries.[23] According to the 1871 census, its population was fully one-third Scottish, making the Scots the largest single national group, followed by the English and then the Irish.[24] In the city of Halifax, by contrast, there were 4,861 persons of Scottish descent, or about 18 percent of the city's population, compared with 11,626 Irish, about 40 percent of the total, and 9,898 English, who constituted about 34 percent.[25] The city's Scottish population had grown up over the years for the most part independently of its fellow countrymen's migrations to the eastern portions of the province, and seems to have had little direct connection with the preoccupations and concerns of the immigrant clansmen of those areas. Certainly the 78th regiment had little to do with the eastern region of the province, despite the obvious Scottish associations. There is a record of the pipe corps making one or two excursions to Pictou, but not much else.[26] A newly constituted militia unit, the Pictou Highlanders, did forge a close link with the 78th, assuming its number in the new Dominion of Canada militia list and adopting its tartan and some of its insignia, but this was because a number of its officers came to Halifax to study at the new federal Military School of Instruction, which was then being run by the 78th.[27]

Despite their small numbers when compared to citizens of Irish and English origin, the Scots of Halifax had always played a prominent part in the city's social, business and economic life. It is well known, for example, that the Guild of Scottish Merchants formed in 1768 was the parent organization not only of the North British Society but of the city's Board of Trade as well.[28] Though their numbers may have been relatively small, the Scots still made up a significant national body. Many of them were very well situated socially, and they were by and large a culturally vociferous group that made its presence in the city felt.

By the mid-Victorian period, the Halifax Scots' sense of their national background seems to have become imbued with the same Highland emphases that had taken hold in Scotland. This is suggested by the following remarks contained in a speech delivered in 1868 to the North British Society, very much a pan-Scottish organization, by the Nova Scotia Chief Justice, the Stirlingshire-born Sir William Young. In summing up the advantages of being Scottish, as opposed to Irish or English, he argued that:

Figure 7.1   Corporal Tulloch, 78th Highland Regiment of Foot and girl on horse, c. 1870, Notman Collection (courtesy of the Public Archives of Nova Scotia)

> They want something that we possess. They want the broad sword and dirk, the picturesque and martial costume, the garb of old Gaul (applause) which attracts with a national interest every man who has Scottish blood running in his veins, and captivates every woman whether she has Scottish blood in her veins or no (loud applause).[29]

There were two Scottish cultural organizations in Halifax at this time: (1) the North British Society, essentially a fraternal organization, described in 1900 as "the strongest and the oldest Scottish organization in Canada,"[30] and (2) the Highland Society, founded in 1838 with a commission from the Highland Society of London. The latter's aim was the "preserving in Nova Scotia of the Martial Spirit, Language, Dress, Music, Poetry, and Athletic Games of the Highlanders of Scotland."[31] To this end it staged annual Highland games and other activities. Naturally there was considerable overlapping between these two groups, and both actively solicited the participation of the officers (but not the rank and file) of the 78th in their activities.

The unpublished records of the North British Society contain an entry to the effect that an approach was made to the 78th's commanding officer, Lieutenant Colonel Alexander Mackenzie, soon after his regiment's arrival in the city, "requesting the Col. & officers to allow themselves to be placed on the Honorary List of the Society."[32] It took sometime for the officers to respond to the invitation, but once they had done so they entered into its social activities with much energy and spirit. Officers of Scottish regiments had been joining in the activities of the North British Society for years, but judging by the number and length of the entries in the Society's published *Annals*, those of the 78th participated more actively and enthusiastically than most.[33] The following entry for the St. Andrew's Day celebrations of 1870 is typical: "Among the distinguished guests were Col. Mackenzie and several officers of the 78th Highlanders. . . . The toast list was disposed of at 2 a.m. and proved a most enjoyable celebration. The [78th] Highland pipers were there in force, and gave in concert several pieces of Highland music which were greatly appreciated."[34] At another meeting on 1 November 1871, the "Col. and officers of the 78th with Regimental pipers" were again present. On this occasion Lieutenant Callander of the 78th "favored the meeting with several marches on the pipes, he being a noted player. The company separated at 2 a.m., delighted."[35]

Reports of an event in which the 78th participated in association with the Highland Society in March 1870 are perhaps indicative of the cultural impact that they were by then having in the city. This was a "Grand Celtic" concert that was advertised as being "under the patronage of Col. Mackenzie C.B. and the gallant officers of the 78th."[36] The Temperance Hall, filled with the so-called "beauty and fashion of Halifax," was draped with tartans and studded with Scottish emblems for the occasion. The pipe corps under Pipe Major Mackenzie, and the band under cornet virtuoso and recent Kneller Hall graduate Andrew McEleney seem to have been the main attractions. Both would have been amongst the finest organizations of their kind in the world at this time. Some of the excitement of the event is conveyed by the following report from the *Evening Reporter* newspaper:

> The martial strains of the Pibroch fired the enthusiasm of Scotia's sons as they recalled the glorious deeds of their ancestors. The dancing which was entered into with vigor by the pipers of the 78th rejuvenated the old, set the young on fidgets, and decorum gave place to responsive "Hi his" and hand clapping accompaniments of the "Reel of Tulloch." The reel was executed by four pipers of the 78th, led by Pipe Major Mackenzie, and called forth enthusiastic vivas and an unanimous *encore*. The sword dance by Pipe Major Mackenzie and the Highland Fling by Corporal Borthwick of the Pipe Corps were the finest specimens of highland dancing witnessed in Halifax for many a day.[37]

This is the view of one reporter, who may have got somewhat carried away in describing the event's Scottish enthusiasm. Nonetheless, similar scenes were repeated frequently enough in Halifax during the years the 78th was in garrison to suggest that the regiment was in fact having a stimulating impact upon the life of the city's Scottish organizations, and an arousing effect on the pride of the Scottish community. This was probably most noticeable in a quintessentially Scottish event that occurred on 15 August 1871—the celebrations attending the centenary of the birth of the great Scottish national poet and author Sir Walter Scott. Although of little consequence in the history of the city as a whole, the circumstances of this event are worth recounting as an interesting example of the unexpected influence that the military could have on community life, as a glimpse into the life of the city's national societies of this period, and for the eddies and crosscurrents that are revealed in the swirl of the city's social and political life.

The importance that Scott had for Victorian Scotland's self-image has already been discussed. As one of the most popular writers of the era and in many ways the original voice behind the Scottish national and world image, festivities in 1871 to mark his birth were planned by Scottish communities in towns and cities around the English-speaking world and were co-ordinated through a central organizing committee in Edinburgh. These were for the most part to consist of Highland games, balls and speeches on aspects of his genius. The Halifax Scottish community threw itself into these commemorations with great keenness, and this undoubtedly had much to do with the presence amongst them of the officers of the 78th.

The possibility of a celebration of Scott's centenary in Halifax was first broached at a meeting of the North British Society on 1 June 1871. At this meeting it was resolved that the co-operation of the Highland Society and the 78th Highlanders be sought, an indication perhaps of the extent to which the latter had come to be viewed as a natural participant in the Halifax Scottish community's national events. When contacted, the two organizations pledged their full support, but especially active in their promotion of the event were the officers of the 78th, and perhaps most notably one of its captains, Colin Mackenzie. Mackenzie was a Lowlander from Edinburgh whose father was the Treasurer of the Bank of Scotland. His grandfather, another Colin Mackenzie, of Portmore House in Peebleshire, had been a close personal friend of Sir Walter Scott's, and earlier ancestors had been Highlanders and founding members of the 78th. That the Colin Mackenzie who served with the 78th in Halifax had a close personal interest in Scottish and particularly Highland antiquity is shown by his post-military career as a writer on Highland cultural themes in publications such as the *Celtic Magazine*.[38] With two other 78th officers, he attended the first planning meeting at the Halifax Hotel on 14 June and actively participated in the proceedings, either moving or seconding a number of resolutions.

When the first general planning meeting was held on 27 June, the officers of the 78th were there in force and had brought along the regimental pipers to add to the Scottish esprit of the occasion. The *Evening Express* noted in its coverage that Captain Colin Mackenzie "embodied the warmth of the 78th in the movement."[39] Most of the 78th's Scottish officers became involved, and indeed the net was cast somewhat wider than usual to include a number of individuals from the regiment who, probably for social reasons, were not usual participants in the North British Society's meetings and activities. Thus bandmaster Andrew McEleney was put in charge of the music, sergeant major Parr Campbell was to manage the procession through the streets and quartermaster Charles Skrine (a promoted ranker) was involved with the event's finances.[40]

The celebration began at 10 am on the fifteenth when the procession began to form up at the eastern end of Province House on Hollis Street. At 11 am it moved off with the band of the 78th, bandmaster McEleney in the lead. Following them came an open carriage bearing the Nova Scotia chief justice, the Stirlingshire native Sir William Young, and the Caithness-born local brewing magnate, president of the Nova Scotia Executive Council, and chief of the Highland Society, Alexander Keith. After them came a procession of the Highland Society, headed by their president, Donald Ross, and by the specially selected orator for the occasion, William Garvie, former editor of the *Citizen*. They were followed by a company of the 78th Highlanders and by the regiment's pipe corps. The members of the North British Society and another company from the 78th brought up the rear. With the band and pipers of the 78th playing "appropriate marches," the procession set off and made its way to the Temperance Hall on Grafton Street north of Duke, where the main event of the morning, Garvie's oration, was to take place.

The hall was filled by what the *Morning Chronicle* termed "the grandest Scottish company ever assembled in Halifax."[41] The morning commenced with remarks from Sir William Young and a concert of Scottish music played by the 78th band, bandmaster McEleney having composed a piece especially for the proceedings, entitled "The Scott Centenary Gallop." Then came the morning's centrepiece, the oration by William Garvie, which, entitled simply "The Genius of Scott," lasted for about an hour and a half. It was evidently a fine effort, for, at least according to the North British Society's *Annals,* when the Scott centenary orations delivered around the world were published by the Edinburgh Centenary Committee, it was pronounced "the finest of all that had been delivered the world over."[42] At its conclusion, the orator was thanked by the Reverend George M. Grant, pastor of St. Matthew's Presbyterian Church, and then the blast of the 78th's pipers played the assembly out of the hall.

In the afternoon, Highland games were held in the Horticultural Gardens; but the culmination of the day's activities was a grand ball held in the city's main skating rink, which was located at the eastern end of the Horticultural Gardens (at a spot about opposite to today's YMCA building). In the hands of the decorations committee, which included Captain Colin Mackenzie and the bagpipe-playing Lieutenant Callander, the rather unsightly interior of this building had been transformed into a sparkling ballroom. A floor of planed spruce had been put down, and gas pipes had been laid along either side, running the entire length of the building. Along both pipes rose about sixty burners, each surmounted by a glass globe. In the centre of the floor stood a fountain, while along the walls was a series of arches, each containing the name of one of Scott's works, with Scottish banners and evergreens filling the intervals. A ceiling was formed of pink and white muslin, covering the rough timbers of the building's roof. The whole, pronounced the *British Colonist*, presented a "brilliant appearance in the dazzle of gas light [produced] by the large numbers of burners."[43] The "Programme du Bal" consisted of quadrilles, waltzes, polkas and gallops performed by the hardworking band and pipe corps of the 78th.

In all, it would seem that Sir Walter's memory had received a fitting tribute from the citizens of Halifax. There can be no doubt that the ardour the occasion generated owed much to the participation of the 78th Highlanders. Thus the North British Society's *Annals* for 1871 observed that "the presence of the 78th Highlanders added greatly to the interest of the commemoration."[44] And the *Christian Messenger* declared that the "presence of the 78th Highlanders with their ancient Scottish costume gave an appropriateness to the occasion and *eclat* which no other regiment of the line could have secured for it."[45]

Yet, there were problems with the Scott centenary celebrations, for they do not seem to have been as great a success as some thought they should have been. Accounts in the newspapers vary, but it does appear, for example, that not as many as were expected came out to view the procession in the morning, while only about half the expected number turned up for the ball in the evening. In part, at least, this was attributed to the notion that the Scottish community had allowed itself to get a bit too carried away with the Scottishness of the event. Given Sir Walter Scott's special significance for the contemporary sense of Scottish national identity, this was perhaps understandable, but in the Halifax of this time it was probably a mistake. Ethnic and religious strife that had existed in the 1850s in the city had largely abated and an amiable but wary truce prevailed amongst its three major national communities—the Irish, English and Scots—each with their own different national/cultural and religious emphases. Although they were prepared to live together in harmony, each community was still very aware of its distinctiveness and sensitive to any undue national self-assertiveness amongst the others, most notably as expressed through their respective national clubs or societies. These were, besides the Scottish Highland and North British societies, the Irish Charitable Society and the English St. George's Society (other national groups were either insufficiently numerous or insufficiently organized at this time to have formed similar societies). The success of major public events staged by any one of these clubs or societies was to some degree dependant upon the co-operation of the other groups, who would necessarily and temporarily need to downplay their own national preoccupations and join in the celebrations. This co-operation seems not to have occurred sufficiently to ensure the unqualified success of the Scott centenary festivities. Probably the *Evening Express*, voice of the city's predominantly Irish Roman Catholic community, put its finger on the problem when, in a critical editorial, it referred to the "too Scottish national character of the celebrations."[46] The Scots' sense of national assertion on this occasion was, of course, not entirely unconnected with the presence amongst them of the 78th Highlanders.

Then there was local politics. It would seem that the organizers had managed to trip one of the numerous political land mines that lay about the ground of post-Confederation Halifax. Confederation had occurred some four years previously, and although "better terms" had in the meantime been negotiated between its chief opponent in Nova Scotia, Joseph Howe, and Canadian prime minister John A. Macdonald, and most of its foes probably had by now accepted it as a fait accompli, it still remained a highly sensitive issue.[47] Resentment continued to smoulder in some quarters, and old animosities could quickly spring back to life. William Garvie, the Scott centenary's special orator, had been, as editor of the *Citizen* from 1863 to 1870 and author of the satirical pamphlet *Barney Rooney's Letters on Confederation, Botheration, and Political Transmogrification,* one of the Confederation scheme's most persistent and sharpest-tongued critics. As recently as November 1870, he had run unsuccessfully as a candidate in a provincial by-election in Halifax on behalf of the anti-Confederation government of William Annand. Here he had been severely critical of Howe's "better terms" and had held up to ridicule his own former partner on the *Citizen*, E.M. Macdonald, who had switched his previous anti-Confederation stance to one in favour of union.[48]

The problem for the organizers of the Scott centenary was that to a certain pro-Confederation and pro-Tory segment of Halifax opinion, Garvie's name was anathema. This view was represented most forcefully in the pages of the *British Colonist*, which was a strong supporter of Confederation and its chief advocate in the province, Charles Tupper. When the choice of Garvie was announced in July, this newspaper put the selection down to the machinations of a clique "composed for the most part of Garvie's personal friends, including himself." With Tupper-like vehemence, it fumed: "We have had enough of this presumption. It is about time that certain people realized that the very name stinks in the nostrils of the citizens of Halifax."[49] Comments of a similarly abusive nature continued to appear in the *Colonist*'s editorials over the next week: "unprincipled political tool of a violent faction," "self-sufficient upstart," "unprincipled venturer" and "political ruffianism" were some of the terms used.[50]

Such controversy prompted the respected and pro-Confederation pastor of St. Matthew's, the Reverend G.M. Grant, to write a letter that attempted to cool the situation down. In fact, he wrote, two orators had originally been asked by the committee to speak: Garvie and himself. He had, however, con-

Figure 7.2   Unveiling of the Sir Walter Scott bust at the Halifax Public
Gardens, Nov. 2, 1931, Allan Fraser Collection (courtesy of
the Public Archives of Nova Scotia.

sidered Garvie the "fittest person" for the honour and had "urged him . . . as a
personal favour to myself to undertake the duty." Grant also observed that his
object was "not only to give Mr. Garvie the commonest fair play, but to give
my protest against the disagreeable habit—too common in Halifax—of seeing
everything through political spectacles."[51] Despite this intervention, however,
the *Colonist* stuck to its guns and continued to hurl abuse at Garvie.

Garvie's choice as orator for the Scott centenary may have been understandable, for he was an enthusiastic Scot (although born in the West Indies,
his parents were Scottish and he had been educated at the University of Edinburgh) and a skilled public speaker. According to the author of the North
British Society's *Annals*, his "commanding presence, agreeable manner, good
gesture, and pleasing Scotch accent made him the very beau ideal of an orator."[52] Still, it seems likely that the tensions generated by his choice as orator
contributed to the generally low turnout for the events of the Scott centenary.
In recording that only 200 of the expected 573 turned out for the ball at the
skating rink, a note of despair seems to be evident in the unpublished minutes
of the North British Society: "The results of the large experiment would show,
what most of the Committee supposed, that a public ball is daily becoming
difficult of success from the present complications of Halifax society."[53]

Although fraught with problems, and poorly attended by Haligonians at
large, there can be little doubt that the Scott centenary was a major event for

the city's Scottish community. The officers of the 78th had given their enthusiastic support to this venture and undoubtedly contributed to whatever success that it had. Yet, paradoxically, because the overweening Scottishness of the celebrations would in part at least have been due to their stimulative presence, they may have also contributed to its wider failure.

There were no signs in mid-Victorian Halifax of that phenomenon, so common in our own era, whereby virtually the entire population seems to some degree prepared to acquiesce in the myth that Nova Scotia is at heart Scottish. Wider national/cultural and political precoccupations were too strong for that. Despite indications of its being present in incipient form amongst the city's Scottish population, there is no evidence of the wider phenomenon of "tartanism" as defined by Ian McKay, of which the present-day incarnation of the 78th Highlanders on Citadel Hill represents such a prominent and colourful manifestation.

Notes

1. The standard source on this remains W.B. Armit, "Halifax, 1749–1906: Soldiers Who Founded and Garrisoned a Famous City," unpublished manuscript, n.d. (ca. 1955), copy on file, Halifax Defence Complex.
2. See Major H. Davidson, *History and Services of the 78th Highlanders (Ross-shire Buffs)*, vols. I and II (Edinburgh, 1901); John Pym, *Seaforth Highlanders* (Aldershot, 1962).
3. H.J. Hanham, *Scottish Nationalism* (Cambridge, Mass., 1969), p. 70.
4. See H.J. Hanham, "Mid-Century Scottish Nationalism: Romantic and Radical," in Robert Robson, ed., *Ideas and Institutions of the Victorians* ((London, 1967), pp. 144–79; Bruce Lenman, *Integration, Enlightenment, and Industrialization: Scotland, 1746–1832* (Toronto, 1981), pp. 129–45.
5. Hugh Trevor-Roper, "Sir Walter Scott and History," *The Listener*, 86, 2212 (August 1971), p. 225.
6. Ian McKay, "Tartanism Triumphant: The Construction of Scottishness in Nova Scotia, 1933–1954," *Acadiensis*, XXI, no. 2 (Spring 1992), pp. 5–47.
7. McKay, "Tartanism Triumphant," p. 14.
8. Hugh Trevor-Roper, "The Invention of the Highland Tradition in Scotland," in Eric Hobsbawm and Terence Ranger, eds., *The Invention of Tradition* (Cambridge, 1983), pp. 15–41.
9. Trevor-Roper, "The Invention of the Highland Tradition in Scotland," pp. 18–25.
10. Tom Nairn, *The Break-Up of Britain* (Thetford, Norfolk, 1977), pp. 123, 116.
11. Nairn, *The Break-Up of Britain*, p. 162.
12. Hanham, "Mid-Century Scottish Nationalism," p. 147. On Queen Victoria at Balmoral and her relationship with John Brown, see Elizabeth Longford, *Victoria R.I.* (London, 1964), pp. 260–61, 265–69; J.D. Mackie, *A History of Scotland* (London, 1982), p. 334.
13. See John Telfer Dunbar, *History of Highland Dress* (London, 1972), p. 10.
14. British Parliamentary Papers (1872) XXXVII (c.171), p. 433, "Army . . . Return showing the number of English, Irish, Scotch, Non-commissioned Officers, Corporals, Privates"; H.J. Hanham, "Religion and Nationality in the Mid-Victorian

Army," in M.R.D. Foot, ed., *War and Society* (London, 1973), pp. 158–81.

15. On the adaptation of the government sett as the official sett for various clans, see I.H. Mackay Scobie, "Highland Military Dress," *Journal of the Society for Army Historical Research*, vol. I, 1921–22, pp. 49–50; R. Money Barnes, *The Uniforms and History of the Scottish Regiments* (London, 1956), p. 277.

16. One of the better recent discussions of the evolution of Highland military costume is Peter Cochrane, *Scottish Military Dress* (London, 1987).

17. See Captain D.R. MacLennan, "Reminiscences of Pipers and Piping," *Proceedings of the Piobeareachd Society Conference*, (Middleton Hall, Gorebridge, 1976,) pp. 5–29. The most comprehensive account of piping in the army remains C.A. Malcolm, *The Piper in Peace and War* (London, 1927); see also Diana Henderson, *Highland Soldier* (Edinburgh, 1989), pp. 245–53.

18. See, for example, the *Acadian Recorder*, 6 May 1869, p. 2.

19. *Morning Chronicle*, 17 May 1869, p. 3.

20. Presbyterian *Witness*, 22 May 1869, p. 164.

21. *Christian Messenger*, 19 May 1869, p. 155.

22. Cameron Pulsifer, "Nationality, Social Background and Wealth in a Mid-Victorian Highland Regiment: The Officers Corps of the 78th Highland Regiment, 1869–71," pp. 6–15, unpublished paper presented at Scottish Studies Conference, Guelph University, September 1995 (to be published in a volume of the conference's proceedings).

23. See D. Campbell and R.A. MacLean, *Beyond the Atlantic Roar: A History of the Nova Scotia Scots* (Toronto, 1974).

24. *Census of Canada, 1870–71*, (Ottawa, 1873), p. 333.

25. *Census of Canada, 1870–71*, p. 326.

26. See the Pictou *Colonial Standard*, 27 October 1871, p. 3. On the pronounced regionality of Nova Scotia in this period, see Carmen Miller, "The Restoration of Greater Nova Scotia," in David Bercuson, ed., *Canada and the Burden of Unity* (Toronto, 1977), pp. 44–59.

27. James Cameron, *Pictonians in Arms: A Military History of Pictou County*, published privately by the author, through the University of New Brunswick Press, p. 72.

28. See David Macmillan, "The Scots as Businessman," in W. Stanford Reid, ed., *The Scottish Tradition in Canada* (Toronto, 1981), pp. 170–202.

29. In James S. Macdonald, *Annals of the North British Society, 1768–1893* (Halifax, 1894), p. 198.

30. Wilfrid Campbell, *The Scotsman in Canada*, vol. I (Toronto, n.d. [ca. 1900]), p. 6.

31. *McAlpine's Halifax City Directory, 1878–79* (Halifax, 1879), p. 568.

32. Public Archives of Nova Scotia (PANS), MG 20, vol. 232, R72, "Minutes of the North British Society, 1867–86," meeting of 5 August 1869.

33. See Macdonald, *Annals of the North British Society, 1768–1893, passim.*

34. Macdonald, *Annals of the North British Society, 1768–1893*, p. 247.

35. Macdonald, *Annals of the North British Society, 1768–1893*, p. 276.

36. *Evening Express*, 7 March 1870, p. 2.

37. *Evening Reporter*, 2 December 1870, p. 2.

38. See Alexander Mackenzie, *History of the Clan Mackenzie* (Inverness, n.d. [1879]), p. 364.

39. *Evening Express*, 28 June 1871, p. 2.

40. PANS, "Minutes of the North British Society, 1867–86," p. 139.
41. *Morning Chronicle,* 16 August 1871, p. 2; Macdonald, *Annals of the North British Society, 1768–1893*, p. 250.
42. Macdonald, *Annals of the North British Society, 1768–1893*, p. 274.
43. *British Colonist,* 15 August 1871, p. 2.
44. Macdonald, *Annals of the North British Society, 1768–1893*, p. 249.
45. *Christian Messenger*, 16 August 1871, p. 2.
46. *Evening Express*, 16 August 1871, p. 2.
47. On this, see K.G. Pryke, *Nova Scotia and Confederation* (Toronto, 1979), pp. 60–119.
48. See Pryke, *Nova Scotia and Confederation*, p. 117; also see P.B. Waite's biography in the *Dictionary of Canadian Biography*, vol. X, (Toronto, 1972), pp. 300–301.
49. *British Colonist*, 27 July 1871, p. 2.
50. See *British Colonist*, 29 July 1871, p. 2, and 3 August 1871, p. 2.
51. *British Colonist*, 3 August 1871, p. 2. It is interesting to note that the *Colonist* had originally refused to publish Grant's letter, and consequently he sent it to the *Morning Chronicle*. Only after it had appeared there did the *Colonist* undertake to publish it as well. The unpublished minutes of the North British Society indicate that Grant's version of events was substantially correct, although in fact three orators had originally been chosen: Garvie, Grant and Chief Justice Young, PANS, "Minutes of the North British Society, 1867–86," p. 135. It is interesting to note that, doubtless because of the controversy it generated, the writers of the Annals of the North British Society, 1768–1893, felt compelled to explain how the orator was chosen. Macdonald, *Annals of the North British Society, 1768*–1893, p. 275.
52. Macdonald, *Annals of the North British Society, 1768–1893*, p. 250.
53. PANS, "Minutes of the North British Society, 1867–86," p. 137.

8

"Advent'rous Merchants and Atlantic Waves":
A Preliminary Study of the Scottish Contribution to Book Availability in Halifax, 1752–1810[1]

Fiona A. Black

The study of the book trade between Scotland and Canada in the eighteenth century has not yet been undertaken. Such a study faces challenges because of a dearth of extant business records which match the richness of sources such as the Strahan-Hall correspondence.[2] Those papers have shown clearly the connections between the London trade (and its satellite operations in Edinburgh) and the "American" colonies. On the Canadian side, the great wealth of research which has been flourishing since the 1960s has focused on the print culture and the intellectual history of French Canada. The history of the development of English Canadian print culture, while not ignored, has lagged behind.[3] MacDonald's study of the Scottish merchant and bookseller James Dawson of Pictou, Nova Scotia, is important in the historiography of Canadian book history because it is the first to delineate direct links between a Maritime bookseller and a Scottish printer/publisher, with no intermediary business connections in either London or America.[4] This chapter attempts to place such (apparently rare) direct book links between Scotland and Canada in the context of the period, a context which included the overwhelming influence of London as not only a centre of book production but *the* centre of transatlantic book distribution. Here I will take a broad approach and outline the boundaries of the longer-term study of which this chapter forms a part.[5]

In the eighteenth century the ties between Scotland and Nova Scotia took many forms in addition to the private and familial links between the old and new homeland. They included both mercantile and cultural ties, and one might assume that nowhere did such links conjoin more naturally than in the book trade.[6] This chapter examines such an assumption by exploring book availability in Halifax, primarily from the evidence in colonial newspapers.[7] This evidence shows the importance of a hitherto unsung group in the history of the Canadian book trade: general merchants.

It has been stated that Scottish booksellers viewed the "American" market as a "beacon."[8] This may indeed have been true for the colonies to the south but, perhaps strangely, the evidence so far uncovered on both sides of the Atlantic does not support the notion that the same held true for the movement of books from Scotland to Nova Scotia. However, within Canada as a whole, there was "an army of Scots and Ulstermen who dominated nineteenth-century printing and bookselling."[9] The entrepreneurial spirit of these immigrants, from the evidence uncovered to date, was not matched by a similar spirit of enterprise among the major printers and publishers in Edinburgh in their dealings with Nova Scotia. This chapter can offer only preliminary findings and possible explanations for this, and further work is ongoing. Nevertheless, the picture which emerges for Halifax provides points for future comparison with other Canadian towns and with provincial towns in Britain.

The questions addressed here include: What factors affected the broader transatlantic book trade? What characterized Halifax's book trade? And who were the key players in making books available in the town? The primary source material is contemporary newspapers, which have been supplemented wherever possible by business and legal (e.g., probate) records. However, the general lack of business records for early Halifax poses a significant challenge for book historians and must be compensated for, not only by the use of contemporary records from other centres, but by a degree of caution in conclusions arising from the study.

Book Exports to Nova Scotia
Within the Transatlantic Context

Since at least the mid–eighteenth century, business networks of Scots in the book trade in London and the "American" colonies had been the means of moving tens of thousands of pounds worth of books to Philadelphia and other colonial towns.[10] These links often involved a Scottish printer in "America" who would sell books as an adjunct to the business of printing newspapers, ephemera and increasing numbers of both reprinted British works and original material.[11] However, Halifax differed distinctively from many colonial towns in the eighteenth century as it could not boast a Scottish printer.[12] Nevertheless there were Scots in the community who played a key role in importing books, Scottish and otherwise.

For those in Britain, Nova Scotia was a new colony for English-speaking settlement and offered fresh trading opportunities. It would be easy to assume that as such it would be an obvious choice as a destination for British books. However, the evidence so far gathered seems to suggest that, other than in a few isolated cases, Nova Scotia was far from being considered a market segment worthy of much investment by Scottish booksellers. In the early days of settlement this is not surprising as the population of Nova Scotia as a whole was only a few thousand compared to, for example, 250,000 for Pennsylvania.[13] By 1817 the population of Nova Scotia was just over 81,000.[14]

Whatever the contemporary perception of market size, between 1750 and 1780 a total of 596 hundredweight and 28 pounds of British-published books (i.e., a total weight of 66,752 pounds)[15] were recorded as being shipped from London to Nova Scotia.[16] The summary figures for exports from Scottish ports detailed in Appendix A offer a picture of book shipments to the Maritimes. However, this picture needs to be treated with caution. Evidence from newspaper advertisements in both Halifax and Saint John shows clearly that books were arriving, apparently from Port Glasgow or Greenock (i.e., according to the advertisement itself), in years when the customs collectors' summary statements indicate no books at all moving to Nova Scotia or New Brunswick from any Scottish port. Appendix B gives examples of advertised shipments not referred to in the summary accounts.[17]

There are several intervening variables, or constraints, which need to be considered in any discussion of the movement of books from Scottish ports to Nova Scotia. As with other periods of transition related to the trade in books, it was "accidental opportunities which characterize[d] any innovation in the commercial sphere,"[18] and such accidental opportunities appear to have been seized upon by some enterprising Scots in Halifax, though by remarkably few of their compatriots in the book trade in Edinburgh and Glasgow.[19] The eighteenth-century transatlantic book trade can perhaps be characterized as presenting more constraints than opportunities, constraints which appear to have had the effect of leading the majority of Scottish printers and publishers to control their risks by avoiding trade to Nova Scotia altogether.[20] These factors can be grouped into various categories to aid a framework for discussion: personal knowledge of the colonial scene; business contacts; distribution and marketing techniques; finance; and information—both general and trade-specific.

Knowledge of the Colonies

Unfortunately for the Scottish trade, there were no Edinburgh booksellers who could claim the direct personal familiarity with Nova Scotia which the Englishman James Rivington could. As early as the spring of 1761, he was in Halifax and, to judge from the lack of newspaper book advertisements in the following few years, he may truly have flooded the regional market in the province. His advertisement does more than hint at the size of stock he had imported, and it stated, in summary:

> James Rivington, Bookseller and Stationer from London, has imported a large and curious collection of books in history, divinity, law, physick, mathematics, classics, architecture, navigation, a variety of the best novels and books of entertainment with a good assortment of Greek, Latin and English School books, a great choice of low priced histories, books of piety, Bibles, Testaments, Psalters, Primers, Hymnbooks and all sorts of articles for the supply of Country stores . . . stationary wares, maps of Nova Scotia, Charts of Halifax and Chignecto Harbours, the Grand Chart of the River St Lawrence . . . great chart of the Sea of Nova Scotia, New England and New York . . . . setts of books for merchants . . . ledger and waste books . . . [and] paper . . . [all] sold at his store . . . [near] the Parade.[21]

It is possibly not overstating the case to say that he had not, in 1761, left much room for competitors. Rivington was from a well-established and financially successful London publishing and bookselling family, from which he had migrated to the "American" colonies in 1760.[22] The evidence suggests that this trip to Halifax was unusual amongst "American" booksellers and unheard of amongst English or Scottish booksellers.

McDougall has described some of the interconnections between the "American" colonies, Scottish publishers and booksellers in London and those in Edinburgh.[23] Extensive research is required to ascertain why the Canadian colonies were apparently not the recipients of Scottish books to nearly the same extent. Direct personal knowledge of the colonies was not a realistic business objective for most in the trade, but the importance of personal and business contacts should not be underestimated in eighteenth-century transoceanic trade.

Known Contacts

Booksellers, like other merchants, had a choice when they made a transaction: they could deal with another firm or they could deal directly with individuals. Scottish book trade members in Scotland itself tended to work through colleagues in London who suggested contacts in the "American" colonies.[24] Two example are the King's Printers in Scotland, Adrian Watkins and then Alexander Kincaid, who shipped Bibles, Testaments and prayer books to Hall in Philadelphia on several occasions. Kincaid and his partner John Bell also sent a variety of other titles to Hall and to others.[25] The Edinburgh men sent the Bibles after a recommendation from Strahan in London.[26] The latter does not seem to have had any contacts in the Canadian colonies, and extant records do not indicate that either Watkins or Kincaid ever shipped Bibles (or any other title) to any town in Nova Scotia or Canada.[27] If David Hall, for example, had lived in Quebec, which was then the centre of book importing in Canada, the picture of Scottish links with Canada may well have been different.)

Wholesaling bookseller/publishers such as Archibald Constable made it clear that they preferred to deal with retail booksellers rather than with individuals whom they did not know, even if that person was only forty miles away in Glasgow.[28] The preference for dealing with someone known (or at least someone recommended by someone known) was for purposes of relative financial security. If booksellers and publishers chose to retain more control in colonial transactions by dealing only with people they knew in the colonies, this would of necessity restrict the number of shipments they could send. Contacts in Nova Scotia, known by Scottish booksellers in London and Edinburgh may have been very rare.

In contrast, general merchants and those trading mainly in single commodities such as tobacco or lumber or sugar had already established networks within the North Atlantic, and Scots interconnections, in particular, have been noted in such networks.[29] Sometimes Scottish booksellers would supply these merchants with small book stocks of primarily standard religious works, history books, schoolbooks and magazines. This occurred with book shipments sent via the tobacco trade to Maryland and Virginia.[30] In these cases it is possible that the impetus for the trade came from the merchants rather than the bookseller. The merchant saw a fairly obvious business opportunity, and the Scottish bookseller had the advantage of dealing with a local merchant/agent. This relatively risk-free system is apparently how at least some of the general merchants in Halifax, described below, acquired their book stock. There is no evidence that they were ordering directly from publishers; rather, it is likely that they bought from local suppliers, at the retail or wholesale level, in the ports where they had agents.

Distribution and Marketing Techniques

London was the hub of the wheel of book distribution in eighteenth-century Britain.[31] London-printed books pervaded the stocks of booksellers in both Scotland and England and, not surprisingly, would have done the same in the colonies. Shipments of books from the Clyde ports were certainly not composed entirely of Scottish imprints but contained both Scottish and English (and possibly Irish) editions.[32] Edinburgh publications which were jointly published with Scottish (and sometimes English) publishers in London had a greatly increased market reach, a fact well-known to Scottish booksellers and authors. Not all of the national methods of distribution, or international methods to the "American" colonies, worked equally well, apparently, for books to the Canadian colonies. The primary reason for this in the early years was almost certainly the youthful state of print culture and the book trade within and between the Canadian towns.

Exchange

One of the common distributive methods after the middle of the eighteenth century across Europe, not just in Britain, was the system of exchange. This worked for books as well as periodical articles. By the 1790s the system of exchange was in regular use by publishers in the "American" colonies also.[33] However, in Nova Scotia in the early days there was little literary periodical production and there was certainly no quantity of book production which could have worked as an exchange.[34] This is not to say there were no literary endeavours: the *Nova Scotia Magazine* was a prime example of a literary periodical.[35] However, its own local market area was not sufficient to support it, nor were its local contributors sufficient to fill its pages with local literary material. Exchange therefore was not really feasible as a way of attracting book shipments to Nova Scotia.

Consignment—Sale or Return

The consignment of books not specifically ordered by the recipient was an established method of marketing by the middle of the eighteenth century within Britain. Although it does not appear to have been a popular transatlantic practice, it was occasionally employed for the movement of books from Scotland to Nova Scotia. For example, in the autumn of 1786, a shipment of books had arrived in Halifax on consignment, possibly from Glasgow, and was offered new for sale by the auctioneer William Millet.[36] Consignments were also sent to New Brunswick in the same year. The Scottish merchants Campbell and Stewart in Saint John advertised a consignment of eighty-three titles and stated that "Being a consignment they will be sold very low for cash."[37]

As with most transatlantic shipments, it is difficult to ascertain the numbers of each title shipped without business records to augment the newspaper advertisements. However, Millet's consignment included thirty-eight distinct titles which indicated a range of materials likely to sell in the town. Practical works for use by seamen, merchants and traders were included, such as *The Seaman's Daily Assistant*, Moore's *Navigation*, Guthrie's *Geographical Grammar*, Trader's *Sure Guide*, Mair's *Book-keeping*, Salmon's *Geographical Grammar* and Hopper's *Measurement*. Such works were advertised regularly in the Halifax papers,[38] but this consignment included, besides the ubiquitous Bibles, Hervey's *Meditations* and Watt's *Hymns*, literary items such as *The Spectator* and yet more recreational fare such as novels by Samuel Richardson, Tobias Smollett and Frances (Fanny) Burney and collections of songs. All of these works were perennial steady sellers in the North American colonies, just as they were in Great Britain.[39] Copies were shipped to the colonies from London and Glasgow and possibly also from Liverpool.[40]

An aspect of consignment which would not have appealed to Scottish booksellers due to the long-distance nature of the transaction was the question of returns. In 1820, Archibald Constable wrote to John Young in Halifax, referring to books and periodicals which had been shipped to Halifax from Greenock: "We regret to find that the Edin[burgh] Review does not suit . . . and . . . rather than be at the expense of receiving it back, we are willing that you dispose of it if you can, at a reduction of 25 per cent from the price charged."[41] This would have led to a financial loss for Constable, but clearly the amount would have been less than the cost of paying for further insurance and packing for a return transatlantic crossing. This is an indication of the relatively narrow profit margins involved in overseas shipments which would have constrained any speculative trade.

Direct Orders

In contrast to consignment shipments, direct orders, whether for wholesale, retail or library use (as with John Young), offered some level of security. One might ask if the Scottish booksellers deliberately sought out such orders. A newspaper advertisement of 1806 promoted the placing of orders directly with a publisher/bookseller in London on the grounds that "in every part of North America, [there is] an increasing taste for English Literature, without a corresponding Increase of Facilities for obtaining the best . . . Publications."[42]

Research to date indicates that no bookseller in Edinburgh or Glasgow ever placed a similar advertisement. However, though possibly not being proactive in seeking out those who would place direct orders, some Scottish publishers certainly responded promptly if orders were sent to them. In 1820, Archibald Constable sent a letter to a Scot, Archibald McQueen, stating that he was filling McQueen's order for books for the library at Miramichi in New Brunswick. Constable said: "We shall be very glad to continue to supply the Miramichi library . . . and as an earnest of our wish to encourage such undertakings we discount 15[%] from the enclosed Invoice. . . . We shall be happy to receive your future orders."[43] Constable also filled orders for the literary agriculturalist John Young of Halifax, who operated a societal library there.[44] Reacting to orders received, then, was an acceptable business practice, and the costs of packing and insurance were added to the invoice. The profit margins among publisher, wholesaler and retailer were not large enough to absorb the costs of transatlantic transportation. Finance was on a relatively precarious footing for most of those involved.

Finance

The pull of London as a centre of production and distribution was also strong for other critical reasons. One of the major constraints of the book trade (or indeed of all trade, especially in luxury, limited-market goods) was the question of payment. Banks with international mechanisms for the transfer of funds in various currencies were still evolving during this period.[45] However, accepted practices were followed by wholesalers and retailers engaged in over-seas trade. One method for reducing financial risk was to insist on a clearly defined method of payment. An example of a British publisher doing this in Halifax comes from 1806. It is an advertisement inserted by a London book-seller, and no equivalent has been found for an Edinburgh or Glasgow book-seller or publisher, even those who had outlets in London:

> To Booksellers and all Lovers of Literature
> Mr Richard Phillips, a well known publisher of books in London, having learnt that there exists in every part of North America, an increasing taste for London Publications, hereby undertakes to ship from London with punctuality and good faith, assortments of the newest and most valuable publications. . . .
> In every instance he expects remittances in good bills, or orders for prompt payment, of which an extra discount will be allowed, or he expects references to good houses in London, where payment must be guaranteed in ten months from the shipping of the goods. No atten-tion can be paid to any application unless the payment is unequivo-cally secured in either [of] these ways.

This notice is an example of the typical requirements of the time. "Remit-tances in good bills" usually meant, in practice, payment from a mercantile house in London.[46] That city was the centre of the credit structure, and the book trade was no different from other businesses regarding the need for relatively secure credit. In short, a London connection was not only important for the financial transactions of the book trade, it was usually vital. The book trades of Edinburgh and Glasgow should thus be seen within this constraining financial context whenever one considers their overseas shipments. One Glas-gow firm had a sufficient number of "American" retailing customers to war-rant setting in type a business letter concerning transatlantic credit, though no references to the letter being sent to Nova Scotia have so far been located.[47]

Even with such clear statements and accepted practices, extracting the payments due from colonial booksellers could be a challenge. In 1798, William Creech, an Edinburgh bookseller and publisher with strong business ties to the London trade, wrote a near despairing letter to W.H. Tod in Philadelphia in which he referred to debts owed to him by six individuals and booksellers in the "American" colonies.[48] He concludes (not unreasonably): "The trouble and delay in getting business settled in America really sickens mercantile people in Britain with regard to answering orders."[49] The "mercantile people" in this case were those within the book trade. Their difficulty lay in the fact that commerce in books was one "in which exceptionally long credit was expected by client retailers and customers,"[50] which was a detriment to the business operations of the supplying booksellers who had to carry, in the interim, not only the production costs of the books but the not inconsiderable freight and insurance costs. For at least some of the London wholesaling booksellers and publishers, their trade to the colonies "was hardly worth" all the effort involved.[51]

There would be a clear advantage in financial arrangements if books were sold (and paid for) on a local level to merchant companies which in turn would send the books overseas through their own distributive network. From evidence uncovered to date, this was the primary route for books moving to Nova Scotia in the early period, and it remained a mode of book distribution even after Halifax acquired its first specialist bookseller, the Scot Alexander Morrison, in the 1780s (see below). In addition, general merchants in the colonies who were by definition dealing in a wide array of goods would not be so dependent financially, as Davie Hall the Philadelphia printer and bookseller was, on a relatively rapid turnover of book stock. The book stocks of general merchants would only form a relatively small proportion of their entire stock. The Haligonian John Kirby (or Kerby) is an example of a merchant for whom schoolbooks and stationery were a staple though not large part of his regular stock.[52]

General and Trade-Specific Information

Booksellers did not just require information about financial reliability. Their information needs were considerably broader. The need for various types of information is apparent, if not self-consciously so, in the letterbooks of such Scots booksellers as John Bell of Edinburgh and Davie Hall in Philadelphia, who were both engaged in international trade.[53]

Fundamental information such as appropriate shippers and their sailing schedules was of importance to book specialists and general merchants. The major coffee houses in London, Glasgow and Edinburgh were the equivalent of the daily trade bulletins of this century—dates of ship clearances and names of captains and shipping agents were regularly exchanged in the commercial and social atmosphere of such emporia. For example, in the 1780s the Tontine Coffee-Room in Glasgow included amongst its patrons "the most influential members of the mercantile community" in the city.[54] The early coffee houses in Halifax had similar patrons and served precisely the same need for the exchange of information.

An example of a potentially vital publication for dealers in books is the following, from a Halifax paper in 1801:

> PROSPECTUS OF A GENERAL SHIPPING AND COMMERCIAL LIST
> Published at the General Post Office conformably to a plan, submitted to, and approved of by His Majesty's Post-Master General. This list exhibits a periodical account of the sailings and arrivals of

merchant ships at all ports, both foreign and domestic. . . . Publication every Monday, Wednesday and Friday. . . . The list will be sent by the post . . . to America at £1. 3s. per annum. . . . Orders will be received . . . by every Postmaster in the British Settlements abroad.[55]

Not only were there periodical publications such as this one, but local newspapers also often inserted shipping information. The Halifax merchants could order a range of goods from British merchants with instructions to have the goods shipped aboard specific ships which they knew on good authority to be heading for Halifax. This was not a hit-and-miss business structure. There was therefore, at least in theory, time to plan what book stock should be ordered.

Other tools for business people in both Scotland and Nova Scotia were locally produced almanacs which ranged from pamphlets of a few pages to yearbooks of surprising sophistication. Scottish almanacs that were available in Halifax,[56] such as the *New Glasgow Almanac for 1806,* included information which might indeed help Halifax merchants, such as lists of banks in Edinburgh and Glasgow and lists of merchants and manufacturers in Glasgow. Although details of the Bookbinders' Society were included, there is no listing of city booksellers that could have been used by colonial merchants who wished to import. From a Scottish perspective, other than distances between various towns in the colonies and tables of stamp duties for bills of exchange, there was little in local colonial almanacs which would be of real aid in the transatlantic book trade.

In addition to almanacs, general mercantile handbooks were printed in several British towns. These handbooks ranged from some which were essentially tables and formulae for the conversion of weights and measures[57] to others which dealt with mercantile and maritime laws and customs.[58] Some of these handbooks were offered for sale in Halifax, for example, *The Merchants' Directory, or Lex Mercatoria.*[59] Although of general use for a wide array of goods and suppliers, all these handbooks lacked listings of wholesale and retail booksellers on both sides of the ocean. Such a tool could have been created, as there had been a useful precedent in the form of a pocket guide by John Pendred.[60]

Basic information, such as population figures in the colonies, that sometimes appeared in London and other British papers, would have also affected whether or not the various colonies were evaluated as potential markets worthy of targetting for book shipments.[61]

Book-Related information

Booksellers required more information than what was in print and from whom was it available.[62] And such bibliographic information would have been of greater importance to specialist booksellers (who included amongst their customers those wishing to place special orders for the latest publications and editions) than to general merchants (who would have been aiming to hold a stock of general, topical and practical interest). In short, general merchants may not have been overly concerned if they did not have the latest edition of the general *London Catalogue of Books*[63] or house catalogues from individual English or Scottish publishers, because they were relying on agents in Scotland and England to ship appropriate titles.

It would have been a business norm in Nova Scotia to expect that the majority of titles would be available in London. However, there is a small body of evidence from newspapers which indicates that some Scottish colonial merchants took advantage of Scottish book information or availability which came their way. Three examples are Hugh Johnston of Saint John, and Archibald McColl and James Beith of Halifax.

The highly successful Hugh Johnston's main mercantile interests involved lumber and fish,[64] but he offered evidence in at least one specialized newspaper advertisement of being able to acquire current information, presumably from contacts in Scotland, about new Scottish publications which might have relevance and therefore a market in a newly settled colony. In autumn 1796, at his wharf on the west side of Water Street in Saint John, Johnston's staff unloaded "several hundred" copies of a new specialist work on agriculture written by James Donaldson of Dundee, *Agriculture, or the Present State of Husbandry in Great Britain*. The books arrived on the ship *Lucy* from Glasgow, and Johnston added a puff to his newspaper advertisement with the words "worthy the attention of every farmer, particularly those in this infant country."[65]

Five years later, Archibald McColl in Halifax advertised Gaelic Bibles and Testaments for sale, along with the same items in English.[66] He had imported these from Glasgow in the ship *Nancy*, and they would almost certainly have been published in Scotland,[67] either by one of the Glasgow or Edinburgh Gaelic printers, or through the auspices of one of the religious societies.[68] McColl was, like Hugh Johnston, deliberately targeting a specific market with these books, and his market was Scottish.

James Beith's company imported "a large collection of books" on the brig *Charlotte* from Glasgow, which arrived in Halifax in June 1802.[69] His history books, ready reckoners, dictionaries and song books might have been published in any part of Britain, but the "Children's Toy Books" he referred to in his advertisement could very easily have come from the local Glasgow publishing house of James Lumsden and Son which specialized in tiny chapbooks and children's books.[70] Books shipped from Glasgow, though they may not have been published locally, would likely have been purchased locally.[71]

Book Availability in Halifax

In spite of all the factors which affected the transatlantic book trade, the spring arrivals of supply ships from Britain regularly brought at least small collections of books. From the evidence in surviving newspapers, over 874 distinct titles or generic collections were advertised in Halifax between 1785 and 1810.[72] Of those titles for which there is shipping information, slightly less than half (372) had been shipped from Glasgow or Greenock, most of the rest coming from London. Although some of the publishing booksellers in Philadelphia were beginning to embark on a national distribution effort within the American colonies,[73] the tense political relationship with both Great Britain and the northern colonies did not encourage much movement of books northward in this twenty-five-year period. Another source of supply for books within the continent might have been the wholesale warehouse of the Scottish printer and bookseller John Neilson of Quebec. Ships from Quebec did sometimes put in at Halifax harbour, but Neilson's market reach seems to have been restricted mainly to the Canadas, and especially to Montreal.[74] Table 1 is a preliminary list of the geographic origins of books arriving in Halifax.

Table 1. Geographic Origins of Book Shipments to Halifax, 1752–1810

Port of Entry	Port of Exit	Number of Shipments[75]
Halifax	London	35
	Glasgow	5
	Glasgow and/or Liverpool	2
	Greenock	1
	Liverpool	1
	Glasgow and/or London	1
	Greenock and/or Liverpool	1
	Philadelphia	1
	Boston	1

This table places London clearly in top place as a book-exporting city to Nova Scotia. The overwhelming centre of book production in Britain was London, but, though lagging far behind, Edinburgh was second in overall numbers of titles and editions. It is possible to gain some idea of the relative importance of Scottish presses compared with those in London by using the electronic files of the *Eighteenth-Century Short Title Catalogue* (ESTC) and the *Nineteenth Century Short Title Catalogue* (NSTC).[76] Searching these files for annual production figures puts Scotland's book trade within a perspective which should not be overlooked when studying the export of books from Scottish ports (see Table 2).

Table 2. Publication Data Drawn from ESTC and NSTC[77]

Years	Place	Number of Titles/Editions
1701–1800	Scotland	23,580
	Edinburgh	17,686
	London	168,891
1750–1800	Scotland	15,381
	Edinburgh	10,371
	London	101,488
1801–1820	Edinburgh	4,622
	London	40,786

Although it is difficult to ascertain the place of publication for many of the titles advertised in Halifax newspapers (typical of their time, the advertisements did not refer to edition or place of publication), a Scottish flavour can be discerned. The first book advertised in a newspaper anywhere in Canada had a

Advertiſements.

London, February 20, 1752

P R O P O S A L S

For Printing by SUBSCRIPTION,

M E M O I R S

OF THE

L I F E and C H A R A C T E R

Of the late RIGHT HONOURABLE

J O H N Earl of C R A U F U R D,

Firſt Earl of SCOTLAND,

Lieutenant General of HIS MAJESTY'S FORCES,

AND

Colonel of the R O Y A L   N O R T H   B R I T I H   D R A G O O N S.

By *R I C H A R D   R O L F,*

Author of *The Hiſtory of the Conduct of the ſeveral Powers of* Europe *engaged in the late General War.*

Any Gentleman who is willing to encourage the Work, is deſired to apply to Capt. Robert Campbell, *at his Houſe near the Parade in* Halifax.

Figure 8.1 Reproduction of bookseller Richard Kidston's advertisement, *Halifax Journal,* May 2, 1799.

Scottish flavour. This advertisement did not refer to a locally printed item, nor to one available in local stores; rather, it was a reprinting of a typical eighteenth-century proposal for printing a work by subscription. The dateline was London, February 20, 1752, and it was inserted in the *Halifax Gazette* on June 27 of that year, London papers having arrived in the three-year-old port with the spring arrivals of goods and people, including military officers. This advertisement, for a book on a Scottish figure, was placed by a Scottish military captain stationed in Halifax, Robert Campbell. Campbell's early initiative in promoting a particular publication possibly reflected his conviction that at least a few residents would be sufficiently interested to subscribe.

By the end of the century, the book culture of Halifax had expanded greatly, and residents could purchase locally the famous works of Scottish (and other) authors in belles-lettres, religion, history, travel, philosophy or economics.

Following is an example of Scottish Works Advertised by Richard Kidston in 1799[78]

Aitken's *Letters*
M'Pherson's *Introduction to the Blair's Lectures History of Great Britain*
Blair's *Sermons*
Ossian's *Poems*
Buchan's *Domestic Medicine*
Robertson's *Charles V*
Burn's *Poems*
Robertson's *History of America*
Edinburgh Dispensatory
Robertson's *History of Scotland*
Edinburgh Musical Miscellany
Ruddiman's *Grammar*
Ferguson's *Lectures*
Ruddiman's *Rudiments*
Hume's *Essays*
Smith's *Wealth of Nations*

Sellers of Books in Halifax

Those who sold Scottish works, whether the products of Scottish or English presses (and they were often the latter, Scottish authors being aware of the importance of London's distributive network for profits), were both inside and outside the book trade itself. Table 3 is a preliminary list of the firms which sold books in Halifax and indicates their primary business.[79] Although many of these businesses have no extant records, the names of the proprietors attest a Scottish element.

Table 3. Firms Advertising Books for Sale or Loan in Halifax, 1752–1810

Occupation	Name
General Merchant	Joseph Anderson
	James Beith & Co.
	George Bell
	Michael Bennett
	Francis Boyd
	George Deblois
	S. Deblois
	Andres Gray
	William Grigg
	John Hemmington
	John Kerby
	James Kidston
	James and Alex Kidston
	Richard Kidston
	William Kidston
	Dobson and Telford Kidston
	James Leaver
	James and Thomas Leaver
	Robert T. Lyon
	M'Kevers
	Archibald McColl & Co.
	William Minns
	Thomas Russell
	John Witham
Auctioneer	James Browne
	William Craft
	Charles Hill
	Thomas Leaver
	William Millet
	Piers and Hill
	W.K. Reynolds
Printer	John Bushell
	Robert Fletcher
	Grant and Howe
	Anthony Henry
	John Howe
Bookseller	David Howe
	Alexander Morrison
	James Rivington
Hardware Merchant	Brymer and Belcher
	Samuel Sellon
Library Proprietor	Thomas Bennett
Ship Chandler	Benjamin Salter
Watchmaker	Charles Geddes

Amongst these diverse sellers of books, and within the larger context of all the challenges of marketing, financing and information requirements, were there any significant Scottish figures in the early print culture of Nova Scotia? There are two examples which do more than hint at a distinctive Scottish contribution. Scotland provided the first specialist bookseller in the Maritimes, Alexander Morrison, as well as a potential network of regional book distribution through the Scottish merchant firm of Richard Kidston and his brothers and sons. Both these businesses are likely to have had connections with businesses and family members in Glasgow and not with Edinburgh, and this in itself may be significant as Glasgow had the enormous benefit of having a direct shipping route to Halifax.

Alexander Morrison[80]

Alexander Morrison's route to Halifax is not known, though we do know that he was from the Glasgow area and probably married after arriving in Halifax, as his wife was the daughter of a Halifax mariner.[81] The familiar bookseller's sign, the Sign of the Bible, swung above his shop, and he was in business in the port from at least 1786, when he was at the corner of the Parade.[82] He then moved in 1799 to a potentially better site for business, the corner of Granville and Duke streets.[83] By the end of his life he had amassed a considerable quantity of land in King's County and held more than one piece of property within Halifax, on top of which he was able to provide not only for his wife but to leave annuities for his widowed sister in Glasgow, besides bequeathing monies to his six nephews and nieces in Scotland.[84] There are hints in sources such as early histories of the city and the province that his role as bookbinder, stationer and bookseller provided a comfortable living.

Did Morrison use his family contacts in Glasgow to arrange for shipments of books and stationery? His brother-in-law was John McCallum, and the linking of the names "Morison and M'Allum" was present in Glasgow at least in the 1770s.[85] Did he ever make trips back to Britain or to "America," as the Scottish bookseller in Quebec John Neilson did? Morrison could have been receiving his book stock and stationery from London and Liverpool as well as from Glasgow, as ships were arriving in Halifax from all three British cities. No book advertisements are extant for his business, other than notices for "A Large Collection of Books," such as one inserted in the *Gazette* in June 1799.[86] The customs accounts do not indicate a shipment from Scotland to Halifax in 1799,[87] but in 1789 a £40 value was placed on book exports leaving Scottish ports for Nova Scotia. It is possible that this refers to a shipment to Morrison. This valuation would have been put on a collection of approximately 540 volumes;[88] such a number of books could have been termed "a large collection." Being the only specialist bookseller in Halifax, Morrison may have had his own catalogues printed, obviating the need to have lists printed in the newspapers. Unfortunately, none of Morrison's catalogues or booklists have apparently survived, so it is not possible to analyse or even speculate about his stock. Further, there are no extant ledgers or day books for Morrison or his successor Eaton that can indicate direct or indirect Scottish sources of supply.

The Kidston Family

As with Morrison, there are no remaining business records from the Kidston firm of general merchants, but the newspaper advertisements for this firm offer useful details concerning book availability and possible geographic sources for its books. Remaining newspapers offer evidence of seven book shipments of widely ranging sizes in an eleven-year period (1789–1799): two from London, three from Glasgow and the remaining two possibly from Glasgow.[89] It may be reasonable to state that the Kidstons were importing some books every spring while they were in business. The evidence certainly suggests that they were importing a greater variety of titles than any other merchant in the 1790s. Between 1752 and 1800, apparently the only other firms or individuals to import books that covered such a wide array of subjects were those within the book trade: the booksellers Rivington[90] and possibly Morrison, and the printer Robert Fletcher.[91]

The first of the Kidston family to advertise books was Richard Kidston,[92] whose advertisement from 1789 indicates that his stock had come from London. On that occasion he advertised 249 titles, including the histories of William Robertson, the sermons of Hugh Blair and a popular family medical handbook by the Edinburgh physician William Buchan. Seven years later, Richard's son James imported books from both London and Glasgow, a clear indication that he (or his British agents) used whichever book suppliers were close at hand when he had a major shipment of general goods being loaded for him.[93] In that year, however, his book shipment from London on the *Enterprize* included forty-one distinct titles or genres (e.g., children's books), including several novels, music books and Burns' *Poems*; whereas only Bibles, Testaments, spelling books and primers had been loaded for him on the *Neptune* at Glasgow.

In 1799, James Kidston advertised a book stock which may have warmed the hearts of educated, expatriate Scots, and on this occasion the shipment may have come from Glasgow.[94] The Kidstons would have numbered amongst their general customers some of their fellow members of the North British Society,[95] which was in many regards "a Scottish mercantile brotherhood."[96] Some of the members met regularly "to read and discuss papers on learned subjects"[97] and would almost certainly have bought books locally, as well as, no doubt, placing private orders by letter, and purchasing books whilst on leave in Britain. The intellectual chaplain to the society, Andrew Brown, lived in Halifax from 1787 to 1795 and may have appreciated having a local supplier of historical works, because he was writing a history of North America himself.[98]

The Kidstons would have dealt with a variety of merchant houses in Scotland and England. It is impossible to know from newspaper evidence alone which British booksellers they purchased from. Were they usually dealing with one of the wholesaling booksellers in London or Glasgow? London wholesalers regularly supplied the Scottish printer and bookseller John Neilson in Quebec with a wide array of British books.[99] How much control did the Kidstons have over the selection of their book stock? It is not yet known whether they sent detailed requests for particular titles or genres, although this was possibly the case, as their larger book stocks were not advertised as consignments (the nature of the consignment system implies that the sender had more control over the content than the receiver).

The sometimes lengthy advertisements for books the Kidstons placed in Halifax papers reveal the nature of at least a portion of their stock. Further, using advertisements and catalogues from Scottish towns in the same period, it is instructive to compare the range of materials covered in the two "provincial" regions.[100] For example, the Highland town of Elgin and the Lowland town of Duns offer data which can be compared with those books advertised by Richard Kidston in 1789. However, this single comparison may not be generalizable and is offered as an example only, pending further research from other towns. The Elgin catalogue of the bookseller Isaac Forsyth[101] lists a total of 577 titles, while the Duns Library catalogue lists a total of 394 titles. Richard Kidston added 249 titles to his book stock in June of that year.[102] Ninety-five titles were common to both of the Scottish catalogues in 1789.[103] A comparison of Kidston's new stock, imported from London on the brig *Ceres* with that of Forsyth in Elgin, shows forty-five titles in common. Therefore, nearly one-fifth of Kidston's stock mirrored that available in a Highland town. The titles common to the two booksellers consist of the subjects shown in Table 4.

Table 4. Titles Common to Forsyth's and Kidston's Book Stocks, 1789[104]

Subject	Number of Titles
Religion	16
Novels	8
History	5
Literary periodicals	3
Travel/voyages	2
Fables	2
Poetry	2
Commerce	2
Belles lettres	2
Philosophy	1
Medicine	1
Drama	1

Of the 193 titles which Kidston imported in 1789 and which are not matched in either Forsyth's catalogue or that for the Duns Library, 39 percent were religious works or tracts. This apparently high proportion is in keeping with overall publication figures for the century, which placed religion ahead of every other subject, including politics and other social sciences.[105] Many of the rest of Kidston's books were histories or works of travel, and several were practical works related to commerce. In Forsyth's specialist bookstore in Elgin, all the same subjects were also found, along with works of local interest in geography and history, and many works of imaginative literature.[106] It is difficult to ascertain how many newer publications in this last category were reaching Halifax. "Plays, latest published" is a phrase familiar to several advertisements in Maritime newspapers, but "Novels" as a similarly generic term is rare; usually novels were listed individually.[107] Contemporary diaries do offer hints that plays and novels were available for sale or loan in Halifax. In 1795, Anna Kearny recorded that in summer she had read plays in her bower, and one evening in October "Read *The Banished Man* till Bed time."[108] Kearny notes that she frequented Kidston's store, but unfortunately she does not state whether she acquired books there.[109]

Although Kidston's stock did not include as many newer works as were available in Elgin (and no doubt in similar country stores in Scotland), many of the older works on the tables and shelves in his store would have been known to literate Halifax residents. It is also likely that Kidston was, like many other Halifax merchants, willing to offer a discount to country merchants. He would have been, in short, a locally and possibly regionally known supplier of books and thus would have served a cultural as well as commercial role of note in the life of colonial Nova Scotia.

Conclusion

In 1817, Lord Dalhousie, a Scot and not a person noted for understatement, complained: "There is not a bookseller's shop in Halifax, nor is there an individual possessed of anything that can be called a Library."[110] His Lordship's comparison of the book facilities of the maritime port with those of London and Edinburgh is clearly unfavourable. However, if a comparison is drawn with provincial towns in Scotland, a rather more realistic basis of comparison for a relatively new colony, the impression one gains is not so negative and possibly more accurate. Although my research has not yet shown whether the situation of book imports to Nova Scotia reflects that of imports to "American" colonies, which was described by Stephen Botein as representing "the detritus of eighteenth-century English culture,"[111] the evidence does indicate that the books sent from Scottish ports were generally neither intellectually nor materially distinctive from those shipped from London.

This chapter has attempted to sketch some of the critical factors in the development of book trade links across the North Atlantic. There is evidence of at least some transoceanic Scottish links with Nova Scotia. The Scottish (and other) merchants in Halifax were acting as competent businesspeople, then or now, would act—they stocked items they felt would sell. The merchants carried primarily the ubiquitous religious works and widely popular practical works, as well as a sampling of imaginative literature, for readers in Nova Scotia. However, their book stocks, especially those of the Kidstons, also included works of philosophy, history and belles lettres that would have had a much smaller market in the colony but certainly offered a Scottish element, in authorship if not in publication. Unlike Lord Dalhousie and his immediate circle, the citizens of Halifax formed a heterogeneous community who may have had only limited expectations of what books should be available, and it is conceivable that the general stores may have been meeting their needs more than adequately.

Considerable further research is required to address some of the larger issues only touched on here. Did Scottish booksellers miss a golden opportunity to expand their market reach to a colony which perforce relied on imports? The picture painted by surviving evidence suggests that publishers and booksellers in Edinburgh were reactive rather than proactive in their export businesses. Negative factors that influenced this attitude include significant concerns with long-distance financial transactions, and a lack of personal knowledge and general information concerning potential markets in the colony.

There is a perennial difficulty in examining the business dealings of any cultural group. Did the booksellers and merchants in Halifax and elsewhere see themselves in terms of their *function* first and their *nationality* second? Whatever future research may reveal on this point, Scottish general merchants may yet prove to be the unsung heroes in the story of the early dissemination of books, both Scottish and otherwise, in Nova Scotia.

Appendix A
Book Exports from Scottish Ports, 1755–1811
(extracted from the annual summary customs accounts)

(Figures extracted from records held at the Kew Public Record Office (PRO), CUST 14/1–23, Board of Customs and Excise, "British and Foreign Goods and Merchandize Imported to and Exported from Scotland."

Data are included only for those years for which "Canadian" destinations are included. For comparative purposes, total figures are also included for shipments to "American" destinations. The term "Canada" refers to shipments to the port of Quebec City.

Quantities, unless in sterling, are by weight, given as "hundredweights(cwt).quarters.pounds" (i.e., one hundredweight = 112 pounds; one quarter = 28 pounds). Bound books were usually valued at £11/cwt., and unbound at £12/cwt., though this varied throughout the period.

Of interest are book shipments in reverse—in some years, books were imported to Scotland from North America, e.g., 1792, 1793, 1800 and 1811.)

Data as Given in Annual Customs Summary Accounts

Year	Canada	Nova Scotia	Newfoundland	"America"
1783		£20		36.2.24
1784		£15		61.3.26
1789		£40		£100
1792	£10	2.2.20		46.3.14
1801	12.3.12		6.0.0‡	£576
1802	2.1.21		1.1.24	9.2.27, £1,753
1807	1.0.0			7.0.8, £15 4s 0d
1810	0.3.0, £2 2s 0d	0.1.0		2.0.12
1811	0.0.20			0.0.10, 0.2.25‡

‡Unbound books only

Annual Summary Customs Data '"Normalized" by Weight

Year	Canada	Nova Scotia	Newfoundland	"America"
1783		1.3.8		36.2.24
1784		1.1.13		61.3.26
1789		3.2.16		9.0.10
1792	0.3.18	2.2.20		46.3.14
1801	12.3.12		6.0.0‡	52.1.13
1802	2.1.21		1.1.24	169.0.12
1807	1.0.0			8.1.16
1810	0.3.21	0.1.0		2.0.12
1811	0.0.20			0.0.10, 0.2.25‡

‡ Unbound books only.

Appendix B

Advertisements for Books from Scottish ports
(for which there is no corresponding entry in
the annual summary statements of exports for customs)[112]

Port of Exit and Ship	Merchant	Newspaper	Advertisement Date	Books
Glasgow Brig *Mary*	George Grant & John Howe, Halifax	*Halifax Journal*	12 August 1790, p. 1	William Gordon's *New Geographical Grammar*
Glasgow *Scipio*	James Kidston, Halifax	*Halifax Journal*	7 January 1796, p. 1	Fenning's and Dilworth's Spelling Books
Glasgow *Neptune*	James Kidston, Halifax	*Halifax Journal*	5 May 1796, p. 3	Bibles, Testaments, Schoolbooks
Glasgow *Ann*	James Hart, Saint John	*Saint John Gazette and Weekly Advertiser*	2 September 1796, p. 3	Bibles, Testaments, Schoolbooks, Small Histories
Glasgow *Lucy*	Johnston & Ward, Saint John	*Saint John Gazette and Weekly Advertiser*	4 November 1796, p. 1	James Donaldson's *Agriculture*
Glasgow *Liberty*	Lang & Turner, Saint John	*Royal Gazette and New Brunswick Advertiser*	22 July 1800, p. 3	"Books and Stationary (sic)"
Glasgow *Nancy*	Archibald McColl, Halifax	*Nova Scotia Royal Gazette*	21 May 1801, p. 3	English Bibles and Testaments, Gaelic Bibles and Testaments
Edinburgh via Saint John *William*	Colin Campbell, Greenock	*Royal Gazette New Brunswick Advertiser*	26 May 1801, p. 3	Music ("Scotch, Italian and other")
Glasgow Brig *Charlotte*	James Beith, Halifax	*Nova Scotia Royal Gazette*	17 June 1802, p. 3	"A Large Collection of Books"
Greenock *Paragon*	James Leaver, Halifax	*Nova Scotia Royal Gazette*	28 April 1807, p. 1	Bibles Schoolbooks

Notes

1. The paper on which this chapter is based was published in the Scottish journal of book history, *The Bibliotheck*, 22 (1997), pp. 35–76. The quoted phrase in the title is taken from the anonymous *Glasgow: A Poem* (Edinburgh, 1824). Although Halifax is the geographical focus of this enquiry, both Saint John and Miramichi have been included in some examples, although after 1784 they became a part of the separate province of New Brunswick.

2. American Philosophical Society (APS), Hall Papers, "David Hall Letter Books, 1750–1771," microform.

3. An impression of the relative state of book history research in various regions of Canada may be gauged from Mark Bartlett, Fiona A. Black and Bertrum H. MacDonald, *The History of the Book in Canada: A Bibliography* (Halifax, 1993).

4. Bertrum H. MacDonald "Scottish Imprints in the Diaspora: The Case of James Dawson & Son, Pictou, Nova Scotia." Paper presented to the fifth annual conference of the Society for the History of Authorship, Reading and Publishing, Edinburgh, July 14–17, 1995.

5. The research reported in this chapter is part of a larger study being undertaken at the Department of Information and Library Studies, Loughborough University, England. The larger study will offer a comparison of book availability in Canada and provincial Scotland, 1750 to 1820.

6. Two secondary sources for the study of local book production in Nova Scotia are Marie Tremaine, *A Bibliography of Canadian Imprints, 1751–1800* (Toronto, 1952) and Patricia Lockhart Fleming, *Atlantic Canadian Imprints, 1801–1820: A Bibliography* (Toronto, 1991). These are descriptive bibliographies of an extremely high standard, detailing every item known to have come from printers in Nova Scotia (and elsewhere). For the book trade in general, see George L. Parker, *The Beginnings of the Book Trade in Canada* (Toronto, 1985). However, no detailed elucidation of the mechanics of book importation has yet been published. For information on Maritime booksellers, the unpublished Shirley B. Elliott and Douglas Lochhead, "A Dictionary of Maritime Printers, Publishers, Booksellers and the Allied Trades, 1751–1900" (1981) excludes merchants, because of the compilers' concentration on those within the trade itself.

7. The reliance on newspapers is evidenced in the time range of this study. 1752 was the year the first newspaper appeared in Nova Scotia and, indeed, in "Canada."

8. Warren McDougall, "Scottish Books for America in the Mid 18th Century," in Robin Myers and Michael Harris, eds.*Spreading the Word: The Distribution Networks of Print, 1550–1850* (Winchester, 1990) pp. 21–46, especially p. 21.

9. Parker, *The Beginnings of the Book Trade in Canada*, p. 25.

10. See, for example, Robert D. Harlan "William Strahan's American Book Trade, 1774–76," *Library Quarterly*, 31 (1961), pp. 235–44; and Robert D. Harlan, "David Hall's Bookshop and Its British Sources of Supply," in David Kaser, ed.*Books in America's Past: Essays Honoring Rudolph H. Gjelsness* (Charlottesville, Va., 1966), pp. 1–24.

11. David Hall is the best known, due to his surviving correspondence and the secondary literature arising from it; see APS, "David Hall Letter Books, 1750–1771." For an indication of the number of Scottish printers in America, see Isaiah Thomas, *The History of Printing in America with a Biography of Printers* (1874; reprint New York; s.d.).

179

12. The two earliest printers were John Bushell, from America with English roots, and Anthony Henry, who was German. All of the early printers printed either the official gazette for the government, or other newspapers. They are all therefore included in Lynn Murphy and Brenda Hicks, compiler and cataloguer, *Nova Scotia Newspapers: A Directory and Union List, 1752–1988*, 2 vols. (Halifax, N.S., 1990). The best-known Scottish printers in Nova Scotia were the Robertson brothers, James and Alexander, who came as Loyalists to Shelburne and printed a newspaper there for a few years before Alexander's death and James's removal of his press to Charlottetown, where he acted as king's printer for a few years before returning to Scotland. See Douglas C McMurtrie, *The Royalist Printers at Shelburne, Nova Scotia* (Chicago, 1933); and *Dictionary of Canadian Biography* vol. 5 (Toronto, 1983) The most detailed research to date on the Robertsons was carried out by Marion Robertson, "The Loyalist Printers: James and Alexander Robertson," typescript, Public Archives of Nova Scotia (PANS).
13. *The Halifax Gazette*, 23 August 1755, p. 1.
14. Wayne W. McVey and Warren E. Kalbach, *Canadian Population* (Toronto, 1995), p. 35, Table 2.2.
15. This weight, using McDougall's method for calculating number of volumes, represents approximately 89,000 volumes; Warren McDougall, "Copyright Litigation in the Court of Session, 1738–1749, and the Rise of the Scottish Book Trade," *Edinburgh Bibliographical Society Transactions*, 5.5 (1988), p. 15. Whether such a number of books could have been absorbed by the relatively small population of Nova Scotia in this thirty-year period, when a proportion of that population could not read at all or, if they could read, could not afford to purchase books, requires further investigation. It is possible that some of these thousands of volumes were being transhipped to ports in the American colonies or in the West Indies. Some preliminary analysis of the numbers of volumes sent to other colonies, compared with Nova Scotia, has been performed, but to draw potentially accurate conclusions requires analysis of a complex set of variables (including literacy rates, trade routes, presence of local book wholesalers, etc.). Such analysis is planned in a further project which will use geographic information systems technology to aid analyses. See Fiona A Black, Bertrum H. MacDonald and J. Malcolm W. Black, "Geographic Information Systems: A New Research Method for Book History," *Book History*, 1 (1998).
16. The customs data are held, in varying formats, at the Public Record Office (PRO), Kew, and the Scottish Record Office (SRO), Edinburgh. PRO, CUST 14/1–23; and SRO, E 504. Collations of some of these figures are given in Giles Barber's meticulous and seminal paper on the topic; see Giles Barber, "Books From the Old World and for the New: The British International Trade in Books in the Eighteenth Century," *Studies on Voltaire and the Eighteenth Century*, 151 (1976), pp. 185–224. The London figures include New Brunswick within the Nova Scotia total, of course. The annual summary accounts from which they are drawn did not detail which port the books were being sent to, simply which colony.
17. Further research is required to check each advertisement against the individual quarterly account volumes which may include data not collated in the summary statements. SRO, E504/13 Glasgow; E504/15 Greenock; E504/22 Leith; E504/28 Port Glasgow.
18. Lisa Jardine, *Worldly Goods: A New History of the Renaissance* (New York,

1996), p. 142. Jardine is speaking of the earliest stages of an international trade in printed books, but her revisionist conclusions regarding the commercial as opposed to cultural forces leading such a trade are relevant for a clear perspective of the new trade across the Atlantic to Canada four centuries later.

19. The Scottish book trade has, perhaps surprisingly, not received the research attention it deserves. Some meticulous studies have been carried out, such as those by McDougall and Beavan, but there can be no synthesis without extensive further groundwork. The proposed "History of the Book in Scotland" project will, it is hoped, address this lacuna in some measure. See Warren McDougall, "Gavin Hamilton, John Balfour and Patrick Neill: A Study of Publishing in Edinburgh in the 18th Century," Ph.D. dissertation, University of Edinburgh, 1975; and Iain Beavan, "The Nineteenth-Century Book Trade in Aberdeen, with Primary Reference to Lewis Smith," Ph.D. dissertation, Robert Gordon University, 1992. Other studies have addressed the book trade from the perspective of the publication of works traditionally considered those of the Scottish Enlightenment; see for example Richard B. Sher, "'Charles V' and the Book Trade: An Episode in Enlightenment Print Culture," typescript, 1996; and, more broadly, Jennifer J. Carter and Joan H. Pittock, eds., *Aberdeen and the Enlightenment: Proceedings of a Conference Held at the University of Aberdeen* (Aberdeen, 1987).

20. The risks were obviously real in business terms, as a perusal of the bankruptcy records for Scottish members of the book trade indicates. The number of booksellers going bankrupt in Edinburgh and Glasgow doubled between the 1790s and the 1800s. SRO, CS.96, includes "sequestrations." For a lucid brief introduction to the topic of bankruptcies, see Michael Moss, "Sequestrations in the Scottish Printing and Book Trade, 1839–1913," *Publishing History*, 15 (1984), pp. 31–64.

21. *Halifax Gazette*, 14 May 1761.

22. Ian Maxted, *The London Book Trades, 1775–1800: A Preliminary Checklist of Members* (s.l., 1977.) Boynton states that Rivington "may have overrated his market for the large stock of books he imported from England" to New York; Henry Walcott Boynton. *Annals of American Bookselling, 1638–1850*, reprint ed. (New York, 1932, New Castle, Del., 1991), p. 111. It is possible that Rivington was offloading some of this unwanted stock in Halifax. For examples of contemporary comments on Rivington's apparently questionable business methods, see Rosalind Remer, *Printers and Men of Capital: Philadelphia Book Publishers in the New Republic* (Philadelphia, 1996), pp. 53–54.

23. McDougall, "Scottish Books for America in the Mid 18th Century."

24. McDougall, "Scottish Books for America in the Mid 18th Century," p. 37.

25. Bodleian Library, MS Eng. Lett. c. 20 and c. 21, "Kincaid and Bell Letter Books, 1764–1773."

26. McDougall, "Scottish Books for America in the Mid 18th Century." pp. 27–34.

27. Bodleian Library, MS Eng. Lett. c. 20 and c. 21.

28. National Library of Scotland (NLS), MS 790, "Archibald Constable Letter Book, 1817–1820," fol. 293, "Constable to J. Brash and Co., Glasgow," 14 November 1818.

29. See especially David S. Macmillan, "The 'New Men' in Action: Scottish Mercantile and Shipping Operations in the North American Colonies, 1760–1825," in David S. Macmillan, ed., *Canadian Business History: Selected Studies, 1497–1971* (Toronto, 1972), pp. 44–103.

30. McDougall, "Scottish Books for America in the Mid 18th Century," pp. 25–27.
31. John Feather, *The Provincial Book Trade in Eighteenth-Century England* (Cambridge,U.K., 1985), Chapter 4, "The Distribution System."
32. I am very grateful to Sandrine Ferré, who carried out an extensive preliminary search in the *Eighteenth Century Short Title Catalogue* at Dalhousie University on my behalf. Her findings show that considerably less than 50 percent of the titles shipped from Clyde ports had Scottish editions within the previous five years from the date of sailing. See also McDougall, "Scottish Books for America in the Mid 18th Century," p. 25. McDougall's examples are from the 1750s, and my own range from the 1780s to the 1800s.
33. Remer, *Printers and Men of Capital*, pp. 79–82.
34. Fleming's work indicates a total of 206 items (including broadsheets but excluding periodicals) printed in Nova Scotia from 1801 to 1820. Although there would have been other items, no references to which have survived, this is nevertheless a clear indication of the relative state of local production; Fleming, *Atlantic Canadian Imprints*, pp. 56–139.
35. There were insufficient subscribers to keep the magazine alive for long. See Thomas Vincent and Ann La Brash, *The Nova Scotia Magazine, 1789–1792: Contents Report and Index*, Occasional Papers of the Department of English, Royal Military College, 4 (Kingston, Ont., 1982).
36. *Nova Scotia Gazette and Weekly Chronicle*, 8 August 1786, p. 3.
37. *Royal Gazette and New Brunswick Advertiser*, 17 October 1786, p. 3.
38. Practical works were advertised by general merchants such as Richard and James Kidston, and by printers such as Robert Fletcher (not a Scot, in spite of his name). This was not just true of Halifax; not surprisingly a similar pattern has been found in Saint John.
39. A useful measure of the popularity of titles is the number of editions which were published. *The Eighteenth Century Short Title Catalogue* and *The Nineteenth Century Short Title Catalogue* are the standard sources for locating numbers of editions. In addition, for fiction, see James Raven, *British Fiction, 1750–1770: A Chronological Check-List of Prose Fiction Printed in Britain and Ireland* (Newark, N.J., 1987).
40. There were only six titles in common between Millet's consignment in Halifax and Campbell's in Saint John, which does not suggest, though it does not preclude, the same bookseller or shipper in Britain.
41. NLS., MS 791, "Archibald Constable Letter-Book, 1820-1822," "Constable to John Young," Halifax, 26 March 1821.
42. *Nova Scotia Royal Gazette*, 17 April 1806, p. 3. The quotation offers one commentator's perception of North American print culture, which possibly reflects more than the eighteenth-century equivalent of advertising "hype." The "increasing taste" referred to may possibly reflect simply the increasing numbers of non-aboriginal residents on the other side of the ocean. The taste of individuals may not have increased at all as there is evidence from the earliest periods of English trading and settlement that individuals craved books and magazines and went to considerable lengths to acquire them.
43. NLS., MS 791, "Archibald Constable Letter-Book, 1820-1822," "Constable to Archibald McQueen," Miramichi, 19 August 1820.
44. NLS., MS 791, "Archibald Constable Letter-Book, 1820-1822," "Constable to

John Young," Halifax, 26 March 1821.

45. Some of the historical literature of banking useful for this study includes Stanley Chapman, *The Rise of Merchant Banking* (London 1984); Duncan McDowall, *Quick to the Frontier: Canada's Royal Bank* (Toronto, 1993); and Joseph Schull, and J. Douglas Gibson, *The Scotiabank Story: A History of the Bank of Nova Scotia, 1832–1982* (Toronto, 1982).

46. James Raven, "Establishing and Maintaining Credit Lines Overseas: The Case of the Export Book Trade from London in the Eighteenth Century, Mechanisms and Personnel," in Laurence Fontaine et al., eds., *Des personnes aux institutions réseaux et culture du crédit du XVIe au XXe siècle en Europe* (Mons, Belgium, 1997), pp. 144–62, passim. Raven makes clear the tedious and costly mechanims involved in the payment for books—these could have involved paper currency, bills of exchange or promissary notes. For a variety of reasons, bills of exchange were used often in transatlantic affairs.

47. The letter gave, in great detail, the reasons why the Scottish bookseller felt forced to shorten the period of credit on the transatlantic shipments of Bibles; Historical Society of Pennsylvania (HSP), "Lea & Febiger Papers," "James and Andrew Duncan, Glasgow, to Mathew Carey, Philadelphia," 1797. I am grateful to Warren McDougall for alerting me to this source.

48. Edinburgh City Library (ECL), Edinburgh Room, "Creech Letter Book, 1798–1809." I am grateful to Rick Sher for alerting me to this source. See also SRO, RH4/26A Dalguise Muniments, Creech MSS. This latter collection includes mainly letters to other booksellers in Edinburgh and London, but Benjamin Franklin and others in the American colonies are also in evidence. What is wholly lacking is any correspondence with booksellers in Canada.

49. "Creech Letter Book, 1798–1809." "Creech to Tod," 28 December 1798. Some of the debts were not inconsiderable—Robert Campbell, bookseller in Philadelphia, owed Creech £166 7s 1d.

50. Raven, "Establishing and Maintaining Credit Lines Overseas."

51. Raven, "Establishing and Maintaining Credit Lines Overseas."

52. "Halifax County Original Estate Papers," J1-J4 [microfilm], "John Kirby, Merchant, Inventory, 1780," PANS. Kirby is described as a chandler and shopkeeper by the registrar for the Probate Court. The inventory of his store's stock on Buckingham Street in Halifax runs to thirty-three pages. His total estate was valued at over £11,000. There is evidence of supplies of Dilworth's spelling books, primers, Testaments, Common Prayer Books, etc.

53. Bodleian Library, MS Eng. Lett. c. 20 and c. 21, "Kincaid and Bell Letter-Books, 1764–1773," APS, "David Hall Letter-Books, 1750–1771.

54. *A Facsimile Reprint of Jones's Directory or Useful Pocket Companion for the Year 1789* (Glasgow, 1973), p. v.

55. *Nova Scotia Royal Gazette*, 20 August 1801, p. 2.

56. The reference for delineating which almanacs were likely to have been available in Halifax is the collection in the library of the Public Archives of Nova Scotia. This is an acceptable way to gauge the presence of almanacs, though some caution is required; the provenance is not always known and therefore some of the almanacs consulted may have arrived in Halifax considerably after their dates of publication. The non-Canadian almanacs examined include W. M'Feat, *The New Glasgow Almanack for 1806* (Glasgow, 1806 [1805?]); *The Aberdeen Almanack*

for the year 1795 (Aberdeen, [1794]); and John Nathan Hutchins, *Hutchins Improved, Being an Almanack and Ephemeris . . . 1782* (New York, [1781]). For the use of almanacs as primary business sources, see Judy Donnelly, "January Hath 31 Days: Early Canadian Almanacs As Primary Research Materials," *Papers of the Bibliographical Society of Canada*, 29.2 (1991), pp. 7–31.

57. See, for example, S. Thomas, *The British Negotiator: or, Foreign Exchanges Made Perfectly Easy* (London, 1791), ESTC, t146850.

58. For example, David Steel, *The Ship-Master's Assistant and Owner's Manual: Containing Complete Information, as well to Merchants, Masters of Ships. . . .* (London, 1788), ESTC, t066545.

59. Robert Fletcher, the printer, advertised this book which he had received from London; *Nova Scotia Gazette and Weekly Chronicle*, 1 September 1772), p. 3. For a listing of contemporary directories covering Scotland, see D. Richard Torrance, comp., *Scottish Trades and Professions: A Selected Bibliography Including a Summary of Scottish Directories* (s.l., 1991), p. 2.

60. This was written specifically for London booksellers wishing to deal with British provincial booksellers and published in 1785; Graham Pollard, ed., *The Earliest Directory of the Book Trade by John Pendred, 1785* (London, 1955).

61. For example, population figures were printed in the *London Magazine* in May 1755. Regardless of their accuracy, they were the figures which businessmen in London and elsewhere would rely on as a source of information about the colonies. On this occasion, Halifax and Lunenberg were credited with five thousand inhabitants, "exclusive of the Military Forces, in the Pay of the Government, and Negroes."

62. The types of queries to which contemporary booksellers required answers are essentially the same as those posed by John Feather for the provincial trade in England; Feather, *The Provincial Book Trade*, p. 44. Feather's explanations and answers form a very useful foundation from which to assess the situation for overseas booksellers.

63. For example, a copy of *The London Catalogue of Books . . . With Their Sizes and Prices* (London, 1791) is held in PANS and may well have circulated amongst Halifax residents and merchants.

64. Hugh Johnston is one of the better-known Scottish merchants in the Maritimes; he arrived in Saint John in 1784 from Morayshire "in a vessel owned by himself and laden with the merchandize with which he commenced business"; William Franklin Bunting, *History of St. John's Lodge, F. And A.M. Of Saint John, New Brunswick, Together with Sketches of All Masonic Bodies in New Brunswick, From A.D. 1784 to A.D. 1894* (Saint John, 1895), p. 221. See also *Dictionary of Canadian Biography*, vol. VI (Toronto, 1987).

65. *Saint John Gazette and Weekly Advertiser*, 4 November 1796), p. 1. Johnston may have heard about this work from contacts in Scotland, or he may have seen the single-sheet prospectus which was published, possibly in Edinburgh, in 1795, ESTC, t096483. The four-volume work was printed in 1795–1796 by Adam Neill of Edinburgh; ESTC, t096464.

66. *Nova Scotia Royal Gazette*, 21 May 1801, p. 3.

67. See Mary Ferguson and Ann Matheson, *Scottish Gaelic Union Catalogue (SGUC): A List of Books Printed in Scottish Gaelic From 1567 to 1973* (Edinburgh, 1984), p. 7. The phrase "almost certainly" is used deliberately, as Gaelic Bibles for the

British and Foreign Bible Society (BFBS) were printed in London (1807, SGUC, 79) considerably before they had an Edinburgh edition (1826, SGUC, 83). However, Testaments and selections (such as Proverbs) were published in Scotland first. See, for example SGUC, 148–49, 271–72, 275–80. For BFBS, see also Leslie Howsam, *Cheap Bibles: Nineteenth-Century Publishing and the British and Foreign Bible Society* (Cambridge, U.K., 1991).

68. There were several such societies, although the BFBS only had one title in its "catalogue." The Society in Scotland for Promoting Christtian Knowledge was an active promoter of Gaelic religious works; see SGUC.

69. *Nova Scotia Royal Gazette*, 17 June 1802, p. 3.

70. The business records of the Lumsden firm have apparently not survived. "There is no hint that any serious attempt was made to invade the English market which was already well provided for by Newbery, Harris, Marshall and others"; S. Roscoe and R.A. Brimmell, *James Lumsden & Son of Glasgow: Their Juvenile Books and Chapbooks* (Pinner, Middlesex, 1981), p. xi. However, shipment of their books from a local wharf may indeed have occurred. Lumsden items are in evidence in Canadian repositories, including the Osborne Collection of children's materials in Toronto.

71. For an overview of the Glasgow trade, especially figures to support the contention that bookselling rather than printing was paramount in the trade after the 1770s, see Roy A. Gillespie, "The Glasgow Book Trade to 1776," in Kevin McCarra and Hamish Whyte, eds., *A Glasgow Collection: Essays in Honour of Joe Fisher* (Glasgow, 1990), pp. 53–63, especially p. 63.

72. This number is exclusive of specialty lists printed separately for circulating libraries or for booksellers, none of which apparently have survived. In addition, these figures represent the state of this research project in September 1996.

73. Rosalind Remer, *Printers and Men of Capital*; and James N. Green, "From Printer to Publisher: Mathew Carey and the Origins of Nineteenth-Century Book Publishing," in Michael Hackenberg, ed.*Getting the Books Out: Papers of the Chicago Conference on the Book in 19th-Century America* (Washington, D.C., 1987), pp. 26–44.

74. John Hare and Jean-Pierre Wallot, "Le livre au Québec et la librairie Neilson au tournant du XIXe siècle," in Claude Galarneau and Maurice Lemire, eds., *Livre et lecture au Quebec, 1800–1850* (Québec, 1988), pp. 93–112; and "John Neilson," *Dictionary of Canadian Biography*, vol. VII (Toronto, 1988). The Neilson Papers, held at the National Archives of Canada, are the richest single collection relating to the early printing history of Canada.

75. This table shows only the number of shipments. A full analysis of the significance of the geographic spread of the trade will necessarily include the quantities of books (at the very least the number of titles) in each shipment.

76. Because of the different data-gathering techniques used in these two files, the figures are not directly comparable over the turn of the century. Within NSTC, which is not as comprehensive in coverage as ESTC, it is not possible to search by country of publication, each town having to be searched separately.

77. NSTC does not offer the facility to search by country of publication and thus differs from ESTC. In addition, and more importantly, NSTC does not claim to be a comprehensive record of publications in that century. Therefore all nineteenth-century figures are, by definition, low.

78. *Halifax Journal*, 2 May 1799, p. 2.
79. The primary, and sometimes only, source for deducing the primary occupation/ business is newspaper evidence. General merchants acting in part as booksellers were not unique to the colonies. An example from Britain at this time is the general shopkeeper, Mr. Dent, whose business, including his dealings in books, is detailed in T.S. Willan, *An Eighteenth-Century Shopkeeper: Abraham Dent of Kirkby Stephen* (Manchester, 1970), especially Chapter 1 and Appendix II. I am grateful to John Feather for alerting me to this source.
80. His obituary referred to him in conventional, unexciting, though clearly respectful terms as "a sincere Christian, steady friend and an honest man"; recorded in *Reminiscences*, 1 February 1896, a scrapbook of clippings in the Legislative Library of Nova Scotia. I am grateful to Shirley Elliott for this information.
81. I am grateful to my colleague Kenneth G. Aitken of Regina Public Library for his genealogical research expertise, which helped delineate Morrison's family links in Scotland.
82. Morrison's earliest known advertisement lists him as a binder and stationer (or more precisely a paper cutter); *Nova Scotia Gazette and Weekly Chronicle*, 5 December 1786, p. 1. "A large collection of Books and a general assortment of paper and other stationary" appears in the *Royal Gazette and Nova Scotia Advertiser*, 18 June 1799, p. 3. One set of the *English Encyclopedia* 10v 4to was advertised by Morrison to be sold for "first cost and charges" in the *Nova Scotia Royal Gazette*, (19 April 1808) supplement. NSTC lists such an encyclopedia with a London publication date of 1802; NSTC, E885.
83. *Royal Gazette and Nova Scotia Advertiser*, 18 June 1799, p. 3.
84. Alexander Morrison's will is held in the Office of the Registrar Probate, District of the County of Halifax, M-163.
85. I am grateful to John Morris and Graham Hogg of the National Library of Scotland for searching the online and card index of the "Scottish Book Trade Index" on my behalf in 1995. I am further grateful to John Morris for since providing me with a copy of the electronic file of the index.
86. *Royal Gazette and Nova Scotia Advertiser*, 18 June 1799, p. 3.
87. For further discussion on the discrepancy between customs accounts and book arrivals as advertised in Maritime newspapers, see below and Appendix B.
88. The method for calculating numbers of volumes from valuation and weight is drawn from McDougall, "Copyright Litigation," p. 15.
89. The first Kidston advertisement appeared in Anthony Henry's *Royal Gazette and Nova Scotia Advertiser*, 23 June 1789. Five of the advertisements appeared in the newspaper of John Howe, the King's Printer, called the *Halifax Journal*: 7 January 1796, 5 May 1796, 16 June 1796, 24 May 1798 and 2 May 1799.
90. *Halifax Gazette*, 14 May 1761.
91. See, for example, *Nova Scotia Chronicle*, 20–27 June 1769.
92. *Royal Gazette and Nova Scotia Advertiser*, 23 June 1789, p. 3. Richard Kidston (elder) migrated from Logie in Scotland to New York in 1781 and thereafter moved north with the Loyalists; PANS, MG 100, vol. 172, no. 5-5d, "Kidston Family—Genealogy." Letter from John Kidston to unknown recipient, 1 January 1824. The Kidston's had a personal interest in books, as well as a commercial involvement, and when Richard's grandson died in 1836 the probate inventory includes amongst his personal possessions "one cow, two steers and ninety vol-

umes of books." PANS, "Halifax County Original Estate Papers," K1-K57 [microfilm], "Kidston Family Estate, 1813–1836."

93. The two advertisements appeared in *Halifax Journal*, 5 May 1796, p. 3 and *Halifax Journal*, 16 June 1796, p. 3.

94. For the 1799 shipment, see *Halifax Journal*, 2 May 1799, p. 2, and "Kidston Family—Genealogy." At some point in the early nineteenth century, one of Richard Kidston's sons, William, went to Glasgow and started a merchant operation there. There is evidence of his firm in the customs records; see, for example, SRO, E504/15/101, Greenock, 29 July 1813. On board the *Jubilee* (Captain John Morrison) British woollens were shipped to Halifax on behalf of William Kidston "merch[an]t in Glasgow." There is, however, no conclusive proof that this is the same Kidston due to a dearth of business records for the firm on either side of the ocean.

95. James S. MacDonald, *Annals, North British Society, Halifax Nova Scotia, 1768–1903* (Halifax, 1905).

96. "Alexander Brymer," *Dictionary of Canadian Biography*, vol. VI (Toronto, 1987).

97. "Alexander Brymer," *Dictionary of Canadian Biography*.

98. Brown's history remained unpublished; Andrew "Brown," *Dictionary of Canadian Biography*, vol. VI (Toronto, 1987).

99. Hare et Wallot, "Le livre au Québec et la librairie Neilson," p. 110, note 12.

100. For further details, see my "Book Distribution to the Scottish and Canadian Provinces, 1752–1820: Examples of Methods and Availability," In Peter Isaac and Barry McKay, eds., *The Reach of Print* (Winchester, 1998).

101. Not much is known about Forsyth's business. He was apprenticed as bookbinder to Alexander Angus of Aberdeen, 1783–87, and opened his business in Elgin in 1788; "Scottish Book Trade Index" [electronic file]. Forsyth is placed in the context of other circulating library owners in John C. Crawford, "The Origins and Development of Societal Library Activity in Scotland," M.A. thesis, University of Strathclyde, 1981, pp. 53–90, especially p. 85.

102. *Royal Gazette and Nova Scotia Advertiser*, 23 June 1789, p. 3.

103. Isaac Forsyth, *A Catalogue of the Elgin Circulating Library* (Elgin, 1789); and *A Catalogue of Books in the Subscription Library At Dunse* (s.l., 1789).

104. Forsyth, *A Catalogue of the Elgin Circulating Library*; and *Royal Gazette and Nova Scotia Advertiser*, 23 June 1789, p. 3.

105. For details concerning subject content of publications in this century, see John Feather, "British Publishing in the Eighteenth Century: A Preliminary Subject Analysis," *The Library*, 8.1 (1986), pp. 32–46.

106. Forsyth, *A Catalogue of the Elgin Circulating Library*.

107. For "plays," see, for example *Nova Scotia Chronicle*, 15–22 May 1770, p. 167, for sale by the printer Robert Fletcher; and *Halifax Journal*, 2 May 1799, p. 2, for sale by the merchant James Kidston. For "novels," no generic advertisements have been located for Halifax, but the stationer Samuel Bent of Saint John advertised them as such; see *Royal Gazette and New Brunswick Advertiser*, 1 August 1786, p. 2.

108. PANS, MG 1, no. 526A, "Kearny Diary, Halifax, 1795 and Sydney, 1802"; 6 August 1795 and 3 October 1795.

109. "Kearny Diary," 10 June 1795.

110. Earl of Dalhousie, *The Dalhousie Journals*, Marjorie Whitelaw, ed. (Ottawa,

1978), vol. 1, p. 75. I am grateful to David Sutherland of Dalhousie University for his insight regarding Dalhousie's propensity for exaggeration; personal communication, September 1996.

111. Stephen Botein, "The Anglo-American Book Trade Before 1776: Personnel and Strategies." in William L. Joyce, et al., eds., *Printing and Society in Early America* (Worcester, Mass., 1983), pp. 48–82, especially p. 49. The implication is that British booksellers were offloading unwanted stock.

112. PRO, CUST 14/1–23.

9

Mediating a Scottish Enlightenment Ideal:
The Presbyterian Dissenter Attack on Slavery in Late Eighteenth-Century Nova Scotia

Barry Cahill

Most studies of the Scottish factor in British North American antislavery focus on the mid-nineteenth century and the Scottish Free Church opposition to plantation slavery in the southern United States.[1] Even studies which purport to examine the role of antislavery in the context of the Scottish Enlightenment, the American Revolution and Atlantic reform tend to project antislavery to the much later period following the statutory abolition of slavery throughout the British Empire in 1833.[2] This chapter examines the central role of the Scottish Enlightenment in forming early Canadian antislavery thought and preparing the ground for the attack on slavery. Its purpose is to help scholars whose interest is in the genesis of the controversy over slavery in British North America, by enabling them to draw upon the ideological roots of antislavery in another society.

John Moir, the leading historian of Canadian presbyterianism, has described the Scottish Secession, an early-eighteenth-century presbyterian dissenting church, as "aggressively mission-oriented."[3] There can be no doubt that the mission to Nova Scotia, which commenced in 1765—a mere twelve years after the first Secession Church missionary was sent to America—was responsible for the introduction and establishment of presbyterianism in the province.[4] By the late 1780s the Secession had also become a vehicle for the introduction of antislavery, one of the commonplace ideas of the Scottish Enlightenment.[5] Its introducer was the young Gaelic-speaking missionary, the Reverend James MacGregor (1759–1830), an antislavery radical whose *Letter to a Clergyman Urging him to set free a Black Girl he held in Slavery*, pub-

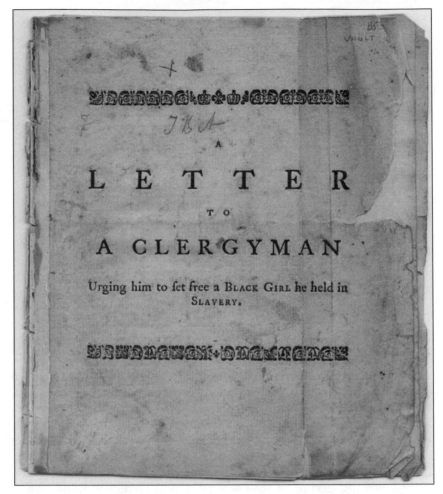

Figure 9.1　Title page of Rev. James MacGregor, *Letter to a Clergyman . . .* Halifax, 1788 (Courtesy of Special Collections,
Killam Library, Dalhousie University)

lished in Halifax in 1788, is the earliest and most outstanding production of
white antislavery literature in Canada.[6] Acquaintance with it will help to make
knowledge of antislavery opinion in the Maritimes a little less fragmentary.[7]

The circumstances of most African-Americans in Loyalist Nova Scotia,
between the mass emigration of 1783 and the exodus of 1791, were so desperate that MacGregor's pamphlet was the spark which set the slow fires of
antislavery to burning. The late 1780s saw the Antiburgher wing of the Secession Church mission to Nova Scotia provide an essential fillip to the antislavery agenda in British North America, which the Methodists (including the

African Methodists) and Quakers had inaugurated in the aftermath of the American Revolution.[8] The Secession Church mission was itself divided along slavery and antislavery lines. The immediate object of the attack was the Burgher minister Reverend Daniel Cock of Truro, who held slaves, while the attacker was the Antiburgher minister MacGregor, who condemned the practice.[9] Both of them were expatriate Scots educated at the University of Glasgow. Yet the real object of the attack was colonial slavery, a moribund social institution in Nova Scotia which had been given a new lease on life by enthusiastic slaveholders among the Loyalist refugees.

But it was neither to Loyalists nor their slaves that James MacGregor had come to Nova Scotia to minister. By birth and upbringing a true child of Ebenezer Erskine's "First" or original Secession of evangelical ministers from the established Church of Scotland in 1733, MacGregor was also a product of the Scottish Enlightenment.[10] In 1779 he matriculated at the University of Glasgow,[11] which had undergone a revival and gained a national reputation thanks to the philosophers and scientists of the Enlightenment.[12] It was the scholars of the Enlightenment who also, according to Duncan Rice, "perfected most of the eighteenth century's rational arguments against slavery."[13] The ideas of Francis Hutcheson and John Millar, both professors at Glasgow University, went directly to the Scottish abolitionists, of whom MacGregor was one, and it was he who in turn introduced the antislavery legacy of the Scottish Enlightenment to British North America. This Enlightenment ideal was also mediated to the young colonial missionary by the evangelical outlook of the so-called "Antiburghers," the branch of the Secession Church of Scotland which was no less inflexible in its antislavery than in its opposition to civil oath-taking and establishmentarianism.[14] During the 1780s, moreover, the Antiburgher wing of the Secession began to change from being a lowland rural phenomenon to becoming an urban one, the chief centre of which was Glasgow.[15]

The eighteenth-century *locus classicus* of Scottish antislavery was John Millar's *Origin of the Distinction of Ranks* of 1771,[16] which contains a long chapter on slavery and which reached its third edition in the same year as MacGregor matriculated at Glasgow University. Millar (1735–1801), whom Duncan Rice describes as "the only major scholar who gave the London [slave-trade abolition] committee any help,"[17] epitomized the Scottish Enlightenment. An advocate (barrister) by profession, he was a liberal Whig who favoured American independence, was sympathetic to the aims of the French Revolution and was ardently opposed to the slave trade. He assumed the chair of civil law at Glasgow in 1761 and held it for forty years. Though MacGregor's antislavery polemic seems not to have been directly influenced by the critique contained in "Millar on Ranks," the intellectual origins of MacGregor's antislavery are to be situated in his two years of undergraduate study at Glasgow, where he would have been exposed to the lectures of Millar and the writings of

Frances Hutcheson, Adam Ferguson (of Edinburgh) and Adam Smith. It was from the writings of the earlier Glasgow professors—especially Hutcheson, who "derationalized" slavery by showing that it was antinatural—that MacGregor derived the philosophical basis of his moral indictment of slavery. Hutcheson, professor of moral science and natural philosophy at Glasgow, counted among his students both Adam Ferguson and Adam Smith, who succeeded to Hutcheson's chair and taught Millar.

The year previous to MacGregor's admission to the university, a decision by the chief court in Scotland had, in the words of Millar, "condemn[ed] the slavery of the negroes in explicit terms, and, being the first opinion of that nature delivered by any court in the island, may be accounted an authentic testimony of the liberal sentiments entertained in the latter part of the eighteenth century."[18] Unlike England and its American empire, in Scotland unqualified or absolute slavery was unheard of, except rarely for condemned criminals. D.M. Walker, the premier historian of Scottish law, states that "slavery and serfdom had disappeared from Scotland long before 1603."[19] Wage slavery, on the other hand, was not colour-based but was an entirely white phenomenon, confined to coal miners and salters whose gradual emancipation by statute began only in 1775 and was not complete until 1799.[20]

The legal rationale of antislavery, which had been articulated in 1760 by the jurist George Wallace, was that perpetual bondage was incompatible with the status of fundamental rights guaranteed by Scottish habeas corpus.[21] How far contemporary Scottish law and jurisprudence had advanced beyond the horizon of their English and colonial counterparts was well brought out by Nan Wilson in her seminal 1970 article, "Legal Attitudes to Slavery in Eighteenth Century Britain: English Myth, Scottish Social Realism and Their Wider Comparative Context":[22] the "English myth" was that the famous *Somerset* case of 1772 abolished slavery, whereas in fact it merely caught up with Scottish law by establishing that habeas corpus was colour-blind; "Scottish realism" was the debatable assumption that common-sense philosophy, rather than the Scottish Enlightenment tradition out of which it developed, provided the intellectual underpinnings of antislavery and slave-trade abolitionism; and the "wider comparative context" was scientific jurisprudence, to which antislavery radicalism was a distinctively Scottish contribution. Wilson's article supports the view that "the contribution of Scottish law to the repudiation of slavery in Britain has been underestimated."[23] The same could be said of the contribution of the Scottish Enlightenment to preparing the attack on slavery in British North America.

In another respect, however, the wider comparative context was not so much the failure of attempts to introduce colour slavery into the kingdom of Scotland as the Scottish attack on the international slave trade, from which not even Glasgow itself was immune. Lord Chief Justice Mansfield's narrow ruling in *Somerset* (1772), which established that an alleged slave could not be forcibly removed from England, had even less impact in Scotland than it did in England because colour slavery did not exist and wage slavery was about to be statutorily abolished.[24] If wage slavery was declared illegal because a state of servitude could not be allowed to exist in a free country such as the kingdom of Scotland, then, *a fortiori*, colour slavery was inconsistent with the principles of natural law on which the law of Scotland was based. The Scotch appeal case, *Knight* v. *Wedderburn* (1778), was everything that England's "Negro case" (*Somerset*) was supposed to be but in fact was not. A Black slave, brought from the plantations, acquired his freedom absolutely upon arriving in Scotland and could sue for wages. Such was not the case in England, where a slave remained a slave, though he was safe from deportation.[25]

The legal "non-status" of slavery in Scotland was only very obliquely referred to by MacGregor, who mentioned in passing "the laws of Great-Britain . . . abolishing slavery";[26] for "Great Britain," of course, one must read "Scotland," and for "slavery" one must read "wage slavery." Colour slavery was no more legislatively abolished in Scotland, where it did not exist, than in England, where it did. As an antislavery thinker and writer, James MacGregor, whose conscientious abolitionism did not really owe very much to natural-law jurisprudence, exemplified "the zealous antislavery propaganda of other Scottish ministers and moralists, such as Thomas Somerville and James Beattie."[27] The latter especially, an "evangelical, common-sense philosopher" who held the chair of moral philosophy at Aberdeen, was untypical of the academy in that, like Professor Millar, he was also an active, campaigning abolitionist. Scottish antislavery, like the Presbyterian dissenters themselves, was aggressively missionary, and its mission field was both England and its American empire. Like that staunch abolitionist and signatory of the Declaration of Independence, Dr. Benjamin Rush (after his return to Philadelphia from Edinburgh University), James MacGregor came to the mission field influenced by the Scottish Enlightenment's critique of slavery. Moreover, as Duncan Rice points out, "For Scottish evangelicals, criticism of the institution and activist commitment to get rid of it were inseparable. By the late [seventeen-] eighties . . . the whole tenor of Scotland's religious life was changing."[28] No sooner had the Antiburgher presbytery reconstituted itself as the General Associate Synod in May 1788 than the new court formally "declared its abhorrence of the slave-trade and urged efforts for emancipation."[29]

When he arrived in Nova Scotia in July 1786, MacGregor was—according to his grandson, biographer and editor, the Reverend George Patterson—"fired with the controversy then agitating Britain on the slave trade."[30] The previous month, Thomas Clarkson, whose brother John was to be instrumental in the exodus of the free Blacks from Nova Scotia to Sierra Leone in 1791, had published in London his celebrated *Essay on the Slavery and Commerce of the Human Species, particularly the African.* . . . MacGregor opposed Black slavery in Old Scotland, where it did not exist; he would now oppose it on practical terms in New Scotland, where it did. It was perhaps easier to be an antislavery radical in Scotland, where colour slavery had no legal or empirical existence, than in British North America, which had recently experienced an influx of not only free-born Blacks and emancipated slaves but slaveholding Loyalists. Some of the latter, who had been dispossessed of their human property, were prepared to use any means available in order to enslave free Blacks or re-enslave fugitives who had been emancipated by the British military authorities during the war. For many Loyalists—not to mention the New England Planters, who had colonized the vacant Acadian lands between 1759 and 1764—the only good Black was a slave.[31] Antislavery, whether its focus was slave trading or slaveholding, lay well beyond their collective psychological horizon. While the marketing of slaves through public auction was a thing of the past in the Nova Scotia of the later 1780s, slaves were still bought and sold, advertisements offering rewards for the apprehension of runaway slaves still appeared and Loyalist port towns, such as Shelburne, participated quietly in the West Indies slave trade.[32] Indeed, the fact that the unnamed addressee of MacGregor's anonymous *Letter* was the seventy-year-old Reverend Daniel Cock, the Burgher Secessionist minister at Truro (a Scots-Irish township), speaks volumes for the enduring respectability and customary lawfulness of Black slavery in the colonies. Cock, an emigrant from Scotland to Nova Scotia in 1770, had gone native by owning and selling Black slave women.[33] When in Nova Scotia, Cock did as the Nova Scotians did; he could not have held slaves in the Scotland from which he had emigrated. What Duncan Rice describes as the "normal antislavery assumption that there should be no pastoral connection with slaveholders and/or their sympathizers"[34]—typical of controversies over slavery in the nineteenth century—was thus foreshadowed in the eighteenth. This assumption strikingly illustrates just how far ahead of his time MacGregor was.

In the antislavery movement, James MacGregor is important both as a polemicist and an emancipator, all the more so because of the publicity given his activities by his co-religionists in Scotland.[35] The Scottish abolitionists were happy to exploit him as a valuable public relations asset in the campaign for the introduction into the British Parliament of a Bill to abolish the slave trade.[36] In view of the fact that members of the Seceder Antiburgher presbtytery of Glasgow involved themselves from the outset in the struggle for slave-trade abolition, they could hardly have done otherwise than welcome the voluntary contribution of one of their own colonial missionaries, labouring in a foreign field where not only had the attack on slavery not yet begun, but also where a *laisser-aller* slaveholder was to be found within the ministry of the Burgher wing of the Secession Church mission.

Though it is not yet known how wide an effect MacGregor's *Letter* had in abolitionist circles in Scotland, he was certainly one of a small group of emigrant Scots—Zachary Macaulay, James Ramsay, William Dickson ("the Clarkson of Scotland") and James Stephen the Elder[37]—who endeavoured to make a practical contribution to the national campaign against the slave trade. Within three months of the publication of his *Letter*, MacGregor was writing about it to clerical friends and supporters back home. "I am happy to hear you are commenced author on such a commendable Subject as the emancipation of our fellow Creatures," wrote one of them in reply in April 1789; "It is thought a Bill will be brought into Parliament for abolishing the Slave trade, or at least for the better treatment of the Slaves, but what will be done in that business is hard to say."[38] MacGregor afterwards enclosed six copies of the *Letter* to his "good friend," the Reverend John Buist, an Antiburgher minister at Greenock, who so approved its contents that he had the following notice inserted in the *Glasgow Advertiser*: "The Rev. Mr James MacGregor, Gaelic Missionary from the Antiburgher Presbytery of Glasgow to Pictou, Nova Scotia, has published in that country against the slave trade, and has since recommended his doctrine by a noble and disinterested philanthropy, in his devoting a part of his small stipend for purchasing the liberty of some slaves." This advertisement, Buist reported to MacGregor,

> was copied in the newspapers through Britain, and your name is famous. Luckily it appeared in that Glasgow paper that the resolutions and subscriptions by David Dale for £10 and other Glasgow gentlemen to the amount of £170, for carrying the Bill for abolishing the slave trade appeared, and was placed just a few lines before their advertisement requesting others to subscribe. I have virtually approved your book.[39]

MacGregor's pamphlet seems to have been well received in Scotland, where wage slavery had been statutorily abolished more than a dozen years before; where the illegality of colour slavery had been reaffirmed, *ipso jure*; and where the movement for statutory abolition of the slave trade was accelerating. Unique in British North America, MacGregor was unusual even in metropolitan Scotland in that he had been exposed not only to the secular Enlightened critique of slavery but also to radical evangelical imperatives of the sort that had impelled the General Associate Synod to take an official and public stand on the issue. In terms of the Scottish abolitionist agenda, MacGregor's timing was perfect; here was a committed and active abolitionist who was also a private emancipator. He had put his money where his mouth was by practising what he preached and using his meagre stipend to ransom and redeem Black slaves from their obliging owners.[40] How unlike those "genteel eighteenth-century Scots," who, according to Duncan Rice, "appear to have shrugged off any responsibility to put theory into practice."[41]

No one reading MacGregor's pamphlet could doubt that its author was a whig-presbyterian, having a good deal in common with the radical literati of Glasgow.[42] What is perhaps most remarkable about MacGregor's abolitionist tract is that it appears to combine the radical evangelicalism of the Antiburgher Seceders (whose opposition to the anti-Jacobite Burgess Oath placed them in a minority in their own dissenting church) with the politics of the radical whigs. That the language of MacGregor's pamphlet is scriptural is simply a reflection of the *ad hominem* and polemical character of the work. He recapitulates, but only with a view to refuting, the various proslavery arguments made on the basis of biblical interpretation. His principal idea, that slavery is so gross a violation of natural law that the master is the greater slave, derives from Hume and ultimately from Montesquieu, whose influence, according to Rice, was farthest-reaching on the writers of the Scottish Enlightenment.[43] MacGregor is indeed a prime example of "the early colonial pamphleteers who absorbed Montesquieu most fully, though they seem to have done so second-hand, through the writings of Ferguson, Hutcheson, Wallace and Beattie."[44]

Stylistically, there are undoubted similarities between MacGregor and Montesquieu. The rhetorical counterfactual argument and sarcastic irony of the conclusion to MacGregor's pamphlet reminds one of the famous fifth chapter ("Of the Slavery of the Negroes") in book xv of *L'Esprit des Lois*:

> As far as I see, Reverend Sir, you are under the necessity of renouncing every thing amiable, divine or human, before the curse of Canaan entitle you to enslave your fellow creatures. You must also grant, 1. That you have hitherto been sinfully negligent in the slave trade; for if it be a duty at all you should do it in whatsoever your hand findeth to do, with all your might, and yet I believe, you might have done ten times more if you had been zealous enough for the glory of God, and the slavery of man. 2. That all men are to be exhorted and commanded in the name of the Lord to enslave their brethren, and that those who are remiss should be censured. 3. That the laws of Great-Britain, France, Pennsylvania, etc., abolishing slavery, laws which are the envy of neighbouring states, are most iniquitous and oppressive, incapacitating the inhabitants from performing the glorious duty of chaining, whipping and killing innocent men.[45]

Nevertheless, MacGregor's letter is perhaps unique among eighteenth-century polemics on slavery, especially in the American colonies and in Scotland, in that he neither quotes from nor alludes to Montesquieu. The unnamed "fine writer" who *is* quoted at the very end—"Let avarice defend it as it will, there is an honest reluctance in humanity against considering our fellow-creatures as a part of our possessions"[46]—is not Montesquieu in translation.

Antislavery, as a conception typical of the Scottish Enlightenment, was introduced into British North America through James MacGregor, who was but one of the many spokes of an Atlantic intellectual wheel, at the hub of which lay the Scottish universities. It was in Nova Scotia that MacGregor adapted the message of the antislavery radicals, such as James Beattie of Aberdeen and the jurisprudent George Wallace, in order to create a work of abolitionist propaganda which in turn would be transmitted back to Scotland. One wonders how many copies of MacGregor's now extremely rare pamphlet were printed,[47] and what became of the six copies that were received in Glasgow in 1791.

MacGregor's polemic casts new light on early antislavery radicalism and is no less revealing of the central role of the Scottish Enlightenment in antislavery thought than is Wallace's legal critique of slavery in the context of scientific-whig jurisprudence. Like Wallace, the MacGregor of the *Letter to a Clergyman* has been viewed both within and outside the Presbyterian Church in Canada as a dangerous radical;[48] indeed, James W. St.G. Walker excluded MacGregor's polemic from his discussion of antislavery in his monolithic 1976 study, *The Black Loyalists*. Robin Winks, however, not only devoted a long chapter of his masterwork *The Blacks in Canada* (1971) to "The Attack on Slavery in British North America, 1793–1833" but also dealt at length with James MacGregor.[49] Although MacGregor's conscientious antislavery was perhaps a little too radical and utopian to play a major role in the British North American abolitionist movement which he helped to launch, it was certainly one of the channels through which the writers of the Scottish Enlightenment influenced the development of antislavery ideology in the colonial period. Unlike the Scots abolitionists in Scotland, moreover, whose contribution before 1833 is severely downplayed by Rice,[50] James MacGregor contributed more to the practice than to the theory of antislavery.

If there is a Scottish factor in the attack on slavery in British North America, then it was first and foremost the antislavery witness of the Reverend James MacGregor. Radical in both his antislavery and his evangelicalism, MacGregor perfected antislavery as an overwhelmingly evangelical sentiment. Unlike his expatriate contemporaries who returned from the West Indies convinced of the immorality of slavery and went on to become abolitionist leaders in Great Britain, MacGregor went out to America a diehard opponent of slavery. His earliest experiences as a young colonial missionary drove him to become a polemicist and emancipationist. For MacGregor, slave-trade abolitionism was a test of evangelical commitment long before the revival of Scottish Evangelicalism in the early nineteenth century turned antislavery into a popular and fashionable movement. Though the urgency of MacGregor's concern over slavery stemmed from his radical evangelicalism, his antislavery was by no means a mere transition from Enlightenment to evangelical reform. This first emigrant Scot translated antislavery criticism into antislavery commitment. If he was influenced by secular teachers, his mentors would have been his professors at Glasgow University. It was natural that he should show some dependence on the sceptical, cosmopolitan world of enlightened Glasgow, which had been propagating a fully developed critique of slavery. The Glasgow

Enlightenment had examined and criticized slavery incidentally to solve the same problems and meet the same needs as those of an early antislavery radical such as MacGregor.[51]

James MacGregor perfectly exemplifies the intriguing late-eighteenth-century phenomenon identified by Duncan Rice, "that those Scots most deeply committed to improvement, to progress, and to the values on which the nineteenth century was to be based, were greatly enthused over the future of American society."[52] Like the free Blacks who came to (and then departed from) Nova Scotia in search of a "promised land," MacGregor envisioned the emancipation of slaves and ultimately the abolition of slavery itself as history's hard lesson taught to the unenlightened British by the American Revolution.[53]

Notes

1. See for example J.S. Moir, *Enduring Witness: A History of the Presbyterian Church in Canada* (Kingston and Montreal, 1987 [reproduction of 1974 ed.]), pp. 38–39, 127; R.W. Vaudry, *The Free Church in Victorian Canada [West: Ontario], 1844–1861* (Waterloo, Ont., 1989), index p. 183, s.v. "Slavery."

2. C. Duncan Rice, "Scottish Enlightenment, American Revolution and Atlantic Reform," in Owen Dudley Edwards and George Shepperson, eds., *Scotland, Europe and the American Revolution* (New York, 1977), pp. 75–82.

3. Moir, *Enduring Witness*, 38.

4. See generally James Robertson, *History of the Mission of the Secession Church to Nova Scotia and Prince Edward Island, from its Commencement in 1765* (Edinburgh, 1847). Modern scholarship on this subject is almost nonexistent.

5. A.C. Ross, "Anti-slavery," in Nigel M. de S. Cameron et al., eds., *Dictionary of Scottish Church History and Theology* (Downers Grove, Ill., 1993), p. 18 (hereafter *DSCHT*).

6. Marie Tremaine, comp., *A Bibliography of Canadian Imprints, 1751–1800* (Toronto, 1952), p. 258. MacGregor's antislavery pamphlet is now available in a microfiche edition published by the Canadian Institute for Historical Microreproductions (CIHM no. 94371). For an analysis, see Barry Cahill, "The Antislavery Polemic of the Reverend James MacGregor: Canada's Proto-Abolitionist as 'Radical Evangelical'," in Charles H.H. Scobie and G.A. Rawlyk, eds., *The Contribution of Presbyterianism to the Maritime Provinces of Canada* (Kingston and Montreal, 1997), pp. 131–43.

7. Greg Marquis, "Haliburton, Maritime Intellectuals and the Race Question," in Richard A. Davies, ed., *Haliburton: A Bicentenary Chaplet [Thomas H. Raddall Symposium No. 4]* (Wolfville, N.S., 1997). For the eighteenth century see Barry Cahill, "Slavery and the Judges of Loyalist Nova Scotia," *UNB Law Journal*, 43 (1994), pp. 73–135; and *"Habeas Corpus* and Slavery in Nova Scotia: *R. v. Hecht, ex parte Rachel*, 1798," *UNB Law Journal*, 44 (1995), pp. 179–209.

8. See generally T. Watson Smith, "The Slave in Canada," in Nova Scotia Historical Society, *Collections*, 10 (1899).

9. See Barry Cahill, "'Colchester Men': The Proslavery Presbyterian Witness of the Reverends Daniel Cock of Truro and David Smith of Londonderry," paper pre-

sented at the Fourth Planter Studies Conference, Acadia University, September 1997.

10. See generally S. Buggey, "MacGregor (McGregor), James Drummond," *Dictionary of Canadian Biography*, VI, p. 457.

11. W. Innes Addison, comp., *Matriculation Albums of the University of Glasgow from 1728 to 1858* (Glasgow, 1913), p. 124. There is no evidence to support the received view that MacGregor attended the University of Edinburgh.

12. See generally Andrew Hook and Richard B. Sher, eds., *The Glasgow Enlightenment* (East Linton, S.C., 1995). I am grateful to Dr. Ned Landsman (History, SUNY, Stonybrook) for drawing this important work to my attention and for pointing out that antislavery radicals in the Antiburgher wing of the Secession were by no means political radicals.

13. C. Duncan Rice, *The Rise and Fall of Black Slavery* (London, 1975), p. 160; see pp. 163–76 for the clearest and most comprehensive statement of the central role of the Scottish Enlightenment in Anglo-American antislavery thought. See also by Rice, "Controversies over Slavery in Eighteenth- and Nineteenth-Century Scotland," in Lewis Perry and Michael Fellman, eds., *Antislavery Reconsidered: New Perspectives on the Abolitionists* (Baton Rouge and London, 1979), pp. 24–48; *The Scots Abolitionists, 1833–1861* (Baton Rouge and London, 1981), pp. 18–22; and "The Scottish Enlightenment and the Atlantic Anti-Slavery Impulse" (unpublished manuscript, 1979). A promised monograph on "the Scottish response to slavery before 1833" did not materialize. (I am grateful to Professor Rice, now principal and vice-chancellor of the University of Aberdeen, for sharing with me information on this point.)

14. See generally David C. Lachman, "General Associate Synod," *DSCHT*, pp. 354–55; Callum G. Brown, "Religion and Social Change," in T.M. Devine and Rosalind Mitchison, eds., *People and Society in Scotland: Volume I, 1760–1830* (Edinburgh, 1988), pp. 150–51. "There is no thorough modern treatment of presbyterian dissent," according to Callum G. Brown, *The Social History of Religion in Scotland since 1730* (London and New York, 1987), p. 258.

15. Despite its dependence on the West Indies trade, Glasgow was a centre of Scottish antislavery, "in part, because from around 1780 onwards Scottish Evangelicalism grew in strength of numbers and also in its influence on educated Scots" (Ross, "Anti-slavery," 18).

16. John Millar, *Origin of the Distinction of Ranks*, first edition (Glasgow, 1771); for a modern critical edition, see W.C. Lehmann, *John Millar of Glasgow, 1735–1801: His Life and Thought and His Contributions to Sociological Analysis* (Cambridge, 1960), pp. 167ff.

17. Rice, *Scots Abolitionists*, p. 21.

18. Lehmann, *John Millar*, p. 322. The reference is to *Knight* v. *Wedderburn*, an appeal proceeding before the Court of Session (Scotland's supreme civil court): (1778), Morison's *Dictionary of Decisions*, p. 14545. Millar quotes the judgment, in which the respondent (the alleged slave, Joseph Knight) was represented by no less a figure than the Lord Advocate and which was declaratory of Scottish law upon the liberty of the subject. The appeal case originated in Knight's action to establish his right to freedom and to recover wages.

See also J.B. Nicholson, ed., *An Institute of the Law of Scotland* [Erskine], new ed. (Edinburgh, 1871), p. 240; A.D. Gibb and N.M.L. Walker, eds., *Introduction to the Law of Scotland* [Gloag and Henderson], 6th ed. (Edinburgh, 1956), p. 219; T.B. Smith, "Master and Servant" [The Stair Society], *An Introduction to Scottish Legal History* (Edinburgh, 1958), pp. 137–38. According to Lord Stair, slavery was against the law of nature but was introduced by means of the *jus gentium*; though not unlawful, it had been abolished in Scotland; see David M. Walker, ed., *The Institutions of the Law of Scotland* (Edinburgh and Glasgow, 1981 [repr. of 1693 ed.]), pp. 80, 97–98, 1013.

19. D.M. Walker, *A Legal History of Scotland, Volume IV: The Seventeenth Century* (Edinburgh, 1996), p. 642.

20. See generally [anonymous], "Slavery in Modern Scotland," *Edinburgh Review*, 189 (1899), pp. 119–48.

21. *Act anent Wrongous Imprisonment, 1701*. See generally D.B. Davis, "New Side-lights on Early Antislavery Radicalism," *William and Mary Quarterly*, 3rd ser., 28 (1971), pp. 585–94.

22. Nan Wilson, "Legal Attitudes to Slavery in Eighteenth Century Britain: English Myth, Scottish Social Realism and Their Wider Comparaive Context," *Race*, 11 (1970), pp. 463–75; cited to good effect by James W. St.G. Walker, *The Black Loyalists: The Search for a Promised Land in Nova Scotia and Sierra Leone, 1783–1870* (Toronto, 1992 [repr. of 1976 ed.]), p. 107 n. 5. For eighteenth-century Scottish legalists slavery was an English—or rather, colonial—phenom-enon, of historical interest only, in relation to the comparative study of the sources of law. See, for example, Lord Bankton, *Institute of the Laws of Scotland in Civil Rights* . . . , vol. 1 (Edinburgh, 1993 [repr. of 1751 ed.]), pp. 76–77.

23. P.C. Hogg, *The African Slave Trade and Its Suppression* (London, 1973), p. 312.

24. *An Act for altering, explaining and amending several Acts of the Parliament of Scotland respecting Colliers, Coal-bearers and Salters* (1775), 15 Geo. 3, c. 28, was really a gradual emancipation Act.

25. See the report of *R. v. Knowles, ex parte Somerset*, (1772) 20 St. Tr. 1 (K.B.), which reprints the report of the *Knight* appeal case as a note.

26. MacGregor, *Letter to a Clergyman*, p. 11.

27. Richard B. Sher, *Church and University in the Scottish Enlightenment: The Mod-erate Literati of Edinburgh* (Edinburgh, 1986), p. 189. Somerville (1741–1830) was a Church of Scotland Moderate.

28. Rice, "Controversies over Slavery," p. 35.

29. Lachman, "General Associate Synod," p. 355; John M'Kerrow, *History of the Secession Church*, rev. ed. (Edinburgh, 1845), pp. 343–4. In June 1788 the Rever-end John Buist, Antiburgher minister at Greenock, wrote, "The General Assembly [of the Kirk] have followed the Antiburgher Synod in two things[:] in not petition-ing the house of commons as to the slave trade but publishing their sentiments in opposition to it.": J. Buist to J. MacGregor, 19 June 1788: James MacGregor fonds, file S.4, Maritime Conference Archives (MCA) (Sackville, N.B.); micro-film at Nova Scotia Archives and Records Management (NSARM).

30. George Patterson, *Memoir of the Rev. James MacGregor, D.D., Missionary of the General Associate Synod of Scotland to Pictou, Nova Scotia*; . . . (Philadelphia, 1859), p. 151.

31. See Gary Hartlen, "Bound for Nova Scotia: Slaves in the Planter Migration, 1759–1800," in Margaret Conrad, ed., *Making Adjustments: Change and Conti-nuity in Planter Nova Scotia, 1759–1800* (Fredericton, N.B., 1991); Allen B.

Robertson, "Bondage and Freedom: Apprentices, Servants and Slaves in Colonial Nova Scotia," in *Royal Nova Scotia Historical Society Collections*, 44 (1996), pp. 57–69, and sources cited in Cahill, "*Habeas Corpus* and Slavery," pp. 205–9.

32. See, for example, Barry Cahill, "Colonel Blucke and Captain Booth: William Booth's 'Rough Memorandums' [1789] as a Source for the History of the Black Experience in Early Shelburne," unpublished paper presented to the Shelburne County Cultural Awareness Society, 25 November 1992.

33. Patterson, *Memoir*, pp. 154–58.

34. Rice, "Controversies over Slavery," p. 45.

35. Patterson, *Memoir*, pp. 152–53.

36. In April 1791 the House of Commons decisively rejected a motion by William Wilberforce, MP, to introduce a limited slave-trade abolition bill; the trade was not to be statutorily abolished until 1807.

37. Rice, "Controversies over Slavery," p. 34.

38. J. Barlas to J. MacGregor, 26 April 1789: James MacGregor fonds, file U.4, MCA.

39. J. Buist to J. MacGregor, 18 March 1791; quoted in Patterson, *Memoir*, pp. 152–53. David Dale (1739–1806) was a prominent industrialist and philanthropist; see article by W.F. Storrar in *DSCHT*, p. 232.

40. Patterson, *Memoir*, pp. 151–52.

41. Rice, *Scots Abolitionists*, p. 21.

42. See Hook and Sher, *Glasgow Enlightenment*.

43. Hook and Sher, *Glasgow Enlightenment*, note 13.

44. Rice, *Black Slavery*, p. 163.

45. MacGregor, *Letter to a Clergyman*, p. 11.

46. MacGregor, *Letter to a Clergyman*, p. 11.

47. Though only one copy is known to be extant, MacGregor's pamphlet appears to have been printed in quantity.

48. On this point see Cahill, "Antislavery Polemic."

49. Robin W. Winks, *The Blacks in Canada: A History*, 2nd ed. (Montreal and Kingston, 1997), pp. 102–5. The commencement date of 1793 refers to Upper Canada (Ontario), which enacted a law prohibiting the importation of slaves.

50. See especially Chapter 1 of Rice, *Scots Abolitionists* ("The Scottish Background and the Atlantic Context"), pp. 18ff.

51. Paraphrasing Rice, "Controversies over Slavery," p. 35.

52. Rice, "Scottish Enlightenment," p. 80.

53. MacGregor, *Letter to a Clergyman*, p. 6.

10

Scottish Influences in Nineteenth-Century Nova Scotian Medicine:
A Study of Professional, Class and Ethnic Identity

Colin D. Howell

Doctors in nineteenth-century Nova Scotia were preoccupied with matters of professional self-definition, concerned about competitors in an uncertain medical marketplace and worried about the shape of a newly emerging commercial and industrial order and their place within it. Much has been written about the process of medical professionalization, the transition from a profession characterized by marginal status and limited public confidence in the first half of the nineteenth century to one of expanded authority and approval in the latter half.[1] In the first half of the century, doctors identified themselves as members of the "gentlemanly professions," which included medicine, law and divinity, and often secured their power through astute political and commercial alliances, by a self-serving rendering of the history of medicine as the vanquishing of ignorance and, for some of the more influential physicians, by reference to their training in Scottish medical schools. By the end of the century, as Nova Scotia's mercantile economy was gradually transformed with the coming of the new industrial capitalist order, medical doctors were more likely to emphasize their "scientific" authority rather than their gentlemanly character and to claim the competence to heal not only ailing bodies but the seemingly diseased body politic.[2]

When understood in a reductionist way, the process of medical professionalization and the discourses that surround it appear simply to be expressions of one interest group's desire to monopolize the provision of health services and to restrict competition in the medical marketplace. This cynical view regards the development of medical licensing regulations, elevated educational standards, the organization of medical associations, and assertions about the profession's social value as little more than a self-serving strategy of market control.[3] Understood more broadly, however, professionalization can be seen as part of a process of class formation, as part of the fashioning of bourgeois identity and its social and cultural hegemony.[4] Indeed, the shifting definitions of the profession's social utility and what doctors considered their public responsibility—first in the mercantile and then in the industrial age—provide interesting insights into the making of the Nova Scotian bourgeoisie in the nineteenth century.

How do ethnicity and, more particularly, Scottish identity fit into this larger context of professionalization and class formation? For many Nova Scotian doctors in the years before Confederation, a sense of professional and class identity was inseparable from their overseas medical training. This chapter addresses the pivotal role that Scottish-trained doctors played in the pre-Confederation professionalization process, and the declining importance of that connection by the end of the nineteenth century. The central questions I will address are these: What connection, if any, can be established between ethnic, class and professional identities among nineteenth-century physicians in Nova Scotia? Did training in Scottish medical schools such as the University of Edinburgh—widely regarded as the finest medical school in Britain—influence the social values, status or therapeutic orientation of Nova Scotian physicians? To what extent did practitioners of Scottish heritage draw upon a sentimentalized and romanticized celebration of the accomplishments of Scottish medicine as a way of confirming their own professional authority and influence? And, finally, to what extent did a shift among Nova Scotia's practitioners from overseas training to training at American and Canadian medical schools in the last half of the nineteenth century reveal a reconceptualizing of professional identity that rendered both the image of the professional gentleman and the celebration of Scottish identity largely anachronistic?

Even though much of the early writing on the pre-Confederation Nova Scotian medical profession amounts to a celebration of the work of heroic doctors and a whiggish chronicling of the profession's progress from marginal status to social prominence,[5] it does reveal the particularly intimate connections between leading practitioners and the merchant community in the colony. This is evident in even the most standard biographical profiles of the province's leading physicians. Prominent members of Nova Scotia's medical profession unabashedly cultivated family connections and marriage alliances that contributed to influence among their peers and connected them to the mercantile elite. At the same time, promotion of Scottish identity and connections, demonstration of medical training at either Edinburgh or Glasgow, and a romantic rendering of the place of Scottish doctors in medical history, from William Cullen and Edward Jenner to Joseph Lister, helped some doctors to dominate the professionalization process in Nova Scotia before Confederation. Given the close connection between the medical profession and the merchant class, and the valorization of Scottish medical education, the more prominent doctors in Nova Scotia generally had more in common with their counterparts in Scotland[6] than with those in England.[7]

The intertwining of professional, mercantile and ethnic identities was most evident in pre-Confederation Halifax, where the leading practitioners of the city were drawn from or forged marriage alliances with leading merchant families and drew upon their overseas medical training as a way to secure their leadership within the profession. Even at the beginning of the nineteenth century when, as Allan Marble has pointed out, many civilian practitioners had difficulty making a living and were forced to take up secondary occupations,[8] aspiring young doctors from the colony's leading families were venturing to Scotland in search of medical training. By 1845, thirteen of the fourteen senior practitioners in the city were Edinburgh-trained, and the fourteenth had been trained at Glasgow.[9] As was true of medical doctors throughout British North America, the influence of these professional men derived in large measure from their "appropriate" education, their political respectability and their gentlemanly character, as much as it did from their skill as practitioners.[10]

The first Nova Scotian–born doctor to train overseas was William Bruce Almon, who graduated from Edinburgh University in 1809. Son of a military surgeon and Loyalist who had come to Halifax during the American Revolution as Surgeon of Artillery and Ordnance in the 4th Battalion of Royal Artillery,[11] Almon belonged to a distinguished Halifax family which would contribute physicians and surgeons to the city for more than a century into the future. When young Almon arrived in Edinburgh in October 1806, he carried letters of introduction that reveal the close contacts that prominent families in Nova Scotia had maintained with their Scottish counterparts. After arriving at the Drysdale Hotel on St. Andrew's Street in Edinburgh, Almon immediately called upon a Dr. Turnbull, "an old and intimate acquaintance of my father," and was invited to lodge with him. The next few days were taken up with more letter-delivering to professional and business contacts of his father's, including Drs. Brown, McIntyre and Reid, described as "erstwhile residents of Halifax." Shortly thereafter, Almon began his course of studies at the university. In addition to training in Chemistry, Anatomy, Biology and Natural Philosophy, he was instructed in the virtues of professional responsibility and public service. Almon's diary makes clear the emphasis that his professors placed upon practical knowledge and the cultivation of the characteristics of a professional gentleman. Almon was particularly impressed by John Bell's discussion of the social responsibilities of the physician, and by his professors' condemnation of those who considered medicine a mere trade, practised "only for the sake of filthy lucre."[12]

After graduation Almon returned to Halifax where he set up a medical practice and drug dispensary in partnership with his father, and served as medical and surgical officer of the poorhouse and the jail. He also demonstrated some of the family's business acumen, investing in a number of successful business enterprises in the city. Almon's untimely death from typhus in 1840, contracted while providing medical services to the crew of a ship that arrived in port afflicted with the disease, would subsequently be employed by doctors as evidence of the selfless behaviour and devotion to service that characterized this "gentlemanly profession."

The Almon family was intimately connected to the commercial and political elite in pre-Confederation Halifax. William Bruce's brother, Mather Byles Almon, for example, was one of the original directors of the Bank of Nova Scotia, and its president from 1837 to 1870, and his sister Amelia married James William Johnston, leader of the conservative forces in the colony and opponent of responsible government.[13] William Bruce's son, William James Almon, was educated at King's College in Windsor, where he was a classmate of Edward Cunard, son of the founder of the Cunard Line, and of Charles Tupper, whose lengthy political career included stints as provincial premier, federal cabinet minister and prime minister of Canada. Like Tupper, who also completed a medical degree at Edinburgh, William James's career married medicine and politics. Almon received a medical degree from Glasgow in 1838, followed by postgraduate training in Edinburgh. Over the next three decades, he practised in Halifax and was actively involved in the establishment of the City and Provincial Hospital and the medical faculty at Dalhousie University. Then politics beckoned. After serving as an MP in the John A. Macdonald government between 1872 and 1874, he became the first medical doctor in Canada to be appointed to the Senate.[14]

This blending of Edinburgh training, adroit marriage alliances, business acumen, charitable work and involvement in politics was a commonplace characteristic of the leading members of the Nova Scotian medical profession before Confederation. Daniel McNeill Parker, who apprenticed with William Bruce Almon during the 1830s, enrolled in Edinburgh in 1842 and graduated three years later with the gold medal in anatomy. Parker also spent a summer as a clinical clerk to Sir James Simpson, who would gain international acclaim for first using chloroform in surgery. In 1845, Parker returned to Halifax, established a lucrative private practice and married Eliza Johnston, the eldest daughter of the aforementioned J.W. Johnston. In addition to various charitable efforts, Parker took a keen interest in promoting the mercantile interests of the province in Britain. He was one of the commissioners who arranged for a Nova Scotia exhibit at the Great Exhibition in 1851 in London, for which he received the Prince Albert Medal, and was largely responsible for establishing the Nova Scotia Industrial Exhibition in 1854. A staunch Imperialist and a Tory in politics, Parker served as a legislative councillor in Nova Scotia from 1867 to 1901.[15]

While Parker and the Almons were Nova Scotians who travelled to Scotland to train for a position of leadership within the colony, Scottish immigrants such as William Grigor followed similar career strategies upon arriving in Nova Scotia. Born in Elgin, Scotland, Grigor had received his medical degree from Edinburgh shortly before emigrating to Nova Scotia in 1819. After a few years of practising at Antigonish and Truro, Grigor moved to Halifax in 1824 and quickly assumed a position of influence among the doctors of the city. In April 1827, Grigor married Catherine Louisa Foreman, the daughter of James Foreman, a prominent local merchant of Scottish origin whose fortune was made in the importation of dry goods from Britain and their distribution throughout the colony. By the first decade of the nineteenth century Foreman was the second largest importer on the Halifax waterfront.[16] Grigor's reputation was further enhanced when he and fellow Scot John Stirling, a former naval surgeon, established the first Halifax dispensary to provide medical aid to the poor and indigent. As an outsider and latecomer, however, Grigor found himself at odds with the Almon group and chafed at Almon's monopolistic control over the poor's asylum hospital. As Allan Marble has pointed out for the late eighteenth century, medicine in Nova Scotia, given the uncommon poverty of the region, was intimately connected to poor relief and, in the years before the opening of the City Hospital in 1859, the Poor House provided an important locus for treating the sick and impoverished.[17] The disagreement with the Almons seems to have arisen out of Grigor's desire that the poorhouse be used as a place for all the city's doctors to gain clinical experience, and William Bruce Almon's refusal to open its doors to other physicians.[18] Whatever the reason, Grigor aligned himself with reformers who attacked the Tory establishment of which the Almons were a part. Grigor joined The Club, a group of Joseph Howe's associates whose political satire and attacks on the government graced the pages of Howe's newspaper, the *Novascotian*, from May 1828 to 1831. For many years Grigor was Howe's personal physician and political ally. With the coming of responsible government, Grigor received his political award with an appointment to the Legislative Council in February 1849. Yet, despite the political differences that divided Grigor and the Almon group, they nonetheless had much in common. Whatever their differences, they shared a broader commitment to elevated professional standards, charitable work, economic development and political leadership, all of which were important to bourgeois hegemony in mid-century Halifax.[19]

At the same time, however, the mid-century medical profession faced considerable public suspicion, and considerable competition in the larger marketplace for medical services. Irregular practitioners, proponents of natural and herbal remedies, and quacks of various sorts challenged orthodox practitioners and their reliance upon the techniques of bloodletting, blistering, and dosing with purgatives, which had been dubbed "heroic therapy." Attempts by the profession to monopolize the dispensing of medical services, moreover,

Figure 10.1 Halifax from the Citadel with a view of the Visiting Dispensary (on the far left), c. 1877, Notman Collection (courtesy of the Public Archives of Nova Scotia)

ran against the growing tide of antimonopoly sentiment that energized liberal reformers' attacks on Tory privilege. Despite his friendship with Grigor, for example, Joseph Howe opposed any attempt by the profession to extend its control over the medical marketplace. Although the profession gained greater influence during the 1850s, as witnessed by the establishment of the Halifax Medical Society in 1854 and the opening of both the Nova Scotia Lunatic Asylum and the Halifax City Hospital in 1859, before mid-century, doctors still struggled to improve the profession's reputation.

In the fight to elevate the status of the profession, Edinburgh-trained doctors played a crucial role. Doctors like Parker, the Almons, Grigor, Tupper, Frederick Morris and James DeWolf involved themselves in politics and charitable work, and in the establishment of institutions which enshrined contemporary definitions of scientific medicine and social improvement. Morris, who like Parker had apprenticed with William Bruce Almon before studying at Edinburgh, was resident physician at the Halifax Visiting Dispensary founded in 1855;[20] Parker was a founder of the Halifax Institution for the Deaf and Dumb and the Halifax YMCA; Grigor was first president of both the Halifax Mechanics' Institute and the Halifax Medical Society, and DeWolf was president of the Nova Scotia Philanthropic Society and first superintendent of the Provincial Hospital for the Insane (while at Edinburgh, DeWolf had been house surgeon to the Maternity Hospital and clinical clerk to Professor Sir Robert Christison and subsequently became the first colonial member of the

Medico-Psychological Association of England.)[21]

It is clear that Edinburgh-trained doctors dominated the medical profession in mid-century Halifax, playing leading roles in the establishment of major institutions such as the Hospital for the Insane, the City and Provincial Hospital, and the Visiting Dispensary. They also took the lead in the establishment of professional associations directed at improving the quality of medical care and advancing the interests of the profession in the legislature. In the years to come, the influence of this elite cadre of physicians would extend beyond provincial boundaries. A number of them would play leading roles in the development of the Canadian Medical Association established in 1867. The CMA's first two presidents, Charles Tupper and Daniel McNeil Parker, were Nova Scotians who had been schooled at Edinburgh, and the minute books of the association during its early years reveal a strong contingent of Edinburgh-trained physicians from the Maritimes, including Rufus Black, James DeWolf, William Bayard, Alexander Reid and William Wickwire.[22]

The influential group of Edinburgh graduates who spearheaded the professionalization process in Nova Scotia before Confederation were later joined by John Stewart and Alexander Peter Reid, both of whom studied in Edinburgh at a time of critical shifts in therapeutic fashion and advances in surgical technique. Reid was a leading proponent of scientific research and investigation, and joined Stewart as an early advocate of Joseph Lister's technique of antiseptic surgery. Although Stewart continued to employ the more traditional rhetoric of the profession's gentlemanly character, both he and Reid extolled the scientific foundation of contemporary medicine. Stewart and Reid would subsequently be joined in the promotion of Listerism by Daniel McNeill Parker and A.W.H. Lindsay, both of whom had received first-hand experience in antiseptic surgery at Edinburgh in the early 1870s. In 1871, Parker had temporarily given up his lucrative practice in Halifax to study antisepsis both at Edinburgh and on the continent. At about the same time, Lindsay, a graduate of the Halifax Medical College and Dalhousie University, began postgraduate studies at Edinburgh. Upon their returns to Nova Scotia, Lindsay and Parker joined Reid and Stewart as disciples of Listerism.[23]

It was John Stewart, however, who would eventually take the lead in promoting Listerism throughout the province. Born at Black River, Cape Breton, in July 1848, Stewart was the son of a Scottish presbyterian minister who had emigrated to Cape Breton a number of years earlier. In 1868, Stewart went to Scotland to take over the operation of a farm for an aunt and, after spending a year at the University of Edinburgh, returned to Nova Scotia to enter Dalhousie. In 1874 he returned to Edinburgh to complete a degree in medicine under the tutelage of Joseph Lister. Stewart was associated with Lister successively as dresser, clerk and house-surgeon and accompanied him to King's College Hospital, London, in 1877 when Lister was elected to the Chair of Clinical Surgery. Stewart and Lister became close friends. In the fall of 1878, Stewart decided to return to Nova Scotia, even though urged by Lister to remain with him. Stewart set up a practice in Pictou County and threw himself tirelessly into a campaign in support of antiseptic surgery, which he regarded as a clear example of the profession's scientific awareness.

Despite Stewart's veneration of the scientific underpinning of contemporary medicine, he continued to rely heavily on more traditional discourses of gentlemanly behaviour, like many of his colleagues. Medical journals such as the *Maritime Medical News*, which published monthly from 1888 to 1911, frequently contained articles extolling the elevated status of medical practitioners and the tradition of public service and selflessness that could be found in the past accomplishments of great medical men. John Stewart's own keynote address to the Canadian Medical Association in September 1902, for example, compared the great accomplishments of Joseph Lister to the navigators of the fifteenth and sixteenth centuries who sailed "out into the vast, unknown, unmeasured, unsounded sea, fearing, but daring Mystery, and hoping for the Hesperides."[24] Like those of the great explorers, the heroic biographies of the great doctors suggested the opening up of new worlds. Stewart's whiggish approach to health and medicine connected notions of progress, imperial greatness, gentlemanly sacrifice and scientific inquiry into a compelling celebration of a triumphant and noble profession. His reminiscenses of Lister approached hagiography:

> Lister was a truly great surgeon—he was of infinite resource. No unlooked-for accident, no complication found him unready. He was pathologist as well as surgeon. And yet one thing more: There is no man who remembers Lister's hospital work who was not impressed by his human spirit, his tender regard for the mental and physical suffering of the poor who came under his care.
>
> As a teacher Lister was peerless. His earnestness, enthusiasm, and energy, were contagious and inspired "such love and faith as failure cannot quell." His teaching at the bedside was invariably interesting and practical, and it had all the novelty of a new-found world. His lectures were models of English speech in clearness and simplicity, and the musical voice in which he spoke made them a delight. . . .
>
> Lister was more than a great teacher, he was a great example. Of him, as of the great Duke, we may say, "Whatever record leap to light he never shall be shamed."

No doubt this went down well with an audience of physicians and surgeons. But as another Scot, Dr. Robert MacNeill, President of the Prince Edward Island Medical Society, had argued in an address to the Maritime Medical Association a few years earlier, doctors might lay claim to "celestial origin" and "divine lineage," but the truth of the matter was that most "people look upon them as enemies, whose sole object is to fleece and rob them."[25] Even as late as the first decade of the twentieth century, doctors faced criticism for their inability to cure diphtheria and tuberculosis, and from anti-vaccinationists and anti-vivisectionists who remained unconvinced of the profession's medical effectiveness. In May 1909, for example, A.C. Northrop wrote to the *Halifax Herald* opposing Alexander Reid's call for compulsory vaccination in the schools. Vaccination, Northrop argued, was just another medical fad, like bleeding or "dosing with mercury until the teeth fall out. . . . When the people refused any longer to be bled, salivated, or burned to death, the doctors found it best to quit."[26]

In the face of these lingering suspicions of medical incompetence, many of the leading practitioners at the turn of the century recognized the need to reshape professional and bourgeois identity in the context of an emerging industrial capitalist order. As we have seen, in the period before Confederation, overseas training often helped launch a young physician into the ranks of the professional and mercantile elite in Halifax, and commitment to philanthropic work and public service was a hallmark of bourgeois identity. With the transition from a mercantile, staples-based and export-oriented economy to the new age of industrialism, the authority of the profession came to rest not so much upon its ties to the Old World or to gentlemanly character as it did upon the application of scientific principles both in medical practice and in the reordering of society. If the medical profession was still unable to treat effectively many of the diseases that struck their patients, they could nonetheless provide useful advice on matters such as the heating and ventilation of homes and buildings, the sanitary conditions of schools and workplaces, sewer drainage and garbage collection, the location of playgrounds, pure water and the adulteration of foods. Doctors at the end of the century not only treated their patients, therefore, but increasingly claimed the expertise to nurse the ailing body politic back to health.[27]

No-one was more aware of the need to make the profession more relevant to modern industrial society than John Stewart's fellow Edinburgh graduate Alexander Reid. The son of a Scottish artisan who had emigrated to London, Ontario, in the late 1820s, Reid received a medical degree from McGill in 1858 before doing postgraduate work at Edinburgh. Upon his arrival in Edinburgh, Reid found himself embroiled in a sometimes acrimonious controversy involving Thomas Laycock and John Hughes Bennett, the senior professor of Clinical Medicine and professor of the Insititute of Medicine at the University of Edinburgh, over the usefulness of bleeding and purging patients. While Laycock believed that bleeding and dosing patients with calomel removed morbid material from the blood, Bennett argued that the accumulation of blood around diseased organs was the body's natural attempt to promote recovery through cell formation.[28] "It is amusing to go round the wards with Dr. Bennett," Reid observed, "as he never allows a chance to escape without

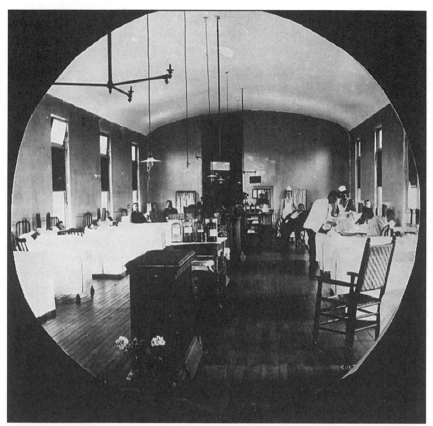

Figure 10.2 Ward 42, Victoria General Hospital, Halifax, Nova Scotia
c.1910, Notman Collection (courtesy of the Public Archives
of Nova Scotia)

uttering a tirade against mercury and bloodletting."[29] Reid's observations upon his experiences there were published in a series of letters to the *Medical Chronicle* of Montreal and reveal a youthful fascination with being at the centre of the medical world and being involved in the current debates in the field. In Reid's opinion, Edinburgh was the leading school of medicine in the English-speaking world, particularly because Bennett had drawn upon continental influences to introduce a tradition of clinical medicine at Edinburgh. London might be the pre-eminent school of surgery, where one could attend operations daily and see the methods employed by the great surgeons of the day, Reid reported, but it could not equal Edinburgh as a school of medicine.[30]

Armed with a commitment to scientific investigation and keeping abreast of the most recent developments in the field, Reid returned to Canada and set up a medical practice near London, Ontario. The drudgery of a rural practice soon had the best of him, and he left on a tour of the continent that took him west to the Pacific, south to California and across the United States again to the east coast. After spending a term at the New York University medical school, Reid settled in Halifax and, in the years that followed, became a leading figure in the professionalization process in Nova Scotia. He became the first dean of the Dalhousie Medical Faculty in 1868, founding president of the Clinical Society of Halifax in 1869, a founding member of the Scientific Branch of the Nova Scotia Medical Society and superintendent of the Nova Scotian Hospital of the Insane in 1879.[31]

A closer look at Reid's career reveals an important transition that was taking place in the process of medical professionalization in the last third of the nineteenth century as doctors increasingly attached themselves to the imagery and ideology of modern science, and argued their social utility in the new age of industrial capitalism. The emphasis on gentlemanly behaviour, charitable work and social concern that had been the hallmark of early professionalism was by no means jettisoned, but increasingly doctors reimagined themselves as medical scientists who could apply their knowledge to the reform of society. Critical to this transition were the advances that accompanied the germ theory of disease and Lister's experiments in antiseptic surgery. Alexander Reid was the first Nova Scotian physician to use carbolic acid as a surgical antiseptic and to accept the germ theory in its entirety. In October 1869, Reid told his colleagues in the Clinical Society of Nova Scotia that Lister's procedures "turned ordinary wounds into subcutaneous ones" and thereby protected patients from germs and post-operative infection. He had been applying Lister's antiseptic techniques for almost a year.[32] The relevance of the germ theory and antisepsis extended far beyond surgery, however; in the years to come it would be incorporated into the construction what Sir James Richardson called "Hygeia," the sanitary city that many saw possible in the future.[33]

For Reid, the virtues of the medical profession rested not so much on its gentlemanly associations as upon its ability to establish a scientific blueprint for ameliorating the unfortunate consequences of contemporary industrial capitalism. Like many of his contemporaries, no matter where they received their training, Reid believed that the medical profession was particularly well-suited to minister to the ills of the community, offering advice on immigration policy, crime, insanity and delinquency, disease prevention, marriage control and eugenics, gender and race relations, healthful architecture and scientific education. Reid's reformist sensibilities involved the extension of medical authority into a wide range of social concerns and was part of what Robert Nye has referred to as the "intrusive medicalization of the twentieth century ... state."[34] By the end of the century the medical profession had come to redefine itself as the handmaiden of a modern, efficient and scientifically managed social order.

In *Poverty Superseded: A New Political Economy for Canada*, Reid offered his design for a more humane capitalist order where professionals and the state would mediate the destructive antagonism between capital and labour.[35] Concerned that the industrial age had spawned a capitalist class whose selfish interests impoverished the weak and contributed to a war between the classes, Reid proposed a new order based upon state regulation of the economy and a system of public works, sanitary reform and eugenics. Because of "those powerful engines . . . capital and combination," Reid wrote, "the ideal state of society has been obliterated." Strikes by workers interrupted production, and capitalists reacted with violence to suppress labour. Only when "society, as represented by Government, undertakes . . . the regulation of industry," Reid argued, would a more effective order be established.[36]

This objective of a more humane economic system, shared by many turn-of-the-century reformers from Edward Bellamy to William Lyon Mackenzie King, implied both a reimagining of the social purpose of the modern bourgeoisie and the reshaping of late-nineteenth-century capitalism.[37] It also suggested a reimagining of the social purpose of the medical profession. If the older tradition of Edinburgh training and gentlemanly service contributed to bourgeois authority in pre-industrial Halifax, the blurring of medical science with social science at the end of the century was an important component of the rehabilitation of the Nova Scotian ruling class in the industrial age.

By the end of the century, Scottish influence upon Nova Scotian medicine had waned significantly. Despite the leadership of Edinburgh-trained doctors in promoting the germ theory of disease and applying antiseptic principles to surgery during the 1870s and 1880s, overseas training was becoming far less important to securing status within Nova Scotia's medical profession than it had been previously. It is also worth remembering that even in the period before Confederation the Scottish connection was largely confined to Halifax. Few Scottish-trained doctors—John Stewart was a notable exception—practised in Pictou County or on Cape Breton Island, which had both been heavily settled by Highland and Lowland Scots. By the 1860s most doctors in Cape Breton were receiving their medical training in the United States, and the number of Canadian-trained doctors was also on the rise.[38] During the 1870s, Bellevue Medical College, McGill, the Halifax Medical College and Dalhousie University supplied the island with most of its practitioners. This shift to North American training, which had the virtue of being more accessible and less expensive, was evident across the province and even in Halifax. Of the 326 doctors in the Nova Scotia Medical Register in 1890, for example, 236 had been trained in the United States, 63 in Canada and only 27 overseas. Twenty years later, 300 of 549 doctors in the province had been trained in Canada, 208 in the United States and only 41 overseas.[39] By that time, the faith that the principles of scientific medicine could be applied to the solution of social problems had become universal, and the importance of overseas training and the cultivation of a gentlemanly persona had diminished considerably.

What, then, should we conclude about the relationships of profession, class and ethnic identity amongst nineteenth-century medical doctors in Nova Scotia? Before Confederation most Edinburgh-trained physicians located in Halifax and, through propitious marriage alliances and the cultivation of a gentlemanly persona, secured an elite position within the profession and considerable political and social influence outside it. For these practitioners there was an obvious connection between their professional and ethnic identities and their positions within the Nova Scotian class structure. For doctors outside Halifax, overseas training and Scottishness exerted a more tenuous influence. And, finally, with the coming of modern industrial capitalism to Nova Scotia in the last quarter of the nineteenth century, the reimagining of the social purposes of the profession in terms of its scientific utility gradually eclipsed the tradition of gentlemanly professionalism and veneration of the demigods of Old World medicine. Not surprisingly, for Edinburgh-trained physicians such as Alexander Reid, it was not one's Scottish heritage or the location of one's schooling that mattered. Rather it was to take the scientific principles that medicine had established for treating ailing bodies and apply them to the reshaping of the modern social order in the name of greater efficiency and a more healthy social environment. Ironically, it was the developments in medical training pioneered at Edinburgh that made such a view possible. Even more ironic was that Edinburgh training, so important at the beginning of the nineteenth century, was partly responsible for its declining significance at century's end.

Notes

1.   Paul Starr, *The Social Transformation of American Medicine: The Rise of a Sovereign Profession and the Making of a Vast Industry* (New York, 1982); John Harley Warner, *The Therapeutic Perspective: Medical Practice, Knowledge, and Identity in America, 1820–1885* (Cambridge, 1986); John S. Haller, *American Medicine in Transition* (Urbana, 1981); Morris Vogel and Charles E. Rosenberg, eds., *The Therapeutic Revolution: Essays in the Social History of American Medicine* (Philadelphia, 1979); Thomas J. Haskell, *American Physicians in the 19th Century: From Sects to Science* (Baltimore, 1972); John Woodward and David Richards, eds., *Health Care and Popular Medicine in Nineteenth Century England* (London, 1977).

2.   Colin D. Howell, "Medical Science and Social Criticism: Alexander Peter Reid and the Ideological Origins of the Welfare State in Canada," in David C. Naylor, ed., *Canadian Health Care and the State* (Montreal and Kingston, 1992), pp. 16–37.

3.   See, for example, Ronald Hamowy, *Canadian Medicine: A Study in Restricted Entry* (Vancouver, 1984).

4.   For a broader discussion of this point, see Colin D. Howell, "Medical Professionalization and the Social Transformation of the Maritimes, 1850–1950," *Journal of Canadian Studies*, 27, no. 1 (Spring 1992), pp. 5–20; and Simon Gunn, "The 'failure' of the Victorian middle class; a critique," in Janet Wolff and John Seed, eds., *The culture of capital: art, power and the nineteenth-century middle*

class (Manchester, 1988) pp. 17–44.

5. Much of the writing about early medicine in Nova Scotia has been done not by professional historians but by physicians with an interest in the development of the profession. Not surprisingly, their efforts have emphasized the contribution of local physicians to medical progress. See, for example, D.A. Campbell, "Pioneers of Medicine in Nova Scotia," *Maritime Medical News*, XI, no. 7 (July 1904), pp. 243–53. The best work of this genre has been done by Allan Marble. See his biographical profiles of medical doctors in *Nova Scotians at Home and Abroad: biographical sketches of over 600 native born Nova Scotians*, rev. ed., (Hantsport, N.S., 1989). An example of this heroic approach to medicine in Scotland can be found in David Hamilton, *The Healers: A History of Medicine in Scotland* (Edinburgh, 1981).

6. On the close connection between the mercantile and professional classes in Scotland, see T.C. Smout, *A History of the Scottish People, 1560–1830* (London, 1972), pp. 342–65. Other work also suggests that Perkin's findings do not fit well with the Scottish experience. See, for example, "A. Allan MacLaren, "The Liberal Professions within the Scottish Class Structure, 1760–1860: A Comparative Study of Aberdeen Clergymen, Doctors and Lawyers," in T.M.Devine, ed., *Scottish Elites: Proceedings of the Scottish Historical Studies Seminar, University of Strathclyde 1991–1992* (Edinburgh, 1994), pp. 77–97.

7. Harold Perkin, *The Rise of Professional Society: England Since 1880* (London and New York, 1989); and *The Origins of Modern English Society, 1780–1880* (London, 1969).

8. Allan Everett Marble, *Surgeons, Smallpox and the Poor: A History of Medicine and Social Conditions in Nova Scotia, 1749–1799* (Montreal and Kingston, 1993).

9. Dr. Daniel McNeil Parker, "On the Completion of Fifty Years Active Professional Work," *Maritime Medical News*, VII (October 1895), p. 209.

10. R.D. Gidney and W.P.J. Millar, *Professional Gentlemen: The Professions in Nineteenth Century Ontario* (Toronto, 1994).

11. Kenneth A. MacKenzie, "The Almons," *Nova Scotia Medical Bulletin* (August 1951), p. 33.

12. "William Bruce Almon Diary, 1806–8," MG 1, vol. 11, "Almon Family Papers, October 12–14, 1806," Public Archives of Nova Scotia (PANS). On Almon's reading of Bell and the responsibilities of the practitioner, see his diary entry of 28 October 1806.

13. Colin Howell, "William Bruce Almon," *Dictionary of Canadian Biography*, VII, p. 16.

14. Kenneth A MacKenzie, "The Almons," *Nova Scotia Medical Bulletin* (Halifax), 29 (1950), pp. 149–54; vol. 30 (1951), pp. 31–36; D.M.L. Farr, "Sir Charles Tupper," *The Canadian Encyclopedia* (Hurtig, 1985), p. 1859.

15. Colin D. Howell, "Daniel McNeill Parker," *Dictionary of Canadian Biography*, XIII, 1901–10, pp. 812–13.

16. David Sutherland, "James Foreman," *Dictionary of Canadian Biography*, VII, pp. 299–300.

17. Marble, *Surgeons, Smallpox, and the Poor.* See also Kenneth G. Pryke, "Poor Relief and Health Care in Halifax, 1827–1849," in Wendy Mitchinson and Janice Dicken McGinnis, eds., *Essays in the History of Canadian Medicine* (Toronto, 1988); Marguerite H. L Grant, "Historical Sketches of Hospitals and Alms Houses

in Halifax, Nova Scotia, 1749–1859," *Nova Scotia Medical Bulletin*, XVII, no. 4, pp. 229–39; Relief Williams, "Poor Relief and Medicine in Nova Scotia, 1749–1783," *Nova Scotia Historical Society Collections*, 24 (1938), pp. 33–56. In Scotland, deep-rooted opposition to indoor relief meant that the poorhouse was at best a marginal institution. See Rosalind Mitchison, "The Poor Law," in T.M. Devine and Rosalind Mitchison, eds., *People and Society in Scotland, Volume 1, 1760–1830* (Edinburgh, 1988), p. 256.

18. Kenneth G. Pryke, "Poor Relief and Health Care in Halifax, 1827–1849," in Wendy Mitchinson and Janice Dickin McGinnis, eds., *Essays in the History of Canadian Medicine* (Toronto, 1988), pp. 44–47.

19. Colin D. Howell, "William Grigor," *Dictionary of Canadian Biography*, VIII, 1851–1860, pp. 348–49. The most comprehensive analysis of the Halifax mercantile elite in the first half of the nineteenth century is David Sutherland, "The Merchants of Halifax, 1815–1850: A Class in Pursuit of Metropolitan Status," Ph.D. Thesis, University of Toronto, 1975.

20. Phyllis Blakely, "Frederick William Morris," *Dictionary of Canadian Biography*, IX (Toronto, 1976), pp. 573–74.

21. Edward G. Salisbury and Evelyn M. Salisbury, "Genealogy of the DeWolf Family, with an appendix by Jame DeWolf, M.D.," microfilm no. D524, PANS.

22. Canadian Medical Association, Minute Book of Annual Meetings, MG 28, vol. 1, *National Archives of Canada*.

23. David L. MacIntosh, "Dr. John Stewart," *Dalhousie Medical Journal* (1940), pp. 6–11; Colin Howell, "Elite Doctors and the Development of Scientific Medicine: The Halifax Medical Establishment and Nineteenth Century Medical Professionalism," in Charles G. Roland, ed., *Health, Disease and Medicine: Essays in Canadian History* (Toronto, 1983), pp. 105–22. Doctors in Nova Scotia still debated the merits of "Listerism" as late as the 1880s. See the report of the debate over Dr. A.W.H. Lindsay's paper on the subject before the Clinical Society of Halifax in July 1880, Clinical Society of Halifax, Minute Book, 20 July 1880, PANS. Lindsay discussed the importance of antiseptic principles in relation to puerperal fever at a later meeting of the society. Puerperal fever, he argued, was to be prevented rather than cured, "by employing the strictest antiseptic precautions possible in even ordinary cases of labour, but especially where manual or instrumental interference is necessitated", Clinical Society of Halifax, Minute Book, 21 December 1880.

24. John Stewart, M.B., Edin., "The Contribution of Pathology to Surgery," the address in Surgery, Canadian Medical Association, 17 September 1902, MG 11, vol. 711, no. 11, PANS.

25. Dr. R. MacNeill, "Higher Medical Education and One Qualification for Canada," a paper read before the Maritime Medical Association, July 1896, in *Maritime Medical News*, XI, no. 7 (July 1899).

26. *Halifax Herald*, 22 May 1909.

27. For a fuller discussion of this process, see my "Reform and the Monopolistic Influence: The Professionalization of Medicine in the Maritimes, 1880–1910," *Acadiensis*, II, no. 1 (Autumn 1981), pp. 3–23.

28. John Hughes Bennett, *Clinical Lecture on the Principle and Practise of Medicine*, 2nd ed., (Edinburgh, 1858), p. 271. The emphasis on clinical observation in Scottish medicine, of which Bennett's career forms an integral part, is outlined in

Guenter B. Risse, *Hospital Life in Enlightenment Scotland* (Cambridge, 1986).
29. Alexander Reid, "A Student's Letter, No. 5," *The Medical Chronicle or Monthly Medical Journal of Medicine and Surgery* (Montreal, 1858), vol. 5.
30. Reid, "A Student's Letter, No. 6," Ibid.
31. Colin D. Howell, "Alexander Peter Reid," *Dictionary of Canadian Biography*, XIV (forthcoming).
32. Clinical Society of Halifax, Minute Book, 27 October 1869, PANS. Reid disagreed with most of his colleagues on the value of Lister's experiments. In Reid's opinion "Lister made out a strong case in his treatment of compound fractures. He said severe injury to joints might take place without suppuration if they were not exposed to the air."
33. J.H. Cassidy, "Hygiea: A Mid-Victorian Dream of a City of Health," *Journal of the History of Medicine and Allied Sciences*, 17, no. 2 (April 1962), pp. 217–18.
34. Robert A. Nye, *Crime, Madness and Politics in Modern France: The Medical Concept of National Decline* (Princeton, 1984).
35. A.P. Reid, *Poverty Superseded: A New Political Economy for Canada* (Halifax, 1891). For a more comprehensive treatment of Reid's life and thought, see Howell, "Medical Science to Social Criticism: Alexander Peter Reid and the Ideological Origins of the Welfare State," in Naylor, *Canadian Health Care and the State*, pp. 16–37.
36. Reid, *Poverty Superseded*, p. 15.
37. The literature on late nineteenth-century reform is voluminous. See, in particular, Robert Wiebe, *Businessmen and Reform* (Cambridge, Mass., 1962); James Weinstein, *The Corporate Ideal in the Liberal State* (Boston, 1968); and Reginald Whitaker, "The Liberal Corporatist Ideas of Mackenzie King," *Labour/Le Travailleur*, 2 (1977), pp. 137–69.
38. Kathleen MacKenzie, "The Development of a Permanent Public Health Care System in Industrial Cape Breton 1880 to 1930," unpublished M.A. thesis, Saint Mary's University, 1991.
39. Figures for 1890 calculated from *Belcher's Family Almanac* (1890), and for 1910 from data contained in *Census of Canada* (1911).

11

Victorian Philanthropy and Child Rescue:
The Career of Emma Stirling in Scotland and Nova Scotia, 1860–95

Philip Girard

At dawn on April 3, 1895, Emma Stirling stood before the flaming ruins of the house at Aylesford, Nova Scotia, which had been her home for nearly a decade, surrounded by some two dozen children and servants who had escaped from the inferno with her. Through its doors had passed some two hundred children who had been rescued from the streets and alleys of Edinburgh and were on their way to supposedly healthier and more secure homes in the Maritimes. The fire, which, it was generally agreed, had been set by Miss Stirling's enemies, was a turning point in her life. After some twenty years of philanthropic endeavour in the fields of child welfare and child rescue in Scotland and Nova Scotia, Emma Stirling had had enough. Within months she sold her Nova Scotian property and took refuge among the Quakers of Pennsylvania, as she put it. The last twelve years of her life were spent in semi-retirement, as she divided her time between Florida and Coatesville, Pennsylvania, where she died in 1907.[1]

What themes can we draw from the life of Emma Maitland Stirling? Engaged as she was in anti-cruelty work on both sides of the Atlantic, Emma Stirling's career allows us to compare both the role of female philanthropists and that of the anti-cruelty movement in Scotland and Nova Scotia. Her writings also permit us to follow the changing reactions of a Scottish emigrant to Nova Scotian society, as her romantic ideals clashed with the realities of life in

Fiigure 11.1 Photo of Emma Stirling from *Our Children in Old Scotland and Nova Scotia* 1892 (courtesy of Special Collections, Killam Library, Dalhousie University)

the province. In this, she exemplified a noticeable trend among the British upper classes, who had often sought refuge from the class conflict and disorder of late Victorian cities in the supposedly purer and simpler environs of Canadian fruit farms.

Emma Maitland Stirling was born in Edinburgh in 1838 or 1839, and was raised at her family home in St. Andrews, Fife, in the shadow of a ruined cathedral. That monument to Scottish iconoclasm is an appropriate symbol for her own life. Although her worldview remained that of a daughter of the Scottish upper class, she rejected most of the options available to such women and did not share the preoccupation with wealth and status which animated the rest of her family. Her Stirling ancestors had participated in both the industrial revolution and colonialism from the mid-eighteenth century, when her great-grandfather had begun to manufacture linens in Glasgow for export to America, and to import Virginia tobacco on the return trip. Ties of marriage soon began to supplement and reinforce those founded on commerce. There was a tradition of intermarriage between the Stirling family and the Willing family of Philadelphia through several generations, which continued with Emma's parents, John Stirling and Elizabeth Willing. The family diversified into London banking and cotton spinning in Manchester, but they also held a place in the landed gentry. Emma's father was referred to as "gentleman of Eldershaw," his country estate, and was entitled to bear the arms of the Stirlings of Cadder, an ancient Scottish house. The Willings were not less distinguished. Elizabeth Willing was the granddaughter of Thomas Mayne Willing, president of the first chartered bank in America and a delegate to the Continental Congress.[2]

The youngest of eleven children, Emma Stirling spent a gloomy childhood and adolescence as she witnessed the deaths of her father and six of her siblings. Two brothers were killed in the Crimean War, aged eighteen and twenty-five; three other siblings died at the ages of seven, fifteen and seventeen; and her beloved sister Mary died at the age of twenty-six in 1852, a year before their father. Three of Emma's surviving siblings were a generation older and led much more conventional lives than she would. Her sisters Jane and Ann married a stockbroker and an advocate, respectively, and moved within Edinburgh's comfortable professional circles. Her elder brother managed the family's many business enterprises and produced thirteen children. Emma's relations with these three siblings seem to have been cordial but distant.

In the face of these continuous bereavements, it is not surprising that Emma Stirling turned to religion. Her family were already devout members of the Scottish Episcopal Church, a dissenting sect which attracted many adherents from the landed classes in the mid-Victorian period, but she experienced a personal conversion the day after the death of her sister Mary.[3] Emma's rock-solid faith motivated her later philanthropic work and she remained a keen believer in the providential ordering of her own life. She was undaunted by an accident which left her a semi-invalid for some six years, but was well enough to care for her blind and increasingly infirm mother until the latter's death in 1874.[4]

Early on, Emma Stirling manifested an interest in children and education. She served as visitor at the Fishers' School in St. Andrews for many years and tried her hand at children's literature in the 1860s. *The History of a Pin*, which appeared under the pseudonym "E.M.S.," enjoyed a measure of success. It was published in Edinburgh and London in 1861, reissued in 1862 and appeared in American editions in 1867 and 1872; most of these editions were illustrated by Robert T. Ross, a member of the Royal Scottish Academy. Stirling used a familiar device in children's literature, telling the story from the point of view of a household object which passes through various owners. The object's reflections on the human situations it witnesses contained moral lessons for the child reader.[5]

Stirling's treatment of one of the central characters in her book, a beggar girl named Bat, shows that her ideas about the role of philanthropy were already well formed at this point in her life. Bat is in the care of her grandmother, a poor but disreputable woman who forces Bat to steal to help them survive. When Bat befriends a kindly man who feels sorry for her, Granny fears that she will confess her crimes to him. To forestall the exposure of her own guilt, the unnatural grandmother arranges for Bat to be killed by a shadowy male figure. He strikes Bat and leaves her for dead in a forest, but she is revived by a friendly dog. Now completely on her own at age nine, Bat is convicted of vagrancy and sent to a "Female Reformatory and Industrial School" for six years. Here she is well cared for: "good regular food, exercise, and sleep, soon told their own tale." At the end of the book, Bat turns up as a domestic in an aristocratic household, where she is well-behaved, useful and "a general favourite both with her ladies and fellow-servants." Stirling embedded a clear message for adults in her children's tale: philanthropic institutions play a key role in rescuing street children from their depraved families, for their own and the public's good.

The death of Emma's mother in 1874 gave her daughter the opportunity to practise what she had preached in *The History of a Pin*. A substantial inheritance enabled her to forsake the familiar confines of St. Andrews for the philanthropic career which beckoned from the broader stage of Edinburgh. Her first efforts were devoted to the creation of what we would now call a day care, the Stockbridge Day Nursery and Infant Home, in early 1877. The Day Nursery was open Monday to Saturday from 6 am to 8 pm for working mothers, and by 1884 had fifty children between two months and five years old in attendance on a daily basis.[6] Mothers had to pay 2d per day for this service, but it was also subsidized by Emma. She had outlined the need for such an institution in her first book some fifteen years earlier: in one of the homes in which Mrs. Pin had found herself, a kindly woman took in the young children of working mothers for 1d per week. These mothers, noted Stirling-as-narrator, were relieved that their children "were not in danger of falling into the fire, or scalding themselves to death with pulling over the kettle, or being drowned in the water-stoup."[7] The Infant Home accepted motherless children from the age of one year on a residential basis, for a fee of 2s 6d per week. It also took in "many Destitute cases for whom no board can be paid" and soon had fifty-seven motherless children in its care.[8] In 1878 Stirling appointed a board of directors to advise her and adopted the name Edinburgh & Leith Children's Aid and Refuge Society (ELCARS).[9]

Stirling began to include abused children within her purview by 1884, when she opened her Shelter from Cruelty at 150 High Street, apparently the first such shelter in Edinburgh. In doing so, she was in the vanguard of the anti-cruelty movement which burst into prominence on both sides of the Atlantic in the early 1880s. In Britain the movement had began with the Liverpool Society for the Prevention of Cruelty to Children (SPCC) in 1883, modelled on the New York SPCC, and was followed by the London society and the Glasgow society in 1884. In Nova Scotia, meanwhile, closer to the epicentre of the anti-cruelty movement of the late 1870s in the eastern United States, the Society for the Prevention of Cruelty (SPC) received statutory powers to investigate and intervene in cases of cruelty to children in 1880 and 1882.[10]

Miss Stirling's plans for a shelter had no sooner been laid than a group of prominent Edinburgh residents met with a view to establishing a local SPCC. Stirling was not amused and her board of directors refused to cooperate with the nascent enterprise.[11] The new society sputtered along and eventually "found that the best way they could benefit the bairns of Edinburgh was to join the Institution of Miss Stirling," which they did in January 1886.[12] For the next few years Stirling was at the zenith of her career. In addition to the Day Nursery, the Infant Home, and the Shelter from Cruelty, she ran two homes for boys, two for girls and leased a farm at Leadburn Park where children of delicate health might be sent for rest and fresh air. In all, she had three hundred children under her care and had spent probably £8000 of her own money on her work in its first decade.[13] In 1885 she had secured the consent of the Earl of Aberdeen to act as patron of her organization. Her board of directors included prominent medical men and city magistrates, and she was on good terms with the police establishment, who came to rely on her Shelter for Cruelty as a place to commit children in trouble. In 1886 she began her boldest venture yet, the establishment of a child emigration scheme which would see dozens of her bairns transported to the farm she purchased at Aylesford, Nova Scotia. In her first book, *Our Children in Old Scotland and Nova Scotia,* she describes her first six years in Nova Scotia in fairly rapturous terms.

Yet, as we have seen, her work in Nova Scotia came to a dramatic and abrupt close only a few years later. More significantly for the historian, per-haps, her pioneering role in child welfare, child rescue and child emigration in eastern Scotland is virtually unknown in the land of her birth. The social history of what is now the Royal Scottish SPC (RSSPCC), published in con-junction with the supposed centenary of the society in 1984, mentions her name only once, and in a misleading fashion. How and why did this decline and subsequent obliteration come about?[14]

In immediate terms, Stirling's fiery exit from Nova Scotia was precipi-tated by her decision to press criminal charges against an Annapolis man who had allegedly impregnated one of her former pupils then working as his do-mestic, and the doctor who had allegedly performed an abortion on her. The significance of the fact that the fire at Hillfoot Farm was started four days after Stirling laid the information was lost on no one.[15] Her enterprise was already in trouble, however, and might not have lasted much longer in any case. Her departure from Scotland had occurred at a time of considerable friction with her board of directors, and relations with them had continued to worsen over

Figure 11.2 Photo of Stirling's Aylesford farm from *Our Children . . .*
(courtesy of Special Collections, Killam Library, Dalhousie
University)

time. And the steady supply of children which she needed for Hillfoot Farm
had dwindled over the years, imperilling its future.

The directors were upset that she had withdrawn from ELCARS with little
notice, leaving them to manage as best they could without her generous subsi-
dies. As well, her decision to emigrate a number of children without their
parents' consent led to lengthy and expensive litigation in both Scotland and
Nova Scotia. When a Scottish court ruled that the directors were responsible
for Stirling's illegal act and must do all in their power to regain the children,
they were effectively forced to subsidize the lawsuit of one bereft father,
Arthur Delaney, against her in Nova Scotia. In this proceeding she was held in
contempt of court for giving evasive answers as to the whereabouts of these
children, which gained her a certain notoriety on this side of the Atlantic.[16] Her
1892 book, *Our Children in Old Scotland and Nova Scotia*, in addition to
describing her work and attempting to raise funds, contains a long justification
of her actions in this matter, just as its 1898 reprint contains a long sequel
presenting her perspective on the events which led to her departure from Nova
Scotia.

Imperious, self-rightcous and prickly Emma Stirling undoubtedly was,
but attributing her eclipse to personality flaws alone would miss much of the
significance of her career. Many men with similar qualities have easily quali-
fied for hero status, while such women are often labelled difficult or overzeal-
ous. In other words, the fate of Emma Stirling illustrates the constraints which
bound the late Victorian female philanthropist. It obliges us to examine the
child rescue movement as a site of gender struggle, which has recently been

suggested in the Nova Scotian context but not, so far as I know, in the Scottish.[17]

The middle-class Victorian sentimentalization of childhood and motherhood laid a solid foundation for women to be involved in child welfare and child rescue work, just as they contributed to the growing prevalence of women teachers, who doubled their numbers in the profession in Scotland from 35 percent in 1851 to 70 percent in 1911.[18] Yet women teachers were contained in a system dominated by all-male hierarchies, while female philanthropists were so many loose cannons, as it were. Emma Stirling behaved exactly as if she were a man, using her substantial financial resources to pursue goals which were important to her, unconstrained by any male authority figure, be he father, son, husband or priest. She herself had appointed her male board of directors, who were advisory rather than supervisory in nature, though they often found this difficult to accept. She created her own female hierarchies, delegating management of each of her homes to a matron, usually a single woman, who in turn supervised servants and volunteers in caring for the children.[19]

Although child-care work was identified with a private and female sphere of activity, the organizational role of the female philanthropist inevitably brought her into the public sphere, where conflict with traditional male modes of ordering was likely.[20] When the rival Edinburgh SPCC was trying to organize in 1884, its chair, General Anderson, asked rhetorically, "When Miss Stirling had done so much in this noble work, what could they not expect to be done by an influential body of men working *con amore*?"[21] In other words, women might accomplish something in this new and exciting field, but men were bound to do much more. In the short term General Anderson was wrong, since his society was forced to join Stirling's on her terms, but, in the longer term, men did succeed in dominating the movement, both at the time and in the historical record. When the Edinburgh & Leith Children's Aid and Refuge joined with the Glasgow SPCC in 1890 to form the Scottish National SPCC (SNSPCC), all the officers and members of the board of directors were male. The Edinburgh branch retained some lady visitors and two matrons for some time, but women occupied no such positions in Glasgow.

Having resigned from ELCARS in early 1888, Stirling was anxious to preserve her pioneering role in the annals of the new society. In 1894 she finally reached an agreement with the board of directors that, in return for reimbursing them £400 for the legal expenses in the Delaney lawsuit, her name would appear as founder of ELCARS on the title page of the annual reports of the new society.[22] Perhaps unbeknownst to her, in the previous year, the directors had named James Grahame, founder of the Glasgow Society, as founder of the new national society. This formula continued to appear in the reports of the society until a few years after the death of Emma Stirling in 1907, when her name was dropped, and James Grahame continued as the sole "founder" of the

SNSPCC and thus of the anti-cruelty movement in Scotland. Stirling contributed to her own eclipse by alienating many of those who might have assisted in keeping her name alive, but sexism also played a role. The respectable businessman James Grahame presented a much more attractive founder figure to contemporaries in the anti-cruelty movement than a prickly and obdurate unmarried woman who did not fit easily into any social category.

Recent scholarship in Nova Scotia also reveals the child protection movement as a site of gender struggle. In a thesis on the evolution of the NSSPC and the emergence of early child protection legislation in Nova Scotia, Beverly Dubinsky has suggested that the SPC discouraged women from being involved in child protection work in all but the most subordinate roles, an option which they rejected. As a result, the society's finances remained continually precarious, since they could not rely on the extensive fundraising work of women which was so important in Ontario and in some of the SPCs on the eastern seaboard of the United States. Eventually, according to Dubinsky, Halifax women became interested in the Children's Aid Society as an organization through which they could make a contribution, leading to the fragmentation of child protection efforts in the province.[23]

Where a feminist analysis of Emma Stirling reveals commonalities between Nova Scotian and Scottish experiences, examination of the other important strand in her life—her Calvinist evangelicalism—reveals significant differences between the two societies. One has the impression that Emma Stirling expected to find in Nova Scotia a more or less faithful reproduction of her own society, transplanted to the western shore of the Atlantic. This image of a "New Scotland" may have inspired the choice of Nova Scotia as the site of her child emigration efforts, although this is pure speculation.[24] The titles of her books— *Our Children in Old Scotland and Nova Scotia*—suggest a somewhat romanticized continuation of the "Old Scotland" in the new, and indeed it was some time before Stirling came to realize that neither her class position nor her religious beliefs commanded the kind of automatic deference in Nova Scotia that she had been accustomed to at home.

When Nova Scotians became aware of the lawsuit launched by the Irish Catholic father of the children whom Stirling had wrongfully transported to Nova Scotia, public opinion by no means rallied to her side. It has not been possible to discover whether the Catholic Church actively supported Mr. Delaney's cause here, but Emma Stirling clearly thought it did. She attributed the lawsuit to a conspiracy by Halifax Catholics to get rid of her by urging their co-religionists in Edinburgh to stir up some trouble there which could be publicized in the province. By assuming that she had the right, more or less unquestioned in Scotland, to convert Catholic waifs under her care to Presbyterianism, Emma Stirling had breached a fundamental taboo of Nova Scotia society. Religious pluralism had been accommodated after considerable struggle by according Catholics and Protestants control of their own separate institutions, particularly those dealing with children. Nova Scotia was not the Calvinist paradise which Stirling imagined it should be.

The circumstances surrounding Stirling's exit from Nova Scotia reveal that she breached another taboo, but this time one which casts her in a more favourable light in modern eyes. By bringing to light scandalous allegations about two prominent citizens of the Annapolis Valley, Stirling revealed herself to the locals as an interfering outsider who had no right to stir up trouble where residents were content to turn a blind eye. Stirling's experience with rough justice in the Annapolis Valley provides a fascinating window on an insular society with its own subterranean legal order, one understood by the local community but not apparent until its norms were breached by an unsuspecting outsider. When a subscription was started to aid Miss Stirling after her loss, it was, revealingly, begun by a former inhabitant of the county, Pastor J. Clark of Turner's Falls, Massachusetts.[25]

Nor was the anti-cruelty movement itself identical in the two jurisdictions. However unprogressive it may have been in refusing to involve middle-class women in responsible positions, the SPC in Halifax was quite alive to the problems of working-class women and intervened on their behalf, as well as on behalf of their children, in a wide variety of situations, from physical and sexual abuse to employment problems. As Judith Fingard has concluded in her study of the SPC, while the society did not advocate radical social change to aid its clients, it did "propose a range of practical solutions for individual supplicants and this accorded them a degree of dignity and choice consistent with a sense of control over their own lives."[26] The *deus ex machina* of emigration simply was not available in the Nova Scotian context; the children of the poor had to be dealt with in the here and now.

In Scottish cities, the SPCC, known as "The Cruelty" among the working classes, came to be widely feared.[27] In keeping with others involved in anti-cruelty work, Miss Stirling could envisage only one solution for her young clients' problems: removal not only from their families but from Scottish society itself. While it is relatively easy to see the progression in Nova Scotia from the SPC's activities to those of state-sponsored social workers, such a link is more difficult in the Scottish instance. The Scottish SPCC only seemed to become more conservative over time, its focus punitive rather than ameliorative. Totally devoid of any social critique, it became an ideal object of aristocratic patronage: the Prince of Wales became honorary president in 1890, and by 1908 honorary officers included five dukes, two marquesses, six earls, five lords, seven baronets and two knights.

A final theme in Stirling's life is the flight from British urban chaos to an unspoiled Canadian Eden symbolized almost too predictably by an apple orchard. Many members of the British aristocracy and landed classes invested heavily in schemes to grow fruit in British Columbia in particular. Indeed, three of Stirling's nephews did just this, emigrating to Vancouver Island to grow fruit in the 1880s and 1890s. Much of the appeal of Hillfoot Farm for Stirling centred on its apple orchard, which she described in idyllic terms in her books: "you would have smiled to see the party of children sally forth to work in the orchard, boys and girls, with large half-bushel baskets, little toddling mites holding up their pinnies, each doing what it could for the farm." She urged her readers to "turn from the sunny Hillfoot Farm with its pure fresh air, and scent of the apples, clover, and pine trees, to the dark and dingy closes of the Old Town of Edinburgh, or the no less unwholesome and airless dens of Leith," and asked rhetorically whether "I have not done my best for 'Our Children' in taking as many of them as I can to Nova Scotia?"[28]

The contrast which Stirling made in her first book between an unhealthy and corrupt Old World and a fresh and innocent New World is a conceit as old as the discovery of America itself. Her usage of this theme takes an ironic turn in view of the experiences chronicled in her second book, where she exposes corruption in the heart of her new Arcadia—the worm in the apple, so to speak. Here again Stirling follows a path well-trodden in both literature and historical experience, joining vast numbers of emigrants forced to exchange the imagined landscape of their destinations for the complex realities of their new homes. Where Stirling diverges from this pattern is in her second migration to Pennsylvania, which provided her with an opportunity to reflect on both Scotia and Nova Scotia.

We are not privy to any of Emma Stirling's reflections during the last dozen years of her life, but her estate papers provide a window on her activities during this period.[29] She seems to have severed all ties with both Scotland and Nova Scotia, leaving no property in either jurisdiction. Stirling acquired a small orange grove in Florida, where she wintered, spending the rest of the year at her farm near Coatesville, Pennsylvania. All the beneficiaries under her will were resident in the United States, and none seems to have been a family member; a major beneficiary was the Florida Humane Association.[30] Some of the beneficiaries under Stirling's will were illegitimate children, which engendered some litigation ultimately favourable to them in light of a liberal state law passed in 1901. This disposition is surprising in light of Stirling's exclusion of illegitimates from her Edinburgh homes; she made exceptions only in cases of physical abuse.

In retirement, Emma Stirling appears, improbably, to have mellowed, and to have adapted to her new American environment. She relaxed her former moral vigilance to such an extent that families with illegitimate children could be admitted into her personal circle. She withdrew from the controversial field of child welfare to the safer sphere of animal protection. She permitted herself vacations in Florida. Perhaps Stirling realized that the immolation of Hillfoot Farm symbolized the end of an era for the maverick Victorian philanthropist. The Maria Ryes, the Annie Macphersons[31] and the Emma Stirlings belonged to a world which was fast fading even before the final explosion of 1914. A new discourse rapidly replaced voluntarism, piety and philanthropy were replaced by bureaucracy, secularism and career professionalism, and Emma Stirling had neither qualifications nor stomach for this new order. In saying goodbye to Scotia and Nova Scotia, Emma Stirling found a kind of peace at last.

Notes

1. The only published sources for Emma Stirling's life are her two books: *Our Children in Old Scotland and Nova Scotia* (London, 1892), and *Our Children in Old Scotland and Nova Scotia, with sequel* (Coatesville, Pa., 1898). These have been supplemented by research in primary sources in Scotland, Nova Scotia and Pennsylvania.
2. The family history is well chronicled in Thomas Willing Stirling, *The Stirlings of Cadder* (St. Andrews, 1933). T.W. Stirling was Emma Stirling's nephew but appears to have been totally uninterested in her. Neither her birthdate nor deathdate is noted, although they are painstakingly supplied for her numerous siblings. His sole comment on his aunt is that she "died unmarried."
3. Stirling describes this experience in *Our Children* (London, 1892), pp. 21–22.
4. Stirling's mother was listed as blind in the 1851 census, General Record Office (Scotland), Census Return 453 (Parish of St. Andrews, Fife, Enumeration District no. 5). The household at that time comprised John Stirling, age 66; Elizabeth Stirling, age 52; John Stirling, age 15; Emma, age 12; and three female servants.
5. Stirling may have borrowed from a work attributed to a Miss Smythies, *The History of a Pin, as related by itself* (London, 1807), which was first published in 1798; see Judith St. John, comp., *The Osborne Collection of Early Children's Books, 1566–1910: A Catalogue*, 2 vols. (Toronto, 1966), vol. 2, p. 942.
6. *Courant* (Edinburgh), 18 April 1884 (advertisement).
7. Stirling, *History of a Pin*, p. 91.
8. In spite of the seemingly benign nature of these interventions, they aroused considerable controversy in the Edinburgh of the 1880s. When the National Association for the Promotion of Social Sciences met in Edinburgh in 1880, a session on "The Day-Nursery Question" elicited criticisms based on both moral and Malthusian arguments, as well as some support. Day nurseries, it was argued, would inappropriately relieve parents of their God-given duties, and encourage excessive births in the lower classes. In the end, participants could agree only that if such institutions were to be founded, it should be through purely charitable efforts and the state must be kept out at all costs. See *Scotsman* (Edinburgh), 8 and 18 October 1880.
9. The Society published annual reports from 1878 to 1889, but they are available only from 1886 at the Scottish Record Office, Royal Scottish Society for the Prevention of Cruelty to Children (RSSPCC) fonds, GD 409/57/5. The *Post Office Edinburgh & Leith Directory*, 1885–89, carried advertisements for the society which contain extensive information about its locations, officers and activities. Leith was an independent municipal unit subsequently incorporated into the city of Edinburgh. The best primary source is the detailed "Minute book of Directors' Monthly Meeting Stockbridge Day Nursery, Infant Home & branches, from May 1, 1884 to [September 5, 1889]," held as part of the RSSPCC fonds, S.R.O.,

GD 409/1, vol. 1. Volume 2 is a more summary minute book for the period November 1888 to October 1895, when Stirling's original society had become the eastern branch of the Scottish National SPCC. These will be referred to as ELCARS Minute Book 1 and 2, respectively.

10. On the work of the Nova Scotia SPC, see Judith Fingard, *The Dark Side of Life in Victorian Halifax* (Halifax, 1989), chap. 8. See also George K. Behlmer, *Child Abuse and Moral Reform in England, 1870–1908* (Palo Alto, 1982); Linda Gordon, *Heroes of Their Own Lives: The Politics and History of Family Violence, Boston 1880–1960* (New York, 1988); Elizabeth Pleck, *Domestic Tyranny: The Making of American Social Policy Against Family Violence from Colonial Times to the Present* (New York, 1987).

11. The dispute can be followed in ELCARS Minute Book 1, entries for November 1884 and March 1885.

12. *Scotsman* (Edinburgh), 4 March 1886.

13. This was her own estimate which seems reasonable (*Our Children*, p. 38). The expenses of Stirling's various homes regularly ran £100 per month over revenues in 1884 and 1885 according to the minute books, and she repeatedly assured her directors that she would pay the deficit personally rather than reduce expenditures. At this rate, she could easily have spent £8000 during her decade-long association with ELCARS. The extent of Emma Stirling's fortune is not known, but it must have been considerable. She inherited virtually all her mother's estate, which was valued in 1874 at £12,368 minus a few small legacies; Scottish Record Office, Commissary Register of Inventories, vol. 45, fol. 970. Her father's estate, in which she was entitled to a quarter share on her mother's death, would have been substantially larger, but there is no inventory contained in his Scottish estate papers; S.R.O., Commissary Register of Inventories, vol. 25, fol. 440.

14. Brian Ashley, *A Stone on the Mantelpiece: A Centenary Social History of the Royal Scottish Society for the Prevention of Cruelty to Children* (Edinburgh, 1985) refers to Stirling only in the following sentence (p. 30): "In 1886 the Edinburgh Society finding that similar work was being done by the Edinburgh & Leith Children's Aid and Refuge Society, which had been founded by the late Miss Emma Stirling in 1877, joined with that Society, and the Society thus re-enforced united in 1889 with the Glasgow Society under the title of the Scottish National Society for the Prevention for Cruelty to Children [SNSPCC]." This passage appears in the 1908 Report of the SNSPCC, when the reference to "the late" Miss Stirling was appropriate, given her death the previous year. The context as reproduced in Ashley suggests that her death occurred in the mid-1880s. Ashley equates the origins of the present-day RSSPCC with the commencement of the Glasgow SPCC in 1884 and gives virtually no recognition to Stirling's seminal work in Edinburgh between 1877 and 1884.

15. Stirling explains the circumstances surrounding her departure from Nova Scotia in some detail in her second *Our Children* book (1898), and the story can be confirmed through local newspapers such as the Bridgetown *Weekly Monitor*, April–June 1895.

16. I have discussed these custody disputes in some detail elsewhere: "Children, Church, Migration and Money: Three Tales of Child Custody in Nova Scotia," in Hilary Thompson, ed., *Children's Voices in Atlantic Literature and Culture: Essays on Childhood* (Guelph: Canadian Children's Press, 1995).

17. This conflict is hinted at in Linda Mahood, "Family Ties: Lady Child-Savers and Girls of the Street 1850–1925," in Esther Breitenbach and Eleanor Gordon, eds., *Women in Scottish Society, 1800–1945* (Edinburgh, 1992), pp. 42–64, but is not explored in any detail. The literature on female Victorian philanthropists says surprisingly little about the male resistance which such women often encountered and their strategies for dealing with it. See F.K. Prochaska, *Women and Philanthropy in Nineteenth-Century England* (Oxford, 1980); Olive Checkland, *Philanthropy in Victorian Scotland: Social Welfare and the Voluntary Principle* (Edinburgh, 1980); Maria Luddy, *Women and Philanthropy in Nineteenth-Century Ireland* (Cambridge, 1995); and Lori D. Ginzberg, *Women and the Work of Benevolence* (1990).

18. Eleanor Gordon, "Women's Spheres," in W. Hamish Fraser and R.J. Morris, eds., *People and Society in Scotland, Volume II, 1830–1914*, 3 vols. (Edinburgh, 1990).

19. When a public meeting was being organized in June 1885 to explain the work of ELCARS, advertisements stated that the "attendance of Ladies is particularly requested" (copies of advertisement pasted in ELCARS Minute Book 1).

20. Mahood, "Family Ties," pp. 42–43.

21. *Courant* (Edinburgh), 22 December 1884; copy pasted in ELCARS Minute Book 1, entry for 8 January 1885.

22. ELCARS Minute Book 2, entry for 18 July 1894.

23. Beverly Dubinsky, "Rescued: Early Child Protection Legislation in Nova Scotia" (M.S.W. thesis, Dalhousie University, 1995).

24. Nova Scotia possessed a number of practical advantages from Stirling's point of view: it presented the closest available high-quality agricultural land in a British dominion. She travelled to North America in 1885 to ascertain "whether a favourable outlet existed in America for the young lads in the Homes who were rapidly growing up and for whom provision would soon require to be made with the view of setting them out in the world for themselves" (ELCARS Minute Book 1, 6 November 1885). It appears that she toured a number of potential sites inside and outside Nova Scotia, but why she chose the Annapolis Valley over the others is unknown. One possible connection is the presence of the young Margaret Marshall Saunders in Edinburgh in the late 1870s. Saunders was the protégé of the Rev. William Garden Blaikie, whose wife was also involved in child rescue work. Mrs. Blaikie sent some of her children to Emma Stirling's home in Nova Scotia in the late 1870s and early 1880s, when the idea of a Canadian home began to take shape in Stirling's mind. I would like to thank Gwen Davies for suggesting this possible link.

25. *Weekly Monitor* (Bridgetown, N.S.), 24 April 1895.

26. Fingard, *Dark Side of Life*, p. 186.

27. Mahood, "Family Ties," p. 56.

28. These two passages are found in an "Our Children" pamphlet included in the 1889 ELCARS annual report and aimed primarily at a Scottish audience. They do not appear in the book versions of *Our Children*.

29. Emma Stirling appears to have left no assets and no estate papers in Scotland. Her will was probated in Chester County, Pennsylvania, where it is held by the Chester County Archives and Records Services, no. 31324, along with the Orphans' Court file, no. 9157, containing records of the litigation which ensued when some of her legacies were contested. I would like to thank Barbara L. Weir, Assistant

Archivist, for making this material available to me.

30. The exact relationship of the beneficiaries to Emma Stirling is unknown. One of the personal beneficiaries was named Jesse Stirling Martin, but it seems unlikely that she was a relation of Emma Stirling. Jesse Martin had two illegitimate children also named in the will.

31. On the work of these pioneer organizers of child emigration schemes, see Gillian Wagner, *Children of the Empire* (London, 1982).

12

Notes From Eastern Canada:
Scottish Immigration to the Maritime Provinces in the 1920s

Marjory Harper

In 1910, Canada overtook the United States to become—as it had been consistently until 1847—the favourite destination of immigrant Scots. Its retention and consolidation of that position throughout the inter-war years were attributable not only to the negative influence of American quotas, but to enthusiastic agency activity, an upsurge of British imperialism, and the unprecedented involvement of governments on both sides of the Atlantic in far-reaching and well-endowed schemes of assisted colonization. Paradoxically, the 1920s also saw the rehabilitation of Maritime Canada, making it a mainstream destination for immigrants, rather than simply the first landfall where transatlantic liners disembarked human cargoes whose destinations lay much further west. It was a phenomenon which partially counteracted the well-attested outmigration which characterized Maritime life in this decade dominated by political and social instability and economic decline in the mining, fishing, farming and lumbering industries, when Atlantic Canada became an early casualty of the ills which were to afflict the entire Dominion in the 1930s.

This essay examines the mechanisms by which the Maritimes were able to circumvent some of the region's manifold internal problems of the 1920s, contributing to the mosaic of Scottish immigration through the cultivation of both formal and informal networks, when philanthropists and promoters were able to draw on the newly available resources of the Empire Settlement Act, not least in the area of juvenile migration.[1]

The most potent stimulus to migration was always personal encouragement from friends and relatives, followed by advice and practical assistance from professional agents. Canadian efforts to develop a co-ordinated immigration policy after Confederation culminated in the decade 1896–1906, when the Laurier government poured four million dollars into promoting settlement, particularly in the Prairie Provinces. The British Isles in particular were carpeted with resident and itinerant agents representing the Dominion and provincial governments, as well as the transcontinental railway companies, laying the foundations of a recruitment policy which continued until the depressed 1930s. For twenty-five years after 1872 the whole of Scotland came under the control of one resident Dominion agent based in Glasgow, with occasional assistance from subagents stationed elsewhere, but by 1907 the volume of business was so great that a second agent was appointed for the north, based in Aberdeen, and in 1923 the number was increased to three, with the appointment of a Highland agent at Inverness. The Dominion agents were responsible for promoting all parts of Canada even-handedly throughout their district, by distributing literature, liaising with booking agents and conducting lectures and interviews. They also oversaw the periodic recruitment campaigns of visiting provincial and railway company agents, including representatives from the Maritimes, despite occasional complaints from these provinces that too much attention was being focused on the prairies.[2]

When an agent representing Prince Edward Island visited Aberdeen in 1910, he was successful, in one case, not simply in translating a vague restlessness into a concrete decision to migrate to his territory, but in the more difficult task of changing a mind that had already been made up. Robert Rhymes, an engine driver with the Great North Railway, was persuaded to purchase a 140-acre farm in Prince Edward Island instead of heading for the prairies. As Rhymes recalled to E.W. Watt, manager of the Aberdeen *Press and Journal*, who was on a CPR-sponsored tour of Canada fourteen years later: "I was intending to go West, but the agent representing the island was in Aberdeen, and I met him at the Kittybrewster Show. His story induced me to come here and look round, and I am not disappointed that I did not go West." Since P.E.I., he claimed, offered farmers, particularly those with a little capital, opportunities equal to Ontario or the prairies and was more sociable than the sparsely populated West, "there never was a better chance than there is right now."[3]

Encouraging correspondence and factual reports published regularly in provincial newspapers and farming journals supported the more direct efforts of paid agents. Readers were assured that labour was much cheaper than in the West, and men of small capital could make, "if not a fortune, a very comfortable living without having to experience the rigours of the Western climate. Any man with a couple of hundred pounds should do well, and more than well."[4] The series of letters from which this chapter takes its title was written by "WRJ," a Scottish settler in an unidentified part of the East, who wrote regularly to the *Scottish Farmer* in the 1920s and 1930s, reporting on farming conditions and prospects in Quebec and the Maritime Provinces. Readers were told about wages, prices, climate, harvest prospects, topical issues in national and regional politics, often with reference to immigration policy, and the benefits and drawbacks of settling in the Maritimes. In May 1924, for example, the correspondent reported on the "antiquated" methods of farming in Nova Scotia,[5] but by February 1926 he predicted that this problem would be overcome, reporting approvingly on a recent conference held between the premiers of Nova Scotia and New Brunswick and representatives of the Canadian Pacific Railway (CPR), with the aim of redirecting the tide of immigration:

> What the Maritimes are in need of is a complete agricultural resurrection, brought about by the introduction of good new settlers, and to secure this an intensive practical immigration policy must be extended without interruption for many years. The opportunities in the Maritimes have never been given the publicity the West has, and, personally speaking, for a man with small capital, the advantages of the Maritimes seem to me easily to surpass anything that can be offered in the West. Farming careers can be carried out under the pleasantest of living conditions, without the extremes of temperature experienced in the West, and as the country is older in every way, schools and churches are already established, and there is no pioneer work to start with, as experienced in the West. If the Maritimes had the same publicity as the West, and also the assistance of the railway companies, they would by this time be the garden of the Dominion. I have great faith in their future, and my advice to intending immigrants is to look into the possibilities in the East, especially Nova Scotia, before making up their minds that nothing can be done unless West of Winnipeg.[6]

In another communication a month later, he upheld the benefits of "a community life much more approaching the Old Country conditions than that which is encountered further West," and by the end of the following year he was writing with satisfaction of the increased immigration to Nova Scotia and New Brunswick. By 1928 he declared that "never since the pioneer days has there been such a steady and sustained flow of new settlers as at present," and in March 1930, just before he was forced to admit the impact of depression and unemployment, he predicted that the next decade would see "a growth in the development of both Nova Scotia and New Brunswick that will exceed all records in the past. I have often said that if the railway companies had had land to sell in the East as they have in the West, Nova Scotia would have now been the 'Garden of Canada,' and although development has been long in coming, the interest that both the railway companies are taking in these provinces foretells a promising future."[7]

Other correspondents' accounts of their experiences generally confirmed

WRJ's positive outlook, although one female settler complained at having been misled by a shipping agent who "was quite ready to swear to us that New Brunswick was the only real paradise on earth," whereas in fact it was cold and barren.[8] More unequivocally positive was a former teacher from Glasgow who, at the age of 37, had moved to the Hebrides to recover her health. At the age of 40 she had married a crofter seven years older than herself, and, inspired by a promotional book they read together, they sailed from Glasgow in spring 1921 to purchase (for $1,000) a farm in New Brunswick, fifty miles from Saint John.

> Our Island friends wished us the best of luck, but many of them thought it was a most foolish and reckless undertaking. One man told us that we were going to certain ruin, that there was no good farming land in New Brunswick, it being a land of rock! Others thought that, as I was entirely ignorant of a farm-wife's duties, I would find it too hard and difficult, and would break down in health. I was pressed to stay and continue teaching, even although I was married, but I was getting pretty sick of the confining life of a teacher and longed for some life and adventure, no matter what hard work it entailed. So we followed the advice of our book and chose a Province which would not be such a radical change for elderly folks as the West. The climate here does not go to such extremes as in the West, and crop failures are almost unknown. Fortunes may not be made, but, to balance that, fortunes are not lost by sudden climatic changes affecting the crops, as unfortunately does happen at times in the West. We also wished to be as near to the Old Country as possible, to give our friends there an opportunity of visiting us without incurring a heavy train fare as well as that of the steamer. . . . We feel much more used now to the Canadian ways of farming, and I believe our hardest days are over. We have had drawbacks, but are ready to begin again all over. It seems to me we took a wise step coming here, at least for people of our maturity. The West may be all right for strong young folks who can work out a while and gain experience before buying a farm of their own. But New Brunswick and its people too are very much more similar to our own land and our own Scotch folks. We have here the Highlands to the north, fine sporting country, and the Lowlands to the south, good farming land, just as at home.[9]

Such glowing commendations of farming opportunities would have struck a discordant note with many Maritimers, for whom the 1920s brought a huge outmigration of 122,000 people, demographic growth of only one percent, and an unequal struggle against exploitation by powerful external economic forces in an increasingly competitive international market.[10] A contracting agricultural sector played an integral role in the Maritimes' relegation to a dependent satellite of the Dominion, as farmers' interests were subordinated not only to the attractions of urban and industrial development on both sides of the American border but also to the competing interests of regional paper, coal and steel companies and the demands of the prairie farming lobby for tariff and freight policies which were opposed to the Maritimers' best interests.

In this climate, the propagandists' advocacy of Maritime farming might be interpreted as a rear-guard attempt to reverse depopulation and restore some credibility and influence to an industry which was becoming increasingly marginalised, and polarised between a few progressive, export-oriented large farmers and a mass of small subsistence agriculturists struggling to survive.[11] Since it was in the interests of the advocates of Maritime land settlement in the 1920s to highlight opportunities rather than threats, their pronouncements tended to focus on the way in which farming was facilitated, first of all, by the Canadian Soldier Settlement Board and later by various schemes developed under the auspices of the Empire Settlement Act. From January 1920 to March 1923 the Soldier Settlement Scheme, orchestrated from London, offered free third-class passages to British veterans and their dependents who had applied to take up farms overseas and had been approved by the government of their chosen dominion, after initial selection by local officials of the British ministries of Labour and Pensions. It was introduced mainly to appease veterans who were restive at unemployment and poor housing in postwar Britain, but in its three-year existence soldier settlement assisted only 86,027 of its 269,696 applicants. Thirty-two percent went to Canada, where they were allocated farms all over the Dominion that had not been taken up by the Canadian veterans for whom they had been earmarked.[12] On 1 June 1922, before this experiment was terminated, the Imperial Parliament passed the Empire Settlement Act, which made unprecedented provision for the British government to spend up to £3 million a year for fifteen years on loans and grants for assisted passages, land settlement schemes, training courses and other approved ventures in partnership with Dominion governments or with public and private bodies in Britain or the dominions. Although Canada ultimately took 46 percent of migrants under the Empire Settlement Act, the Liberal government was at first reluctant to participate, fearing that selective assistance would upset the powerful western farming lobby and drive Canadians south to the United States. In 1923, however, it allocated $600,000 to assist the immigration of domestic servants, agricultural workers nominated by Canadian farmers, and child migrants sponsored by private societies. The introduction of passage rebates in 1924 was followed by the 3,000 Families Scheme in 1925, under which land originally purchased for soldier settlement which had been abandoned or never taken up was made available to three thousand British families who, if they had £25 for immediate use on arrival, were to receive advances of up to £300 each from the British government for the purchase of stock and equipment. In 1928 a similar scheme was introduced in New Brunswick, where the Farm Settlement Board was to settle one hundred British families per year for five years on vacant farms which the Board had purchased and improved before reselling them at cost price. The farms, which were located in old, established districts, varied from 75 to 200 acres, and were generally suitable for mixed farming.[13]

In 1925, Flora McKenzie, the correspondent who had earlier complained about the New Brunswick climate, wrote to the *Scottish Farmer* criticising soldier settlement in New Brunswick on the grounds that the land was overpriced and the scheme badly managed, but William Forbes, the settler whose experience she had used to illustrate her argument, immediately wrote back to refute her allegations:

> What the idea of this article was I don't know. Was it trying to raise a scandal about the Land Settlement Act; or was it only an advertisement for the farmers in Scotland who don't like to see so many of their farm workers leaving the country? Some people have a strange way of helping others. The worst feature about the whole article was where it said that the "agent" had neglected his duty. That is not true, for the "agent," as Flora calls him, has done his very best for our welfare, and any of my neighbours could verify this statement. The article also went on to say that my wife was unable to bear the strain of hard work and loneliness, and broke down and had been sick ever since. The next time "Flora" wants to write an article about us she will have to be better informed on my wife's sickness and several of her subjects she touched on, and not write a lot of stuff which is hardly correct. . . . We have got a splendid chance through this scheme of making a home for ourselves—a chance we could never get in the Old Country; and my wife and I feel very grateful for the kindness of all the officials connected with this branch of the Land Settlement Board, and I think that the agent who was accused of not doing his duty is certainly entitled to an apology by the person or persons who wrote this article.[14]

Forbes' commendation reinforced the satisfied comments of a correspondent of the Aberdeen *Press and Journal* two years earlier, who praised the assistance which his father, a doctor, had received from the Soldier Settlement Board's field supervisors when he brought his wife, son and daughter to Nova Scotia.[15] Equally positive was John Jackson, a one-time tenant farmer at Lesmahagow, Lanarkshire, who, having seen the New Brunswick Family Settlement Scheme advertised in the *Scottish Farmer*, emigrated in April 1931. Five months later he wrote to James Malcolm, the Canadian government agent in Glasgow, full of praise for the land settlement officials who had met the family at each stage of the journey from Halifax. The 250-acre farm he had been allocated, although empty for about a year since its occupants died suddenly, was "in the best of condition," with about 120 acres cleared, and he was "liking it very well."[16] In all, 349 British families were settled under the New Brunswick scheme in the teeth of the Depression, 172 of whom were still on their farms fourteen years later, having presumably weathered the worst of the economic storm.[17]

In August 1927, WRJ's "Notes from Eastern Canada" had made passing reference to the appointment of a new Scottish manager at the Cossar Farm in New Brunswick and outlined the scheme whereby boys were selected in Scotland under the terms of the Empire Settlement Act for farm training and subsequent employment in Canada.[18] The assisted migration of juveniles to Canada was not new but, like subsidized farming settlement, was given extra momentum by the Empire Settlement Act. Since at least the 1870s several British philanthropists had incorporated assisted migration of needy men, women and children into a variety of rescue and rehabilitation programs which attempted, in the absence of state welfare provision, to alleviate problems of destitution, overpopulation and unemployment. Undergirding most of the relief programs was an evangelical Christian commitment to offer both practical and spiritual help to needy individuals, increasingly reinforced by a eugenic confidence that the future of Britain and the Empire could best be secured by the judicious transfer of suitable recruits from debilitating urban environments before their constitutions had been irreparably damaged. None of these sentiments was eroded either by the First World War or by the hesitant beginnings of state-funded welfare, although eugenic, imperialist arguments steadily overtook Christian concerns. Organizations like Barnardo's and Quarrier's Homes, which were established as part of the late Victorian enthusiasm for evangelical philanthropy, continued to combine domestic rescue work with assisted migration throughout the 1920s, when they were joined by a variety of new enterprises eager to capitalise on the shared funding opportunities made available by the Empire Settlement Act.[19]

The best-known philanthropist in the Maritimes was probably George Cossar, whose farm at Lower Gagetown in New Brunswick had begun to recruit Scottish trainees in 1910. Like his contemporaries, he promoted juvenile migration as a means of both relieving domestic difficulties and addressing the Canadian clamour for agriculturists, but his activities remained fairly low-key until funding from the Oversea Settlement Department allowed him to purchase a selecting centre in Scotland in 1922. For sixteen years the Gagetown enterprise was wholly owned and run by Cossar himself, but between 1926 and 1931 it was managed and subsidised by a Council of Management in Scotland, assisted by a Canadian committee, though Cossar himself continued to provide most of the funding. Although his name never became as well known as that of Barnardo or his fellow countryman and probable model,

William Quarrier, Cossar's influence on youth training and employment in both central Scotland and the Maritimes was not insignificant, and in 1948 he was accorded a glowing posthumous tribute. "In Eastern Canada," it was asserted in a radio broadcast, "no person has done more for immigrant boys, no name is held in such respect and regard as that of the late George Carter Cossar, C.B.E., M.C. . . . To the Maritimer the name 'Cossar' has become synonymous with integrity, uprightness and Christian endeavour."[20]

Born into a wealthy Glasgow family in 1880, Cossar attended Rugby School and Oxford, where he graduated in civil and mining engineering before taking up a temporary post in Peru. His charitable conscience had been aroused in his student days, when he had seen the plight of homeless men sleeping on the Thames Embankment, but it was disadvantaged juveniles whom he sought to rehabilitate on his return to Glasgow, opening missions, soup kitchens and clubs in the city centre and purchasing a training farm in Ayrshire, Todhill, to instruct and then place boys in farm service at home or abroad.[21] To facilitate Canadian placements, in 1910 he purchased a 700-acre farm with an eighteenth-century colonial farmhouse at Gagetown, New Brunswick. Recruits were sent there for training, either directly or via Todhill, before being placed out with individual farmers in the province, and Cossar managed to persuade the Canadian immigration authorities to grant him the statutory commission of one pound sterling per head, on the grounds that they were legitimate agricultural labourers required to work on his farm. In 1911 he escorted his first recruits to Gagetown, along with a man and wife from Stirlingshire to superintend the venture, and he subsequently purchased three adjacent farms to increase his holding to one thousand acres. By 1913, when G. Bogue Smart, Canada's Chief Inspector of Juvenile Immigration, submitted a report on the farm, 250 boys had passed through its doors, and by 1922 this number had risen to 800. Although Smart suggested that Cossar was naive in expecting his recruits to repay their fares, he reported that each boy, when interviewed individually, had expressed enthusiasm for his work, and concluded that "Mr. Cossar's plan of supplying a good class of young Scotch immigrants is not only commendable but advantageous to Canada and deserving of encouragement."[22]

Until 1922, Cossar—who during World War I had retrained as a doctor and won the Military Cross in France—assisted emigration entirely at his own expense. Then, encouraged by the funding made available under the Empire Settlement Act, he purchased for £2000, with the aid of private donations, the 36-acre Craigielinn Estate near Paisley, to be used as a basic Scottish training farm.[23] As before the war, trainees were to be mainly "city boys of the poorer classes" who would be referred by schools, labour exchanges, Presbyterian churches or individuals. Craigielinn was given a grant in return for testing one hundred boys per annum with a view to their permanent settlement as farm workers in either Canada or Australia. The farm's directors were to admit only those applicants who showed potential to be successful colonists, and from such trainees they were subsequently to make an initial selection of candidates for presentation to the colonial selecting authority. Cossar was interested not only in impoverished youths, for he acted as a Scottish agent for the British Immigration and Colonisation Association from its inception in 1924, welcoming the opportunity both to orchestrate the migration of self-financing boys from affluent families and to extend his influence by arranging placements in provinces other than New Brunswick. After 1924, Canada replaced Australia as the primary destination of Craigielinn trainees, who were sent not only to the association's receiving hostel in Montreal but also to Lower Gagetown farm, which was used by the association as its reception centre in New Brunswick.[24]

Eighteen months after Craigielinn's establishment on a subsidised basis, Cossar was in no doubt that it constituted a successful assault on poverty and unemployment and was therefore worthy of supplementary public support. In making an appeal for £2000 through the Scottish press, he pointed out that of more than 250 lads tested at Craigielinn, 160 had gone overseas, while others had been passed as fit and were waiting their turn to go, many of them "after several years of idleness."[25] Cossar's canvassing did not fall on deaf ears, for Craigielinn was well supported by public subscriptions, and by 31 October 1928 it had expanded its premises and trained a total of 1,076 boys, of whom 535 had been sent to Canada and 199 to Australia. The directors were well satisfied with their work, which had grown despite competition from more glamorous agencies which offered boys immediate transfer overseas without the apparent drudgery of preliminary testing. Although the directors were mostly Glasgow-based, Craigielinn's recruitment field was Scotland-wide:

> We have taken boys from every part of Scotland, ranging from the Shetland Isles to Berwickshire, and, while most of the boys were from the cities, we were glad to have a leavening from the country, who helped to make the others more contented by their outlook on life away from the crowd. From the advantage that has been taken of our extended accommodation, it is evident that there is an increasing desire among many boys to get overseas, and that the thoughtful parent values the opportunity of a preliminary testing. A satisfactory feature is the number of younger brothers coming, whose brothers were at Craigielinn before emigrating.[26]

Like most of his contemporaries and predecessors, Cossar attempted to generate public support by peppering his annual reports with letters of gratitude and recommendation from successful migrants. Included in the 1926 report, for example, was the following contented account of life at Irishtown, New Brunswick:

Although Scotland is the land of my birth and childhood, I must say that the Canadian country life has got it beat all to pieces as far as weather, work, and opportunity goes. On the fine winter days we have snow shoeing, ski-ing, sleighing, also skating if there is any ice near. I like the autumn—there is hunting, big or little game, trapping, and lots of fun in the woods for the outdoor man or boy. I feel that Canada is the country for me. Mr. M___, an Irish Protestant, heard through his sister, who lives in the Shediac Road, that I was looking for work. Being quite clanish [sic] to the Old Country people, Mr. M___ came and offered to teach me the most delightful business of breeding silver foxes for their fur, and help to install me in the fox business myself later. Mr. and Mrs. M. send a cordial invitation to you, through me, to visit their home next autumn, and I, most of all, would be delighted to see you.[27]

The following year's report included ten illustrated letters from Cossar boys in New Zealand, Australia and Canada, and while the three Australian letters included reservations as well as recommendations, the New Zealand correspondent and six correspondents in Canada were unequivocal in their praise. One of three boys writing from the Maritimes passed on his mother's request that his brother could be located in the same part of Nova Scotia when he came out to Canada, since "This is just what you said, a great country. I like the work, like the people, and in fact, I like everything." The second, located on a farm in New Brunswick after only three days at Lower Gagetown, urged Cossar to "tell the boys at Craigielinn that they could not come to a better country." And the third expressed delight with his domestic arrangements: "The people I am with think the world of me, they call me their son. They have a private car, and when they go out they take me with them. I am earning 12 dollars a month, they give me 6, and put the rest in the bank for me, and I think they are doing the right thing, for in later years I will need it, not just now."[28]

Not surprisingly, selected success stories and positive accounts of chain migration present only a partial picture of Cossar's activities. Even the propagandist annual reports contain some hints of bad conduct, the "abandoning" of colonial life, and the damaging opposition raised against Cossar through negative press statements made by those who, he claimed, "were failures in the Colonies and, in many cases, misfits at home."[29] Canadian Immigration Department files contain more explicit complaints about the deficiencies of Cossar boys—and their sponsor. As early as 1913, sixty citizens of Gagetown petitioned the immigration authorities in Ottawa "with a view to stopping the frequent crimes which have been committed in our community, by the boys brought out here from the Old Country by Mr. Cossar and others," asking that checks should be made to ensure that no recruits had a criminal record or had been inmates of a reformatory. Cossar dismissed the complaint as sectarianism on the part of the hostile Anglican majority in Gagetown and pointed out that only two of his two hundred recruits (neither of whom had a previous record) had turned out badly.[30] Boys were periodically deported for vagrancy, criminal convictions, illness, laziness, unadaptability or, in one case, because the recruit was "thoroughly unsatisfactory and a bad influence on other boys." Others were criticised for absconding from the Gagetown farm, whose reputation suffered further when in 1925 the British Immigration and Colonisation Association decided to send all its delinquent boys there instead of returning them to Scotland.[31] Employers sometimes complained that boys were undersized or spendthrift. One such derogatory comment on recruit John Wemyss by a farmer at Andover, New Brunswick, was made to G. Bogue Smart and passed on by him to the superintendent at Gagetown:

> John has but recently arrived. He is all legs and arms, and with the ever present cigarette, he looks like a centipede. Like all or more of Cossars Glasgow boys, he is an inverterate [sic] smoker. In fact Farquhar [the employer] tells me he has drawn the entire $6.00 for clothes and pocket money and spent it on cigarettes—leaving nothing to go towards clothes. He may pull through but it will take time. He is also very apt to tell lies. He is of good manners and attractive personality.[32]

In November 1924 a scathing attack on the management at Gagetown was made in a report by a former matron Margaret Waugh, to G.G. Melvin, the chief medical officer in Fredericton:

> Dr. Cossar, a medical doctor in active practice in Glasgow, and who goes about preaching at times as well, collects boys in Scotland for emigration to his farm in the county of Queens at Lower Gagetown. These boys are supposed to be fed and clad and to get $10 a month and supposed to remain one year on the farm, at the end of which time they are supposed to be free of debt and to be trained to hire out to farmers. . . .
> These boys seem never to be out of debt. After hiring out so many months there is always something to be paid out to the Meiklejohns. . . . Mr. and Mrs. Meiklejohn have been in charge of the farm for 14 or 15 years. . . . There is nothing to work with nor to cook with and the boys do their own cooking and washing. There is no sanitary arrangement; one lavatory which is used only by Mr. and Mrs. Meiklejohn to which they hold the key. No patent water-closet. The only water laid on is in the kitchen, by tap. There is no bathroom; no means of bodily washing; no tanks, no boilers, no hot water system. . . . The boys are neither well-fed nor properly clad. . . . They get neither butter nor

milk and no meat except once in a long while. Meal and water and bread, stewed apple cooked without sugar, constitute their food. A boy of about 16 [is] at present doing the cooking. They are obliged to carry water from the Meiklejohn kitchen and if it does not suit Mrs. Meiklejohn when they come for water or food to give it, they do not get either until she is ready to do so. Last week end, there was no bread and the boy doing the cooking was ordered to make scones. He did so and Mrs. Meiklejohn, wishing the oven, took the half baked scones out of the oven and put them on the boys' table to be eaten by them. Mrs. Meiklejohn is apparently suffering from asthma or consumption and is not careful respecting sanitary aspect of the matter. The boys appear to be much afraid of both Mr. and Mrs. Meiklejohn. No one will remain as matron in the home. The boys rise at 5 a.m., and have no light in the morning. At night a stable lamp is placed on the table. The house is cold. Mr. Meiklejohn made the statement to Mrs. Waugh that the boys were liars and thieves and had been taken out of reformatories and gutters.[33]

Although Margaret Waugh's claims contradicted Dr. Melvin's earlier impression that the boys were well nourished, and were challenged by Cossar on the grounds of the matron's unsuitability for the post of assistant to the sickly Mrs. Meiklejohn, G. Bogue Smart did find some of her complaints substantiated and advised Cossar to renovate the buildings and improve procedure.[34]

Official opinion was divided about the calibre of the Meiklejohns' successor, John Jackson, a noted shorthorn breeder who arrived with his wife in 1927. M.J. Scobie, manager of the British Immigration and Colonisation Association, spoke highly of the new superintendent, perhaps not surprisingly, given Cossar's close relationship with the association. The Cossar farm was "the finest conducted Boys' Farm which I have seen," his only criticism being "that great care must be taken else the boys will find that the surroundings while at the farm are so pleasant they will not be ready to put up with the conditions as found on the ordinary New Brunswick farm and will be constantly returning."[35] Jackson came in for criticism from the Canadian immigration authorities, however, for his lax attention to selection of employers and after care, being more concerned with farm management and agricultural experimentation than with the welfare of the boys. He admitted that pressure of time sometimes prevented him from checking employers' references, homes were not always visited in advance and almost never thereafter unless trouble arose, and there was no clear procedure for indenturing the boys, ensuring regular payment of their wages, answering their enquiries or even keeping track of them.[36] Although deficient inspection was addressed by the appointment of one Captain Clingo in 1930, his task was complicated by the fact that Cossar's recruits were mostly older boys who, having "knocked about Glasgow for two or three years after leaving school," resented regulations about compulsory saving of wages and tended to find their own situations.[37] The scathing observations of D.J. Murphy, the Canadian Immigration Department's representative in Saint John, suggest that matters had deteriorated rather than improved by 1930. Writing to Bogue Smart, he claimed that his hard-hitting report simply reflected the opinions of many complainants.

> There is no doubt but the boys in many cases are being exploited by employers, and in others, Cossar throws them in without a semblance of investigation. I find boys all over the country working on roads for their employers who give the lads none of the earnings although these same boys do the chores at night and morning in addition to milking etc. . . . In far the majority of cases I find Cossar's lads are farmed out without agreements, and seldom or ever do they get any real notice (outside of prayer circulars) and the loose check is not doing any good. Jackson lives in luxury and yet he can't keep boys about the place to give them some sort of idea of Canadian ways. I saw last year when there, grass growing out of his potato planter, that is not what boys should see on landing at the farm. Boys leave one job and find another on their own and it is all the same to Mr. J. As long as he is not worried, all is well. He is a farmer on the stock side, and has no real time for the most important of all work—the welfare of the boys. I also notice so often that I fear there is truth in my conviction, that after he gets the amount owing to Cossar for outfit, he is no longer vitally interested. It is only too self-evident.
>
> Then this awful heavy outfit. The hobnailed boots are a constant irritant to the woman of the house and of no real use on Canadian farms where there are no paved roads or stone floors to barns. In they bring heaps of manure stuck to the soles and the woman starts to whine, the boy starts to talk back, she calls him saucy, he asks for his pay and the man of the house comes in and throws him out. All due to Cossar's boots. . . . Now this is not imagination, and if the Dr. on his visits would talk to the family instead of the boy behind the barn, and tell the family he wanted their view point he would get some of the truths I am writing.[38]

Bogue Smart's annual inspection in 1931 confirmed some of Murphy's complaints, revealing a "quota of misfits and problem cases" amongst the boys during the year, in spite of "careful selection." Twenty boys had been returned to Scotland, while 14 of the 188 remaining in New Brunswick had left their farm placements and were awaiting relocation. However, Bogue Smart felt that, despite the intractability of some of the recruits, "Dr Cossar's efforts to provide the farmers of the Maritime Provinces, more particularly New Brunswick, with juvenile farm help, are generally appreciated by employers," and that Jackson's record-keeping had improved considerably.[39]

Complaints were also made by a few dissatisfied boys and their parents. Glaswegian Hugh Paterson, 14, who went to the Cossar Farm with his 17-year-old brother William in July 1924, resented being pressurised to sign a contract which would prevent the brothers from moving to Toronto where two sisters and another brother were already settled, and where his widowed mother was about to emigrate with two younger children. He also hinted that W.J. O'Brien of the British Immigration and Colonisation Association was the real power behind the Cossar enterprise:

> Dear Mother,
> I don't like starting this wrong but I've got to. The people from some Association here are trying to get us to sign a contract for a year, or rather to consent to the farmer signing it, to keep us for 1 year, the best pay being $10 a month with some given to us for pocket money and some put in a bank somewhere nobody around here has heard of. Willie and I refused to consent until we had heard from Alec or you. He led us to believe it was his scheme but its the Orangemen here with a guy called O'Brien at the head of it, that's bringing us Protestant boys out. Cossar's only an agent, darn him. He never told us about contract or anything else and he said he would come round and see us all, but he came and just visited one fellow as far as I've heard, and he was a chap that came from 28 Monteith Row, do you see through it? [Cossar lived at 23 Monteith Row, Glasgow]. They're just twisting the contract business round so as the farmer could have us for a year and work us like—like—the dickens for $10 a month. I believe I could stick it for a year but I don't know about the boss sticking me. I'll sign the contract if you and Alec want me and so will Willie but if they come funny will show them how far a Scotsmans neck can shoot out. The man also mentioned that we might be deported if we didn't sign. I asked him what for and he couldn't say.[40]

Cossar and his staff not only defended themselves against allegations of neglect, lax policy and deception; they also attacked restrictive dominion regulations which, in both Canada and Australia, led to the rejection of many applicants on the grounds of underdeveloped physique. Disputes with the Canadian immigration authorities increased after 1928, when—on Cossar's own suggestion—New Brunswick handed over to Gagetown Farm the responsibility for processing all the province's assisted juvenile immigrants, making it the provincial training centre for the reception, distribution and placement in New Brunswick of all boys recruited in the United Kingdom for that purpose under assisted passage agreements. Cossar was henceforth required to bring out one hundred boys per year under his own auspices, as well as receive those recruited by other organizations, but his heightened role was a mixed blessing. On the one hand, he seemed to have secured the future of his colonial training farm in an era of increasingly restricted operations, when it was awarded an annual federal grant of $500, paid through the province, with the provincial and Dominion governments also shouldering responsibility for placement and after-care.[41] On the other hand, he felt the new arrangements had seriously reduced his independence and control over the venture which bore his name.

Because the farm at Gagetown had been turned into a provincial reception centre, Cossar was unable to require all recruits—particularly those from rural areas—to undergo preliminary training at Craigielinn, as both he and John Jackson wished, and he suspected that his preference for "city boys of the poorer classes" was being eroded by the federal and provincial governments' tendency to select rural recruits or boys who had received a secondary education. Craigielinn trainees were then put at a further disadvantage, he claimed, by stringent new federal medical regulations, and after 1928 he complained frequently that enforcement of a minimum height requirement of five feet was resulting in two out of every three such trainees being rejected. Although he admitted that city-bred boys were often of below-average height before emigrating, he claimed that this did not impair their farming skills or their popularity with New Brunswick's farmers. But his threat to close down the Craigielinn centre and his proposal to take responsibility for the repatriation of any under-sized boy who failed to find employment cut no ice with the Dominion immigration authorities, which argued that since the farm at Gagetown had been designated the provincial training centre, it should set an example in securing only "strong, robust boys."[42]

Far from lowering standards, the federal immigration authorities responded to the deepening depression by encouraging juvenile migration societies to discontinue operations on the approach of winter. In 1929, Cossar had persuaded the New Brunswick authorities to allow his work to continue, but when he proposed to send out sixty boys between September 1930 and February 1931, the federal authorities warned the provincial government that it would be financially answerable for any concessions it made, and stated vehemently:

> We killed the assisted farm labour movement by allowing unsuitable men to be included for assisted passage who were not farm labourers and never intended to be. This was on the pressure of transportation and other interests. The agricultural family movement was practically killed for the same reason. The trainee movement has come to an inglorious end because we allowed men to come who were not fit. Now pressure is concentrated on the juveniles and if we allow other interests than the interests of the boys themselves and the Province to which they are going, to govern the movement, we will put the juve-

nile movement where the others have gone.[43]

Increasing tension between Cossar and the Canadian immigration authorities was reflected in a long-running correspondence about the criteria on which boys were to be judged. James Malcolm, the Canadian government emigration agent in Glasgow—whom Cossar accused of both inconsistency in selection and a "blasphemous and rough" attitude—complained that Cossar knowingly submitted delinquents and boys who were medically unfit. He cited two cases from Edinburgh: one was of an epileptic who had been referred to Cossar by the Scottish Society for the Prevention of Cruelty to Children (SSPCC) after having been rejected earlier by the Canadian medical officers; the other was of an illegitimate boy who, having been put on probation for theft, was one of forty "problem cases" referred to Cossar by the Edinburgh Juvenile Organisations Committee between 1929 and 1931 with a view to emigration. According to the boy's mother, "he had the choice of going to Canada or going to gaol, and he chose to go to Canada under Dr. Cossar's scheme."[44]

The Canadian immigration authorities, while sympathetic to Cossar's desire to befriend "unfortunate waifs," were, not unnaturally, anxious "that the material he helps from the gutter should be absorbed on the other side rather than sent to this country. . . . if he is fishing in such muddy waters in Edinburgh, he is likely to be doing it elsewhere and the percentage of runts and failures that he sends out absolutely justifies us in applying all the tests that have been applied in the past and probably a few more."[45] The Canadians also alleged that Cossar was guilty of double standards, pressing for relaxed entry regulations while at the same time abusing the government-subsidized charity rate by returning boys whom he deemed unsuitable on some trifling and precipitate excuse. In 1931 twenty boys were sent back to Scotland, including eleven "failures" and four on health grounds. As one Canadian civil servant commented crossly, "It is somewhat of an anomaly to find the Cossar people on the one hand asking us to help some more boys out this year and on the other hand having them send boys home whose only undesirability so far as I can see is requiring several placements."[46]

Cossar was unmoved by senior immigration official F.C. Blair's advice to "declare a holiday until conditions improve" and remained determined to proceed despite the cessation of Empire Settlement funding in 1931.[47] In 1932, however, Craigielinn's increasing financial difficulties led to its free transfer to the Church of Scotland's Social Work Committee, and it was subsequently used as a training centre for youths on probation and potential delinquents until it was sold to Paisley Town Council in 1937.[48] At the same time the farm at Lower Gagetown—rebuilt after the original eighteenth-century building had been destroyed by fire in December 1929—functioned independently as a training centre for unemployed boys from eastern Canada, under Cossar's renewed personal control and John Jackson's superintendence. By 1938, Cossar was involved in what a New Brunswick newspaper called "a cloak and dagger drama," rescuing more than two hundred Jewish children from Nazi Germany, but in 1942 he died in Scotland, as a result of heart disease and exposure suffered two years earlier when the ship on which he was escorting evacuee children to Canada was torpedoed in the Atlantic. Much of his estate was bequeathed to the juvenile rescue work he had so long supported, and in 1945 Jackson and two associates purchased the farm from Cossar's trustees, although in the changed postwar climate they were unsuccessful in their intention of re-establishing assisted immigration from Scotland.[49]

Perhaps the most appropriate epitaph on Cossar was penned by New Brunswick immigration agent Major D.J. Murphy, who, having observed his work in both Scotland and Canada, concluded in 1933 that "he means well but does not know how to go about it."[50] He was naive both in expecting recruits to repay their fares and in his failure to see that some boys who had families in Canada were simply making use of his facilities in order to rejoin their relatives, absconding from the Gagetown farm and leaving him out of pocket for fares and outfit. More importantly, he remained largely oblivious to the fact that his rescue work was not supplying the type of recruits demanded by either Canada or Australia. By 1926 he had fallen out with the Australian agents over their reluctance to accept Craigielinn trainees, despite repeated efforts by the Oversea Settlement Committee to explain the reasons and work out a compromise, and he never achieved his intention of establishing a training and distribution farm in Australia.[51] Having operated the Canadian farm at his own expense and by his own rules from 1910 to 1928, he never really understood or accepted the principles of assisted migration under the Empire Settlement Act and was irked at the restrictions placed on his activities after Gagetown became a provincial training centre.

Cossar's problems raise the wider question of whether state involvement assisted or impeded migration and settlement, particularly when it impinged on enterprises which were established well before 1922. For Cossar, the Empire Settlement Act was a two-edged sword, offering financial assistance with one hand while taking away freedom of selection with the other, and in 1930 he complained to the secretary of state for Scotland that Canada was dictating policy to the Oversea Settlement Committee, so that "it is much harder for me to get boys away than it was before the Government gave assistance in the way of fares."[52] G. Whiskard of the Oversea Settlement Department summed up the whole problem of state-assisted migration when he responded—sympathetically but negatively—to a request by Cossar in 1930 that the department should help him finance the passages of boys whom he regarded as suitable, but who had been rejected by the Canadian authorities:

I am afraid that we must look at this question from a rather different point of view than you do. You, of course, are concerned with the individual boy and are anxious to give him a better chance. We are concerned rather with the whole movement from the point of view of the economic advantage to the various parts of the Empire.[53]

However, by that time the onset of worldwide depression had rendered assisted migration an economic burden rather than an asset to the Empire, and in 1932 Cossar estimated that expenditure at Gagetown exceeded income by about $6,000. His misfortune in being confronted with economic circumstances beyond his control is also illustrated by the plight of one of his recruits, Henry Allan from Glasgow, who, four years after being sent to New Brunswick, appealed to the secretary of the British Emigration Hostel in Montreal to arrange for his repatriation on the grounds that he was penniless and could not obtain work. Both he and his erstwhile employer had fallen victim to the Depression.

> I was forced to walk the road for a while this winter until Mr. Dunn gave me shelter for the time being. Mr. Dunn cannot keep me very long as he is an English settler himself and has a hard time to make ends meet himself at present. My mother is anxious for me to go back home to Glasgow and she wrote and asked me to apply to your department to repatriate me, as I have stated I have no money and cannot obtain work and had it not been for Mr. Dunn's kindnes [sic] in giving me shelter I would have to become a public charge.[54]

Cossar's success was impeded not only by his own naivety, the limitations of the Empire Settlement Act and the impact of international depression. Throughout the 1920s he had tried to implement his colonization scheme in a region beset by multifaceted economic, social and political problems, where internal initiatives such as the disparate Maritime Rights movement and attempts to create a federal university or develop a coherent policy on prohibition had all fallen on stony ground. In view of the discouraging Maritime environment in which he operated, it was therefore little wonder that Cossar's campaign failed to match his claims or expectations. Yet although his vision was frustrated and his name does not rank in the history books alongside those of Barnardo or Quarrier, his achievements were not insignificant. For more than two decades his work, which saw around nine hundred boys sent to Canada and two hundred to Australia, was relatively untainted by complaints from employers or accusations of exploitation from recruits. He established the farm at Lower Gagetown both as a reception centre and also to set a fair wage level for the province, and some of his recruits preferred to stay there to "have a good time" on ten dollars a month rather than seek independent employment elsewhere.[55] Not only were disadvantaged urban youths given opportunities which Scotland could not afford them thanks to training in the farming skills which the dominions required; the good reputation earned by Cossar also enabled him to exercise exceptional influence over the wider juvenile migration policy of the province of New Brunswick even as other philanthropists began to retreat from that type of enterprise, and it is remarkable that Scottish youths continued to be absorbed into New Brunswick society despite the deep-seated and increasing economic malaise that afflicted Atlantic Canada. Surprisingly, the great majority of his recruits—he alleged— became successful farmers in the Maritimes, while others attained prominent positions in a variety of professions. One boy became a Beaverbrook scholar at the University of New Brunswick, one became a leading fox rancher on Prince Edward Island; one held high office in the New York City Police Force; one returned to Scotland to serve on the staff of the Craigielinn Farm; and one became a squadron leader in the Royal Canadian Air Force during the Second World War.[56] But Cossar's influence went beyond the sphere of juvenile migration, for his long-running enterprise made a significant contribution to the general rehabilitation of Maritime Canada as a mainstream destination for immigrants both before and after the Empire Settlement Act redrew the boundaries of public policy on both sides of the Atlantic. It was a remarkable achievement, wrested out of a background of chronic economic problems, labour unrest and outmigration, as well as an endorsement both of the power of informal networks and the lingering role of Imperial administration in dominion affairs.

Notes

1. For discussion of problems in the Maritimes in the 1920s, see John G. Reid, "The 1920s: Decade of Struggles," in his *Six Crucial Decades: Times of Change in the History of the Maritimes* (Halifax, 1987), pp. 161–89, and David Frank, "The 1920s: Class and Region, Resistance and Accommodation," in E.R. Forbes and D.A. Muise, eds., *The Atlantic Provinces in Confederation* (Toronto, 1993), pp. 233–71.
2. The activities of emigration agents are discussed in detail in Marjory Harper, *Emigration from North-East Scotland*, vol. 2, *Beyond the Broad Atlantic* (Aberdeen, 1988), pp. 15–41.
3. *Press and Journal*, 20 September 1924.
4. *Scottish Farmer*, 17 January 1925, p. 74.
5. *Scottish Farmer*, 17 January 1925, p. 74.
6. *Scottish Farmer*, 20 February 1926, p. 234.
7. *Scottish Farmer*, 27 March 1926, p. 430; 12 November 1927, p. 1540; 17 November 1928, p. 1533; 29 March 1930, p. 444.
8. *Scottish Farmer*, 29 March 1924, p. 396.
9. *Scottish Farmer*, 10 May 1924, pp. 590–1.
10. Frank, "The 1920s," p. 234.
11. Frank, "The 1920s," pp. 238–3.
12. Kent Fedorowich, "The assisted emigration of British ex-servicemen to the dominions, 1914–1922," in Stephen Constantine,ed., *Emigrants and Empire: Brit-*

ish Settlement in the Dominions between the Wars (Manchester, 1990), p. 63.

13. For further discussion of Empire Settlement in relation to Canada, see John A. Schulz, "'Leaven for the lump': Canada and Empire Settlement, 1918–1939," in Constantine, *Emigrants and Empire*.
14. *Scottish Farmer*, 26 September 1925, p. 1244. See also Flora's letters of 25 July 1925, p. 983, and 7 November 1925, p. 1471.
15. *Press and Journal*, 5 December 1923.
16. *Scottish Farmer*, 24 October 1931, p. 1453.
17. G.F. Plant, *Overseas Settlement. Migration from the United Kingdom to the Dominions* (Oxford, 1951), p. 109. Fifty families returned to the United Kingdom and 127 families remained in Canada but followed occupations other than farming.
18. *Scottish Farmer*, 27 August 1927, p. 1163.
19. For further discussion of juvenile migration schemes, see Marjory Harper, "Making Christian Colonists: an evaluation of the emigration policies and practices of the Scottish Churches and Christian organisations between the wars," *Records of the Scottish Church History Society* 28(1998) pp 173–215.
20. Provincial Archives of New Brunswick (PANB), MC 2402, Vera Ayling Records.
21. Cossar to W.J. White, Dept of the Interior, Ottawa, 3 November 1909, in National Archives of Canada (NAC), RG 76, C-10647, vol. 568, file 811910, part 1.
22. Report by G. Bogue Smart on Gagetown Farm, 15 September 1913, in ibid.
23. *Glasgow Herald*, 3 August 1922. See also Agreement between the Secretary of State for the Colonies and Craigielinn Farm, 28 August 1922, NAC, RG 76, C-7821, vol. 282, file 234636.
24. *Montreal Star*, 15 August 1924.
25. *Press and Journal*, 15 April 1924.
26. Annual Report of the Cossar Boys' Training Farms Inc., 1927–28, NAC, RG 76, C-7831, vol. 282, file 234636.
27. Annual Report of the Cossar Boys' Training Farms Inc., 1927–28, NAC, RG 76, C-10646, vol. 567, file 811910, part 2.
28. G.M., J. McI. and J. McC. in Annual Report of the Cossar Boys' Training Farms Inc., 1927–28, NAC, RG 76, C-7831, vol. 282, file 234636.
29. Scottish Record Office (SRO), AF/51/171, Annual Report of the Cossar Boys' Training Farms Inc., 21 December 1923.
30. Rev. William Smith, Gagetown, to Dept of the Interior, 14 October 1913; Cossar to W.D. Scott, Superintendent of Immigration, Ottawa, 6 December 1913, NAC, RG 76, C-10647, vol. 568, file 811910, part 1.
31. Deportation order of 26 March 1929, NAC, RG 76, C-7831, vol. 282, file 234636; Cossar to F.C. Blair, Assistant Deputy Minister, Ottawa, 8 August 1931, and John Jackson to Blair, 15 August 1931, NAC, RG 76, C-10646-7, vol. 567, file 811910, part 2; J. Obed Smith to W.D. Scott, 22 August 1917, and Mr. Meiklejohn to G. Bogue Smart, 23 October 1925 in ibid., part 1.
32. G. Bogue Smart to John Jackson, 17 August 1928, NAC, RG 76, C-10647, vol. 568, file 811910, part 1.
33. Waugh to Melvin, 14 November 1924, in ibid.
34. Memo by Smart, 20 January 1925; Cossar to W. J. Egan, Deputy Minister of Immigration, Ottawa, 6 March 1925, in ibid.
35. Scobie to Blair, 13 January 1932, NAC, RG 76, C-10646-7, vol. 567, file 811910,

part 3.
36. Report by G. Bogue Smart on Cossar Farm, 21 September 1929, in ibid., part 3.
37. Jackson to Bogue Smart, 6 April 1932, in ibid.
38. D.J. Murphy to Bogue Smart, 4 July 1930, in ibid.
39. Report by Smart on Cossar Farm, 13 October 1931, in ibid, part 2.
40. Hugh Paterson to his mother, "Sunday 6th" [September 1924], in ibid.
41. J.A. Murray, Minister of Immigration and Industry, New Brunswick, to W.R. Little, Commissioner of Emigration, 7 October 1927, NAC, RG 76, C-7821, vol. 282, file 234636. See also internal memorandum of the Dept of Immigration and Colonisation, Ottawa, 3 January 1934, NAC, RG 76, C-10260, vol. 356, file 397430.
42. Annual Report of the Cossar Boys' Training Farms Inc., 26 April 1929, NAC, RG 76, C-7821, vol. 282, file 234636.
43. Blair to Egan, 8 September 1930, NAC, RG 76, C-10647, vol. 567, file 811910.
44. Immigration and Colonisation Department Memorandum, 10 April 1930; Malcolm to Little, 21 May 1931; Cossar to Little, 30 May 1931, in ibid.
45. Blair to Murray, 24 June 1931, in ibid.
46. Blair to Little, 25 August 1931, in ibid, part 2.
47. Blair to Cossar, 31 August 1931; Little to Blair, 7 September 1931, in ibid.
48. Church of Scotland, Minutes of the Committee on Social Work, 11 March 1931, and 19 October 1932; Minutes of the Committee on Christian Life and Work, 7 April and 27 May 1937.
49. *Saint John Telegraph Journal*, 18 December 1929, 13 October 1948; Vera Ayling Records, PANB, MC 2402; Cossar's Will, registered in the Books of the Lords of Council and Session, Edinburgh, 26 August 1942, copy in PANB.
50. Murphy to Blair, 14 June 1933, NAC, RG 76, C-10647, vol. 567, file 811910, part 1.
51. G.F. Plant to Cossar, 16 February 1926 (Scottish Record Office, AF 51/174).
52. Cossar to Hon. William Adamson, 26 March 1930, in ibid.
53 Whiskard to Cossar, 24 February 1930, NAC, RG 76, C-10647, vol. 567, file 811910, part 1.
54. Allan to British Emigration Hostel Secretary, 24 January 1933, in ibid.
55. Blair to Little, 27 March 1933, in ibid., part 2.
56. Vera Ayling Records, PANB, MC 2402.

MEMORY

13

On Remembering and Forgetting:
Highland Memories within the Maritime Diaspora

Rusty Bitterman

This chapter concerns memory and change within the Highland communities that developed in the Maritimes as a result of the agrarian transformation of the Scottish Highlands. It explores how the Highland past was remembered and how it was forgotten. As well, it considers the relationship of remembering to the choices Highland emigrants and their descendants made as they established a new world on the western side of the Atlantic. I argue that, to understand the construction of historical memory among Maritime Highlanders, we must be sensitive to how visions of the past changed over time as well as to the contested nature of that construction.

The rough outlines of the agrarian transformation of the Highlands are well known. In the wake of Culloden, market forces penetrated the Highlands at a pace that far outstripped earlier economic shifts, and social changes which would see the extinction of the clan system proceeded at an unprecedented pace. In short order, in a matter of a few generations, communal land use lost out to individualistic control; and social organization rooted in martial values, reciprocity and a subsistence ethic was swept aside and replaced by commercial mores and practices. The rapidity of the change reflected the impact of war and the growth of an industrial society to the south. It also reflected the extraordinary powers that Highland landlords enjoyed. Under Scottish law, there were virtually no restraints on the ability of Highland chiefs—landlords—to dispose of their lands as they saw fit.[1] Confronted with the pressures and opportunities of a new economic order, there was little to prevent them from deploying their land assets in new ways. The exercise of that power emerged in the evictions and removals that have come to be known as the Clearances.

In the county of Sutherland, a quarter of the rural population were removed from their homes within 12 months.[2] In the Highlands as a whole, somewhere between one-half and two-thirds of the rural population were uprooted over the course of fifty years. Some remained on the coastal fringes of the great estates, ultimately creating the crofting communities that persist to this day. Some migrated southward to various locales in the British Isles. Thousands of others took to the sea to make new homes abroad. Among these emigrants were those who made the Maritimes their home.

In his masterful exploration of the history of those who remained in the Highlands—*The Making of the Crofting Community*—James Hunter suggests that it was decades before the lower orders of the old society, the "commons of the clans" as he has called them, recovered from the shock of the vast changes that agrarian transformation wreaked on their lives. Coping with a new capitalist order, with chiefs who had been transformed into simple landlords, and with clearance and relocation, was a psychological challenge of the greatest magnitude, one that required a refiguring of the past and a vast sorting of what was to be retained and what rejected. Until this was done, the clutter of memory, Hunter argues, impeded the ability of Highlanders effectively to construct a new world for themselves. In short, they had to relocate themselves culturally and socially as well as geographically.[3] This was true not just for the "commons of the clans" but for the upper ranks as well.

Gaelic poetry provides us with one way to understand how Highlanders reconstructed their world. We can start with works from the 1760s and 1770s, when the spread of commercial farming, and the beginning of out-migration as a response, were just getting under way. In the songs of this period, we see a nascent bitter critique of the changes occurring in the Highlands. John MacCodrum, for instance, spoke of the emergence of a "nobility without feeling for poor folk." The Sutherland bard Donald Matheson vehemently denounced the changing ethos of the northeast Highlands in the 1760s. Landlords, he lamented, were altering the social relations which used to prevail. They were treating their tenants as chattels, evicting them and "forcing them" to migrate overseas. In the works of John MacRae of Kintail, two hundred kilometres to the southwest, we hear similar sentiments. MacRae condemned the new attitudes that were shaping landlord behaviour. He complained that chiefs had come, in his words, to "prefer gold to a brave man." While both Matheson and MacRae were optimistic concerning the futures emigrants might make for themselves overseas, such optimism did not dilute their condemnation of those who were forcing Highlanders to look elsewhere for a place to live. In a ballad composed on the eve of his own departure to the Carolinas, MacRae invoked "A curse upon the landlord" who had sent them to sea "for the sake of a paltry rent."[4]

Themes emerging in these ballads are echoed again and again in songs of subsequent decades as other bards explained outmigration in terms of unsought and unwelcome changes, condemned the profit-oriented behaviour of land-lords and hearkened back to a time when Highlanders were valued for their loyalty in battle. What of those who emigrated to British North America? What do we know of their responses to the transformation of the Highlands and of the adjustments they made as they constructed and reconstructed their vision of the past?

We can see in the poetry of the emigrants who made their way to the Maritimes in the late eighteenth and early nineteenth centuries the bards' grief and outrage over changes that violated their sense of a just order. Donald Chisholm witnessed decades of clearances in Strathglass before emigrating to Antigonish County, Nova Scotia, in 1803. In his song "We shall go to America," he called for "A plague on the landlords" who "with their greed for money . . . prefer flocks of sheep/to their own armed" men. Allan Macdonald, who left Lochaber in the early nineteenth century to settle first in Cape Breton and later in mainland Nova Scotia, condemned the "treatment/endured by the poor peo-ple" in the Highlands as lairds enhanced their status by amassing riches at the expense of the rural populace. The Highlands, he claimed in a telling phrase, had become "A land without kindness." Rory Rory MacKenzie, an emigrant to Prince Edward Island, expounded upon the decline of the old military culture of the clans and its replacement by capitalist agriculture. With gleeful bitter-ness he predicted: "When the arrogant Bonaparte comes/with his heavy hand,/ the shepherds will be badly off,/ and we will not grieve for them."[5]

As in earlier works, such as those of Donald Matheson and John MacRae of Kintail, this poetry expressed a yearning compounded of loss and hope. On one hand there is a critique of the new order in the Highlands where landlords would "prefer gold to a brave man," and on the other there is the promise of a new world where things will be different. The backdrop for the critique of the changes in the Highlands in the late eighteenth and early nineteenth centuries is a remembered and reconstructed "other," a Highlands in which commercial considerations were not at the forefront of social relations. What had gone wrong in the Highlands, or at least part of what had gone wrong, was that rents and sheep and profits had come to matter more than people. That was one of the perceptions of the past that Highlanders brought to the Maritimes.

But *whose* voices do we hear in this poetry? By and large, the speakers are not drawn from those whom Hunter would describe as the "commons of the clans." Rather, they tend to be men associated with the middle and upper echelons of Highland society.[6] Among the bards cited, John MacRae and Donald Chisholm had served as foresters and mountain rangers for their chiefs. Donald Matheson was a cattle dealer of substance. Rory Rory MacKenzie was supposedly the hereditary chief of the MacKenzies of Applecross.[7] To note their status in Highland society is not to deny that they could express the sentiments of those below them. John MacRae of Kintail explicitly undertook this task. In his song "Since I have ceased to pay rent," he assumed the voice of the evicted about him and spoke as if he were one of them. In yet another of his ballads he took the voice of the landless. Surely, too, bards of the emigrant stream, composing songs on the eve of departure, on board ship and upon arrival, spoke to and on behalf of their audiences in attempting to describe common experiences. Nonetheless, as they wove strands of the present and the past into a coherent tapestry that might speak to shared feelings, they imbued the product with the values of the strata of Highland society with which they were associated. One notes, for instance, the lamentations for the decline of military values, and nostalgia for the life associated with stag hunting and salmon fishing.

In the New World, men from the middle and upper strata of Highland society would play a central role in establishing pioneer communities and providing leadership in the early years of settlement. Given the critique some of these men articulated of the spread of commercial values in the Old World and their defence of traditional culture, we might expect New World communities to reveal strongly the imprint of their interpretations and their memories. Certainly they helped to transfer to the New World a bitter condemnation of the agrarian transformation of the Highlands, portraying unwanted changes as arriving in the garb of alien commercial goals and lamenting the decline of a culture rooted in traditional values.

What became of this perception of Highland history? What happened to the idea that putting profits before people—"gold before a brave man"—violated an essential aspect of what it was to be a Gael? What became of the notion that Highland history carried a message about the risks inherent in the full-blown development of a commercial agricultural economy?

It seems to me, from the fragmentary evidence I have found, that these messages carried greater lasting significance and resonance for some Highlanders than for others—some wanted to remember and remind, and others wanted to forget. What Highlanders chose to do, I believe, was intimately related to the positions they came to occupy in colonial society.

A letter posted from Portree on the Isle of Skye in the 1830s touches on this dynamic, even though it concerns another issue. The recipient was Murdo MacLeod, a recent immigrant to Prince Edward Island. The letter writer began by noting her pleasure at learning that MacLeod had made it to the colony safely and, indeed, that he was prospering there. It then noted reports that MacLeod was about to get married. The warmth and enthusiasm of the opening passages of the letter abate markedly here. Indeed the tone becomes rather tart. It concludes: "your affectionate wife, Effy MacDonald." Clearly there were things in his past that MacLeod wanted to distance himself from and to forget, memories that had become inconvenient. Clearly as well there were things in his Highland past that Effy shared, and which she did not intend to forget or let Murdo forget.[8]

I believe that on a larger plane this was the case with memory among communities of Highlanders in the New World, and that similar tensions emerged within them concerning remembering and forgetting, and between what was to be rejected and what was to be retained and reconstituted. Although members of the upper echelons of Highland society helped to construct an anti-commercial critique of the agrarian transformation of the Highlands and to transfer it to the New World, they and their descendants would over time distance themselves from key aspects of this construction. Having arrived in a new environment and assayed some of the possibilities of the New World, many, like Murdo MacLeod, must have found certain aspects of their past inconvenient and dispensable.

Although the arrival of a commercial economy in the Highlands may have offered little opportunity for the strata between the chiefs and the "commons of the clans," this was not so in the New World.[9] In British North America, Highlanders who came with skills and capital found an environment in which they could prosper by active participation in the same commercial economy that had been the cause for distress in the Highlands.

It strikes me, following Rosemary Ommer's line of argument here, that the letters of Captain John MacDonald of Glenaladale speak to this tension. And they speak as well, to use Ommer's word, of the "guilt" which it induced.[10] Glenaladale was second in command among the Clanranald chieftains when he organised a migration of Highlanders to Saint John's Island (now called Prince Edward Island) in the early 1770s.[11] Having purchased a twenty thousand-acre estate on the Island, he had to grapple with the challenges of assuming the role of chief and landlord in a New World context. In some of his letters, Captain MacDonald speaks of his desire to serve his tenants "so as to cultivate them and their children." In other letters, he curses the life of being "head of a damned tribe." It is, he says, "the life of a dog."[12] At times MacDonald dreams of being through with the obligations that went with clanship, free simply to pursue the commercial possibilities of his lands on Prince Edward Island.[13] MacDonald's views of the transformation of the Highlands, while not as critically pointed as those of Donald Chisholm and Allan MacDonald, nonetheless carry some of the same messages. When, on a return visit to the Highlands, he describes the movement of sheep into Knoydart and discusses increases in rent and depopulation, his letters do not celebrate the progress heralded by agricultural improvement. Rather, he, like the poets I have cited, speaks of the negative consequences for the lives of those who once lived on the land: "farms which formerly have supported 15 families have now only four or five grey plaided shepherds, and as many thousand sheep. Cows and men will in 40 years be as rare to be seen as deer in that ill-fated country."[14]

MacDonald's dilemma with regard to the management of his Prince Edward Island estate was not dissimilar to that which had confronted chiefs in the Highlands as they weighed the advantages of commercial farming. He has caught between the obligations of the past and the possibilities of the present and the future, between the old order and the new. MacDonald's discomfort, as he considered whether it would be best to sever old connections with his followers, was not unlike that which, at least in some cases, chiefs had felt as they grappled with guilt and the burden of the past. His children, like those of others prominent in the Highlands, were less troubled by notions of paternalism and less bothered by commitment to the idea of collective responsibilities.

It appears that Highland identity was being redefined in the Maritimes in the second quarter of the nineteenth century and, to some extent, Highland history was being recast. I have used MacDonald as an example because the splendid collection of his letters permits us some insight into his thinking, but surely he was not alone in his struggle to adapt, even though unusual in his prominence and the extent of his holdings. Others of more modest station surely also felt such tugs between old and new ways of relating to their fellow kinsmen and to the world about them. Some explored the commercial possibilities of agriculture and trade, others took advantage of the openings available for them in the professions, politics, the military and the church. Success in most of these ventures hinged not just on the skills and capital these men commanded, but on maintaining links with broader communities of Highlanders, and others who might be recruited into this collectivity.

What, though, in changed New World circumstances, would constitute a Highland collective identity? What symbols, traditions and history would serve to bind and to unite in a new context? And what remnants of the past were best discarded?

Looking at the generation after Captain John MacDonald provides some evidence with which to answer these questions. In the late 1830s and early 1840s, Captain John's son, Roderick C. MacDonald, charted one of the ways forward with the establishment of Highland societies throughout the Maritimes. These organizations assumed a leadership role in creating a Highland identity and in constructing a Highland past that would permit prominent men like MacDonald to garner support from more humble Scots on the basis of ethnic loyalty. In the late 1830s, he helped to found Highland societies in Nova Scotia, with a central organization in Halifax and branch societies in Antigonish, St. Mary's and Pictou.[15] In the 1840s, he assisted in the establishment of Highland societies in Charlottetown, Prince Edward Island, and in the New Brunswick towns of Chatham, Newcastle and Saint John.[16] He spoke of his efforts on behalf of these societies in terms of stirring a "movement of Highland feeling" in the region at this time.[17]

The Maritime Highland societies received their charters from the Highland Society of London, which had been founded in 1778. Like the London society, and those it spawned in the British Isles, the Maritime offshoots were broad in their membership, bringing together a wide variety of prominent men having either Highland or Lowland connections. The symbols and traditions that helped to unite the members included banners evoking the arms of the London society, the music of the pipes, the wearing of tartan plaid and the reiteration of achievements associated with martial glory. Being garbed in plaid was mandatory for all Prince Edward Island society members, both at their meetings and at "other public occasions." The Miramichi society in New Brunswick allowed for more latitude, simply requiring that office bearers wear "scarfs of Highland tartan" at all general meetings "in order to keep up the national appearance of the Society."[18]

Like the British societies from which they drew their inspiration, Maritime Highland societies included charity, education and improvement among their stated objects. For example, the Newcastle Highland Society described its goals as educating and improving their countrymen, "perpetuating Highland manners, language and feelings, and to recommend sobriety and industry."[19] As well, Highland societies promoted patriotism and adherence to conservative values.

Some of what we see here is the nineteenth-century foundation of elements of the Scottish tradition that Ian McKay describes in his *Acadiensis* article "Tartanism Triumphant," as the Maritime societies used tartans, the music of the pipes and memories of military glory as reference points for the construction of a Scottish identity. Constructing identity, of course, involves exclusions as well as inclusions. McKay notes in his analysis of the public presentation of Highland traditions in Nova Scotia in the twentieth century that the Clearances and the capitalist transformation of agriculture were not included in the tradition. They were "deftly written out of the official public history." This happened, he argues, because memories of these events did not fit well with the needs of those whose constructions of Scottishness were grounded in an "anti-modernist idea of the organic clan unity of the Scots (the imperishable bonds of kin-folk and clan)."[20] Arguably, this erasure began in the nineteenth century. Although Maritime Highland societies concerned themselves with providing charity for the impoverished emigrants who continued to arrive from the Highlands in the 1830s and 1840s, the causes of their exodus and their poverty do not appear to have been issues for public discussion.

Roderick C. MacDonald's 1843 publication, *Sketches of Highlanders: with an Account of Their Early Arrival in North America*, provides a sense of the inclusions and exclusions of the reconstructed Highland tradition. More than half of his eighty-page book describes the military prowess of Highlanders. The focus is primarily on the courage and loyalty of Highlanders in the Jacobite rebellions, but he includes as well discussions of their loyalty to the British crown during the American Revolution, the War of 1812 and the Rebellions of 1837. Attention is given to the role that Highland gentlemen, such as his father, Captain John MacDonald, played in establishing Highland settlements in British North America, and considerable emphasis is placed on the persistence of traditional loyalties to their betters that were to be found among the Highland population of the Maritimes. MacDonald spends less than one sentence on agrarian transformation and clearance, events that were of central importance to the migration of Highlanders to the Maritimes and to the experience of Highlanders in the eighteenth and nineteenth centuries. He does, however, provide an updated list of clan chiefs and their residences for the benefit of their North American kinsmen.[21]

The timing of the establishment of Highland societies in the Maritimes, and elsewhere in British North America, suggests their role in reconciling the lower classes to their place in the new order, as a flurry of organizational activity followed the social, political and military challenges of the late 1830s.[22] The Highland Society of Canada was initially founded after the crisis of the War of 1812. It slipped into torpor in the 1820s but was resurrected in the wake of the Rebellions.[23] The Highland games held in Lancaster in 1840 were staged in conjunction with a ceremony unveiling a plaque commemorating the role of the "gallant Glengarries in repressing the rebellious and disloyal who threatened the subversion of our present mild and beneficent government."[24] In the hands of the colonial elite, the construction of Highland traditions and their public celebration went hand in hand with affirmations of loyalty and deference to authority. The pronouncements of the Highland societies in the Maritimes make references to strengthening "the feelings of loyalty to the British government," resisting the spread of republicanism and fostering a "new race of Scotchmen" who "will maintain the unsullied form of their chivalrous, patriotic and noble minded ancestors."[25] The Prince Edward Island society described its interest in fostering education on the Island in terms of promoting the "surest means of imbuing youth with sound British principles." The secretary of the Newcastle society spoke of the society cultivating "the purest and most ardent loyalty and attachment to Queen and country," a sentiment which would, should the need arise, induce those inspired by the society to stand "shoulder to shoulder" in defence of British institutions.[26] Charles W. Wallace, president of the Highland Society of Nova Scotia, articulated similar concerns in his correspondence with the London Society in the early 1840s.[27]

Many forces converged in the construction of Highland history and traditions promulgated by the Maritime Highland societies. Some, such as the impact of the Rebellions of the late 1830s, are best understood in terms of the specific British North American context. But the construction needs to be understood as part of a broader development involving elites on both sides of the Atlantic. Although Maritime and Canadian Highland societies in many ways took their lead from the parent society, they also helped to shape it, staying in touch both by correspondence and through the movement of elites between London and its peripheries. As well, there were many direct connections between the Highland notables who were involved in the development of a romantic Highland tradition in the Old World and the colonial elites who were engaged in similar constructions.[28]

Family connections between developments in British North America and those in the British Isles are particularly striking in the case of the Old World/New World Glengarry linkages. As Marianne McLean has noted, the powerful in colonial Glengarry tended to be sons of the traditional leaders who held sway in Glengarry, Scotland.[29] Alastair MacDonnell—the Glengarry chief who graces the cover of John Preble's *The Highland Clearances*—was a central player in the promotion of Highland traditions in the British Isles, with a passion for Highland costume that rivalled his enthusiasm for evictions.[30] MacDonnell and his elite friends founded the Highland Society of Inverness, Scotland, in 1815. Their Canadian relatives, with whom they maintained regular contact, were instrumental in founding a comparable society in Cornwall, three years later.[31] Roderick C. MacDonald, whose role I have described in the establishment of Maritime Highland societies, was the son-in-law of MacDonnell of Glengarry.[32]

Roderick C. MacDonald's efforts show one way that Highland traditions and the Highland past were reconstructed in the Maritimes of the 1840s. This construction was sustained by the prominent and well-positioned in colonial society. As well, it distanced and subdued some of the themes that emerged in the Gaelic poetry of the emigration years—the elite tradition and history did not highlight agrarian transformation or the betrayal of ideals that had once placed men before gold.

Was there another version of the past and of Highland history that challenged this mid-nineteenth-century version? Was there an Effy MacDonald saying, "No Murdo; you cannot forget important things about the past and about our collective identity"?

The story of Highland emigration to the Maritimes is the story of the movement of people drawn from varied social backgrounds: people from the upper echelons of Highland society, tacksmen and tenants of substance, and people much closer to the bottom of the heap. While some Highlanders realised the commercial and professional opportunities of the New World, others fared less well. Marianne MacLean's observations concerning the social contours of the Glengarry migration are in keeping with the Maritime experience as well. Many Highland immigrants to the Maritimes, like their counterparts who moved to eastern Ontario, would find property and power concentrated in the hands of the descendants of the upper ranks of the Highland society they had but recently left.

Did those at the bottom accede to the construction of Highland identity that was being crafted by these elites? Did they readily adopt a version of Highland identity that embraced commercial values and improvement? Did they accept a construction of the past that seems to have had less and less space for the story of the agrarian transformation of the Highlands? Or did they construct differently?

Again, the evidence we have is suggestive but not conclusive. In a poem describing circumstances in the Highlands and composed, it would seem, in the late 1830s, Allan MacDonald, who was from Glengarry country, noted: "The nobles got it [the land] for themselves/to enhance their status;/they hold the sons of the tenantry as slaves/in dire need/Although one may go to a festivity in the tartan,/properly dressed on the occasion,/the rest of the time one is only a dupe,/timid, wretched, poor."[33] This does not sound like endorsement for the sort of festivities that were popular with Highland societies on both sides of the Atlantic. Bitter songs about clearances, rent increases and elite betrayals of common values were kept alive in oral traditions that persisted across the nineteenth century.[34] This suggests to me that the sentiments they contained had a continuing resonance. A letter to the editor of the *Pictou Observer*, written in the 1830s, castigates a Highland paper for praising the Countess of Sutherland for her charity, because it was the Countess's abuse of power which gave rise to the need for charity. Charity was needed, the authors argued, because the family of Sutherland had "deprive[d] the tenantry of their farms, held for services performed, and burn[ed] their cabins about their ears." A central theme of the letter is that the evictions on the Countess's estate and her betrayals of her tenants must never be forgotten.[35]

The land struggles on Prince Edward Island also provide us with evidence concerning alternative readings of the Highland past. In a key pamphlet, published at the height of the 1830s agitation against landlordism on the Island, the Highland experience is used as an example of what must be resisted in the New World. The author of the pamphlet, William Cooper, was an Englishman. His constituency, though, was predominantly Scottish. Cooper never explicitly identifies his example as the Highlands. Indeed, he speaks to the broader dynamic involved in the transformation of the Highlands, a dynamic that would, one imagines, have resonated with some of his Irish, English, Acadian and Lowland Scot constituents as well. The Highland grounding for his critique of agricultural improvement and the economic logic that went with it, however, are unmistakable. Cooper juxtaposes an old economy in which land was used to provide sustenance for a hardy race who might support and defend their country, with a new system in which lands are seen as the property of proprietors and as the means by which the proprietors make profit. Under the logic of the new system, land would "yield more if cultivated by a few useful hands, without women or children." In the Old World, their improvement had meant that the general population had been "turned off to the manufacturing towns and the colonies, and villages are turned into sheep pastures and pleasure grounds."

Those who worked the land in Prince Edward Island faced the same fate if they could not change the system. Cooper warned of a New World clearance in which tenants would yet again lose their livelihoods and be pushed from the land: "We have the right to expect from the improved method that as soon as the lands are cleared, the present inhabitants will be turned off to make room for large farms, which will either sell or let at a greater advantage."[36]

Cooper's perspective takes us back to where this chapter began, with a critique of the agrarian transformation of the Highlands and the social relations that went with it. It takes us back, too, to the poetry of men such as Donald Chisholm and Allan MacDonald, and to the early traditions of the Highland communities of the Maritimes. Assuming that Cooper was articulating the sentiments of the tenants and squatters who accepted his leadership, it seems that his voice provides yet more evidence concerning alternative readings of the central messages of the Highland past, readings that diverged from those being promulgated by the Highland societies of the region being led by men such as Roderick C. MacDonald. And it suggests yet again the ways in which remembering and forgetting were grounded in New World experiences. It is worth noting that Cooper's reading of history, like the messages of the Highland societies of the elite, broadened the possibilities for non-Gaels to take ownership of the Highland past.

Notes

1. Eric Richards, *A History of the Highland Clearances*, vol. 1, *Agrarian Transformation and the Evictions, 1746–1886* (London, 1982), pp.16, 25–26. I am grateful to Ted Cowan and Elizabeth Ewan for feedback on an earlier version of this paper. They are not, however, responsible for its shortcomings.
2. Eric Richards, *A History of the Highland Clearances*, p. 33.
3. James Hunter, *The Making of the Crofting Community* (Edinburgh, 1976).
4. James Hunter, *A Dance Called America: The Scottish Highlands, the United States and Canada* (Edinburgh, 1994), p. 39; Margaret MacDonell, *The Emigrant Experience: Songs of Highland Emigrants in North America* (Toronto, 1982), pp. 27, 37, 43.
5. Margaret MacDonell, *The Emigrant Experience: Songs of Highland Emigrants in North America* (Toronto, 1982), pp. 63, 89, 91, 117.
6. Samuel MacLean, "The Poetry of the Clearances," *Transactions of the Gaelic Society of Inverness*, 37 (1939), pp. 293–324, makes note of the social position of the bards and considers the role it may have played in muting some of the critiques; see in particular pp. 299 and 307.
7. Margaret MacDonell, *The Emigrant Experience*, pp. 20, 26, 31, 62–63, 112.
8. Effy MacDonald to Murdo MacLeod, 30 March 1832, Public Archives of Prince Edward Island (PAPEI), 2727/2.
9. For a fine analysis of the limitations of the economic opportunities available to Highlanders of modest means within the new agrarian economy of the Highlands, see Marianne MacLean, *The People of Glengarry: Highlanders in Transition, 1745–1820* (Montreal and Kingston, 1991).
10. Rosemary Ommer, review of J.M. Bumsted, *The People's Clearance, 1770–1815* and Stephen P. Dunn, *The Fall and Rise of the Asiatic Mode of Production*, in *Labour/Le Travail* 14 (Fall 1984), pp. 291–96.
11. F.L. Pigot, "John MacDonald of Glenaladale," *Dictionary of Canadian Biography*, vol. 5 (Toronto, 1983), pp. 514–17; J.M. Bumsted, *Land, Settlement, and*

Politics on Eighteenth-Century Prince Edward Island (Montreal and Kingston, 1987).

12. John MacDonald to Nelly, 6 March 1784, PAPEI, 2664/8; John MacDonald to sister, 29 March 1789, PAPEI, 2664/16.

13. John MacDonald to sister, 26 June 1781, PAPEI, 2664/5; John MacDonald to Nelly, 6 March 1784, PAPEI, 2664/8; John MacDonald to Nelly, 4 July 1792. PAPEI, 2664/20.

14. John MacDonald to Donald [MacDonald], 29 June 1785, PAPEI, 2664/14.

15. *Constitution and First Annual Report of the Highland Society of Nova Scotia with a List of the Members and Office-Bearers for the Year 1839* (Halifax, 1839).

16. *Constitution of the Highland Society of Prince Edward Island, and an Address Issued by the Committee in Favour of Branch Societies: With a list of Office Bearers for the Year 1840* (Charlottetown, 1840); James Caie to Lt. Col. R. C. MacDonald, 11 January 1842; R.C. MacDonald to Secretary, London Highland Society, 3 May 1842; R.C. MacDonald to London Highland Society; Correspondence, Highland Society of London, National Library of Scotland (NLS), Deposition 268/19.

17. R.C. MacDonald to Secretary, London Highland Society, 3 May 1842, NLS, Deposition 268/19.

18. Correspondence of the Highland Society of New Brunswick, Miramichi, to the Highland Society of London, 22 March 1849; *Constitution of the Highland Society of Prince Edward Island*, 9.

19. Extracts from Records of Highland Society of New Brunswick, 13 January 1844, NLS, Deposition 268/19.

20. Ian McKay, "Tartanism Triumphant: The Construction of Scottishness in Nova Scotia, 1933–1954,"*Acadiensis*, 21:2 (Spring 1992), p. 32.

21. R.C. MacDonald, *Sketches of Highlanders: with an Account of Their Early Arrival in North America; Their Advancement in Agriculture; and some of their Distinguished Military Services in the War of 1812, &c with Letters containing Useful Information for Emigrants from the Highlands of Scotland to the British Provinces* (Saint John, 1843). Much of this book is drawn from Chambers' *History of the Rebellion of 1745*.

22. For an overview of some of the challenges occurring in Atlantic Canada, see Rosemary E. Ommer, "The 1830s: Adapting Their Institutions to Their Desires," in Phillip A. Buckner and John G. Reid, eds., *The Atlantic Region in Confederation* (Toronto and Fredericton, 1994), pp. 284–306.

23. A.J. MacDonell to Secretary, London Highland Society, 18 March 1843, NLS, Deposition 268/6.

24. Scotus to editor, *Cornwall Observer*, 16 July 1840.

25. Charles W. Wallace to Secretary, London Highland Society, 9 March 1842; R.C. MacDonald to Secretary, London Highland Society, 28 February 1843, NLS, Deposition 268/19.

26. Extracts from Records of Highland Society of New Brunswick, 13 January 1844, NLS, Deposition 268/19.

27. Charles W. Wallace to Secretary, London Highland Society, 9 March 1842, NLS, Deposition 268/19.

28. On the construction of these traditions in the British Isles at this time, see Hugh Trevor-Roper, "The Invention of Tradition: The Highland Tradition of Scotland,"

in Eric Hobsbawm and Terence Ranger, eds., *The Invention of Tradition* (Cambridge, 1983), pp. 15–42; John Preble, *The King's Jaunt: George IV in Scotland, 1822* (Glasgow, 1988); Charles Withers, "The Historical Creation of the Scottish Highlands," in Ian Donnachie and Christopher Whatley, eds., *The Manufacture of Scottish History* (Edinburgh, 1992), pp. 143–56.

29. Marianne MacLean, *The People of Glengarry*.
30. John Prebble, *The Highland Clearances* (London, 1963), p. 142; John Prebble, *The King's Jaunt*.
31. John Prebble, *The King's Jaunt*, pp. 114–15, A.J. MacDonell to Secretary, London Highland Society, 18 March 1843, NLS, Deposition 268/6.
32. George Seymour, "Journal of Tour of Canada and the United States (1840)," Warwick County Record Office (WCRO), CR114A/380.
33. Margaret MacDonell, *The Emigrant Experience*, pp. 89–91.
34. For some of the victims of clearance who relocated in the Maritimes, the memories were, it would seem, too painful to be retold. David Craig, *On the Crofters Trail: In Search of the Clearance Highlanders* (London, 1990), pp. 102–3.
35. Late Emigrants from Sutherland to the editor, *Pictou Observer*, 21 November 1832.
36. [William Cooper], *Legislative and Other Proceedings on the Expediency of Appointing a Court of Escheats in Prince Edward Island* (Charlottetown, 1836), p. 93.

Figure 13.1 Female Highland Emigrant, Hector Museum display, Pictou, Nova Scotia (D. Smith photo)

Figure 13.2 78th Highlanders re-enactment (courtesy of the Citadel Museum, Halifax, Nova Scotia)

14

"Lochaber no more":
A Critical Examination
of Highland Emigration Mythology

Michael Kennedy

Mo shoraidh bhuam an diugh air chuairt
Thar chuan do bhràigh' nan gleann,
Gu tìr nam buadh, ge fada bhuam i,
Tìr nam fuar bheann àrd.
'S e tigh'nn a thàmh do 'n àit s' as ùr
A dh' fhàg mo shùilean dall.
'N uair sheòl mi 'n iar, a' triall bho m' thìr,
A rìgh gur mi bha 'n call.

Dh' fhàg mi dùthaich, dh' fhàg mi dùthchas;
Dh' fhan mo shùgradh thall.
Dh' fhàg mi 'n t-àite bàigheil, caomh,
'S mo chàirdean gaolach ann.
Dh' fhàg mi 'n tlachd 's an t-àit' am faict' i,
Tìr nam bac 's nan càrn.
'S e fàth mo smaointinn bho nach d'fhaod mi
Fuireach daonnan ann.

My greeting from me today
over the sea to the head of the glen,
to the land of heroes, although far from me,
land of the cold, high mountains.

It is coming to live in this new place
that has left my eyes blind.
When I sailed west, departing from my land,
O Lord, that was my loss.

I left my country, I left my heritage;
my mirth remained over there.
I left the friendly, hospitable place,
and my beloved relatives there.
I left the beauty and the place where it was seen,
land of the hollow and the cairn.
It is the cause of my reflection that I could not
stay there forever.[1]

With these words, the Lochaber poet Iain Sealgair (John the Hunter MacDonald) began a mournful lament describing his unhappy arrival at Mabou Ridge, Cape Breton, in 1835. The images he created more than a century and a half ago of struggling to survive, with eyes blinded by tears, in an inhospitable new environment, while longing for the country and heritage left behind, strike a powerful chord with Scots and those of Scottish descent overseas today. Indeed, they are the very essence of the famous paintings of unhappy exile, such as "Lochaber no more" or Thomas Faed's "The Last of the Clan."

It may come as a shock, therefore, to discover how those same sentiments of longing and heavy-hearted exile were received by the Gaelic community in Cape Breton at the time they were first given voice. Ailean an Rids[2] (Allan the Ridge MacDonald), John the Hunter's own cousin, who had come out from Lochaber to Mabou Ridge some twenty years earlier, responded with a biting condemnation:

Chuir thu bòilich sìos 'us bòsd
Air cùisean mór 'nad rann;
Searbh do ghlòir leam cainnt do bheòil
Oir bha mi eòlach thall,
An Albainn fhuar ge fada bhuam i
Suarach leam an call;
B' e fàth a' ghruaim an càradh cruaidh
Bh' air truaghain bhochd a bh' ann.

'S i 'n tìr a dh' fhàg thu 'n tìr gun chàirdeas,
Tìr gun bhàidh ri tuath;
Ach gu tùrsach iad 'ga fàgail
'S ànradh thar a chuan.
Daoine bochda, sìol nan coiteir,

Bha gun stochd gun bhuar;
'S mairg a chàin i, tìr an àigh,
'S an dràsd' iad 'nan daoine uaisl'.

You have put down lies and boasts
about many subjects in your song;
Sour to me your idle talk, the speech of your mouth,
for I was knowledgeable over there
in cold Scotland; although it is far from me,
trifling to me the loss.
It was the cause of sadness, the cruel treatment
of the oppressed poor that were there.

The land that you left is the land without kindness,
without humanity for the tenantry;
but they are sorrowful leaving it
and [facing] the storms over the sea,
poor people, descendants of cottars,
who were without stock, without herds of cattle;
it is despicable to slander it, [this] land of prosperity
where they are now men of worth.[3]

When sifting through the historical record of Gaelic experience, it quickly becomes apparent that we must exercise caution when attempting to divine any sort of common "Highland migration mythology." The example provided by John the Hunter and Allan the Ridge is proof enough of that, as the two men could scarcely have shared more in common, yet could hardly have created a more violently opposed assessment of a shared event of great significance not only to themselves personally but also to their society as a whole. The saga of the Highland migrant has its roots in a period of intense social change and heavy migration spanning a period of slightly more than one hundred years from roughly the middle of the eighteenth to the middle of the nineteenth century. Virtually every community in the large, disjointed region of the Scottish Highlands was affected by a massive exodus of people which led to the establishment of new communities in far-flung, sundry political states and disparate geographical areas around the world. These facts, in themselves, should caution us not to expect the narrative of Highland migration to be a uniform one.

Arguably the most important of these New World settlement areas was, and is, the large Gaelic district of the Maritimes, comprising the contiguous regions of Prince Edward Island, the northern mainland of Nova Scotia and the island of Cape Breton.[4] The importance of this community lies in the fact that its history spans the emigration period (although emigration around the mid-nineteenth century was lighter than in some other areas); that a large, distinctively Gaelic community emerged; and that Gaelic is still spoken in the area, maintaining a vital intellectual link, stretching back almost 230 years, to the arrival of the first Highland immigrants. If there is any place in the world which can shed light on the mythology of Gaelic migration, it is here.

While the form and vigour of the accounts provided by John the Hunter and Allan the Ridge alert us to the diversity of the Gaelic migrants' experience in the Maritimes, they also draw attention to the fact that the creation of a Gaelic migration saga was a highly public affair with a strongly communal forum for discourse. As Gaelic scholar Derick Thomson has described:

> The organization and practice of poetry had clearly reached such a pitch that they deeply affected society. We may suspect strongly that this influence was at one time restricted largely to the richer and more powerful sector of society, but whether by the breakdown of the native order, and the resulting democratization of Gaelic society, or by other means also, the influence of the poetic tradition spread much more widely, producing in earlier times, and to some extent down to the present, an unusually high level of literary awareness and appreciation in the populace at large.[5]

There is no doubt that when John the Hunter put his thoughts into verse he was expressing his own very personal outlook, but he fully intended to shape public opinion as well. He expected his completed work to be sung and intelligently discussed by his fellow immigrants at their social gatherings in New World communities and probably by those who had remained behind in Scotland. Equally, Allan the Ridge used his own considerable poetic abilities to express his personal feelings, but with an obvious eye to preventing the sentiments of John the Hunter from becoming the dominant theme of the general Gaelic migration narrative. He did this not only by directly challenging the content of John the Hunter's poem, but also in a more subtle if equally important way by mimicking his poetic structure, meaning that his song could and would be sung to any air which suited John the Hunter's.[6] As a result, any time John the Hunter's song was sung, listeners would immediately be reminded of Allan the Ridge's alternative offering, even if it were not actually sung at the time (as it undoubtedly was on more than one occasion). In this way, Allan the Ridge effectively countered and undermined the influence of John the Hunter's sentiment.

Because sung poetry was the chief form of Gaelic literary expression, and because it operated in a dynamic oral social setting, it is particularly reflective of community opinion, perhaps more so than the accounts of any other immigrant group to North America, giving us a remarkable insight into the intellectual workings of Gaelic society.[7] It is primarily here that we are able to divine something of the Gaelic mythology of migration and settlement in the New World and of how that mythology was formed and transmitted. Intriguingly, what emerges from our insight into that Gaelic past is a narrative which is very much in agreement with Allan the Ridge's characterization of the Gaelic immigration experience and very much in contradiction to John the Hunter's portrayal. This provides us with a dilemma, since the mythology coming to us from past generations with its depiction of the Gaelic immigrant happily meeting the challenges of life in the New World is in direct contradiction to our own modern mythology (of which the academic historical record is an important part) which depicts that same immigrant in a constant state of nostalgic mourning for a lost Highland homeland.

The simplest explanation for the dichotomy is that the different narratives merely reflect the Gaelic perspective at different points in history. There is a substantial body of external and circumstantial evidence from the mid-nineteenth century, for instance, which might suggest that the Gaelic migration experience of that era was somewhat more confused, and its mythology more negative in tone, than that of the preceding generations. Gaelic society was by then in considerable disarray; those coming to the traditional settlements in the Maritimes often found that they could no longer obtain good land; and those going to areas where there was more space for migrants, such as Australia, often found that the different socio-economic structure there made it much more difficult for them to establish the distinctive Gaelic communities that earlier Highland migrants had shown such a marked tendency to build elsewhere.[8] Gaelic evidence, however, is inconclusive.

Negative accounts of the sort composed by John the Hunter may be somewhat more in evidence by the mid-nineteenth century than in the decades preceding; however, there continued to be a tradition of narrative celebrating migration in the vein of Allan the Ridge, such that it would be difficult, with the evidence we currently have, to argue that the mythology in the Maritimes was generally a negative one. There is, in fact, no difference in the relative antiquity of the two narratives, as they have existed side by side for quite some time without ever overlapping. The root of the contradiction is that there is no common origin for the contending mythologies. They have sprung from entirely separate sources: one, derived from Gaelic, represents the impressions of the people at the centre of the migration saga, while the other, derived from English, represents the external observations of a neighbouring society with a long history of hostility towards the Gaels. The prominence of the English-derived narrative today owes less to the passage of time than to the domination of Gaelic culture by its English neighbour; a domination not limited to the interpretation of history but evident in virtually every facet of Gaelic cultural expression.[9]

I

The selective and often inaccurate interpretation of Gaelic history, and the exclusion of any sort of Gaelic voice from that historical discourse, present a very lopsided view of the Gaelic world and a serious obstacle to our understanding of its people and events. This problem has long been recognized and commented upon by Gaels themselves. As early as the 1600s we find the issue of slanted anti-Gaelic historiography being raised bluntly and clearly by Gaelic scholars, such as Cathal and Niall MacMhuirich, Scots poets and historians to the Clan Donald, and by the Irish historian Seathrùn Céitin (Geoffrey Keating). Keating, for example, colourfully described the essentially negative character of the historical commentary on Ireland that was being produced by English scholars, attributing it to an anglocentric cultural hostility towards Gaels and their society that he believed to be the product of almost perfect ignorance and a great deal of idle speculation. Sadly, these charges have not lost much of their force or relevance in the intervening three and a half centuries:

> . . . beaganach, an phroimpiolláin doghníd, ag scríobhadh ar Eireannchaibh. Is eadh, iomorro, is nór do'n phroimpiollán, an tan thógbhar a cheann i san samhradh, bheith ar foluamhain ag imtheacht, agus gan cromadh ar mhion-scoith d'á mbí 'san machaire, nó ar bhláth d'á mbí i lubhghort, gémadh rós nó lile uile iad, acht bheith ar fuaidreadh go dteagmhann bualtrach bó nó otrach capaill ris, go dtéid d'á unfairt féin ionnta.

> . . . inasmuch as it is almost according to the fashion of the beetle they act, when writing concerning the Irish. For it is the fashion of the beetle, when it lifts its head in the summertime, to go about fluttering and not to stoop towards any delicate flower that may be in the field, or any blossom in the garden, though they be all roses or lilies, but it keeps bustling about until it meets with dung of horse or cow and proceeds to roll itself therein.

The appearance of critiques such as this in both Scotland and Ireland during the seventeenth century was no mere coincidence, but a reaction by the Gaelic intelligentsia to very specific circumstances. They were an attempt to protect the history of the Gaels at a time when it appeared that it was to be taken from them and mauled over by a foreign people hostile to them and ignorant of their ways. As a consequence of military campaigns and government intrusions in native Ireland and Highland Scotland, the Gàidhealtachd began to be erroded, largely from the top down, with the intrusion of an anglicized, and anglicizing, elite. Outside the basic family unit, the chief forces for social conditioning in the Gàidhealtachd would, for the most part, be of English origin and cultural orientation and would be operated primarily and in many instances exclusively by English-speakers, reflecting and imposing the values of a society which was not only non-Gaelic but overtly anti-Gaelic.[10]

The tendency to look to the elite as spokespeople for a society is a common historical problem, but it clearly presents more serious difficulties for anyone dealing with Gaelic history. As a result of top-down anglicization during the subsequent eighteenth, nineteenth and twentieth centuries, the distinction between Gaelic and English culture became blurred in the historical record. In particular, during the nineteenth century the landed elite in Scottish Highland society grew to be extraordinarily out of touch with the bulk of the population and with Gaelic culture. In his examination of the poetry of An Clàrsair Dall (The Blind Harper, or Roderick Morrison), who flourished c. 1656–1714, Derick Thomson revealed how early this top-down rot began to set in and provided a Gaelic take on just how absurdly unrepresentative this new elite had become by the nineteenth century:

> The sad transformation of the clan chief to a foreign cockatoo is well portrayed. Of course all the detail of later times could not be included: the loud discourteous talk in foreign accents, the offensive flaunting of Highland dress, the appalling ignorance of Gaelic language and literature, the loathsome sycophancy and the laughable parades at Highland Games, nor did An Clàrsair Dall see the later development of the nouveau riche who were to win a (relatively) cheap stake in this ersatz society. But he saw enough to see the danger. He was lucky to see no more.[11]

Even if we restrict our examination to material directly related to the emigration saga, it is impossible, in this short space, to delve into the many ramifications of this social manipulation in the nineteenth century, particularly into the increasing fascination the English elite displayed in creating Gaelic fantasies and the increasing success they had in overwhelming the Gaelic voice in the process. However, the extent of the impact of these combined forces on our perception of the culture and history of the Gaels is of the utmost importance because it has directly determined why the Gaelic perception of the past has been almost entirely ignored and is today so badly misunderstood. Fortunately, this effortless domination of the historical record can be demonstrated fairly concisely with one example, that of "The Canadian Boat Song."

First published in *Blackwood's Edinburgh Magazine* in 1829, this anonymous "Canadian Boat Song" is supposed to have been "from the Gaelic," specifically from the singing of Highland boatmen working on the St. Lawrence River, and has become, arguably, the single most popular commentary on the Highland immigrant experience. Today it is encountered at virtually every turn, whether found hanging on the walls of tiny pubs in Scotland, decoratively inscribed on tea towels and posters, brightly printed in tourist brochures on both sides of the Atlantic, or stirringly quoted in the seemingly endless published commentaries on the Highland Clearances and settlement in the New World. In addition to its huge popularity, the poem has been the inspiration for the creation of a "Lone Sheiling" in the Cape Breton Highlands National Park in Nova Scotia and for the title of a high-quality Scottish television documentary on the Gaelic diaspora, "The Blood is Strong."[12]

In spite of its enormous popularity today, "The Canadian Boat Song" is of value only in demonstrating how easily the Gaelic experience is manipulated, because the poem was a complete invention. Several literary figures (all English-speaking) have been advanced by scholars as the possible composer of this piece. The most plausible author is David MacBeth Moir, a physician and life-long resident of Musselburgh, in the Scottish Lowlands, who occasionally submitted poetry to *Blackwood's*.[13] As neither a Gael nor a Canadian immigrant, Moir would have had to rely on second-hand accounts and on his imagination to concoct his literary description of the Gaelic immigrant's experience, but this apparently was more than enough for the general public.

Although we may never conclusively attribute the poem to Moir, there can be absolutely no doubt that "The Canadian Boat Song" was a work of the imagination and of English, and not Gaelic, literature. This is most obviously evident in the fact that the poem is known only in English and not at all in Gaelic, not even in poetic fragments—a suspicious development, considering the strength of the Gaelic oral tradition and the fact that the poem was supposed to have been so commonly sung in Canada.[14] There is also very clearly a great lack of technical sympathy between the poem and any other in the contemporary Gaelic poetic tradition. The style, the imagery and, most importantly of all, the romanticism of the poem all trace their origins directly to the English literary tradition. None of this, however, has stopped the patently non-Gaelic "Canadian Boat Song" from smoothly assuming its position as the pre-eminent literary depiction of the Gael in the New World. Indeed, it is its very unrepresentativeness that has made it so popular among English-speakers, as it so perfectly reflects the tastes and concerns of their own society.

And yet, despite such overt romanticizations, the hard edge of disciplined eighteenth-century Gaelic poetry continued to maintain some degree of its keenness and momentum into the nineteenth century, and a considerable amount of the poetry from both centuries, along with its associated traditions, has found its way down to the present day. Continuity appears to have been particularly evident in the traditions of the immigrant community in Canada, which had escaped from at least some of the pressure being exerted upon Gaels in Scotland. The sense of this continuity was stated in fairly unequivocal fashion in Sorley MacLean's assessment of probably the most famous nineteenth-century poet to emigrate to Nova Scotia: "John MacLean was in every sense but the chronological a poet of the eighteenth century, though he was alive until 1848."[15] Some of this continuity remains evident, both in terms of the clarity and power of expression of that earlier era and in the poet's commitment to stand up defiantly for Gaels against the perceived slander and encroachment of the English world. Indeed, to this day, this latter concern has not disappeared from Gaelic poetry. The challenge for the historian looking back over two centuries of societal decline and historical manipulation is to try to find this voice.

II

The absence of a Gaelic voice in the historiography of Highland emigration and settlement in the New World has not been lost on the present generation of scholars working in that field. As J.M. Bumsted declared when examining the phenomenon of emigration from the Highlands to Canada: "One of the most obvious features of this discussion of the conflicting interest groups is that it does not include the Highlander himself."[16] Eric Richards was even more definitive in his work, *A History of the Highland Clearances*, claiming that no less than 95 percent of the population of the Scottish Highlands was excluded from participating in the historical commentary on the clearances.[17] It quickly becomes apparent, however, and for the reasons outlined earlier, that even those who have become aware of the exclusion of Gaelic accounts from the historical record rarely realize that this is primarily a problem of English historiography rather than Gaelic. Witness Bumsted and Richards' assessments:

> In part this silence was the result of their own inability to put their thoughts on paper in ways useful to future historians.[18]

> This has been a difficult business because the common people of the Highlands, like those elsewhere, have been careless of posterity: poor and mostly illiterate, they have left little of direct record of their lives either before or after the clearances.[19]

Such remarks are in fact rationalizations for a failure to analyze Gaelic commentary and betray a lack of appreciation for the volume and quality of historical material which Gaels did actually manage to preserve; a failure to explain why this corpus has been almost entirely ignored by historians; and a fundamental misunderstanding of what the lack of Gaelic representation in the formal historical record signifies.

Ironically, this fundamental flaw in the historical method, and the historian's inability to perceive it as such, leads rapidly back to the formulaic depiction of the Gaelic world as inherently inept. The peculiar lack of Gaelic representation in what is supposed to be a Gaelic story, rather than being attributed to a weakness in the English historical record, can be dismissed as an inherent weakness in Gaelic society and, according to Bumsted, little more than the silence we should expect from a society peopled by "illiterate semi-barbarians."[20]

> Attempting to deal with the motivations of a population which largely lacked the skills of writing and the ability of fluent self-expression is no easy task.[21]

This characterization of the Gaels is surprising. The confidence of the assessment, considering that it is made by someone who does not understand the Gaelic language and is not very familiar with the Gaelic literary tradition, demonstrates the depth of the chasm separating English scholars from the Gaelic world and harkens back to the criticisms of Keating three hundred years earlier. It certainly stands in marked contrast to the conclusion drawn by folklorist MacEdward Leach, whose assessment of Gaelic literature hardly confirms some historians' depiction of Gaelic migrants as an inarticulate group of savages:

> Cape Breton was settled by a superior people who came from a rich cultural background of story, poetry and song. The beauty, the imaginative power, the dramatic quality, the richness of detail of the old Celtic lore is unsurpassed in Western Europe.[22]

What is most intriguing here is that even when identifying the lack of Gaelic voices in historical scholarship, professional historians are unaware of their own perpetuation of centuries-old stereotypes. Richards, for example, in spite of his laudable and expressly stated desire to use every opportunity at his disposal to give the "common" people of the Highlands the voice they had been so obviously denied in previous commentary on the Clearances, chose to favour the more readily available English language sources. In his impressive two-volume compilation on the Clearances, consisting of such diverse sources as the writings of Samuel Johnson and Karl Marx, and amounting to one thousand pages of text, Richards reproduced only one piece of Gaelic evidence—a single page—and not even a page of annotated text. Instead, the sum total of Gaelic input in his study of the Highland Clearances was used merely as a decorative leaf separating two sections of English commentary, without even a page number. The result is hardly a balanced view of life in the Gàidhealtachd.

By ignoring virtually the entire body of historical commentary supplied by Gaels, the wealth of evidence is supplied, by default, by English observers. Even were it not for the long history of conflict and prejudice between these two groups, such an externally derived framework makes the remaining evidence selected for examination extremely volatile and as vulnerable to becoming a mere reflection of the common preconceptions of the past observer and the latter-day analyst as it is likely to be a source of clear, unequivocal data. Consider, for example, the conclusion Richards reached concerning the general environment of the Scottish Gàidhealtachd during the early stages of emigration:

> The poverty of the old regime in the Highlands may well have been liable to exaggeration by contemporary writers infected with the philosophy of improvement. But there is far too much unanimity in the evidence to allow real doubts about such descriptions as that of John Knox who, in 1786, wrote: "Upon the whole, the Highlands of Scotland, some few estates excepted, are the seats of oppression, poverty, famine, anguish, and wild despair."[23]

The first striking point about this assessment is Richards' belief that he has discovered a balance of proof—a "unanimity in the evidence"—when, as we have already seen, evidence from within the community that is the subject of discussion has not even been brought to light, let alone analyzed. Ironically, the one piece of Gaelic evidence he did reproduce—a poem composed by Donnchadh Bàn (Duncan Ban MacIntyre) at almost the exact time Knox[24] was making his observations on the Highlands—directly contradicts Richards' supposedly unanimous evidence.[25] If there is unanimity in the Gaelic evidence from this period, it is in the condemnation of the new, rather than the old, regime, which Gaels saw as the cause of the deteriorating socio-economic conditions in the Highlands. Gaelic commentary, apart from being replete with praise for life in the Highlands under the old regime, gives a clear and powerful articulation of a Gaelic resistance to a new economic order which Gaels saw as imposed from the outside for the benefit of others and which would lead to their ruination. Intriguingly, this is consistent with the conclusions drawn in a colonial government–sponsored report (also contemporary with Knox's writing) which sought to explain the reasons for heavy migration from at least one district in the Highlands:

> They are industrious people & lived on small farms which they rented at Arasaig and the Island of Egg, containing about 50 acres each, more or less: that the proprietors of those lands[,] able to procure higher rents than those people could afford to pay, found it in their interest to throw those small Farms into grazing grounds [i.e., for sheep], letting a number of them together to one responsible person from whom he can collect his rent with ease & certainty.[26]

By 1790 this tradition of heavy emigration from the Highlands, with its attendant commentary in Gaelic and English claiming dissatisfaction with the new regime, was already some two decades old. The fact that those observations should be ignored seems to owe less to sober, neutral anlysis than it does to the historian applying the English conceptual framework to Gaelic experience, a framework which seeks an inherent decrepitude in Gaelic society.

From an anglocentric perspective, which views the Gaels as a barbaric, backward, miserable and largely inarticulate people resistant to any form of social evolution, it is understandable that the entire Gaelic resistance to outside domination was reduced to a sullen rejection of some benign form of "modernity." It is also understandable that an attendant and fundamental societal upheaval such as emigration should be expected to spawn a mythology which reflected those same qualities. A mythology essentially negative and contradictory in nature, clumsily expressing despair, a sense of helplessness and an unrealistic longing for a romanticized homeland, would be perfectly consistent with such a cultural disposition. Some historians have made an heroic effort to demonstrate this essential coherence:

> The Highlands *were* undergoing rapid alterations in the period 1770–1815, and Highlanders who sought to escape the new order required some legitimisation of what was, after all, a radical step to take. Attempting to explain the complexities of the modernisation process and their own response to it would have been exceedingly difficult, especially in the oral tradition in which they operated. Thus the pressure of the lairds was simplified, heightened, and focused on the easy slogan "CLEARANCE FOR SHEEP." Undoubtedly conscious that they were being attacked by others for deserting the ship and guilt-ridden about their abandonment of traditional lands and clan-ties, the Highlanders sought an explanation for their behaviour which eliminated the necessity for guilt and responsibility: they had not chosen to leave, they were forced to depart. . . . A similar sense of guilt undoubtedly explains the concurrent heightening of the suffering experienced on the North American side of the Atlantic.[27]

This is a peculiar conclusion to reach, no less so because its author, J.M. Bumsted, has drawn our attention to the exuberant spirit of the earliest emigrants preparing to depart from the Highlands. He has reprinted the descriptions, from the famous tour of Samuel Johnson and James Boswell, of emigrants so happy to leave Scotland that they were not only dancing at the sites of departure but had invented an entirely new dance called "America" which appears to have been created to demonstrate the contagious nature of emigration in the Highlands. In these accounts, it is those remaining in Scotland who are wracked with anguish, comforted only by the hope that they would soon follow their friends and relations to the New World.[28] For a people supposedly overwhelmed by the complexities of migration and guilt-ridden for their actions, Gaelic emigrants appear to have been a remarkably happy group!

When we examine the evidence from the pioneering communities on the New World side of the Atlantic, we find that it too is consistent with this picture and gives no impression of a change in attitude among the immigrants after arriving. One of the oldest Gaelic literary descriptions of the New World, if not the oldest, was produced by Mìcheil Mór (Big Michael MacDonald), one of the immigrants in the Glenaladale expedition to Prince Edward Island in 1772. His song "O 's àlainn an t-àite" ("O, fair is the place") fits in perfectly with the scene of excited pioneers looking forward to a new life. Big Michael describes with delight streams full of fish, tall maple trees producing sugar, and the potential of the land: "'S cha bhi annas oirnn 's an earrach,/Chuirinn geall, chuirinn geall" ("We will not suffer scarcity in the spring,/I will wager, I will wager").[29] He also takes time to revel in the society that has been established, describing the sound of fiddles and pipes playing, the sight of men flirting with their sweethearts, and the beautiful courteous behaviour of the children found in his new community. His obvious sense of pleasure and his blunt conclusion that "'S gu'm b'e 'm baothair nach tug oidheirp/ Air bhi ann, air bhi ann" ("He was a fool who did not attempt to come/to be here, to be here")[30] hardly suggests a community plagued by guilt for having "deserted the ship."

Similarly, if we look at the somewhat more communal efforts that were made to record accounts of early emigration, such as the community histories which were recorded from Gaelic tradition bearers in the nineteenth century and written up in English, we again see the same depiction of the Gaels as a people making active, rational choices to emigrate in order to protect their independence and maintain repsonsibility for the running of their communities as they saw fit. We learn, for example, that an emigration to P.E.I. from South Uist in 1787 was carried out against the direct orders of the landlord and in spite of his threats to tear down the homes of any who would assist the potential emigrants by buying the stock and implements they intended to leave behind in Scotland.[31] Likewise, another large Catholic emigration in 1790, the first to include Nova Scotia as a destination, was recorded as having been sparked by MacNeil of Barra's attempt to prevent his tenants from repairing or rebuilding a local Catholic church. According to the accounts, an angry argument ensued between MacNeil and community leaders in Barra and they threatened to leave for the New World if he refused to stop meddling in their affairs—a threat not made idly, as the heavy emigration which followed clearly showed.[32]

Once again, these descriptions of community emigration do not depict a helpless people swept out of Scotland against their will, but an active people making a positive decision to start a new life. Weighing the wide diversity of evidence left by immigrants from the Highlands—poems, stories, anecdotes, letters and so on—one is struck by just how overwhelmingly favourable they are. These positive accounts even find their way into sources composed in

English, such as the early-nineteenth-century musings of Maighstir Uisdean (Father Augustine MacDonald), a priest in Moidart who was persuaded to try his own luck in the New World settlements in Prince Edward Island and Nova Scotia by the quality and consistency of information which had been passed back to the Highlands from the New World:

> America must surely be a Choice habitation or they must be all Scoundrels to a man that have got to it. For for these thirty years past no letters have been sent from thence no mouth opened but lavished without a single exception in the praise of it.[33]

Even with much accessible evidence demonstrating that the Gaelic community could act rationally, positively and consistently, historians have had great difficulty in fully realizing the scope and meaning of such proof and incorporating it into their analyses, since it so dramatically contradicts the English concept of the Gaelic world. In the rare instances where Gaelic sources are used by historians, there is a marked tendency to take highly atypical viewpoints as being generally definitive of the Gaelic experience if they happen to fit the stereotype of melancholia and nostalgia. A poet such as John the Hunter, for instance, would be taken as a spokesman for Gaelic immigrants generally because his poem is nostalgic and exaggerates suffering in the New World, just as Gaelic mythology is imagined to do. Since he is typical in the mind of the historian, the wider narrative tradition may then be casually dismissed, including the contrary song of Allan the Ridge. The manner in which this occurs is readily apparent in the misuse of the one piece of Gaelic evidence with which almost everyone who has an interest in Highland immigration will be familiar: John MacLean's poem "A' Choille Ghruamach" ("The Gloomy Forest").

John MacLean, known both as "Am Bard Thighearna Cholla" ("The Bard to the Laird of Coll") and more generally in the New World as "Am Bard Mac Ghill' Eathain" (The Bard MacLean), was arguably the most gifted Gaelic poet to cross the Atlantic; and his poem "A' Choille Ghruamach" ("The Gloomy Forest"), composed shortly after his arrival along the Gulf shore of Nova Scotia in 1819, is one of the most powerful Gaelic immigration songs ever composed. There can be no doubt that MacLean's verses of utter dismay came straight from the heart and that the longing he felt for his home and friends in Scotland was one shared by more than one immigrant who first confronted the virgin forests of the New World. Commentator after commentator has taken "A' Choille Ghruamach" to be the definitive Gaelic literary account of migration, and it has been reproduced ad nauseum. Indeed, even Gaelic poet and literary critic Sorley MacLean considered "A' Choille Ghruamach" to be a corrective to at least the more "absurdly" idyllic picture of America sometimes encountered in Gaelic emigrant song;[34] and Gaelic scholar Charles Dunn quoted from it on no fewer than six occasions in his book *Highland Settler*, claiming that MacLean "might have come to be considered a classic exponent of the pioneer life which has formed this continent if he had composed his songs in English, rather than in his native Gaelic."[35]

With his condemnation of the New World and his wish to return home to Scotland, in spite of the Gaels' increasingly constrained existence back there, MacLean appears to fit the stereotype of the complaining Gael, unhappy in Scotland but equally unhappy in the New World, retreating from the challenges of modernity by wallowing in romantic, nostalgic versification about a lost golden homeland. However, this impression actually owes most of its force to the manner in which English chroniclers have mishandled MacLean's story, allowing their own mythology effectively to smother what the bard actually had to tell us about his experience in the New World. When MacLean's first New World poems, "A' Choille Ghruamach" and "Am Mealladh" ("The Deception") arrived in Scotland, his friends and his old patron, the Laird of Coll, were very concerned for his welfare and offered to bring him back to Scotland and restore him to his position as Coll's poet. MacLean, however, in spite of having departed from his former patron on the best of terms, refused to leave Nova Scotia.

John MacLean did not return to Scotland because he preferred to live in a fantasy world of hazy, distorted memories, but because he very quickly got over his stunned reaction to the conditions he encountered in Nova Scotia, concluding that his decision to immigrate had not been a mistake after all. He then almost immediately began composing poetry consistent with his revised attitudes and actions, but this flow of composition appears to have been utterly ignored. In fact, one of MacLean's new poems, "Am Bal Gàidhealach" ("The Gaelic Gathering") which begins with the line "Bithibh aotrom 's togaibh fonn" ("Be light-hearted and raise a song") was specifically singled out in Gaelic tradition as having been composed by MacLean out of regret for his earlier accounts of life in Nova Scotia. In direct contradiction to the poetic figure encountered in the more famous "A' Choille Ghruamach" who is so overwhelmed by the oppressive forest that his thoughts have been smothered and his ability to express himself in verse has been suffocated, we find in MacLean's new song a poet who has made a complete recovery:

> Fhuair mi sgeul a tha leam binn,
> Dh' ùraich gleus air teud mo chinn,
> 'S bidh mi nis a' dol 'ga sheinn,
> Ged tha mi 'sa choill am falach.
>
> Gur h-e 'n sgeul a fhuair mi 'n dràsd,
> 'S a dhùisg m' intinn suas gu dàn,
> Bhi 'gam iarraidh dh' ionnsaidh bhàil,

Th' aig na Gàidheal tùs an Earraich.

I heard news that was sweet to me
that refreshed the tuning of the strings of my mind;
I am going now to sing,
although I am hidden in the forest.

It is the news I just received
that has awakened my mind to verse
to be invited to go to a gathering
for the Gaels at the beginning of Spring.[36]

Even more revealing than this cheerful and upbeat description of life in
the New World, however, is the remarkable poem "Seann Albainn agus Albainn
Ur" ("Old Scotland and New Scotland").[37] This poem begins much like
MacLean's earlier verses, in dispraise of the New World, but feature an imagi-
nary confrontation between the poet and Colonel Simon Fraser, the emigration
agent who brought him to Nova Scotia. As the bard presents his grievances, the
colonel admits that the New World presents difficult challenges but slowly
proves verse by verse that they are not only smaller than the challenges to be
encountered in "Old Scotland" but also offer infinitely greater opportunities as
well. In the end, bested in the argument, the bard admits that the difficulties he
encountered in "New Scotland" were nothing more than the stuff of life. Most
tellingly of all, however, is the determination he expresses never again to
dispraise the New World, lest he be taken as a faulty informant by his fellow
Gaels. The sentiments contained in that particular stanza are a prime example
of the Gaelic poet's sense of responsibility as a moulder and reflector of
community opinion and reveal MacLean's ultimate satisfaction with the New
World and his sense that this is also the consensus of his fellow immigrant
Gaels.

Placed in the context of MacLean's own body of poetry, it is clear that the
frequent citation of "A' Choille Ghruamach" by English writers as the definitive symbol of the Gaelic immigrant's experience with the New World owes
little to the actual mythology of Gaelic pioneers of the time, including that of
MacLean himself. Although the song is still known and its poetic value is
respected by Gaelic speakers today, it is rarely sung, while "Am Bal
Gàidhealach" is virtually a standard at any gathering of Gaelic singers in Nova
Scotia.

Fixation on negative imagery is the reason why MacLean's poetry has
been so badly mishandled, but the obsession with melancholia is hardly a true
reflection of all the Gaels had to say about their experience. As Margaret
MacDonell said of Gaelic emigration mythology in her book, *The Emigrant*

Experience:

> Almost all emigrant songs, even those which reveal the deep sorrow
> of the emigrants on leaving home, evince a strong urge to venture into
> a new and prosperous land and to enjoy the freedom and abundance
> to be found there. . . . [Emigration] elicited an extensive repertoire of
> songs in which its tragic aspects received due notice, but not to the
> exclusion of other considerations. The bards, many of them emi-
> grants, usually tempered their compositions with a note of optimism
> as they looked to a more prosperous future abroad.[38]

Important contemporary observers, such as Nova Scotian scientist Abraham
Gesner, who, as a surveyor, had extensive experience in the pioneer settlements of the Maritimes, corroborate this assessment. He concluded that no
immigrant group seemed to face the challenges of pioneering with as cheerful
an attitude as the Gaels.[39]

If we return to Gaelic literary accounts from the nineteenth century, we
cannot help but be struck by their consistent tone of defiance and optimism, as
well as their realism and lack of romanticism. Though MacLean's critique of
the weakening of the Gaelic poetic tradition towards the middle of the nineteenth century must be borne in mind, there remains a strong and largely
unequivocal tradition of Gaelic poetry that condemns the new order in Scotland and praises the immigrants' experience in the New World. Indeed, it was
during the nineteenth century that a real tradition of local praise poetry flow-
ered in the Maritimes, but, as these poems are often the product of the descendants of immigrants rather than of the immigrants themselves, they will not be
examined here. It is easy to see from the immigrant poetry which follows,
however, that that new tradition, with its comparative lack of nostalgia for a
romanticized Scotland, did not represent a sea change in attitudes.

We find, for example, an early-nineteenth-century Ross-shire immigrant,
Ruairidh Ruaidh MacCoinnich (Red Rory MacKenzie), expressing his contempt for conditions in Scotland in very unsentimental fashion and looking
forward (with a much more realistic appreciation of the challenges ahead than
his contemporary John MacLean) to freedom in the New World:[40]

> Tha luchd-riaghlaidh an àite
> Nis 'gar n-àicheadh gu dlùth,
> 'S gur h-e an stiùr a thoirt an iar dhi
> Nì as ciataiche dhuinn.
>
> Gheibh sinn fearann 'us àiteach
> Anns na fàsaichean thall;
> Bidh na coilltean 'gan rùsgadh

Ged bhiodh cùinneadh oirnn gann.

Tha mi deònach, le m' phàisdean,
Dhol gun dàil air na tuinn.
Siud an imrich tha feumail
Dhol 'nar leum as an tìr s'
Do dh' America chraobhach,
's am bi saors' agus sìth.

The overseers of the place
now refuse us unrelentingly,
so that to give her a lead to the west
shall be the most sensible for us.

We will get land and habitation
in the wilderness yonder,
the forest will be cleared
although our coins will be scarce.

I am most willing, with my children,
to go without delay on the waves.
That emigration is necessary
to burst forth from this land
to wooded America
where there will be freedom and peace.[41]

A contemporary of Ruairidh Ruaidh, the Skye poet Calum Bàn MacMhannain, described similar deteriorating economic conditions on his island, which he attributed with absolute certainty to the new social order:

Thàinig maighstir as ùr
Nis a stigh air a' ghrunnd,
Sin an naigheachd tha tùrsach, brònach.
Tha na daoine as falbh,
'S ann tha 'm maoin an déigh searg';

Ciod a bhuinnig dhomh fhìn
Bhi a' fuireach 's an tìr,
O nach coisinn mi nì air brògan.

'S ann a theid mi thar sàil,
'S ann a leanas mi càch,

Fiach a faigheamaid àite còmhnuidh.
Gheibh sinn fearann as ùr,
'S e ri cheannach a grunnd,
'S cha bhi sgillinn ri chùnntas oirnn dheth.
'S math dhuinn fasgadh nan craobh,
Seach na bruthaichean fraoich,

A new master has come
upon the ground now,
that news is sad, mournful.
The people are leaving
their wealth has faded away.

What advantage to myself
to be staying in the land where I do not profit making shoes?

I will go across the sea,
I will follow the rest,
to find myself a worthy dwelling-place.
We will get new land,
to be purchased outright,
and not a penny [of rent] will be charged to us.
And better for us the shelter of the trees
than the heather-covered hillsides.[42]

Composing from his new home in Prince Edward Island, Calum Bàn can hardly be accused of looking romantically back to a golden Scottish homeland nor of heightening the suffering experienced by the newly arrived settlers in order to ease his guilt for having deserted the Highlands, because his poem is directed to the people left behind and concludes with a description of the bounty of his new home and an invitation to join him:

Ach ma theid thu gu bràth
A null thairis air sàil,
Thoir mo shoraidh gu càirdean eòlach.
Thoir dhaibh cuireadh gun dàil
Iad a theicheadh o'n mhàl,
'S iad a thighinn cho tràth 's bu chòir dhaibh.
'Us nam faigheadh iad àm
'S dòigh air tighinn a nall,
'N sin cha bhiodh iad an taing MhicDhòmhnuill;
'S ann a gheibheadh iad àite'

Anns an cuireadh iad bàrr,
'S ro-mhath chinneadh buntàta 's eòrn' ann.

'S e seo Eilean an àigh
Anns a bheil sinn an dràsd.'

But if you ever go
over the sea,
bring my blessings to my close friends.
Bring to them an invitation without delay
that they should come as soon as they decently can.
And if they could find the time
and the ways and means of coming over
then they would not be obligated to [Lord] MacDonald;
they would get a place
in which they would sow crops,
and very well would potatoes and barley grow there.

This is the island of happiness
in which we are now.[43]

Even as we move into the post-1820 period, where we should begin to expect more obvious signs of a poetic tradition in decline, there is little evidence of a serious lack of realism, increased intellectual shuffling or a reversal in attitudes among immigrants in the body of accounts they left in the Maritimes. Instead, we find a striking consistency with earlier commentary. Tormod Bheag Sgoirrebhreac (Little Norman Nicholson of Scorrybreac) was a contemporary of John the Hunter of Lochaber and shared his love of hiking and hunting in the mountains and valleys of the Highlands, in his case, in the Isle of Skye. His pragmatic assessment of the changed conditions in his homeland, however, and his blunt condemnation of the new order which had brought them about stand in stark contrast to John the Hunter's wistful reminiscences and longing to be home hunting the deer:[44]

Thug na h-uachdarain uainn le ceilg,
An t-saorsa sheilg bh' againn uile.

Cùl mo làimh ri laghan fiar,
tha toirmeasg biadh thug Dia do'n duine.

Fàgaidh mi an nis an tìr seo
Chan fhaigh m'inntinn sìth innt' tuilleadh.

The chiefs took from us with treachery
the freedom to hunt that belonged to us all.

The back of my hand to unjust laws,
forbidding food God gave to the people.

I will now leave this land,
[where] I can no longer get peace of mind.[45]

It is worth pointing out that it was just this sense of reality which Allan the
Ridge found lacking in John the Hunter's rosy depiction of the life he left
behind in the Highlands:

Ged 's mór do bhòsd à fear na cròic
Ma ni thu a leòn dhuit fhéin,
Ged is staoigeach, tioram' fheòil,
Bidh tòireachd as do dhéidh.
Theid breith air amhaich ort gu grad
'Us gad a chuir 'ad mhéill,
'Us d'fhògairt thar a' chuan air falbh
Chionn bhi sealg an fhéidh.

Although great your boast of the antlered one
if you shoot him for yourself,
though his dry flesh is abounding in steaks,
you will be arrested.
You will be quickly seized by your neck
and a lash put to your cheek,
you will be banished over the ocean
for hunting the deer.[46]

It is also noteworthy that while John the Hunter's poetry is obviously
flawed by its romanticism, even here the immigrant's arrival in the New World
is not attributed to any sort of compulsion. Rather, John the Hunter takes full
responsibility for his actions, emphasizing that it had been his own decision
which took him to the New World:

'S truagh, a Rìgh, gu'n d'chuir mi cùl
Ri m' dhùthaich le m' thoil fhìn,
Le bhith an dùil 's an àit' as ùr
Nach faicinn tùrn 'gam dhìth;
Ach còir air fearann, òr, 'us earras

Bhith aig gach fear a bh' innt'.
Bha chùis gu baileach òrm am falach,
'S mheall mo bharail mì.

It is a pity, O Lord, that I turned my back
on my country by my own will,
thinking that in the new land
not a penny would I need;
but the right to land, gold, and wealth
would be there for everyone in her;
the [true] circumstance was completely concealed to me,
my expectations beguiled me.[47]

It is the active quality of rational choice, specifically pointed out by John the Hunter, however, which goes some way towards redeeming him as a figure in the Gaelic immigrant mythology and certainly in the eyes of his cousin Allan the Ridge, who attempts to comfort him with the assurance that he made the right decision:

'S tu rinn glic 's nach deach am mearachd
'S cha robh do bharail faoin;
Tighinn do dhùthaich na fear glana,
Coibhneal, tairis, caomh.
Far a faigh tu òr a mhaireas,
Còir air fearann saor,
Gach nì bu mhath leat bhi mu d' bhaile,
Earras 'us crodh laoigh.

You did wisely, and made no error
and your opinion was not unfounded;
coming to the country of the righteous,
the friendly, the gentle, the kind,
where you will find lasting gold,
the right to free land;
everything that would be good for you would be about your farm,
wealth and herds of cattle.[48]

The prominent consideration of the practicalities of life evident in Allan the Ridge's verses of encouragement to his despairing cousin remains a feature of Gaelic immigrant literature, even into the 1840s, when Gaelic poetic expression in the Maritimes appeared to be at a low ebb. Even poets known for

their particularly passionate and evocative descriptions of the natural beauty of
the Highlands maintain their ability to see the larger picture and determine on
action appropriate to their actual circumstances rather than paralyzing themselves with a retreat into romantic lyricism. One of the most popular emigration songs ever composed, "Slàn le beanntan mo ghaoil" ("Farewell to my
beloved hills"), dates from this era, and although it undoubtedly owes much of
its popularity to its powerful depiction of the splendour of the Highlands (in
this case Glendaruel, Argyll) it remains resolutely centred in reality. John
Sinclair, the young school teacher who composed the poem after witnessing
the clearance of the young people from his valley for sheep, did not let his love
for his native land obscure the tragedy he saw unfolding there:

> Ged tha 'n tìr seo lan bhuadh,
> 'S iomadh diomb' tha rith' fuaight';
> Cha chum ceileir na cuaich rium lòn.
> Tha na fearainn ro dhaor,
> 'S na tuarasdail saor,
> 'S chan eil farraid air saothair dhaoin' òg.
> Ach fo shiùil ris tha 'n long
> Tha gam' aiseag thar thonn,
> Gu Australia, fonn an fhéoir.

> Although this land is full of virtues,
> there are many resentments attached to her;
> the warbling of the cuckoo will not keep me in food.
> The land is very expensive
> and the labour free,
> and no one is asking the young to work.
> But the ship is now under sail
> that is to ferry me over the waves
> to Australia, land of grass.[49]

Sinclair did not in fact follow the increasingly large numbers who were
beginning to make their way to the Antipodes from this period but instead
opted for the large Gàidhealtachd of the Maritimes, settling on Prince Edward
Island in 1841. After more than three decades in the New World, his realistic
outlook and positive opinion concerning the benefits of emigration were as
unchanged as the poem he sent back to Cowal in 1874 reveals:

> Ma 's e 's gu 'm bi iad grìdeil
> 'Us dìchiollach, oidhirpeach,

Gun mi-fhortan bhith 'n dàn dhaibh,
Ach slàn, làidir, adhartach,
Mu 'm bi iad fad' 's an tìr seo,
Cho cinnteach 's tha coill' innte,
Bidh aca crodh 'us caoraich,
Biadh, aodach, 's mór ghoireasan.

Ged a tha 'n geamhradh cruaidh,
Reòta, fuar, sneachdach, gaillionnach,
Bidh aca taighean blàth,
'S teine làidir a gharas iad.
'S cha bhi cùram fuachd dhaibh,
'S coille bhuan ri gearradh ac'.
Ma thig sibh nall à Còmh'll,
Tha mi 'n dòchas nach aithreach leibh.

If they are hardy,
diligent, perservering
without misfortune in their destiny,
but healthy, strong, progressive,
before they are long in this land,
as sure as there is a forest in it,
they will have cattle and sheep,
food, clothing, and abundant household goods.

Although the winter is severe,
frosty, cold, snowy, stormy,
they will have warm houses,
and a powerful fire to warm them.
They will not worry about the cold,
and they will have a lasting forest to cut.
If you come over from Cowal,
I expect you will have no regrets.[50]

John Sinclair's song in praise of Prince Edward Island and in fond memory of his homeland was composed at a comparatively late date compared to most emigrant literature in the Maritimes. Nevertheless, by his day, many of the songs had been passed on by the earlier emigrant generation. Just as they made a concerted effort to inform their friends and loved ones in Scotland about their experiences in the hope that they too might benefit, they took great care to pass on the narrative to their descendants. While some of these carefully preserved anecdotes were published in widely accessible sources such as the Gaelic newspaper, *MacTalla*, in most cases they were passed down orally in Gaelic.[51] They appear no less detailed or accurate, for that, than those written accounts recorded roughly a century earlier and concentrate on similar themes: defiance and the search for freedom, dissatisfaction with the new order in Scotland, a conscious decision to search for a better life in the New World and, most importantly of all, the conclusion that that decision had been well made.

On rare occasions, when a wider community effort was made to comment on the migration experience, it was just such sentiments that were expressed. One of the best pieces of evidence of such communal attitudes towards settlement in the New World (and one of the very rare accounts from the mid-nineteenth century) comes from Strathalbyn in central Prince Edward Island and has been handed down in Gaelic until the present day. The Strathalbyn area had first been settled in the mid-1830s, primarily by immigrants from Raasay and the Isle of Skye. This first wave settled about a generation before the arrival of the "Late Comers" who suffered through the Highland Famine before coming out in the 1850s. According to the Rev. Donald Nicholson, a Gaelic speaker from that district, one of the young men who came out with the last wave of settlers was homesick for Raasay and determined to return. Even ignoring the exceptional stress Gaelic emigrants of this period were under, and the fact that most of the best land in Prince Edward Island and Nova Scotia had long since been claimed by earlier arrivals, it is hardly noteworthy that an individual emigrant should be dismayed by the New World and decide to go home. What is noteworthy, however, was the community's reaction to that particular decision.

The people of Strathalbyn felt that the recently arrived immigrant was making such a serious error and believed so strongly that he would change his mind about the New World once he had spent a little time there that they determined to trick him into staying. In order to carry this out, they gathered to formulate a plan and decided that the best man to execute it would be the most gifted Gaelic raconteur in the community, Rev. Nicholson's grandfather, Big Murdoch MacLennan.[52] Big Murdoch agreed to drive the young man to meet the ship he intended taking back to Scotland. On the appointed day, he arrived promptly with horse and wagon and made no effort to discourage his comrade from carrying out his plan to leave, but instead of going directly to the landing after picking the young man up, he took the most circuitous route he could possibly find, distracting the homesick immigrant's attention from the peculiar length of what should have been a short journey with an unending flow of fascinating material from his deep fund of Gaelic stories and traditions. By the time they arrived at the landing place, the ship could be seen at some distance off the coast under full sail. As this was the last vessel leaving before the winter freeze-up of the gulf, the young man was forced to rejoin his brother in Strathalbyn and together they wintered with an uncle who had come out earlier. In the spring he began clearing land in the Strathalbyn district and was said never to have mentioned returning to Scotland again.[53]

Whether the details of this particular story are true—and there is no reason to doubt that they are—is ultimately less important to our attempts to divine a Gaelic mythology than the fact that this particular immigrant community wished to pass these particular impressions on to their descendants, and that they are generally consistent with the material selected for preservation by other Gaelic communities. It is also notable how consistent this account is with the actual actions of immigrants. Moreover, the way in which these accounts are rendered also reveals the intimate connection Gaels made with their own history, even in the case of episodes of considerable antiquity, shedding some light on the importance Gaels placed on their historical record and its accurate preservation. One account from Blackstone in the parish of Mabou, Cape Breton, one of the last strongholds of Gaelic in the New World, gives a particularly vivid picture of this.

Dan Angus Beaton, "Dan Angus, Fhionnlaigh Iain 'ic Iain 'ic Fhionnlaigh Mhóir" (Dan Angus, son of Finlay John, son of John, son of Big Finlay), gave a quite detailed account of the arrival of his forbears at Rubha Fhionnlaigh (Finlay's Point), Cape Breton, at the dawn of the nineteenth century. He described their initial attempts to join their brother at Beaton's Point, Prince Edward Island (frustrated by the lack of freehold land), and skipped rather quickly over their subsequent arrival in Cape Breton, including an account of their first nights spent on the beach under the shelter of their overturned boat and what must have been the frightening loss of most of their provisions to a marauding bear. In Dan Angus's account, Big Finlay's wife simply concludes that they will have to do the best they can, treating the bear attack as a minor setback. The main focus of his account is not on the hardships of the New World but on Big Finlay's humiliation of the abusive landlord who had made life so miserable for the Beatons and their friends and neighbours in Brae Lochaber. Although the account of Big Finlay forcing the landlord to lick his feet before laying him out cold with one mighty blow from his giant fist was nearly two hundred years old at the time of Dan Angus's telling, it was as though Dan Angus had been there himself, helping his great-grandfather strike the blow against the tyrannical landlord. When a listener commented "Rinn e math" ("He did good"), Dan Angus replied, with obvious passion, "Rinn e Damainte math!" ("He did damn good!").[54]

III

Unfortunately, those who grew up in an environment where Gaelic was the language of home and community and where such Gaelic experience was articulated on a daily basis are now very few and very elderly. They are the last in the legacy of Gaelic tradition-bearers well schooled in the history and culture of their people and committed to the telling of the Gaelic story. That they have not been able to pass on more of their vast store of knowledge to the present generation is a tragedy, but it is not one of their own making. Centuries of anglicization have eroded the formal and informal means Gaels used to educate the members of their society to the point where even the most important defining feature of that society, their own Gaelic language, has been all but eliminated.

In spite of these setbacks, the paths to Gaelic history are not yet closed and a little exploratory work might yet shore them up considerably. In the case of the mythology of migration from the Highlands, it is not so much that those Gaelic paths are closed as that the information moving along them has been so studiously ignored by historians. If we take the care to examine that information, we will find that the Gaels in Scotland and the Maritimes have been able to describe the broad scope of migration to the New World in their own language and have an unbroken tradition of describing their migration as a conscious, rational and positive choice made to realise freedom. Whether it was to escape from religious persecution, abusive landlords or other sources of exasperation, the search for liberation from oppression is a prominent theme encountered time and again in Gaelic immigration traditions.

The mythology of being swept out of Scotland helplessly and against their will to make room for sheep is not a tradition invented by Gaels in the New World but owes its popularity to the dominance of English narratives. The Gaels themselves have given us a body of clear accounts of carefully considered, logical decisions which demonstrate a lucid understanding of the goals of the Highland elite and an equal understanding of where tenants could apply pressure to protect their rights. The Gaelic-derived accounts in the New World reveal clearly a desire to find the freedom which was being lost in Scotland, an aspiration to maintain the responsibility for directing the course of their lives so that their own values and goals would be respected and realized, and a clear sense of satisfaction about having succeeded in finding a better home. This, as far as we can reliably determine with all its permutations and combinations, represents the Gaelic mythology of emigration from Scotland and settlement in the New World. Perhaps it is worth concluding with one of the most powerful and eloquent statements from that tradition, a poetic fragment inscribed on a memorial plaque in the large Gaelic district of Belfast, Prince Edward Island. The thoughts captured there, chosen by the community from its own Gaelic song tradition, reveal how Gaels really felt about starting a new life in a New World. Thankfully, this time, those thoughts have been carved in stone:

> Slàn le tir nam beann 's an fhraoich
> Tìr ar sinnsre tìr ar gaoil
> Tha i 'n diugh gu teann fo dhaors'
> 'S airc is gaoir 's gach àit,
>
> Biodh ar n-earbs' an righ na glòir

'S gheibh sinn fearann saors' is lòn
Anns na coilltibh farsuinn mòr
'S theid gach bròn ri làr.

"Is leis an Tighearna an talamh agus an làn."

Farewell to the land of the hills and the heather,
the land of our ancestors, land of our love,
it is today firmly enslaved
with distress and cries of woe in every place.

The King of Glory will be our hope
and we will find land, freedom and sustenance
in the great wide forests
and every sorrow will disappear.

"The Earth and all that it contains belongs to God."

Notes

1. John the Hunter in Margaret MacDonell, *The Emigrant Experience: Songs of Highland Emigrants in North America* (Toronto, 1982), p. 80. My translation.
2. This is an estimated spelling based on its oral rendering.
3. Allan the Ridge in MacDonell, *Emigrant Experience*, pp. 88–90. My translation.
4. Prince Edward Island was part of Nova Scotia until 1769, when it was granted self-governing status. Cape Breton was also made a self-governing colony for a brief period at the turn of the eighteenth and nineteenth centuries before it was reunited with Nova Scotia.
5. Derick Thomson, *An Introduction to Gaelic Poetry*, 1974; 2nd ed. (Edinburgh, 1989), p. 13.
6. The air which singers would be most inclined to use for these poems is a very popular one in the Maritimes. As an instrumental tune (a jig), it is known as "Cha dean mi obair" ("I won't do the work") and is still frequently heard, particularly at square dances in Cape Breton. The tune was also used by Allan the Ridge in another song, the more famous "Duanag do Mhàbu" ("Song for Mabou") which is still well known to Gaelic singers in Nova Scotia. The air also made the transition into the English song tradition as the melody for a turn-of-the-century Prince Edward Island temperance song: "Come Ronald, come Donald, come Paddy O' Connell/Come Jonathan, Jack and Sandy/We will become teetotallers all/We'll bury the rum and the brandy." This last verse comes from the singing of Stewart MacIntyre of East Point, Prince Edward Island.
7. For the importance of Gaelic poetry as an historical source giving insight into Gaelic society, see also: Alexander MacLean Sinclair, *Comh-chruinneachd Glinn a' Bhàird: The Glenbard Collection of Poetry* (Charlottetown, 1890), p. vi; Sorley MacLean, "The Poetry of the Clearances," *Transactions of the Gaelic Society of*

Inverness 38 (1937–41), pp. 293–324; Charles Dunn, *Highland Settler: A Portrait of the Scottish Gael in Nova Scotia* (Toronto, 1953), p. 73; Eric Cregeen, "Oral Sources for the Social History of the Scottish Highlands and Islands," *Oral History* 2, no. 2 (Autumn 1974), pp. 23–24; MacDonell, *Emigrant Experience*, p. 15; Brendan O Madagáin, "Functions of Irish Song in the Nineteenth Century," *Bealoideas* 53 (1985), pp. 175–76; William Gillies, "Gaelic Songs of the 'Forty-Five,'" *Scottish Studies* 30 (1991), p. 19; John Shaw, "Gaelic Cultural Maintenance: The Contribution of Ethnography," unpublished paper presented to the Fasnag Conference, Sabhal Mór Ostaig Gaelic College, Isle of Skye, Scotland, c. 1993.

8. See Stephen J. Hornsby, *Nineteenth Century Cape Breton: A Historical Geography* (Montreal, 1992).

9. The term "English" will be used throughout this article in its linguistic and cultural rather than nationalistic sense and will be applied to any area where the English language and its associated culture predominates.

10. This was particularly true of two of the main "local" institutions in the Scottish Highlands, the parochial school system and the Church of Scotland, both of which began to make their presence heavily felt in the Gàidhealtachd after the '45 and both of which articulated their intention not only to operate in English and reflect an English cultural viewpoint but to destroy what they considered to be the barbaric Gaelic language and culture of the Highlands. The most complete studies of this theme are John Lorne Campbell, *Scottish Gaelic in Education and Life: Past, Present and Future*, 2nd ed. (Edinburgh, 1950), p. 47; and Victor Edward Durcacz, *The Decline of the Celtic Languages* (Edinburgh, 1983), p. 2.

11. Thomson, *Introduction to Gaelic Poetry*, p. 153.

12. See Ian McKay, "Tartanism Triumphant: The Construction of Scottishness in Nova Scotia, 1933–1954," *Acadiensis* 21, no. 2 (Spring 1992), pp. 33–34.

13. Some other prominent candidates are John Wilson (an editor of *Blackwood's Magazine* at the time who wrote under the pen-name "Christoper North"); James Hogg; Dr. William Dunlop (a physician in Canada); Hugh Montgomery, the Earl of Eglinton (a soldier who spent some time in Canada and was reputed to have Gaelic); Sir Walter Scott; J.G. Lockhart (Scott's son-in-law); and Scottish novelist John Galt, who spent an interesting part of his life in Canada. Interestingly, there is correspondence from Galt to Moir suggesting that Moir, as a better writer than Galt, should consider writing a piece on Canada, using for inspiration the Gaelic-speaking boatmen so frequently encountered in the New World.

14. Material from the Gaelic oral tradition rarely survives in English translation when the Gaelic original has ceased to exist; indeed, it is rarely translated into English even while the Gaelic text is still extant. Moreover, the literary standard of the poem is quite exceptional for a work supposedly translated from a lost Gaelic original. This author is not aware of a similar documented occurrence.

15. MacLean, "Poetry of the Clearances," p. 304.

16. J.M. Bumsted, *The People's Clearance: Highland Emigration to British North America, 1770–1815* (Edinburgh, 1982), p. xiii.

17. Eric Richards, *A History of the Highland Clearances: Vol. 1, Agrarian Transformation and the Evictions, 1746–1886*; Vol. 2, *Emigration, Protest, Reasons* (London, 1982 and 1985), vol. I, preface.

18. Bumsted, *The People's Clearance*, p. xiv.

19. Richards, *History of the Highland Clearances*, vol. I, preface.
20. J.M. Bumsted, "Captain John MacDonald and the Island," *Island Magazine* (spring-summer 1979), p. 16.
21. J.M. Bumsted, *The People's Clearance*, p. xiv.
22. MacEdward Leach, quoted in "A View From the Ridge," *Am Braighe* (autumn 1994), p. 5.
23. Richards, *History of the Highland Clearances*, vol. I, pp. 105–6. My italics.
24. John Knox, *A Tour through the Highlands of Scotland and the Hebride Islands in 1786* (London, 1787).
25. Duncan Bàn MacIntyre's "Oran nam Balgairean" ("Song to the Foxes"), was composed c. 1793, according to the historical background given in A*n Gàidheal* 61–72 (1877), p. 205.
26. NA, RG4, A1, 15917, report to Dorchester from the Government of Quebec on causes of emigration from the Highlands, 1790 (reel C-3006), in Marianne McLean, *The People of Glengarry: Highlanders in Transition, 1745–1820* (Montreal, 1991), p. 118. MacLean's work is a model for the use of Gaelic-derived knowledge to provide context for the more traditional sources of English historiography.
27. Bumsted, *The People's Clearance*, p. 220.
28. James Boswell, *The Journal of a Tour to the Hebrides with Samuel Johnson*, L. F. Powell, ed.(London, 1958), p. 189.
29. Big Michael MacDonald in MacDonell, *Emigrant Experience*, p. 58. My translation.
30. MacDonell, *Emigrant Experience*, p. 60.
31. The account of these settlers is reproduced in *History of Indian River*, 2nd ed. (Indian River, P.E.I., 1964; revised ed., Indian River Women's Institute/Centennial Project, 1973); and *Wandering Back: History of Dock – Hills River – Mill River –Rosebank* (Summerside, 1983).
32. Rev. A.E. Burke, "Mission of Saint Patrick (Grand River West)" (Charlottetown; manuscript, also published as a series in the *Guardian*, c. 1881), n. p; Raymond MacLean, *History of Antigonish*, 2 vols. (Antigonish, 1976), vol. I, p. 62.
33. Bumsted, *The People's Clearance*, p. 100.
34. MacLean, "Poetry of the Clearances," p. 304.
35. Dunn took care to point out that MacLean, like most Gaelic poets, came to praise the New World, but the strength of this assertion was somewhat undermined by his own fascination with the bard's more negative imagery. Dunn, *Highland Settler*, p. 60.
36. Alexander MacLean Sinclair, ed., *Clàrsach na Coille*, revised by Hector MacDougall (Glasgow, 1928), p. 118.
37. Sinclair, *Clàrsach na Coille*, pp. 94–100.
38. "They were careful to record many of the factors incident to emigration and did so with remarkable accuracy, so much so that many of their songs are an illuminating supplement to contemporary sources as well as to later historical studies." MacDonell, *Emigrant Experience*, p. 15.
39. Dunn, *Highland Settler*, pp. 24–25.
40. Ruairidh Ruadh would eventually settle along the Gulf shore of Nova Scotia.
41. MacDonell, *Emigrant Experience*, pp. 114–16. My translation.
42. MacDonell, *Emigrant Experience*, pp. 108–10. My translation.
43. MacDonell, *Emigrant Experience*, pp. 110–12. My translation.

44. Tormod Bheag first emigrated to the Miramichi region of New Brunswick but soon joined his contemporaries from Scotland who were settling in Australia.
45. This song appears to have been very popular and exists in many variants. The text quoted here is excerpted from one based mainly on Alexander MacLean Sinclair's version from Prince Edward Island, which appears to be the most complete. Alexander MacLean Sinclair, ed., *The Gaelic Bards from 1825 to 1875* (Sydney, N.S., 1904), pp. 51–53. My translation.
46. Allan the Ridge in MacDonell, *Emigrant Experience*, p. 90. My translation.
47. John the Hunter in MacDonell, *Emigrant Experience*, p. 84. My translation.
48. Allan the Ridge in MacDonell, *Emigrant Experience*, p. 92. My translation.
49. Iain Sinclair in Alexander MacLean Sinclair, *The Gaelic Bards from 1825 to 1875*, p. 86. My translation.
50. Iain Sinclair in Alexander MacLean Sinclair, *The Gaelic Bards*, p. 89. My translation.
51. *MacTalla*, published in Sydney, Cape Breton by Whycocamagh native, Jonathan G. MacKinnon, was the longest-running Gaelic weekly (terminating as a bi-weekly) in the world. It was published from 1892 to 1904 and was widely read. Much of the historical and poetic material published within its pages came, ultimately, from the Gaelic oral tradition.
52. Rev. Nicholson was also related to the young man who wished to return home to Raasay.
53. Interview, Rev. Donald Nicholson/Mike Kennedy, August 1990, Clyde River, P.E.I.
54. Dan Angus Beaton in Ellison Robertson and Jim Watson, eds., and trans., *Sealladh gu Taobh: Oral Tradition and Reminiscence by Cape Breton Gaels* (Sydney, N.S., 1987).

15

Above and Below Ground:
Metaphors of Identity in Fictional Texts from Scotia and Nova Scotia

Uwe Zagratski

Any cross-cultural comparison of Canadian and Scottish literature in a postcolonial context soon comes up against limiting factors. The primary reason is Scotland's critical status in the ongoing debate about its role in relation to other cultures and literatures in the former British Empire and Commonwealth. It can be argued that the internal colonialism exercised by the English state after 1700 forced an original Lowland literature onto crooked paths of self-expression and finally destroyed an independent Highland culture after 1746[1]. Having been colonized through anglicization, the professional members of the ruling class in Lowland Scotland willingly incorporated themselves into British culture. They helped to generate the academic subject "English Literature" and a hybrid British literature in the eighteenth century under the auspices of Enlightenment intellectuals and poets.[2] Throughout the colonial history of Britain they participated in the material and literary colonization of the countries of the British Empire.[3] Nevertheless, these colonizing attitudes caused a strongly patriotic reaction from the ranks of the popular culture, which in the course of time tended to form a decolonizing strategy. Chris Gittings sums up:

> By decolonizing, I mean a challenging and dismantling of colonizing systems of thought that seek to subordinate Scottish and Canadian writings to English and American models. The paradoxical role that Scottish and Canadian descendants of white, European invader-set-

tler cultures play as both agents and subjects of imperialism—the colonizers and the colonized—is visible in Scottish and Canadian historical and literary discourses.[4]

Gittings is able to trace three different practices of decolonizing writing in Scottish and Canadian literature: (1) translation of Scottish discourses into Canadian perspectives, (2) creation of a literature of dislocation/displacement and (3) production of metafiction.[5]

More specifically, we find that at the heart of the fiction by Lewis Grassic Gibbon, Ian Macpherson, James Barke and others, is a challenging of British preconceptions about Scottish identity. Scottish issues are brought up for the sake of redefinition by these regional writers, according to their particular treatments of history and the literary traditions within which they write. Their elemental fiction places them on the peripheries of the British literary canon because it uses the "land" as a metaphor for the tenacity and viability of Scottish cultures. These authors root their characters in the soil of Northeast Scotland to reconnect them with a spiritual tradition considered to be an authentic source of counter-hegemonic Scottish identity. Places ignored by London's modernists and Edinburgh's anglicized literary elite are thus put back on the literary map by Lowland Scottish voices from the rural Northeast.[6]

Translated into a new context, Scottish discourses are also found in modern Canadian literature, in particular from Nova Scotia and especially Cape Breton, a territory colonized in large part by Scots. There the characteristic Northeast Scottish experience and its metaphorical referents undergo an alteration related to the experience of Nova Scotian invader-settler society. Alistair MacLeod, Sheldon Currie, Angus MacDougall and others put their Highland Scottish and non-Scottish figures underground, in what can be regarded as a symbolical act of uncovering an identity different from that of the Lowland tradition. Their mining literature originates from a Gaelic as well as, occasionally, a non-Gaelic background but always stands in stark opposition to the centres of English: Britain, the Scottish Lowlands (as seen from the Highlands) and the United States. In short, two marginalized cultures write against imperial predominance, and it is my intention here to analyze and compare the structures and strategies of this resistance.

Postcolonial Strategies from Northeast Scotland

Lewis Grassic Gibbon's essay "The Land," written in 1934, can be read as a manifesto of a Northeast Scottish line of rural fiction because it specifies the physical and metaphysical agents of a mode of writing directed against subordination to a British centre.

> *That* is The Land out there, under the sleet, churned and pelted there in the dark, the long rigs upturning their clayey faces. . . . And the

voice of it—the true and unforgettable voice—you can hear even such a night as this as the dark comes down, the immemorial plaint of the peewit, flying lost. *That* is The Land—though not quite all. Those folk in the byre whose lantern light is a glimmer through the sleet as they muck and bed and tend the kye, and milk the milk into tin pails, in curling froth—they are The Land in as great a measure. Those two, a dual power, are the protagonists.[7]

The land and the peasants working on it constitute, most significantly, Gibbon's counter-hegemonic strategy against the ideologies of Britishness. The Calvinist doctrine, one of the ideological pillars of the Anglo-Scottish establishment, and especially its discipline of work, is deconstructed by Gibbon's prose. This is most clearly demonstrated when Gibbon's peasant figures strive for liberation from Calvinist bonds of guilt and sin by means of self-determined work to their own taste and fulfilment. The central statement from a crofter-protagonist in one of the short stories is: "Show me a thing that is worth my trauchle, and I'll work you all off the face of the earth," which hints at a self-willed violation of the dogma which relates all human activities to God's glory and praise.[8] Gibbon's subversion includes two parallel modes of rewriting: (1) a Marxist-inspired secularization of the Calvinist doctrine by focusing on the free act of working and (2) a radical portrayal of the crofter as a free agent ennobled by closeness to his work materials which, allusively, further his sense of "belongingness" to and natural feel for the land. It speaks of a pre-Reformation Scotland undisturbed by rigid authoritarian dogmas and, by implication, of a genuine democratic tradition lost in the process of proselytization. Spiritual attachment to the land, from which all but the peasants themselves are excluded, is the basic assumption of Gibbon's trilogy, *A Scots Quair*. Chris, the female protagonist, has an insight about the land:

> And then a queer thought came to her there in the drooked fields, that nothing endured at all, nothing but the land she passed across, tossed and turned and perpetually changed below the hands of the crofter folk since the oldest of them had set the Standing Stones by the loch of Blawearie and climbed there on their holy days. . . . The land was forever, it moved and changed below you, but was forever, you were close to it and it to you, not at a bleak remove it held you and hurted you.[9]

Rooted in the land, the peasants are rooted in the tradition of their Pictish ancestors. This becomes obvious in other Gibbon stories such as "Clay", in which the protagonist, Rob, uncovers an earth-house of old (*eirde*) and shows sympathy for his farming ancestor.

Following the analysis of Craig Cairns, we can see Gibbon's work as part of a "composed history," not to be mistaken for historical reality but to be acknowledged for its conflicting nature. According to Cairns:

> Thus the novelist of progressive history finds himself inextricably bound into a conflict with the very medium of his writing: to *imagine* the past is to encourage those very forces which have been exiled by the establishment of a composed history. The novel may seek to *assert* a civilised linear history, but what it *enacts* is a circle that insistently takes us back to the "barbaric" as the process of narrative makes the past present again.[10]

The silent sides of history, which according to Hume are not part of a composed order and are left outside narration and history, are voiced in Gibbon's counter-historical fiction.[11] "Barbarian" modes of living, working and thinking repressed or forgotten by the dominant historical discourse thus find their way into literature. A radical spirit of freedom is inscribed into the land and presented as an original feature of Northeasterners. Individualism married to a metaphysical rootedness is a hallmark of Gibbon's regional literature and serves as a basis upon which he can, particularly in "Grey Granite," integrate larger social orders into his construction of a Scottish authenticity. Marxism is presented as a "natural" complement to the libertarian philosophy portrayed in the short stories, so the synthesis of the two modes in *A Scots Quair* is a logical consequence. The result of all this is the construction of a "democratic" line in Scottish culture down from the prehistorical Picts to the 1930s and opposed to the colonial-imperial discourse of the British Union.

The "democratic" line extends even to the writing style, wherein a collective folk voice narrates events in a synthesized Scots without a narrator's intrusion. And it extends to metafictional digressions about the relevance of the Scots language as a literary medium, such as the following:

> Rob was just saying what a shame it was that folk should be shamed nowadays to speak Scotch. . . . Every damned little narrow dowped rat that you met put on the English if he thought he'd impress you—as though Scotch wasn't good enough now, it had words in it that the thin bit scrachs of the English could never come at. And Rob said, You can tell me, man, what's the English for sotter, or greip, or smore, or pleiter, gloaming or glanching or well-henspeckled?[12]

Gittings refers to such repetitive textual practices in Scottish literature as "a rewriting of history that traces dislocating cultural moments."[13] Certainly, Gibbon's trilogy tells of dislocating historical moments experienced by his Lowland crofters in the face of agricultural capitalism and imperialist wars, hence the impressions that the Lowlands are colonized territories and that its spokesman is writing against ideological concepts that maintain this colonial status.

Other Northeast writers of the same period responded similarly. Of his four novels, Ian Macpherson's first, *Shepherds' Calendar* (1931), is of major interest when viewed with a postcolonial focus.[14] Set in the Glensaugh area and close to the life and work on a Northeast croft, Macpherson's *Entwicklungsroman* (apprenticeship novel) is built around the issues of rootedness and displacement, and silence and its causes. Like Gibbon's crofters, Macpherson's are creatures of the land who feel that "out of the earth strength flowed into" them.[15] Their devotion derives from an atavistic urge. John Grant, the novel's youthful protagonist, is its principal exponent:

> The land called him. His promise and his mother's affection held him. The earth called him, to be its master and its slave, to break it and to use it, to glory in his strength pitted against its strength, and be broken at last. The peasant blood of his race cried out against his treachery. . . . The valley did not die as mortal mothers died. . . . He knew his days would pass in discontent, were he divorced from the valley. . . . But the land, the land, everything that did not change and did not seem to care.[16]

Macpherson and Gibbon apparently share a common knowledge about their region's spiritual traditions and the crofters' and farmers' significant roles as part of them; and the structure of their respective prose follows the same rhythms of the seasons. They differ where Macpherson renders the act of displacement complete due to his characters' lack of speech. They are silenced, "racked with the agonies of silence."[17] John's dilemma is indicative of the fate of a subdued and voiceless people:

> In his search for words to express his emotions, he came always to the store of what other men had said. . . . He could never find words for himself. . . . He meant to say so much, so much. The words scrambled and cried in his head, seeking exit, and finding none.[18]

At the heart of John Grant's voicelessness lies his alienation from his own body as a consequence of Calvinist hostility towards sexual pleasures.[19] Although a joyful union of John's and his lover's bodies is not in accordance with strict Calvinist rules, an enforced union of two political bodies much to the advantage of Calvinist ideologues is symbolically re-enacted in one passage. Macpherson alludes then to a sensitive historical moment, when an independent Scottish state was overpowered by English threats and machinations in 1707 and forced into a subordinate position.

> He remembered the night they'd taken him to the crow-woodie, and there had been two lassies passing. They came over and laughed at him. He lay on his face on the needled moss and sobbed, when they had gone. He swore then, . . . hiding his face from the light of day that its burning shame might not be seen by the day, that he'd get at them, one by one, for what they had done. . . . And he'd done nothing—nothing.[20]

Parabolically, John's personal shame after the first sexual assaults on his body has political connotations in relation to Scotland's incorporation into the British Parliament. A political reading is also epitomized by John's father-son conflict: "The battle was joined again. Youth in revolt sat down to besiege ancient authority, son to break his father's spirit. . . . Daily, John took from his father some outlying province of his dominions."[21]

Being deprived of their rights to dominion over their own bodies, both physical and political, the Lowland Scottish crofters in Macpherson's novel are emasculated, shamed and left numb by their inability to break the cycle of suppression. Unlike Gibbon, however, Macpherson focuses on the act of silencing, without stating an alternative in words that would be felt to be unavoidably inauthentic.[22] Whereas Gibbon suggests a counter-discourse based on what he thinks are authentic alternatives rooted in the "democratic" soil of his country, Macpherson's decolonizing response reveals the dilemma at the core of any colonized literature.

Although James Barke's saga, *Land of the Leal* (1939) is set in the Southwest, like the other two Lowland Scottish novels dealt with briefly here, it begins in a rural district of Scotland and narrates the successive displacement of rural labourers; this time, farm workers rather than crofters. The life of Jean Ramsay, the novel's heroine, is summed up as follows: "She had worked and laboured a long time, coming up out of Galloway and across the Borders and through Fife towards the city that had finally shut its walls round her. . . . It had been a long arduous pilgrimage from the farm cot-house to this small window in the city wall."[23] The emphasis in Barke's epic, in contrast to Macpherson's *Entwicklungsroman*, is on a group with a shared experience of historical change. The farm workers' expulsion from the land is not simply described in the novel, but is linked to other economic and social changes caused by capitalism. In line with Sir Walter Scott's historical novels, Barke's characters reflect the historical passage from agricultural production to industrial capitalism. Consequently, levels of antagonism between classes in historical states are the textual markers: lairds or farmers vs. farm labourers or crofters, Presbyterianism vs. Chartism, capitalism vs. socialism.

In *Land of the Leal*, we learn about the characters' gradual progress from an individualized Scottish radicalism strongly associated with Robert Burns[24] to a mature socialist attitude. David Ramsay, the protagonist, "would not have been the lover of Burns he was without being a rebel."[25] His knowledge of Burns paves the way to an emotional reaction against his social superiors. But emotional radicalism alone is not sufficient to understand the complex nature of Glasgow's industrial society: "His heart was to remain forever in the country; his habit of thought and speech was ever to be that of the countryside."[26] David's strong links with an older way of seeing the world do not allow him to analyze and explain class society in the same way as scientific socialism. When Andrew, his eldest son and a socialist of his own hue, realizes that his father is what he calls "inarticulate,"[27] he mentions his father's incapability of "translating" his rebellious spirit into the rhetoric of socialism. David's resulting speechlessness is then overcome by Andrew's translation of his father's rebellious legacy into socialist notions. Thus a radical tradition in opposition to the conservative, hegemonic concepts of the British ruling class is retained and adapted to changing conditions. Seen from the perspective of historical materialism, the farm labourers' displacement is a logical step towards social progress, as it is a prerequisite for a revolutionary change of society by the industrial working class. As a result, Andrew joins the Republican side to fight fascism in the Spanish Civil War. Barke's suggestion is thus close to Gibbon's.

Postcolonial Strategies from Nova Scotia

> Cape Breton is an island, although a big island, and I think you seem to have these people who are kind of on the edge of the world or something where the sea meets the land, and then here they are generations or centuries later on the edge of the world where the sea meets the land again and I think that it's always hard to make a living on the edges of the world.[28]

Alistair Macleod thus describes precisely the historical, geographical and inferred cultural situation of the Cape Bretoners in his two collections of short stories, *The Lost Salt Gift of Blood* (1976) and *As Birds Bring Forth the Sun and Other Stories* (1986). Pushed to the peripheries, exposed to the elements and squeezed between land and sea, his predominantly Highland figures struggle for material and cultural survival. Macleod's cultural pocket is inhabited by farmers, loggers and fishermen. I have outlined elsewhere the metaphorical significance of the sea in Macleod's prose.[29] My focus in this chapter is on the "land," or rather the "earth," as much of Macleod's fiction, set "between the ocean and the coal-mining town,"[30] goes underground.

A new mental region is charted in Nova Scotia's miners' literature in general and in Macleod's writing in particular. A sense of loss appears to be its most striking feature, linked to a strong concern for "unhiding the hidden"[31] Highland Scottish culture of Cape Breton. The lilt and flow of the stories' narrations are unmistakingly Gaelic, exemplifying Macleod's method of recording the vestiges of a subordinated culture within the bounds of a larger one.[32] Miners, by means of their occupational skills, hold a privileged position comparable to Gibbon's "rulers of the earth"[33] in recording declining cultural practices: they go underground in order to uncover their spiritual and linguistic roots which have been overlaid by English speech and culture. Symbolically, through their work they explore and recover places turned into dark spaces, into something outside history, by the imperial culture, and they retranslate them into settings for human interaction once again. Parallel with the symbolic reappropriation of suppressed ways of life, Macleod's figures gain greater insight into their collective psyches. The young hero of "Vastness of the Dark," for instance, comes to admit in the end that he cannot simply escape of his own free will from the horrid Cape Breton mining village, because the past of the older generation is inextricably bound up with his own present. His discovery takes up the central metaphor of the miners' lives, "their lives flowing into mine and mine from out of theirs."[34] Where the cultural links have already snapped, as in "The Return," the young protagonist from Montreal is "re-turned" to his Cape Breton mining community by a ritualistic initiation:

> I can feel the pressure of his [the grandfather's], calloused fingers squeezing hard against my cheeks and pressing my ears into my head and I can feel the fine, fine, coal dust which I know is covering my face and I can taste it from his thumbs . . . unable to see or hear or feel or taste or smell anything that is not black.[35]

Macleod's concern with collective values and his focus on deterritorialization bring him within the range of Deleuze and Guattari's definition of minor literature.[36] There is a sense of exile in the stories, a lingering evocation of the Highland Clearances and the crofters' subsequent ordeal of exodus up to the point where economic pressures turn them into miners on the far-flung shores of Cape Breton. Seen in the light of dislocating historical moments, Macleod's fiction concludes more recent chapters of a tormented people's tale of woe. His "urge to memorialize"[37] includes description of mutilated bodies, high death tolls, ugly accidents, the high level of danger on the job and the atavistic urges of the Scot wandering for employment, all directed towards showing the miners still in the iron grip of the capitalist forces which caused their ancestors' hardships. Conversely, Cape Breton's Gaelic culture is not to die without its mining community–based resistance being steeped in Gaelic orality and mythology.[38] Nearly blinded by the darkness of their people's history, Macleod's allegorical miners chronicle the past and present by groping for an understanding in the "mines" of a collective unconscious. Much has been buried since the dislocation of Highland culture, and because of the complexity of the other cultural layers on top of it— Lowland Scottish, British/English, American and Canadian—and the progress of time, "cultural archaeologists" are needed to salvage a decolonizing discourse from oblivion. Compared with Gibbon's peasants, these miners have taken a step further in history towards the final stage of a culture. The miner's elegiac description of his outmigration from Nova Scotia to a South African coal mine in "The Closing Down of Summer" points to their conserving role:

> We go by the scarred and abandoned coal workings of our previous generations and drive swiftly westward into the declining day. The men in the back seat begin to pass around their moonshine. . . . After a while they begin to sing in Gaelic, singing almost unconsciously the old words that are so worn and so familiar. . . . I begin silently to mouth the words myself. There is no word in Gaelic for good-bye, only for farewell.[39]

Macleod's figures stem from tribal, Celtic families and they have this genealogical link in common with characters from Sheldon Currie's, Angus MacDougall's and Hugh MacLennan's prose.

Currie's "The Glace Bay Miners' Museum"[40] is set in the heartland of Nova Scotia's mining industry and is another good example of "minor literature." Currie emphasizes the collective values of the community, focuses on politics and places his figures by way of a hint in the context of past and present dislocations. On the one hand, like Macleod, Currie translates the signifying practices of an oral culture into a system of resistance against the deadly effects of the dominant industrial system. On the other hand, Currie's counter-discursive strategy deciphers colonizing patterns.

Mutilation and death are the miners' constant companions and growing accustomed to them is an appalling feature of bereaved families' lives. Currie's curt style is more than suggestive here. This is how Margaret MacNeil, the young protagonist, relates her husband's and brother's deaths: "Soon as the house was finished, we got married and moved in. Him and my brother, Ian, were buddies by then, working the same shifts. They both got killed the same minute."[41] Against the culture of death, Currie places the vitality of ceilidhs, storytelling, bagpipes and the Gaelic language:

> What they fought about was politics and religion. . . . Every night he'd come and play and sing. Me and my grandfather would tell or write stories. My brother even would sing when he was on day shift or back shift.[42]

This is meant to be a way of mending what has been physically and culturally dismembered. The strongest expression of preserving an endangered culture is Margaret's pickling of parts of Neil's, Ian's and her grandfather's bodies in jars to be exhibited in her miners' museum. Her act of active

remembrance, grounded in a somewhat bizarre working-class humanism, re-
claims her right over the bodies of her beloved ones that she was denied by the
mining companies while they lived. She reconstructs her community's cultural
symbols and resists its death by preserving the "means of production" required
for its survival: tongues, fingers, lungs and sexual organs are retained for
better times and in stubborn opposition to Neil's pessimism about the Celtic
Cape Bretoners' fate: "Came here and lost their tongues, their music, their
songs. Everything but their shovels."[43]

A second reading of Currie's "product of damage"[44] reveals a fierce,
Swiftian sarcasm towards the *tartanization* of Nova Scotia. The term points to
the reconstruction of the Nova Scotian identity, involving the invention of
traditions on the basis of ethnic Highland stereotypes, for tourist consumption.[45] But, Currie takes tartanism to its utmost extreme while simultaneously
parodying the final result. A sanitized and commercially tamed culture represented by dead miners is eventually exposed to the very middle-class propaga-
tors of the ideology of industrialism which helped to kill it off: the colonialization
of provincial minds and bodies is seen to be an all-embracing process.

Angus MacDougall has also taken up the issues of victimization and
resistance in "An Underlying Reverence."[46] The reverence of the title is, according to the protagonist Gibbo Marenelli, an Italian-born miner from Sydney Mines, to be paid to his two nephews who were killed in a mining accident
in 1944. When he has fulfilled his mission fifteen years later, he has dug up
"some earth from every church on Cape Breton Island" and buried it "in the
ground above the boys on the little lot in Sydney Mines."[47] Macdougall weaves
together three levels in this story. On an ethnic level, Cape Breton's diverse
nationalities are fused into an international mining community. On a social
level, antagonistic class relations patterns prevail between the international
workforce and the Scottish-English management. The tensions of class society
are best exemplified by the monument for the Prince of Wales, commemorating his only visit to Cape Breton, and Gibbo's "invisible monument" to the
ordinary man's dignity, which stands in sharp contrast to the public display of
imperial prestige. The story attains its full narrative power, however, on the
symbolic level. Similar to Gibbon's peasants, Macdougall's miners hold privileged positions because they handle life-giving material and work close to the
"heart and soul of the earth . . . of the town and of Cape Breton itself."[48] Like
Gibbon's figures, they are inextricably interwoven with the cycle of life and
death: they return in death to the earth whence they were born and are thus
signifiers of a quasi-religious discourse. As a result, Macdougall's counter-
hegemonic prose thematizes the charting of a new cultural province inspired
by a Christian concept of equality and rooted in a pragmatic working-class
humanism.

As he went from place to place, Gibbo noticed how well-cared-for and cultivated the earth and fields looked in farming areas like Mabou and the Margaree Valley, compared to the stark, empty appearance of the mining towns. . . . They spoke to him silently and effortlessly about how his life as a miner blended in with so many other different lives in Cape Breton, although they hardly realized what they shared.[49]

Disparate elements of a mining community torn apart by the dehumanizing forces of materialism are brought together again by a spiritual tradition meant to heal the wounds. Like Gibbon's, Macdougall's search for wholeness includes a desire to ennoble man: "He planned . . . to create a bond which would unite his nephews and all the victims of the mines with the places on the Island which were considered holy and important."[50] In the end the three levels combine. The miners, nationally uprooted and socially ill-treated, not only have their dignity restored against capitalist notions of profit, but, through Gibbo's remembering, shaping and worshipping, their allegorical significance within the community is reinforced. That Gibbo's rebellious act of burying the earth takes place on Dominion Day invites a critical reading of established texts about Canadian and Nova Scotian history, just as it reminds official Nova Scotia of the ordinary immigrant's contributions to the cultural and religious diversity of the province's identity. Macdougall's story then is, like Currie's, another decolonizing response from the lower depth of society to the colonial textualization of Nova Scotia.

Conclusion

"There's more to Cape Breton than the mines. . . . They're only a—a corruption."

"Yes, there's more here in Cape Breton than that. And each year the best of the island emigrates. We're a dispersed people doomed to fight for lost causes."[51]

The dialogue between these two figures of Highland Scottish descent in MacLennan's *Each Man's Son* encapsulates the characteristics of the literary examples from Nova Scotia examined in this chapter. Dislocations, emigrations, enclosures and further dislocations form a literature of continuous exile. We started with Northeast Scottish metaphors of the land and attempted to analyze their strategies of writing back against British appropriation. Forming a new identity more in line with Scottish discourses and rejecting English axioms of universality involves a literary resistance which, according to Stephen Slemon, is defined by "the untranscendable *ambiguity* of literary or indeed *any* contra/dictory or contestatory act which employs a First-World medium for the figuration of a Third-World"[52] or Second-World resistance.

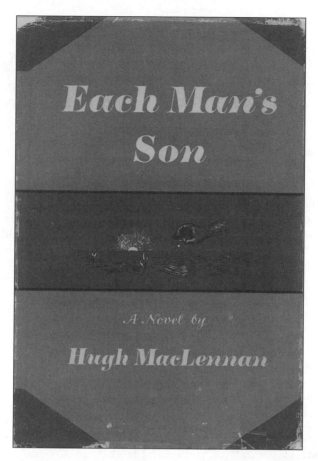

Figure 15.1 Cover of the 1951 edition of *Each Man's Son*, a novel by Hugh MacLennan, published under the Little, Brown and Company imprint (reproduced with permission of Time Warner Books)

Ambiguity has marked Scottish fiction because a pure colonizer/colonized duality is no longer a quality of Scottish culture. Having been colonized by British literary and cultural models, a democratic Lowland culture struggled to rid itself of centralist concepts. But because metaphors of the land had already become ambivalent, thereby revealing the reconstitutive power of the dominant discourse, Gibbon and Barke employed "unbiased" political concepts from outside Scotland and Britain in order to erode imperial control. In contrast, Macpherson's counter-discourse denotes the silencing effects the dominant culture's possession of language has on the marginalized one.

When "land" is translated into "earth" in Nova Scotia's mining fiction, the stain of ambivalence is not removed. MacLennan points to this when he writes of a "Highlander lost in the lowlands of the shrewd men."[53] Having been colonized by the imposition of British, Lowland Scottish, and North American mainstream axioms, Nova Scotia's mining authors dig deep in their regional earth to uncover forgotten layers of their Gaelic past. Since the translation of a Scottish past into a Canadian present requires the English language on top of Gaelic musicality[54] and references to Gaelic cultural practices, the decolonizing texts examined here are dialectically provisional. They acknowledge the impossibility of sounding their authors' protests in Gaelic, and they seem deliberately to abstain from overturning or inverting the dominant "in order to become dominant in their turn."[55] We can therefore claim that these postcolonial responses reflect imperial strategies, as well as decolonizing counter-patterns that seek to avoid imperial pitfalls.

One final remark about the ambiguous character of these texts. As the textual expedition into the earth of Nova Scotia does not extract any cultural signifiers of Native Canadians (e.g., Mi'kmaq), the colonizing nature of a colonized literature is promptly revealed.[56] The irony of the minor literature of Cape Breton and the Scottish Northeast is that their ambiguities, provisional characters, deterritorializations, political biases and collective representations allow them to act effectively as both decolonizing and colonizing texts.

Notes

1. Cf. Michael Hechter, *Internal Colonialism. The Celtic Fringe in British National Development, 1536–1966* (Berkeley, 1975).
2. Cf. Robert Crawford, *Devolving English Literature* (Oxford, 1992).
3. Chris Gittings, "Canada and Scotland: Conceptualizing 'Postcolonial' Spaces," in Diana Brydon, ed., *Essays on Canadian Writing*, 56 (Fall 1995), pp. 134–61. See also Berthold Schoene, "A Passage to Scotland: Scottish Literature and the British Postcolonial Condition," *Scotlands*, 2.1. (1995), pp. 107–22.
4. Gittings, "Canada and Scotland," pp. 138–39.
5. Gittings, "Canada and Scotland," pp. 150–151. Not all of these practices can be dealt with here, and it remains to be seen if the rest apply to the fiction under consideration, since particularly the decolonizing nature of the literature from the northeast of Scotland in the 1930s seems to stem from other dislocating experiences than those of the Highlanders Gittings referred to.
6. I use the term "place," which denotes "a setting for human interaction . . . as social fact," in contrast to "space," which denotes "something chiefly physical, outside, external." See Konrad Groß, "North of Canada—Northern Canada: The North in 19th-Century Juvenile Fiction," *Zeitschrift für Kanadastudien*, 15, Jahrgang, Nr.2, Band 28 (January 1995), p. 22.
7. Lewis Grassic Gibbon, "The Land," in Lewis Grassic Gibbon and Hugh MacDiarmid, *Scottish Scene* (London, 1934), pp. 242–55. Here quoted from Ian S. Munro, ed., *A Scots Hairst* (London, 1967 and 1983), p. 67.
8. "Sim," *The Free Man*, 10 June 1933. Quotation taken from Munro, *A Scots Hairst*, p. 41; see also "Clay," *A Scots Hairst*, pp. 16–27.
9. Lewis Grassic Gibbon, *Sunset Song* (1932) (London, 1982), pp. 117–18.

10. Craig Cairns, "Out of History," *Etudes Ecossaises*, 1 (1992), p. 217.
11. Craig Cairns, "Out of History," pp. 214, 227.
12. Gibbon, *Sunset Song*, p. 153.
13. Gittings, "Canada and Scotland," p. 151.
14. The other three are *Land of Our Fathers* (1933) and *Pride in the Valley* (1936), both dealing with the Highland Clearances, and *Wild Harbour* (1936), an antiwar dystopia.
15. Ian Macpherson, *Shepherds' Calendar* (Edinburgh, 1983), p. 196.
16. Macpherson, *Shepherds' Calendar*, pp. 271–74.
17. Macpherson, *Shepherds' Calendar*, pp. 33–34.
18. Macpherson, *Shepherds' Calendar*, pp. 34, 266.
19. Macpherson, *Shepherds' Calendar*, pp. 30, 156–59.
20. Macpherson, *Shepherds' Calendar*, p. 30.
21. Macpherson, *Shepherds' Calendar*, pp. 109–10.
22. Cf. Bill Ashcroft, Gareth Griffiths and Helen Tiffin, *The Empire Writes Back* (London, 1989), p. 141.
23. James Barke, *Land of The Leal* (Edinburgh, 1987), p. 612.
24. James Barke wrote a sequence of five novels about Burns' life. *Immortal Memory*, (London, 1946–1959).
25. Barke, *Land of the Leal*, p. 194.
26. Barke, *Land of the Leal*, p. 448, see also p. 95.
27. Barke, *Land of the Leal*, p. 548.
28. Chris Gittings, "A Conversation with Alistair Macleod," *Scotlands*, 2.1 (1995), pp. 101–02.
29. "Neil Gunn and Alistair Macleod: Across the Sea to 'Scotland'," in Wolfgang Hochbruck and Jim Taylor, eds., *Down East*: Critical Essays on Contemporary Maritime Canadian Literature (Trier, 1996).
30. "In the Fall," in Alistair Macleod, *The Lost Salt Gift of Blood* (Toronto, 1976), p. 8.
31. This is Robert Kroetsch's term. Quoted in Ashcroft et al., *The Empire Writes Back*, p. 141.
32. See Gittings, "A Conversation with Alistair Macleod."
33. See Gibbon, "The Land," p. 71.
34. "The Vastness of the Dark," in Macleod, *The Lost Salt Gift of Blood*, p. 49.
35. "The Return," in Macleod, *The Lost Salt Gift of Blood*, p. 84.
36. Deleuze, Gilles; Guattari, Felix, *Kafka. Pour une litterature mineure.* (Paris: Les Editions de Minuit, 1975).
37. Joyce Carol Oates in her "Afterword" in the McClelland edition of Macleod, *The Lost Salt Gift of Blood*, p. 159.
38. Cf. the story "Vision," in Alistair Macleod, *As Birds Bring Forth the Sun*, (Toronto, 1986) pp. 128–67.
39. Alistair Macleod, "The Closing Down of Summer," in *As Birds Bring Forth the Sun*, p. 30.
40. First published in *The Antigonish Review*, 24 (Winter 1975). The text used here is from James O. Taylor, ed., *An Underlying Reverence* (Sydney, N.S., 1994), pp. 33–47.
41. Currie, "The Glace Bay Miners' Museum," p. 45.
42 Currie, "The Glace Bay Miners' Museum," p. 45.

43. Currie, "The Glace Bay Miners' Museum," p. 42.
44. Abdul R. JanMohamed and David Lloyd, "Toward a Theory of Minority Discourse: What is to be Done?" in Abdul R. JanMohamed and David Lloyd, eds., *The Nature and Context of Minority Discourse* (New York, 1990), p. 4. Here from Sherrie A. Inness, "'They must worship industry or starve': Scottish Resistance to British Imperialism in Gunn's The Silver Darlings," *Studies in Scottish Literature*, 28 (1993), p. 135.
45. See Ian McKay, "Tartanism Triumphant: The Construction of Scottishness in Nova Scotia, 1933–1954," *Acadiensis*, 21, no. 2 (Spring 1992), pp. 5–47; also see Ian McKay, *The Quest of the Folk* (Montreal, 1994).
46. Angus MacDougall, "An Underlying Reverence," quoted in Taylor, ed., *Underlying Reverence*, pp. 49–62.
47. MacDougall, "An Underlying Reverence," p. 58.
48. MacDougall, "An Underlying Reverence," p. 53.
49. MacDougall, "An Underlying Reverence," pp. 60–61.
50. MacDougall, "An Underlying Reverence," p. 58.
51. Hugh MacLennan, *Each Man's Son* (Toronto, 1951 and 1991), p. 67.
52. Stephen Slemon, "Unsettling the Empire: Resistance Theory for the Second World," *World Literature Written in English*. vol. 30 no. 2 (1990), p. 37. For Slemon, the Second World is "that neither/nor territory of white settler-colonial writing" (p. 30).
53. MacLennan, *Each Man's Son*, p. 113.
54. Janice Kulyk Keefer, *Under Eastern Eyes* (Toronto, 1987), p. 182.
55. Helen Tiffin, "Post-Colonial Literatures and Counter-Discourse," *Kunapipi* 9, no. 3 (1987), p. 32.
56. Slemon, "Unsettling the Empire," p. 30. For the cycle of dislocation in Cape Breton, see also David Craig, *On the Crofters' Trail* (London, 1990), Chapter 8.

Index

Index

Index

Red Thunder 59
Red River 59, 98, 99, 100
Reformation 31
regiments 14, 63, 73, 143-4
42nd Foot (Black Watch)
143, 144
72nd Duke of Albanyís
Highlanders 144
72nd Foot 142
78th Highlanders 141-56
Seaforth Highlanders 142
Reid, Alexander 208, 210-
13, 214
Reid, Alexander Peter 208
Reid, John 18
Reid, W. Stanford 57-8
religion 66, 84 see also
Calvinism, Church of
England, Church of
Scotland, Free Church of
Scotland, Presbyterianism,
Roman Catholics, Scottish
Episcopal Church
religious pluralism 225-6
rent increases 137
Rhymes, Robert 233
Rice, C. Duncan 191, 193,
194, 195, 196, 198
Richards, Eric 21, 105-26, 275,
276-7
Richardson, Sir James 212
Richardson, Samuel 162
Ridge, Alan the 30, 268-71,
280, 287, 288
Rivington, James 159-60, 171,
173
Robertson, Alex 65
Robertson, Angus 20
Roman Catholics 21, 83, 93,
98, 99, 152, 279
Romantic movement 16-18, 29,
36
Ross, Alexander 102
Ross, Donald 150
Ross, Jack 17
Ross, John 119
Ross, Robert T. 220
Ross and Cromarty 118, 142
Applecross 255
Loch Broom 20
Royal Canadian Air Force 250
Royal Scottish Society for the
Prevention of Cruelty to
Children 222, 226, 247

Rush, Benjamin 193
Rye, Maria 227
St Andrewís Day 100, 148
St Andrews societies 61, 99
see also Highland societies,
Scottish societies
St Francis Xavier University 98
St Kilda 121, 125n45, 125n45
Saskatchewan 101
sawmillers 23
Scobie, M. J. 243
Scotland
Aberdeen 120, 233
University 193
Annandale 65
Banffshire 23
Caithness 22
Coll 113, 281
Dumfries 59
Duns 174, 175
Elgin 122, 174, 175, 206
Eriskay 76
Forres 120
Fort William 116
Galloway 50
Glengarry 261, 262
Greenock 159, 168, 195
Hawick 65
Invergarry 143
Inverness 36, 62, 233
Keith 23
Kingussie 116
Kintail 254, 255-6
Kirkcudbright 50
Knoydart 257
Lesmahagow 237
Lochaber 255
Lochbuie 115
Menstrie Castle 53
Moffat 65
Moidart 280
Orkney 58
Pitlochry 36, 65
Port Glasgow 159
Raasay 73, 291
River Clyde 23, 53
St Andrews 219
Strathglass 255
Tiree 60, 68, 116
Ulva 120
see also Argyll, Barra,
Benbecula, Edinburgh,
Glasgow, Harris, Hebrides,
Highlands, Lewis, Lowlands,

North Uist, Ross and
Cromarty, Skye, South Uist,
Sutherland
Scots
criticism of 55, 58, 218,
222-4, 225-6, 241-5, 247
drinking customs 94, 99, 99
see also identity
Scotland on Sunday 17
Scott, John 64-5
Scott, Sir Walter 16, 18, 32,
36, 57, 60, 67, 92, 142, 143,
149, 303
Halifax Centenary celebra-
tion 23,149-54
Scottish Enlightenment 24,
189-201
Scottish Episcopal Church 220
Scottish Privy Council 53
Scottish societies 49, 60, 61
see also Highland societies,
St Andrews societies
Scottish Tourist Board 47n69,
67
Secession Church 189-91
Second World War 102, 250
Selkirk, Earl of 59, 89
Sellar, Patrick 111, 122
Service, Robert 61, 71n40
Sharp, William (Fiona
Macleod) 49
sheep farming 76, 112, 257,
278, 289, 293
ships
Ceres 174
Charlotte 167, 178
Enterprize 173
Hector 20, 34, 60
John Dunscombe 113
Mayflower 20
Nancy 167, 178
Neptune 173, 178
St George 116
Sebim 119
Skelton 113
Sierra Leone 193
Simpson, Sir James 205
Simpson, John 64
Sinclair, John 289-90
Skrine, Charles 150
Skye, Isle of 17, 19, 68, 74,
284, 286, 291
Dunvegan Castle 17
Portree 256

319